THE
GREAT
ESCAPER

THE
GREAT
ESCAPER

THE LIFE AND DEATH
OF ROGER BUSHELL

Simon Pearson

Skyhorse Publishing

Library of Congress Cataloging-in-Publication Data is available on file.

Cover design by Daniel Brount

Print ISBN: 978-1-5107-4896-5
Ebook ISBN: 978-1-5107-4897-2

Printed in the United States of America

This book is dedicated to the memories of Squadron Leader Roger Joyce Bushell and Lady Georgiana Mary Curzon; the pilots of 601 and 92 squadrons, RAF; the heroes of the Czech resistance, particularly Blažena Zeithammelová, her father Otto and her brother Otokar; and the men of many nations who waged war on Nazi Germany from within the prisoner of war camps, notably the officers from the North Compound, Stalag Luft III.

Contents

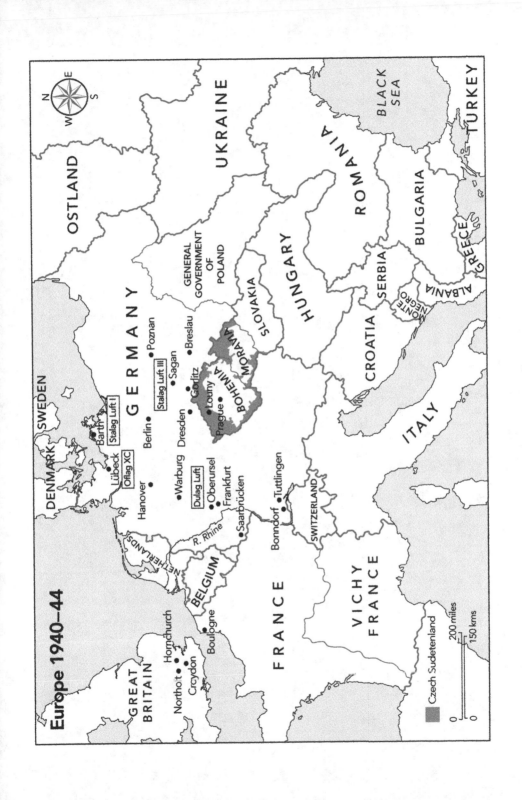

Europe 1940–44

GREAT BRITAIN
Northolt
Hornchurch
Croydon
Boulogne

FRANCE

VICHY FRANCE

NETHERLANDS
BELGIUM
R. Rhine
Saarbrücken
Bonndorf
Tuttlingen
SWITZERLAND

DENMARK
SWEDEN
Lübeck
Barth
Stalag Luft I
Oflag XC
Hanover
Berlin
Warburg
Dulag Luft
Oberursel
Frankfurt

GERMANY
Poznan
Sagan
Stalag Luft III
Görlitz
Breslau
Louny
Dresden
Prague

BOHEMIA
MORAVIA

OSTLAND

UKRAINE

GENERAL GOVERNMENT OF POLAND

SLOVAKIA

HUNGARY

ROMANIA

CROATIA
SERBIA
MONTE NEGRO
ALBANIA
BULGARIA
GREECE

ITALY

BLACK SEA

TURKEY

Czech Sudetenland

0   200 miles
0   150 kms

Prologue

In the late afternoon of Saturday, 29 September 2012, I sat amid the remains of a wooden hut in the forests of Western Poland that was once the prison of a man who'd come to fascinate me – an unorthodox warrior who spent his life breaking rules.

Seventy years ago, this place was a prisoner-of-war camp – Stalag Luft III – about two miles from the German town of Sagan, which is known today by its Polish name of Żagań.

The pines have reclaimed much of the North Compound. Only the foundation blocks made of red brick and the concrete floors of wash-rooms remain of the prison huts once inhabited by the Allied airmen who are central to this story.

Shafts of sunlight flickered through the pines; a breeze ebbed and flowed. I was alone and, for a moment, felt overwhelmed.

As I sat on one of the foundation blocks, my thoughts were interrupted by the bark of a dog and the sight of a man running towards me. Wearing the uniform of a Russian soldier from the Second World War, he was followed by a group of about twenty children.

'You're the Englishman who's writing a book,' he said. 'I'm from the museum.'

I told him I was trying to find out about the life of Roger Bushell.

'Big X!' he answered with a broad smile. 'The head of the escape committee! He lived here . . . you can celebrate this story,' he said. 'This was a POW camp, not a concentration camp. There are no monuments made of bodies here. This was run by the Luftwaffe, not the SS. There was honour in this place.'

The children listened. Many of them said 'Hello'; some of

them shook my hand. Eventually, the Pole in Russian battledress bade me farewell. The children had to get back to the museum for a re-enactment, he said.

Once again, I was left alone in the forest. Roger Bushell, the leader of 'the Great Escape' from Stalag Luft III in 1944, remained an enigma to me.

Almost exactly fifty years ago, I sat with my father, a former airman, in a cinema in the English Midlands and watched a film that gave a dramatic account of events in the forest south of Sagan. As with so many boys of my generation, the Hollywood epic left an indelible mark. A year or so later, I found Paul Brickhill's book of the same name among my Christmas presents.

Perhaps it was not surprising that in a house where bookshelves were lined with the biographies of airmen, and bombers and fighters made from Airfix kits hung from ceilings, I should be interested in this story, but my curiosity about events at Stalag Luft III remained with me and, if anything, became more intense.

My hobby became a quest. When the King's Cup flying competition was held at Tollerton aerodrome near Nottingham, where my father flew at weekends, I met former RAF pilots who had known Bushell. My father took me to Biggin Hill, the fighter base where Bushell had been based at the start of the war. I read many books, but none of them told me much more than Brickhill had done.

In one of the war stories most cherished by the British, the man at the centre of events was largely forgotten. While the main characters in two of Brickhill's most popular books – Wing Commander Guy Gibson, who led the Dambusters, and Douglas Bader, the disabled fighter ace – became national icons, Roger Bushell, the hero of a third, faded away. Brickhill was an Australian journalist who had himself been a prisoner in the North Compound. He sketched the outline of an intriguing man but the image was frustratingly short on detail.

Bushell did not make the transition from paperback to celluloid in the same manner as Gibson or Bader did in British-made films. Hollywood chose composite characters for *The Great Escape* rather than real people and Roger Bushell – played by Richard Attenborough in the film – became Roger Bartlett. He appeared in cameo roles in dozens of books, but no one told the story of his life. Why was this? Who was Roger Bushell?

Years later, while working at *The Times*, I came across a memorial notice in the archive, which marked the anniversary of Bushell's birth and celebrated his life. It quoted Rupert Brooke: 'He leaves a white unbroken glory, a gathered radiance, a width, a shining peace, under the night.' It was signed 'Georgie'.

At that moment, I realised there was a love story to be told as well as a war story. A friend at *The Times*, the author Ben Macintyre, told me to stop dabbling: the time had come to write the book.

Within a few hours, I had written to the Imperial War Museum, outlining what I wanted to do and asking whether the staff could help. In one of those remarkable twists of fate that can define the outcome of any endeavour, the museum's reply thrust open the door to the story of Roger Bushell's life. His family was, at that moment, corresponding with the museum, with the intention of donating his archive. The museum would be happy to pass on a letter from me . . .

Over the years, the Bushell family had been approached by several people who wanted to make films or write books about Roger, but little emerged until 2010 when his niece, the South African film director and anti-Apartheid campaigner Lindy Wilson, made a documentary. She gave her film the title, *For Which I am Prepared To Die*, echoing the words of a speech by Nelson Mandela.

I met Lindy Wilson in November 2011, when she presented her uncle's archive to the Imperial War Museum. For the family, this was a major decision. 'To give Roger's archive to the Imperial War

Museum is an acknowledgement of who he was and that he didn't just belong to us,' she said, 'but also to the country for which he died.'

She hoped that her uncle, who was born in South Africa but lived in Britain from the age of fourteen, would gain greater recognition. 'My hope is that his role will be truly acknowledged – finally acknowledged – by the country he loved and fought for and that he will become part of its culture, its history. This is where he belonged.'

Roger's father, Ben Bushell, shared her belief. When asked to provide an epitaph for his son's gravestone, he sent the following response to the Air Ministry in Whitehall:

A LEADER OF MEN,

HE ACHIEVED MUCH,

LOVED ENGLAND,

AND SERVED HER TO THE END.

The archive, which contains a collection of letters, his mother's diary, newspaper cuttings and photographs, provides a partial – and often fragmented – record of Roger Bushell's life, but it yields three substantial veins of information.

The first is the diary of Bushell's early life, written by his mother, Dorothe, which sets out the extraordinarily close relationship between mother and son. It is an important document, and chronicles the development of a man who clearly needed a woman's love at every point in his life. Dorothe's personal diary, and what appears to be passages written contemporaneously in other notebooks, was cut and compiled with photographs, years later, by her youngest daughter, Elizabeth. Her words are the rich testimony of a mother who loved her son and regarded almost every event in his life as significant.

Many of the letters Bushell wrote to his family during the four years he spent as a prisoner of the Germans are also contained within the archive. A handful of these provide insights into his state of mind at critical periods of the war. Others mask his true intentions, but display the wit of a Cambridge graduate even in adversity. All of his letters are beautifully written.

A third strand of information – often in the form of clarification – is provided by Ben Bushell's notes in the margins, added after the war as he created the archive and tried to make sense of his son's life.

Some events are well documented; some are not. Research can be frustrating, with hours spent in libraries and archives, but the life of Roger Bushell was rarely dull and I was often blessed by the company of generous people – who also wanted to know more about him – and by a number of remarkable coincidences.

Bushell's letters from Germany contained several references to Graham and Mildred Blandy, whose family made fortified wines in Madeira. Mildred was a friend of Bushell's from South Africa who dispatched food parcels to him in Germany. Her son, as it turned out, was a colleague of mine at *The Times*.

When I was invited to have lunch with the grandson of Bushell's guardian, Harry North-Lewis, the family asked several friends to join us. Among them was a nephew of one of the Great Escapers, Mike Casey, and another man whose father, George Dudley Craig, ran the escape committee's intelligence operation in the East Compound. He handed me coded letters and silk escape maps from Stalag Luft III. He had a boxful of the stuff at home.

Similarly, after visiting the site of Tangmere aerodrome, where Bushell had commanded a fighter squadron, I visited my brother-in-law who lived nearby and told him about the story I was trying to write. As the evening wore on, it became clear that his wife's father, born in 1907, had gone to school with Bushell.

In England, Wellington College was preparing for the bicentenary of the Battle of Waterloo in 2015. Archives that had been forgotten in boxes for the best part of a century were being opened. Among these papers were some of Roger Bushell's school reports.

In the Czech national archive, it can sometimes take weeks to get hold of documents. I was lucky. One of the members of staff, who spoke some English, was interested in Bushell. She found Czech and German papers relevant to the case – including a Gestapo file. I had the phone number of the taxi driver who had picked me up in central Prague. He was a law student from Charles University who spoke fluent English and agreed to translate.

In South Africa, the Bushell family shared letters and photographs as well as hospitality. We visited the places where Roger grew up: the family house on the gold reef, his first school in Johannesburg and the home to which his mother and father retired in Hermanus on the Cape coast. A memorial to Roger sits on the seafront at the old harbour. And, each year, Hermanus High School awards two prizes in his name, in recognition of character and linguistics.

Many doors opened, although some remained resolutely shut, and still do, but gradually the details of a remarkable life emerged.

This is the story of Roger Bushell, a young man bent on the pursuit of pleasure and excitement who emerged as a war hero – a somewhat flawed hero, perhaps – but a war hero nonetheless, who was loved by many people, men and women alike. His story deserves to be told.

1

The Great Escape

In the village of Penn in England's Chiltern Hills, a woman waited. She had been waiting a long time – two years since the collapse of an unwanted marriage, nearly nine since the giddy summer of 1935.

Elegant, aristocratic, a former model, she was quite a catch.

Like many women the world over on the night of 24 March 1944, she was waiting for a man to return from the war. His letters had dropped several hopeful hints that he might soon be on his way; the Christmas just past, he wrote, would definitely be his last as a prisoner in Germany. Sitting in her country home, she yearned to have him back.

To the east, some 700 miles away, close to the border between Germany and Poland, a black and white photograph of the same woman hung on the wall of a sparse wooden hut. It was one of many such huts in Stalag Luft III, a vast camp built to house thousands of Allied airmen who had been shot down over Occupied Europe and taken prisoner by the Nazis.

That night, the picture of Lady Georgiana Mary Curzon looked down on an empty room. The usual occupant was waiting impatiently in a tunnel known as 'Harry', thirty feet below the frozen German countryside. His name was Roger Bushell. The other prisoners knew him as 'Big X', the chief executive of the camp's escape committee. Born in South Africa of British parents, Bushell was thirty-three years old. He was a powerful man, not quite six foot, with a thick mop of dark brown hair, a strong, deep voice and striking, bright blue eyes that seemed to shine in the dark.

In her journal, his mother, Dorothe, was moved to write:

He was so good to look at; his face growing more like my people's, but a figure a replica of his father's when young – broad-shouldered, slender-hipped, long but beautiful hands and feet, and a natural grace of movement.

Bushell lived in the North Compound of Stalag Luft III, a group of twenty-odd buildings set behind watchtowers and walls of barbed wire 120 miles south-east of Berlin – about as far from a friendly border as an Allied prisoner could find himself within Nazi Germany.

The tunnel in which he waited that night was one of three – 'Tom', 'Dick' and 'Harry' – built by the prisoners during the previous eleven months as Bushell, a Cambridge graduate, barrister and international skier with a compelling love life, put the business of escaping on an industrial footing. 'Harry' bore witness to Bushell's power, his organisational genius and the respect with which he was held by his fellow prisoners of war.

In the North Compound, Bushell had 'nationalised' the escape industry. All the resources of the 'state' – certainly British, and many German too – were used by the 600 prisoners from many nations who volunteered to support this Allied operation against the Nazis. Private enterprise tunnels had been banned.

The entrance to 'Harry' was just two feet square, but big enough to take a big man in a big coat. Running north for 320 feet from Hut 104 into the pine forest that surrounded the camp, the tunnel was shored up with more than 3,000 panels taken from beds, tables and wooden walls; it was lit by electric bulbs and ventilated by an air-conditioning system. Tracks like a railway made it relatively easy to move backwards and forwards from the entrance shaft to the face of the tunnel. 'Harry' was an inspirational piece of improvised engineering, built in secret and hidden from the Germans.

Squadron Leader Bushell had joined the escaping business within a few weeks of being shot down four years previously when he had been leading the Spitfires of No. 92 Squadron over northern France. He was confident that this, his third escape of the war, would be his last.

He had some good reasons to be optimistic. Preparation for the escape had been thorough. The 200 men Bushell planned to get out of the camp that night – the biggest mass escape of the war by Allied airmen – were better equipped than any prisoners had ever been. They had been issued with forged papers, compasses, maps, and escape rations, and wore civilian clothing or German uniforms. Most of the equipment was produced by the prisoners. The quality of much of their work was good. Only the weather was against them.

The head of the escape committee had advantages over most of the men who were attempting to get out that night. Travelling in the guise of a French businessman working for the aircraft manufacturer Focke Wolf, Bushell wore genuine civilian clothes: a well-fitted continental suit picked up in Prague in 1942, and a trilby hat smuggled into the camp from England. His French papers may well have been authentic and he carried letters of accreditation. He was fluent in French, one of the nine languages he spoke, and also German. Big X intended to travel west towards France. His travelling companion was a Frenchman, Bernard Scheidhauer, a twenty-two-year-old fighter pilot whose family had connections with the Resistance. Scheidhauer was also familiar with the border that they would have to cross. The two men were scheduled to be among the first out of the tunnel and planned to catch a train from Sagan station, a two-mile walk from the camp through the pine forest.

If anyone stood a chance of getting home, many thought it would be Roger Bushell.

But Big X also carried many burdens and secrets. Unusually, Bushell combined two key roles in the North Compound: he was in charge of all escape activity, but he was also a significant intelligence asset, with a special brief on Germany, and his influence carried far beyond the confines of the North Compound. By March 1944, his name was familiar to British military intelligence, which had registered him in 1940 as a potential contact. He was one of the first RAF prisoners to establish links with London and he helped to develop the use of coded letters and radio signals to such an extent that intelligence gathered by prisoners of war became a useful source of information for the Allies.

The name of the British squadron leader was also familiar to the German secret police, the Gestapo. Two earlier escape attempts had raised his profile, and Bushell was under no illusions about the fate that awaited him if he were to be caught again. He would be shot.

It was 9.30 p.m. Everyone was nervous.

As Bushell contemplated his position that night and planned ahead, the wind made just enough noise to muffle the sound of a spade breaking through frozen ground. There was no moon.

Sixteen prisoners waited in the tunnel with Bushell. Some men lay on trolleys, waiting to be pulled towards the exit. Others waited in sidings known as 'Piccadilly' and 'Leicester Square', halfway houses that were wider than the main tunnel.

Up above, in Hut 104, another 173 men waited in rooms and corridors for their turn to enter the tunnel and begin the journey home. Men wore thick civilian jackets and coats made from military uniforms and blankets. They carried cases and other luggage. Anxious and overdressed to cope with the intense cold, they sweated as they waited. Hearts pumped hard. Sometimes it seemed that the walls of the tunnel would burst open as boards creaked and the air thickened with the prisoners' breath. These were the most frightening moments, dangerously claustrophobic, as men waited in the tunnel, deep underground.

In Hut 104, where the entrance to 'Harry' was built into a concrete shaft under a stove, the strain showed, too. Men in many guises drew on cigarettes. Amid the smoke, airmen wearing suits posed as Dutch or French businessmen. Others were dressed as workers from Bohemia and Moravia and the Baltic states. One airman had entered wearing the uniform of a German officer; for just a moment, there had been a hint of panic.

The escape should have started at 9.30 p.m. but it was already nearer 10 p.m. For many it was just like the hours before a big raid on Germany when airmen sat around their bases in England, waiting for the bombers to be armed and fuelled, well aware that the odds on getting back alive were not too good.

Bushell lay close to the far end of the tunnel where two men, Lester Bull and Henry Marshall, both known as Johnny, struggled in the darkness to loosen the tightly packed boards that protected the exit shaft. Swollen with water from melting snow, the boards were jammed.

On that Friday evening, as Bull and Marshall struggled to open the exit to 'Harry', the Allied armies were still not certain of victory: the British and Americans were under attack on the Anzio beach-head south of Rome as they struggled to advance in Italy; the Allied invasion of northern France had not yet taken place; and their air forces were still suffering heavy losses over Germany, with the number of airmen entering captivity on the Silesian Plain rising steadily. The Russian armies were still fighting within their own territory.

Roger Bushell's own war had seemed equally tumultuous; it had been shaped at times by his relationships with three women. The first was his fiancée, Peggy Hamilton, an ambitious woman from Henley; the second was a Czech patriot called Blažena Zeithammelová; and the third was a beautiful debutante called Georgie, who yearned for his return. She had loved and lost him in the mid-1930s, and in the months that Big X planned and organised this most audacious of Allied escape attempts, it was her letters from England that had strengthened his resolve.

The mass escape would not enable many men to get back to Britain. Most of those who would crawl through the tunnel that night knew they stood very little chance of being at large for long in Occupied Europe, particularly in winter. But Bushell had made it clear to the occupants of the North Compound that it was just as important to disrupt the German war effort – 'to make life hell for the Hun' – and that a breakout on this scale would help the Allied war effort.

As Bushell waited, Adolf Hitler was at the Berghof, his mountain headquarters in Bavaria, where, the following morning, he would conduct the daily war conference with Field Marshal Keitel, chief of the German High Command, and other leading Nazis.

At a few minutes past 10 o'clock, Johnny Bull stripped to his underpants as he heaved and sweated, loosening one of the boards barring the prisoners' way into the Sagan forest. The other boards came away more easily. Johnny Marshall took over and removed the last few inches of soil. Within a couple of moments, he could see the stars.

Roger Bushell felt the blast of cold air almost immediately. The Great Escape was on.

2

A Taste of Freedom

Roger Bushell hated tunnels. He always avoided the London Tube. He had been a deeply claustrophobic boy who feared enclosed spaces, even though he grew up on a South African gold mine. He had no intention of following in the footsteps of his father, Benjamin Daniel Bushell, a mining engineer who had learnt his business in the Canadian Klondike and managed some of the most dangerous and difficult mines on the gold reef east of Johannesburg.

Ben was a man who demonstrated both great authority and great courage and was always on site, often underground, whenever the miners hit trouble. His employer, the fledgeling Anglo-American Corporation, built its wealth on the back of the mines managed by him at Daggafontein, and Springs in the Transvaal.

The company, founded by Ernest Oppenheimer, was quick to pay tribute to the man responsible, as the minutes of the seventh general meeting of Springs Shareholders, held on the second floor of the Corner House in Johannesburg at 10.45 a.m. on 26 May 1924, show:

Mr Bushell, the Mine Manager, and his staff have earned our warmest thanks. They have done excellent work throughout the year. The rapid progress made, both underground and on the surface, is worthy of the highest praise; indeed, it is only through Mr Bushell's personality and the whole-hearted support of the staff and employees that we have today reached the producing stage.

Ben's first child, Roger, was slow to reveal similar traits. When it came to 'tunnelling' or other games in the gardens of the various family homes, it was his sister Rosemary who, goaded by Roger, led the way. He teased her relentlessly, even going so far, one memorable day, as to burn her dolls at the stake.

Roger Joyce Bushell was born on 30 August 1910, just as the Union of South Africa was granted independence. His birth was both difficult and propitious: he was delivered by an alcoholic doctor as Halley's comet passed through the South African sky.

In her journal of Roger's early life, his mother, Dorothe, wrote:

After hours of raging storm when lightning ripped the heavens open and thunder crashed above our house on Springs Mine, Roger was born.

Moving across the room, the attending nurse had drawn back the curtains at the window to reveal a flaming gold torch on the deep blue heavens. She turned towards me and said: 'Do you know that when Halley's comet is in the sky a great man dies and a great man is born?' I understood the inference, smiled at the apparent absurdity of it; but loved her for saying it.

Roger's mother, Dorothe Wingate White, was related to General Sir Francis Wingate, who took part in the historic mission to rescue General Gordon at Khartoum in 1885, but whose principal work involved military intelligence. Roger's cousins included T. H. White, author of *The Once and Future King*, and Major General Orde Wingate, the inspirational leader of the Chindits, the unorthodox guerrilla army that confronted the Japanese in Burma.

Roger's father could trace his forebears to the knights of William the Conqueror: one of them is said to have been named on the Battle Abbey roll of William's chief lieutenants after the victory at Hastings in 1066. The founder of the modern branch of the family was Sir Alan Busshell of Brodmerston in

Gloucestershire (a name that would resonate for Roger Bushell throughout the Second World War). Sir Alan died in 1245. The family motto, '*Dum spiro spero*' ('While I breathe, I hope'), was strangely portentous.

Ben was born in Britain and Dorothe in India, but they met in South Africa. He was looking for a position in the mines; she was visiting her brother who had fought in the Boer War at the turn of the century, when Britain made a grab for the gold and diamonds controlled by the other white tribe there, the Dutch-descended Afrikaners.

Ben Bushell was a tall man, with strong sinewy limbs, high cheeks and a firm jaw line; he was thirty-one when Roger was born. He dressed immaculately: beautiful shoes and shirts, often bought in London, and tweed jackets. He fussed about discipline. Dorothe bore an inner serenity. Dark and striking, she was modern and intuitive, having grown up with privileged relatives while her father served the Empire. She was twenty-seven when she gave birth to her son, and she adored him.

Dorothe nurtured him tenderly.

> *He was a delicate baby,* she wrote in her journal. *His body never seemed strong enough for the robust spirit within him and I had to watch over him with very special love and care.*

Indeed, amid fears that he might not live, the infant Roger was christened by his Catholic nurse when only a few days old. He was christened again at six months at St George's Anglican Church in the Johannesburg suburb of Park Town. It was a grand occasion.

By the standards of most South Africans, the Bushells were wealthy. Nadine Gordimer, the author, political activist and Nobel Laureate, grew up near the Bushells' home in the town of Springs. The family made a significant impression on her. In an interview in 2012, she described them as 'aristocracy'.

In 1912, at the age of two, Roger made his first trip to England. He was accompanied by Rosemary, his six-week-old baby sister, who became known as Tods after one of the characters in an American book, *Budge and Toddie*, about two naughty children.

> *By now Roger could run at such speed that his old Mummie could not cope with him, and the stewards spent much of this time chasing him down corridors and returning him to our cabin.*
>
> *When possible the steward would carry him round the deck and then into the bar where he received an uproarious welcome. Then and there, I think Roger decided that a bar was a friendly place.*

Roger was also becoming increasingly aware of his own powers and pushed at the boundaries of acceptable behaviour. Among friends and relatives in England, his mother tried to get her son to eat food he did not like and to be quiet when he wanted to make a noise, but Dorothe often spoiled him, and the boy complained loudly when he did not get what he wanted. And when defeated, he quickly moved on to challenge his mother in new ways. 'His blue eyes sparkled with devilment,' she wrote in her journal, thankful to get him back home.

In time, the Bushells moved to a new house that stood in the middle of a vast garden, almost an estate, on the outskirts of Springs. It was an extensive single-storey building, with a colonnaded veranda, the sort of classic colonial architecture built across India to protect British families from the heat. In the grounds were a stable, garages and a tennis court. Next door was a golf course. The family had a car, a chauffeur, many gardeners who would help Dorothe replant the estate in an English style, and kitchen staff and servants.

The family photograph albums shed light on a privileged childhood; a loving family; holidays on the coast where the boy overcame his fear of the sea; and pet dogs, including his beloved fox terrier, Tuppy. Roger fairly beams out of the pictures.

His 'baby days were very happy ones', wrote Dorothe. 'Brain and body became increasingly active and were combined with a personality which was loving, responsive and fearless.'

Dorothe also noticed a curious thing about her son's striking blue eyes: 'They shone in the dark; not so brilliantly as an animal's, but quite luminously.'

Roger's sense of mischief and adventure was growing. Trouble inevitably loomed when the Bushells bought their first car. 'It was a Ford,' wrote his mother:

The child took the greatest interest and delight in it and always wanted to help if any repairs had to be done. When he came out with me I let him switch on the engine, put his hand on mine as I changed gear and hold the steering wheel with me as we drove along.

I realised my stupidity in doing this one morning when I got out of the car and left the engine running. In a few seconds the young monkey was in the driving seat and the Ford was moving slowly down the street. Fortunately, he had only just put her into first gear so that by running I caught him up and switched off the engine.

Roger got a good scolding, but took little notice of it, for as soon as he got home he told his father with great pride of what he had done and I got a far worse wigging than he did.

Dorothe's journal and the family photograph albums remain the only known sources of information on this period of Bushell's life, but – even allowing for a mother's lack of objectivity – they paint a clear picture of a boy with an increasing appetite for life and all the advantages his privileged background afforded:

*During the next few years, Roger tried to learn everything
within his orbit and we encouraged him to do so.
Partridges and snipe were plentiful on the land around and
wild duck only a mile or two away, so that his father often
took him with him when he went shooting,* Dorothe
wrote. *At the coast they used to go out in a boat on
Walker Bay and fish together. I taught him to ride and
drive the ponies and Abram, the old coloured boy in
charge of the stables, taught him, when he was eight years
old, to drive the Springs ponies with the mules, and bring
them all to a halt. Quite a fine effort for a child of that
age.*

At about this time, the family discovered Hermanus, a small
resort on the Western Cape, a thousand miles from Johannesburg
and more than a day away by train. The town consisted of just a
handful of houses with thatched reed roofs. Its verdant coastline
includes long stretches of sandy beach broken by dramatic
outcrops of volcanic rock. Behind the town, a range of mountains
rises steeply. Hermanus looks out over a great bay in which
Southern Right whales enter in the spring to calve, and where
Orcas can sometimes be seen rising out of the sea, showing off
their great white bellies.

Dorothe's children were enchanted by the resort.

The days were joyous ones, she wrote. *They all surfed on
the Cape rollers, launched boats in the lagoon, and fished
the inlets. The sea there is perilously unpredictable. It can
be compelling in its turbulent magnificence: a threatening
swell at first, then a raging white storm turned against the
coastal granite, almost certainly fatal for a little boy caught
in its path.*

   *Roger learnt to fish from the great rocks, a skilful
and dangerous pastime,* wrote Dorothe, *but his father
and his old ghillie watched him with unceasing care*

and were very stern with him if he did anything foolish.

As he passed his eighth birthday at the end of August 1918, just as the First World War was coming to an end, the curtain was falling on Roger's idyllic early childhood during which he was given the freedom to roam on untouched beaches and ride across unfenced veldt under vast blue skies.

Dorothe and her two children had lived largely in isolation, cocooned from the global conflict in which millions had died, and possibly even oblivious to the jealousies and growing social tensions on their own doorstep.

Nadine Gordimer remembered quite clearly the conspicuously affluent family living near her in Springs: 'Here was this road with our little suburban colonialist houses and at the end of the road – it was a dead end – the Springs mine was at the very end of the road and in front of one of the shafts was a big garden with great hedges and fences around it and that was the Bushells', the mine manager's residence in this little dorp [town]. This person was the most important person in the town; this was the aristocracy – and of course we were all very curious what his house was like.

'I don't know how it came about but I did discover it had something I'd never heard of as a child, and that was that he had his own billiards room! Nowadays everyone has a swimming pool, but here was a billiards room. So there was our little palace, our little royalty from Springs mine at the bottom of the road where, indeed, I lived.'

Gordimer, the daughter of an English mother and a Latvian father, observed life on the opposite side of the street from the Bushells. Black mine workers, many of them immigrants, were badly paid and badly housed far away from their families; they lived in compounds and were discouraged from visiting shops in Springs town centre, twenty minutes from the mine. White girls were taught to live in fear of black miners.

The author and political activist hated Springs. 'It was incredibly closed off. I have no happy memories of it at all. There was nothing there for me . . . Roger Bushell is a legend, but the family were colonialists,' Gordimer said.

In 1919, the decision was taken to send Roger to Park Town Prep, a boarding school forty miles away in Johannesburg. He was eight and a half years old. Until this time, Roger had been taught at home by his mother. 'He was a delightful child to teach, so interested in everything and particularly history,' she noted.

Dorothe had two concerns about sending her son away to school in Johannesburg, and both concerned two babyish habits that might lay him open to bullying. One was an almost 'unbearable' habit of sucking his thumb; the other 'an almost absurd devotion' to a small teddy bear that he had been given on his fourth birthday. It went with him everywhere and was always clasped in his arms when he went to sleep.

The introduction to Park Town School was traumatic for mother and son.

He asked me to stop the car before reaching the entrance to the school. There, both of us in tears, we hugged each other and said goodbye. When at school the moment for parting came, he shook hands with me and said, 'Goodbye, Mummie' and marched off.

Roger had assured his mother he would not suck his thumb when he went away to school and, indeed, the habit had gone by the time he came home for his first holidays. The teddy bear, however, was a more intractable problem: Roger had insisted on taking the bear to school in spite of Dorothe's fears. If there was any trouble, he would fight the boy who caused it. This happened on more than one occasion, but in the end he was left in peace. Teddy slept with him every night and, eventually, the bear was looked on as a mascot in the dormitory.

A majestic building, the school commanded the heights of Johannesburg, with a breathtaking view over the veldt looking to the north. If the boys, all from wealthy white families, did not have a sense of their own superiority before they arrived, they would surely have done so afterwards. New boys approaching PTS, as it was known, would have driven down a road lined with jacaranda trees, a regal guard of honour in purple bloom.

The school was built in 1904 as the personal residence of Percival Tracey, a mining magnate, and was intended to impress, with sparkling white gables in the Cape Dutch style and an expansive veranda wrapped around the building. The entrance hall is equally impressive. A grand staircase made of solid Burmese teak sweeps down into the main hall, the largest of forty rooms found on three levels.

Wearing distinctive cherry-red jackets with 'PTS' emblazoned on the breast pocket, and floppy red bush hats in the same colour, the boys were allocated to one of four school houses whose names resonated with the power of Empire: Haig, Kitchener, Jellicoe and Beatty – the triumphant British generals and admirals of the great global conflict that had drawn to a close just a year before Roger took his place in the school.

The experience of Park Town School had a profound effect on the boy. It hardened him. Dorothe confided in her journal that, although Roger had 'rather a little temper', he never sulked or bore malice and 'took punishment cheerfully'. Indeed, she wrote – no doubt with plenty of maternal pride – from a young age Roger had two outstanding characteristics: 'courage and truthfulness, both of which often got him into trouble'.

By 1921, Ben Bushell's six-month leave in Britain was due again and, despite a determined rearguard action by the Park Town headmaster, Dorothe succeeded in taking Roger out of school to accompany her to Britain:

The headmaster of PTS insisted that if we went to England we should leave Roger behind. His father also thought this wise; but for years I had promised my small son that one

day I would show him the historic places in England I had
talked about and also some of the great shows like
Olympia. I could not let him down, so as the two men
continued to argue about the importance of his education I
said that I would not go either.

I felt that I could not leave him for six months when in
two years' time he was to go to Wellington College.
Needless to say, we all went and although later in life Roger
teased me about the endless sightseeing I dragged him to,
he was intensely interested in all he saw and I am sure that
it laid the foundation of wide interests.

For one term, Roger swapped the grandeur of Park Town for the greater magnificence of London and the somewhat less ambitious timetable of a school in Margate, 'where he put on weight and was very well and happy'.

When the Bushells returned to South Africa in 1922, they found a country in turmoil. The Rand Revolt, an armed rebellion by white miners, threatened the state after the mining companies tried to cut costs when the price of gold collapsed in late 1921. They wanted to cut the miners' pay and weaken the colour bar to promote cheaper black miners to skilled jobs. The strikers' cause was typified by the slogan: 'Workers of the world unite and fight for a white South Africa.' They were crushed by military force. More than 200 people died.

Roger threw himself back into life at PTS, where he started to prepare for the English public school entrance exam. He was also encouraged in many sports: rifle pellets can still be found embedded in the shooting range wall even though the school closed more than half a century ago. There were swimming galas and rugby matches, and the boys embarked on other adventures too. Several were beaten by the headmaster for using a fire escape that overlooked the staff bedrooms to watch the matrons undress; others used the entrance to the heating shafts outside their dormitories on the third floor to make illegal forays downstairs at night. The exit shaft in the dining room is two feet square and lined with teak, and looks rather familiar to anyone who has seen photographs of the tunnel 'Harry'.

3

England Beckons

In January 1924, at the age of thirteen, Roger Bushell sailed with his mother for England to take up his place at Wellington College. He would return to South Africa on only a handful of occasions and never lived there again. His love affair with England would last the rest of his life.

Roger had scraped through his Common Entrance at the end of 1923 – as he would with most of the exams he took over the next ten years.

The journey by sea was memorable. As they sailed past the West African coast towards Europe, two significant events occurred: one posed an immediate threat to Roger's life, the other had portents for the future.

Far to the north-east, Adolf Hitler was facing trial in Munich after his national socialist party's failure the previous November to take control of the city in an armed rebellion known as the Beer Hall Putsch. He was imprisoned but used his incarceration to write *Mein Kampf*, the influential autobiography that set out his vision for a new Germany and established the ground for his rise to power.

The Bushells were almost certainly oblivious to these developments as they headed for the Bay of Biscay and the weather changed. The ship was suddenly hit by fierce storms. Lifeboats were provisioned and slung out in preparation for an emergency; passengers were drilled over the use of lifebelts and their places in the boats. 'Roger was thrilled and never showed any fear, although the cold was intense and the sea looked wicked,' wrote Dorothe.

At Plymouth, the ship was not allowed to dock because of a strike. So the Bushells were taken to Tilbury and had to make the journey into London in an old charabanc. By the time Dorothe had bought Roger's school uniform and other items for his room, the Lent term was well under way.

Thousands of miles from their home in South Africa, the Bushells found that Wellington College was a world away from the cosy, familiar corridors of Park Town. The school was vast; an imposing place built in nearly 400 acres of heathland near Crowthorne in Berkshire. It was steeped in history and had a distinctly military bearing.

Even though her brothers had been educated there, Dorothe was concerned.

Not to know even one of the seething mass of schoolboys into which Roger was suddenly thrown must have been a great ordeal for a 13-year-old South African, she wrote in her journal. *At the moment of my leaving, he broke down. The housemaster was very kind and gentle and took him to the housekeeper's room where Roger told me there was a lovely fire and she gave him a steaming hot tea.*

A fortnight later, the housemaster, Karl Stocken, wrote to Roger's mother.

Don't worry about him any more. He has already organised the new boys in the House, and is very fit and full of himself. I know the type well. He will be beaten fairly often, but he will be much liked and perfectly happy.

Many of the boys with whom Roger mixed and became friends were the sons of soldiers. The school was founded in 1859 on the initiative of Queen Victoria and her husband, Prince Albert, to commemorate the life of Arthur Wellesley, First Duke of Wellington, the victor of Waterloo. Over the years, the school has provided the British Army with thousands of officers and men. Six hundred of them were killed in the First World War.

The Master of the school was Frederick Blagden Malim, a classics scholar from Trinity College, Cambridge, who was largely unapproachable. Malim was an authoritative figure. About 5ft 10in, thickset, with grey hair, he was an outstanding preacher and a demanding man. He ran a good school, according to Patrick Mileham, the college historian, but it was nevertheless 'an open prison for boys'.

Pupils with strong gifts in body and soul, those who were intelligent and good at games, did well. Roger flourished. He joined Wellesley House, one of several 'houses', which were almost schools within the school, and around which Wellington was organised. The boys in Wellesley lived in cubicles on the second floor; each partitioned either side of a long corridor, so that they had a degree of privacy, which was unusual in English public schools. There was a bathroom with three baths and four showers. A matron looked after their clothes.

Discipline was enforced by house prefects who had several measures for doing so at their disposal. The main punishment was a form of 'forced labour' – jobs carried out for the senior boys – under a system known as fagging, which would have been familiar to readers of *Tom Brown's Schooldays*; detention for poor work; and beatings for general slackness. The boys were beaten often. Senior boys demanded respect and got it, but there was an underlying resistance to the authority of the school that Roger would probably have embraced.

Dorothe remained in England until after the Easter holidays. During these, she took her son to Jersey, where it rained a good deal, but they picnicked and swam regardless of the weather and were joined by her husband's sister, Eleanor North-Lewis, and one of her sons.

We had anxious moments for the Jersey tide is treacherous and the boys attached themselves to a fisherman who took them up almost perpendicular cliffs after gulls' eggs. One afternoon, Roger was taking an egg from a nest when the

*father gull returned and with screaming fury attacked him.
The fisherman was close by and soon drove off the angry
bird, but he told me later that the boy's sense in lowering
his head and flattening himself against the rock saved his
life.*

The incident gave Dorothe a moment of reflection:

*I was often criticised for letting Roger do risky, dangerous
things, but I always felt that I must never undermine the
courage that was an integral part of him. Also, I don't
think that any moaning on my part would have stopped
him. He was not that fearless type who seems unaware of
dangers; for often after facing and overcoming it he would
look very white, but his eyes would be alight and the
blueness of them intensified.*

In the autumn of 1924, Roger found a new ally at the school in
Michael Fitzwilliam Peacock, another boy who had spent his
early childhood in South Africa and who was comfortable with
both the academic and athletic worlds in which they were forced
to exist. The two boys hit it off immediately.

Nearly ninety years on from those days at Wellington, one of
their contemporaries recalled the two boys when his memory of
most others had faded. David Wilkinson arrived at Wellington in
1925, the year after Bushell and Peacock, and joined Hopetoun, a
different, and therefore distant, house. 'Bushell was a very active
chap. Dark, really quite athletic, good looking,' he said. 'Peacock
was always in the news doing something. He was an extraordi-
nary-looking chap. He was a good sportsman, too. They were
both very colourful characters.'

Roger found he had a talent for languages, a voracious appetite
for reading and – with the skills he had acquired at home learning
to hunt, shoot, fish and live off the land – the potential to be an
outstanding Boy Scout. His confidence grew.

Photographs of him in the Wellesley House journal show a handsome boy, a natural cavalier with a swagger about him, a cockiness that sometimes irked authority, and which the author Paul Brickhill, who knew him at Stalag Luft III, called 'suave belligerence'.

The house prefects who wrote the journal of Wellesley's sporting life were among those who took exception to the colonial boy's demeanour. They seem to have been reluctant to praise him and are critical of his judgment, with different authors repeating similar phrases over the four years he was at Wellington. On the other hand, they may have been a source of telling observations.

Roger was not regarded as a great team player. One rugby report read:

```
He has an excellent physique and unbounded
confidence in himself. He can run straight and
hard, deliver a telling hand-off, and tackle with
workmanlike precision; but he has yet to learn the
finer points of the game. He often stood too far up
to his scrum-half, and as a consequence against
close marking shewed [sic] a tendency to run
across the field, and he must cultivate the art of
making openings for others as well as for
himself.
```

Another grudgingly acknowledged a fine performance:

```
Bushell played a most resourceful game, and his
outstanding faults - selfishness and lack of
judgment - were seldom in evidence.
```

Cricket reports recorded a similar inconsistency.

```
As a cricketer he at present lacks stability. He
could at times bowl an almost unplayable ball,
```

28

whilst at others he sent down incredible loose
stuff. He has the power of swinging and breaking
the ball both ways. A very useful hitter with
powerful driving strokes on both sides of the
wicket. A fair ground field but an unreliable
catch.

Another stated:

He is still too apt to lose control of the ball in
trying to attain unnecessary speed without paying
sufficient attention to length. A moderate ground
field but an unreliable catch. His batting was weak
at the beginning of the term and even at the end
he never scored as he did last year. On the whole
he has not come up to expectations.

Roger disliked cross-country running and failed to make a great
impression at athletics. He almost cost the Wellesley team victory
in the house relay competition: 'Holland gained the House a
small lead over the first quarter, which was retained by Harries-
Jones and Bushell. But a poor exchange between Bushell and
Adams lost us five yards, and Adams had a terribly gruelling
battle with Rose down the straight, before beating him finally by
three yards.'

Despite the misgivings, Roger scored many tries, took many
wickets and hit many runs, and was eventually selected for the
College's 1st XV rugby team and his House's first teams at both
cricket and rugby. He represented the House at tug of war and
shooting and won the middleweight boxing title. He was clearly
capable of being ruthless:

Shaw tried to rush Bushell off his feet, *records
the house journal*, but Bushell soon stopped him,
and by the end of the first round Shaw was nearly

done. He made a great effort in the second round
but Bushell was much the better boxer, and the
fight was stopped. In the final, Bushell attacked at
once and battered Kingzett, till the referee
stopped the fight before the end of the first
round.

Most of Roger's early holidays were spent in a large, rambling old house near Saffron Walden in Essex, owned by a great uncle. Full of young people of all ages, they played games, produced plays and danced. The old man, a naturalist, took Roger on walks and bird-nesting expeditions.

Roger's mother returned to England in the summer of 1925, which was spent with him in Devon. She was struck by the changes in him.

> *I saw a great deal of my darling boy and we had long talks*
> *together. Even though he was only fourteen, I found that he*
> *had developed a good deal in the time we had been*
> *separated. He had very definite ideas of his own and*
> *expressed them with force and clarity. It made for great*
> *companionship and I realised Roger was a thinker and*
> *often what he said was well worth listening to. It is quality*
> *in people that counts, and there was quality in him even at*
> *this young age.*

But a more difficult side to his character was also developing, even in the company of his mother, who wrote:

> *Often he was thoughtless and trying and there was nothing*
> *of the saint in him; but there was something that was rare*
> *and some deep intuition warned me that I must never grasp*
> *or hold him and that certain things in his nature must have*
> *freedom in which to be fulfilled, whether I approved or*
> *not.*

30

She tried to get him to show some appreciation of music but he became bored with the classical concerts at Wellington and gave his tickets away.

> *He liked popular tunes,* wrote Dorothe, *and on a rather flat note would cheerily join in community singing, but buying a banjolele and learning to play something about a super girl was the height of his musical attainment.*

At the age of fifteen, Roger was given control of his own finances. The school fees were paid, but otherwise his allowance was put straight into his bank account.

He was sent to France for two Easter holidays to improve his French and lived with a family near Tours. In winter he travelled to Mürren in the Bernese Oberland to learn to ski. The annual holiday in Switzerland and his growing prowess at skiing were a source of great joy. 'His letters describing those happy days had the crispness and sparkle of snow which he loved so dearly,' wrote Dorothe. 'The invigorating air combined with the vigorous exercise had much to do with making him the robust young man he became.'

An article in the school magazine by Roger pulsates with his passion for skiing, a passion that would define the next period of his life, and his love of the mountains. Under the headline, 'The Kandahar', it reads:

A wonderful morning with the sun just rising over the Schilthorn ridge and the snow-laden trees glistening. High up on the Schiltgat one can see a bunch of figures and two flags. They look like so many ants on the side of a gigantic, white sheet that is dented and raised by some colossus taking his rest beneath.

Down in the valley a number of excited people and two men with stopwatches. High up the

mountainside a flag waves and half-a-dozen black
dots shoot off down a seemingly perpendicular
slope. Soon they become larger, and one can
clearly see the cloud of snow shooting out
behind their flying skis. Now they are at that
difficult shoulder and two fall in a smother of
snow and skis. The remaining four flash on,
almost sitting on their skis, with heads bent
forward and bodies straining. Veritable modern
Mercuries!

The leader executes a lightning Christiana and
just misses a half-concealed rock; but the next
man is not so lucky, and one hears a crash of
splintering wood, and a human form shoots
through the air landing in a huddled, senseless
mass in the snow. By this time the others have
shot past down that last stretch to Martha's
Meadow - the ruin of so many hopes. A flashing
black form races between two large flags, a
glorious Christiana and all is over. The
Kandahar is lost and won!

Roger, who was due to go up to Pembroke College, Cambridge,
the following autumn, made his last appearance in the Wellesley
House journal under the heading 'Lent Term 1929', which
recorded that the boys had returned to school after their Christmas
holidays on 18 January.

The parting shot was a generous one:

R. J. Bushell was the only person to leave House
last term. He was a dormitory prefect, a member of
the 1st XV, a first-class scout (incidentally, the
first 1st-class scout that the college troop has
produced) and a member of the House XV and cricket
XI. He duly lived up to his scout's motto and was

```
always prepared for everything - from big side
runs to a free fight.
```

His popularity both in House and College was due, it said, 'to his indomitable spirit'.

4

Pembroke and Piste

The young man with mesmerising eyes and the hundred-watt smile was yearning to embrace a high-octane life by the time he left Wellington College at Christmas 1928, two terms earlier than many of his contemporaries.

On the advice of Frederick Malim, the Master at Wellington, Roger Bushell spent two terms at Grenoble University, where he learnt to speak French, not only fluently, but in the manner of a Frenchman.

By this time, he had acquired one great passion, skiing, and he seems to have been working on a second – the female sex. At Grenoble, he pursued both interests with vigour. How much time he actually spent studying is not known, but the photographs in his album are of skiing and his new friends.

Afterwards, in the gap between Grenoble and Cambridge, he made a short trip to South Africa to see his parents and two sisters – Elizabeth, known as Lis, had been born in 1922 – but the visit was not a success: Roger would clearly have preferred to have been elsewhere.

In her journal, Dorothe wrestled with the problem:

I think he loved being in the house again and seeing his sisters. But the weather was atrocious. Howling gales and dust, tennis often impossible, the golf course hard and dry. He had become unused to family life and its necessary dovetailing.

The question of his future was discussed and to no purpose; for he still had no definite idea of what he wanted to be. This indecision was exasperating for his father, who had had to earn his living at a young age and was a man of action and quick decisions. He tried to persuade the boy to go in for mining; but it was the one profession for which Roger had a fear complex, as going underground gave him claustrophobia. I assured him that his father would never force him to do anything he hated; but I know that he was glad to go back to his beloved England and the delights of Cambridge and university life.

His application for Pembroke College was written almost two years previously, on 11 November 1926, in what appears to be his father's hand. The form, which was sent to W. S. Hadley, Master of Pembroke, stated that the boy wanted to study for Engineering Honours, starting at Easter 1929, with the intention of pursuing a career as a mining engineer. In fact, the young Bushell enrolled as a member of Cambridge University on 1 November 1929 to study law.

Even in the 1930s, the cobbled paths and flagstones of Pembroke must have summoned up a bygone age for the young South African. The undergraduates milled around elegant ancient courtyards and, from time to time, worshipped in the perfect symmetry of the college chapel designed by Christopher Wren. Like many a Cambridge college, its wine cellars were generous. But if an invitation from a don to drink from them was not in the offing, the college was well-placed for some of the city's most famous watering holes, including The Eagle in Benet Street, where the ceiling of the bar would later be decorated with the signatures of American airmen stationed near Cambridge during the Second World War.

Undergraduates roamed the immaculate gardens in the warm embrace of one of the university's smaller and more intimate colleges, snuggled in at the end of King's Parade next to Corpus Christi College. Rooms were assembled around alphabetically named staircases where, on arrival, young men – more often than not from public schools – would find their name beautifully inscribed in white painted lettering.

No record seems to exist of where Bushell lived during his first year at Pembroke, but he is believed to have occupied M7 in the Pitt building, named after William Pitt the Younger, during his second year. In his third and final year, he is thought to have lived in D9 above the Hall. Women known as 'bedders' tidied and cleaned for the budding lawyers, doctors, engineers and linguists, a luxury many took for granted.

Away from college life – the silence of the library, the laughter and earnest discussion of the wood-panelled communal dining room, the beauty of its gardens overlooked by a statue of Pitt – Pembroke men lived within easy reach of the Backs, where many a drunken summer afternoon was spent punting the river or picnicking on the meadows. The bicycle was the chosen mode of transport, which brought pastures further afield within range, including the big colleges of King's, St John's and Trinity, or even the village of Grantchester, a favourite destination outside the city.

The man who was one of the most influential at this stage of Bushell's life was Charles Hugo Ziegler – C. H. Ziegler – the director of law studies, known to his students as 'Charlie'. His teaching enabled Bushell to start his career working with some of the most prestigious lawyers in England.

Ziegler had himself been an exceptional student at Pembroke; he took a first in both parts of the Law Tripos, coming second in the first part and first in the second. He graduated in June 1912, and took his Masters in November 1918. He was a legal powerhouse who took an unorthodox approach to teaching.

Another of the young men to benefit was Hugh Saunders, who enrolled as a law student at Pembroke at the same time as Bushell, after being educated at Harrow. Ziegler made a deep impression on them both. Saunders said he had the 'deserved reputation' of being able to get the dullest people through their

law exams, and he coached across the university from 1913 to
1952.

There are some people whose words of counsel one can remember almost audibly even after many years to the extent of seem-
ing actually to hear a speaking voice. Ziegler was such a man and
I vividly remember meeting him in his tutorial room on the
ground floor of Red Buildings. There he sat at the head of a long,
baize-covered table in a Victorian room whose walls were
festooned with photos of countless undergraduates who had sat
at his feet learning the elements of English and Roman Law over
many years. It was indeed a gallery of the good and the great,
whose names formed part of Pembroke's tradition of athletic
prowess.

He beckoned me to sit down beside him, a rather wizened
little middle-aged man with a smiling face and a quiet calm
about him that at once made you feel at home. I shall never forget
his words. 'You come from Harrow – I don't expect you to be
clever, I don't expect you to work hard – but I do expect you to be
a good chap.'

For three years, Saunders and Bushell sat around his table once or
twice a week to hear him declaim on Roman Law, Common Law,
Equity and Constitutional Law. Each week they were supposed to
study, to use obscure passages in learned works, and each week he
expounded upon them and made them clear.

In the centre of the table was a black box containing a deaf aid
wired to headphones which Ziegler wore, *wrote Saunders in the
College Review years later*. Every now and then the box would
emit loud squeaks and buzzes as he adjusted it. He was wont to
ask a question about a subject in hand and often there would be
mutters of our distaste for the subject and the question in particular. He would say, 'Take care, gentlemen. I have a new battery
this morning and can hear everything.'

He would test his students suddenly, throwing down a question that often they would be at a loss to answer. Saunders remembered one vivid moment when Ziegler suddenly said, 'Gentlemen, what is jurisdiction?'

There was silence – none of us seemed to have a clue – then P. C. Yu, a Chinese member of the college, spoke from the depth of his Mandarin culture: 'Jurisdiction is the length of the sword-arm of the ruler.' We were all spellbound. Yu's father had been in the college and his son brought to us something of the culture of his home, and the value of having an oriental mind in our group. Ziegler well understood the benefits to be derived by English public school boys from working with men whose minds had a different background. We all benefited by this mixture, which Ziegler seemed to embody, as it was said that he himself was half-Burmese and half-German.

He so often said to us, 'I don't want to teach you facts, gentlemen. I want to teach you principles', and these were understood as his teaching went on. Ziegler made us all contribute from our backgrounds, diverse as they were: P. K. Mistri the Parsee; E. S. Fay from Canada, R. J. Bushell from South Africa. All saw the world of law from different viewpoints. But it was Ziegler who welded us together without our knowing it and gave us vivid pictures of the great figures of the past. Justinian, Henry II and Edward I were people he knew and admired, just as if he had met them and known them.

Although Bushell was undoubtedly clever, and he listened intently to Ziegler, he did not spend a great deal of time on his studies. One of his peers at Pembroke in 1929 was Max Aitken, son of Lord Beaverbrook, the wealthy Canadian who owned the *Daily Express*, an influential newspaper at this time, and a close friend of Winston Churchill.

Bushell, the cavalier South African, and Aitken, the millionaire Canadian, became friends. Aitken opened the first doors to high society and the world of debutantes, unleashing what Roger's mother later described in her journal as 'his joie de vivre – and touch of joie de vice'.

In the spring of 1930, Dorothe sailed for Europe again, this time with her elder daughter, Rosemary. They were planning to go to Italy for a month before Rosemary started finishing school in Switzerland. They were met at Waterloo station by Bushell, who enveloped them in bear hugs, and they spent a week together in London.

> *Roger had written to me of a certain lovely and her Mamma, so as soon as I arrived I was whisked off to see them. As Roger was at the age and stage of culture where he shuddered at a split infinitive, I had no qualms at the type of woman I was going to meet.*

But Bushell's girlfriend and her mother came as a 'considerable shock' to Dorothe. With a candour and snobbery that is in itself somewhat shocking, Dorothe wrote:

> *The girl was a pretty creature, well-mannered and polished by a good school; but there was a glint in her green eyes and a hard line between her small lips which I did not like. Mrs X with her plucked eyebrows, scarlet lipstick which strayed well beyond her larger mouth, and the horrid smell of drink, which pervaded her once luxurious flat, was quite breathtaking.*
>
> *However, as I talked to her, looked into her candid eyes, listened to her noisy blathering, I saw beneath the cheap glitter, a heart too big and generous to be wise. I felt sure that she made the best of life as it came, without criticism of those who fail, without envy for those who succeed and that she was ready to share her material good fortune on all who crossed her path.*

An interesting exchange ensued between mother and son. Roger asked her opinion of the two women.

Dorothe answered frankly.

'Mamma,' he replied, 'you are full of surprises. I imagined you would place Mrs X beyond the pale, but you are dead right about them both. Mrs X has a heart of gold and I love her; but the sweetie has the nastiest little claws beneath those soft paws.' He added, kissing me, 'So you've got nothing to worry about, darling.'

Dorothe's apparent attempt to avoid a direct attack on a girl she did not think was good enough for her son, and to deflect criticism instead on to Roger's potential mother-in-law, are among the least appealing passages in a journal that is otherwise an entirely charming recollection of her son's life. She remains discreet, however, even though the journal was probably not written at the time, but Mrs X and little Miss X were clearly not people like the Bushells, and Dorothe's shameless snobbery is there for all to see. This part of the journal, at least, seems to be filtered through hindsight but not through rose-tinted spectacles. As much as she loved him, Dorothe's journal recognised her son's faults and many of her own shortcomings.

After dinner and dancing at the Berkeley Hotel, where Mrs X drank heavily and entertained Dorothe with 'incredible stories', the Bushells left.

We spent five days in Paris and Roger stayed on after our departure with undergraduate friends. I introduced him to an Englishman I knew, who lived there with a charming Parisian wife, and begged them to take an interest in my very young son, in case he got into trouble. My fears were unfounded, but they were very kind to him and Roger found Madame entertaining.

Dorothe left Paris 'in a blaze of shame' after packing her railway tickets and presenting hotel coupons at the barrier. 'An awful French fuss ensued,' she recalled. Bushell was clearly embarrassed by his mother. He explained to the ticket collector in fluent French that she was actually sane but did suffer from eccentricity. 'I could have slapped him,' wrote Dorothe.

'We caught the train and departed, waving to Roger, who looked a darling in his rough tweed coat and grey flannel trousers among the upholstered-looking Frenchmen.'

Despite the obvious pride and love for her son, Dorothe was becoming increasingly aware of the hedonism that sometimes gripped him.

When I reached England again, I hired a small blue Morris and drove myself around the Southern Counties to visit friends and relations. But first of all I went up to Cambridge to see Roger. He snatched my baby car from me, trod on the accelerator, making colleges and houses flash by as one blurred picture, jammed on brakes at corners, shaving our tyres by inches. The whole air was filled by the noise of screaming machinery.

Dorothe also met his closest friends and dined with them.

In spite of knowing the university so well in my youth, I felt rather shy at first; but they were so conversational, so full of nonsense and so like the men twenty-odd years ago that I very soon felt completely at home with them. Roger looked so fit, his blue eyes so full of devilment that I knew he was perfectly happy; but when he answered me that he was working very hard, I laughed and refused to believe that one.

He was working hard, though, in one area of his life – skiing – and, during the early 1930s, he emerged as a star of the Cambridge team and one of the great characters of the highly aspirational, but downwardly mobile, Alpine clique.

Arnold Lunn, a pioneer of modern ski competition who founded the Alpine Ski Club in 1908 and the Kandahar Ski Club at Mürren in 1924, reckoned that, as a racer, Bushell had more courage than judgment and threw away many races by recklessness. The young man certainly had a style of his own.

> Strong men turn pale beneath their tans when he skis for Britain, *wrote one observer in an unidentified newspaper from Bushell's clippings*. He makes his way over trees, down precipices, across ice and through boulders at a uniform maximum speed. His wish is to get to the bottom as quickly as possible after leaving the top.

Bushell was a member of the Cambridge team that beat Oxford in 1930, and he won the Langlauf – a cross-country race over seventeen kilometres – by nearly three minutes at the annual British ski championship at Wengen in 1931. His greatest triumph, however, probably came in Canada when, in the early months of 1932, he captained the combined Oxford and Cambridge teams against McGill University, some of the best collegiate skiers in the Americas.

The Canadians expected to win, but Bushell was in form and had just won the slalom title in the annual meet against Oxford, staged while they were at St Margaret's in Quebec, in the build-up to the international fixture.

After winning the team slalom by a narrow margin on the first day, every point counted for Oxford and Cambridge in the cross-country.

> The unexpected part of the whole business was that the Britishers simply refused to stand by and take the complete licking that all and sundry expected them to get, *wrote a correspondent for the Quebec Star*. The first outstanding example of their

determination became evident when captain Roger Bushell cracked up on a slope known to Quebec skiers as 'Hill 70'.

Pursuing an opponent, Bushell had thrown caution to the wind, risking everything to catch the leading Canadian skier, who was way ahead of him. Something inexplicable went wrong: Bushell had tumbled head over heels, broken both his skis, shaken himself generally, and severely cut his face and nose.

Yet when the group of 'Posters' had picked him up, he announced his intention of going on, *continued the Quebec Star report.* 'The team needs every point,' he protested. 'They will lose if I don't continue.'

Fortunately for this stout-hearted Englishman, the others prevailed and he was carried back to the lodge in a painfully injured state.

The tip of one of Roger's skis had gashed his cheek and damaged the corner of his right eye, but he refused to undergo surgery until he returned to London. The eye drooped slightly thereafter, giving him a 'sinister look' in certain lights.

'We had a marvellous time,' Bushell told the Canadian press a few minutes before the gangplank was raised on the ship taking them back to Britain.

Arnold Lunn did not particularly like Roger, according to Ben Bushell, but he recognised the young man's spirit. In an article for the *British Ski Year Book*, he wrote:

```
[Roger] was only fifteen when he first appeared at
Mürren, but I never think of him as a small boy.
Even in those days he counted in any company in
which he found himself. In later years, he was one
of the great characters of St Moritz, and
uncrowned king of the fashionable Italian skiing
centre Sestrieres within a fortnight of his
```

arrival, not because he broke the record on the most popular of the Sestrieres runs, but because the cosmopolitan clientele of the resort were captivated by his boisterous charm.

Charm, however, is too weak a word to describe Roger's magnetism, *wrote Lunn*. He did not achieve his effects by subtle understatement. I remember once hearing (from a distance) Roger describing to a sympathetic group in the Palace lounge the precise nature of the 'lousy skiing' which had lost him an important slalom. As I approached I hinted that he might either adopt a slightly less robust turn of speech, or drop his voice. 'Christ, Arni!' he exclaimed. 'I never swear.'

It would be idiotic to suggest that Roger was nothing more than an attractive skiing tough. He was an exceptionally able young man.

Bushell was also a sensitive man who maintained a loving concern for his family, which he never lost in spite of tensions with his father, and having many other interests. He had a great sense of humour. In letters that remain from his days at Pembroke, addressed to Kerstie and Rubbish, the two dogs belonging to his youngest sister, Lis, Roger thanks them for their correspondence. He gives Kerstie some robust legal advice:

This business of your divorce is really shocking. I am deeply grieved and I feel sure that you are passing through an unhappy time. Of course I agree that it was a marriage of convenience but all the same I think your husband's conduct has been disgraceful and in my opinion you are entirely justified in taking divorce proceedings . . .

Frankly, I consider fifty bones and ten packets of dog biscuits a year reasonable and I think it is highly probable

*that a special jury in the hands of a good counsel will give
you considerably more.*

He was clearly beginning to think like a lawyer.

Roger then turned his attention to Rubbish, telling him that he
had little news from Cambridge:

*While watching a game of football today I sat next to quite
a nice fellow. Hardly blue-blooded, of course, but friendly
all the same. I fear however that he had fleas but he took a
lively interest in the game, making several attempts to join
the players on the field. These were frustrated by his master,
but nothing dismayed, he gave considerable vocal
encouragement from the touchline. A true touchline critic!*

He finished the letter with a word on Crufts:

*They have been having a big show for you fellows at a
place called Crufts in London. The beauty prize went to a
lovely Labrador but he was, I feel certain, a frightful snob.
The very best of hunting, old man, till we meet again.
Roger.*

A year after entering Pembroke, in the winter of 1930–31, Roger
decided to pursue a career as a barrister. 'I was delighted,' wrote
Dorothe in her diary of this time:

*The Law had always intrigued me and I considered that he
already showed a balanced judgment and could talk lucidly.
It was not a profession that appealed greatly to his father,
but he was relieved that a decision had been made.*

The Bushells in South Africa sailed for England again in the spring
of 1931. Elizabeth, now aged eight, travelled with Ben and
Dorothe. So did Nannie, otherwise known as Evelyn Enden, a

Londoner who had joined the family when Roger was a boy and would spend the rest of her life with them.

Ben set down the rules. They were not to stay anywhere near London, but very definitely somewhere in the country, and he stipulated the level of rent. Dorothe found a 'roomy' house in Sussex called Oakdene. It was lamp-lit, but had an efficient hot water system and with it – 'Thank God!' wrote Dorothe – came a cook. But she fretted still:

Both Roger and Rosemary had written that they were delighted by the idea and I think Roger longed for a few months of home life. I also felt certain that my beloved offspring were both planning adaptability to the point of selflessness so that the holiday should be a success. Could it be done when clashing needs and interests arose by two young creatures full of independent thought and action and opposed to their father's rather Victorian conception of parents' privileges?

At first, all went well. Rosemary travelled from Switzerland, and Roger joined them as soon as he had finished his exams. The garden was flooded with sunshine and shadows stretched across the lawns and softened the brilliance of the herbaceous border. Rhododendrons were in bloom and the air was heavy with the scent of lilac and roses.

The first few days 'were days of pure enchantment', wrote Dorothe:

We were all in accord, talked outside about the family and told jokes and laughed over them as if we have never heard them before. My husband was full of good stories at which he is adept. Roger teased and hugged Nannie intermittently every few hours and was enchanted with his baby sister. Together they had fights with the garden sprinklers, played with the pedigree guinea pigs and let them escape into the rhododendron bushes so that it took the whole family to entice them out and back into captivity. I wondered how I could have imagined that difficulties might arise.

Roger returned to Cambridge where he was joined a week later for the Rag week festivities by Dorothe and Rosemary. Ben allowed them to take the car, leaving him stranded in Sussex. Dorothe told Roger that they could throw two dinner parties, one for the Trinity Ball and one for the Pembroke Ball, and for each he could bring six guests to the party. Among them was Jeanette Kessler, one of Roger's skiing friends.

After the first party, Dorothe went back to her hotel. Roger went on to the Trinity Ball and took the car. He planned to breakfast in Huntingdon.

The next morning there was a rap on Dorothe's door. It was Roger and Jeanette, both looking white and shaken. Roger's hands were bandaged; Jeanette's frock was stained with blood. 'The car is smashed up,' said Bushell. 'It was not my fault, the other fellow was drunk and three cars are involved.'

The incident changed the tone of the holiday. Roger was suffering from shock and his hands were painful. Dorothe offered to phone her husband to explain what had happened, but Roger insisted on doing it himself, 'which was right and courageous'.

Roger was determined to go ahead the next night with the second dinner party for the Pembroke Ball, but he was distracted. The phone call with his father had not gone well.

He was obviously suffering from delayed shock and could not talk unless he was spoken to, when he made an effort to respond, wrote Dorothe. His hands were very swollen and he had difficulty in using them; but I knew that the thing that was hurting most was his father's anger over the accident. In spite of, at times, doing things against his father's wishes, spending more than he should and arguing aggressively, he was very devoted to him. I didn't know

*what my husband had said but it had upset Roger terribly.
When he told me how angry he was, I asked if he had
explained the accident and how it really was nothing to do
with him and he replied angrily. 'Don't be silly, of course I
did. He had every right to be angry, I was a BF not to stop
sooner and let the fellow who was drunk get right ahead of
me. For God's sake, let's drop the subject,' said Roger, who
got up, and walked away.*

At Oakdene, they were met by a very angry Ben. He would not
believe that Roger was not to blame. 'Even the fact that he had
danced until the sun was up and driven miles out of Cambridge
for breakfast was reprehensible,' wrote Dorothe, who blamed her
husband's own upbringing for his lack of tolerance: 'The irre-
sponsible gaieties of youth had not come his way when he was
young.'

Worse still, Roger became arrogant and difficult. 'To me he had
said, over and over again, how grieved he was; but he could not
say it to his father.'

Nor was the car as badly damaged as Roger had thought. In the
end, the family hired another car and went to Wimbledon virtually every day to watch the tennis. Roger visited friends in London.
Tension between father and son eased.

In a telling entry in her journal, Dorothe wrote:

*During the difficult adolescent years, he had missed the
beneficial and natural discipline of family give and take
and was, in consequence, if not unhappy, [then] resentful
and impatient of parental interference, advice or criticism.*

*My husband had seen much of the world and had had
much experience of dealing with men; but not with callow
youth and he sometimes condemned things which were
more harmless than he thought them to be. He is a man of
great integrity and unusual courage, qualities which were
developing in Roger also; but their temperaments were*

*different and they took different roads to reach the same
goal, so that although they loved each other, they did not
always understand each other.*

The court case that resulted from the accident was heard, and the
cloud lifted: a witness stated that Roger's quick judgment had
prevented the accident from being far worse and he was cleared of
all blame. More good news came with the announcement of his
exam results. Charlie Ziegler had worked his magic: Roger had
passed.

As July gave way to August, the family headed for Saint-Lunaire
on the Brittany coast, where Dorothe's sister-in-law, who was
'prone to terrible economising', had booked them not into a hotel,
but a pension, 'and a second-rate one at that'. Existing on a diet
of veal and sardines, they had French servants, but it was difficult
to get a bath. 'The place was full of middle-class shopkeepers
from Lyons with their undisciplined, noisy children,' wrote
Dorothe, allowing her social mask to slip once again.

For Roger, there was one bright spot: the company of a young
English actress, 'who entertained us all with racy descriptions of
far worse places that she had endured while touring the prov-
inces,' wrote Dorothe.

In September, they returned to Sussex where Ben and Dorothe
spent the last month of their holiday in England. The actress
turned up again. And Roger introduced his parents to Viscount
Knebworth – more commonly known as Antony Bulwer-Lytton
or Tony Knebworth – described by Roger to his mother as 'a very
rare personality'. The young aristocrat was a fellow skier and
Roger held him in great affection. He would also play a decisive
role in Bushell's life – the fast lane was about to become a lot
faster.

5

High Society

Tony Knebworth invited Roger Bushell to join the part-time pilots of No. 601 (County of London) Squadron, an Auxiliary Air Force unit known as 'the Millionaires' due to their ostentatious wealth. Flying, it seems, had become a natural extension of skiing.

In an era of unemployment, widespread poverty and social dislocation, 'the Millionaires' were, for many people, a source of jealousy and opprobrium as well as admiration. The squadron was founded over supper at White's Club in St James's in 1924 by Lord Edward Grosvenor, a veteran pilot of the First World War. Ostensibly, it was formed as part of a plan by Lord Trenchard, the founder of the RAF, to create a reserve force of part-time pilots. Five squadrons were set up: two in London, one in Birmingham and two in Scotland.

To be a member of an Auxiliary Air Force squadron was to belong to a 'jealously guarded elite', access to which was barred by social and financial hurdles that were impossible for many who might have wished to fly with them. The squadrons were gentlemen's flying clubs for rich young men who read *The Times* and used them, particularly the London squadrons, as an extension of their social lives. They assumed the character of crack cavalry regiments from an earlier era.

Asked about recruitment policy, one commanding officer said: 'I gave each applicant marks for his school record in scholarship and athletics; and if he could ride a horse, or drive a car or a motorcycle, or sail a boat, or ski, or play the piano, I gave him more marks.'

A couple of months after Viscount Knebworth invited Roger to join 601 Squadron, on 21 October 1932, he graduated with a Bachelor of Arts with third-class honours in law after putting skiing above his studies and being absent for the Lent terms in both of his last two years at university.

In January 1933, Hitler became Chancellor of Germany at the head of a coalition government. His aims included the re-armament of the country and the creation of a powerful new air force, in defiance of the peace treaty signed at Versailles after the First World War.

If Bushell was concerned by events in Germany, he showed little sign of it. For almost three years after graduation, he appears to have lived in a social maelstrom. It began with the Knebworths.

The viscount represented the world to which Bushell aspired at this time, including much that would have irritated the martinet in his father. Educated at Eton and Oxford, the eldest son of Victor Bulwer-Lytton, 2nd Earl of Lytton, and his wife, Pamela, Tony Knebworth was tall and suave, the heir to the family title that sat almost at the pinnacle of British society. He had been a stockbroker, briefly, and then gone into politics. In 1931, he was elected Conservative MP for Hitchin at the age of twenty-seven.

A photograph of the two young men embracing in Switzerland bears witness to their friendship. On several occasions, Roger was a guest at Knebworth House, a Gothic mansion thirty miles north of London that had been home to the Lyttons since 1490.

To Roger, 'they were perfection in family life', wrote Dorothe in her journal. 'No restrictions except those of consideration for others, no destructive criticism.'

The Knebworths were part of an aristocratic elite unencumbered by Ben Bushell's strong sense of discipline, who enjoyed their hedonistic apogee before the First World War and warmed to the pursuit of sensual pleasures. For Roger, they were fellow souls.

It was about this time, as autumn gave way to winter, that Roger met 'Georgie' – Lady Georgiana Mary Curzon – probably through the Knebworths. Georgie was strikingly beautiful with a smile that matched Roger's and what appears to have been a similar appetite for life. The daughter of Francis Curzon, the 5th Earl Howe, she moved easily among royalty and aristocracy.

For Roger, however, life was not quite so grand. He shared a rented flat in Tite Street, Chelsea, with his elder sister, Rosemary, who was studying at the Slade School of Fine Art, and later, with Michael Peacock, his great friend from Wellington. It was, however, riotous fun. Rosemary was a big hit with Roger's friends in London, including the pilots of 601 Squadron: boisterous show-offs to a man. They eschewed the discipline of the regular service and lined their tunics with red silk. They played polo on Brough Superior motorbikes and drove fast cars. Some owned their own aeroplanes. Roger stood out even in this crowd – and it was not just because he was broke. 'His charm was magnetic and universal,' wrote Tom Moulson, chronicler of the squadron's history.

Roger seems to have made less of an impact as a junior barrister, and little is known of what he achieved in 1933. He had been admitted to Lincoln's Inn, one of the Inns of Court, in January 1930, when his application was supported by Aubrey Attwater, his tutor at Pembroke, and the Master of Wellington. To keep his place, he had to attend a number of dinners each year and pass the Bar exams set by the Council of Legal Education.

The council offered lectures but these were not compulsory and many students relied on private study. The annual calendars of those passing the Bar exams include only those who were awarded first or second-class passes; needless to say, Bushell's name does not appear. Most students were awarded third-class passes.

Just as Bushell started to pursue his legal career, tragedy struck: Viscount Knebworth lost control of his Hawker Hart biplane while flying in formation with eight other aircraft on the eve of the annual air pageant at Hendon aerodrome at the beginning of May. The Hawker Harts, state-of-the-art fighter aircraft flown by 601 Squadron, were diving in formation at 250 miles per hour, practising the final salute. Eight aircraft pulled out of the dive in the twilight, but Knebworth 'dipped too low, and struck the ground with great force'. Both he and his crewman were killed. Knebworth was twenty-nine.

According to press reports of the time, Lady Lytton was told of the accident by an attendant as she sat in the stalls at the opening night of the Covent Garden opera season. 'Pale and trembling, she went to the foyer, cried, "Tell me the worst", and collapsed in the arms of Lord Lytton.' She kept in touch with Roger and sent him a eulogy to her son written by the historian Arthur Bryant, who described him as valiant, beautiful and generous.

Bushell was awarded his pilot's wings with 601 Squadron in June 1933, shortly after Knebworth's death. Eight months later, he was promoted to the rank of Flying Officer – just as the Nazis stepped up the secret training of their own fighter pilots at glider clubs. He represented Great Britain at skiing in 1934, and was called to the Bar in November, just a few months after Reinhard Heydrich, an ambitious SS officer, had added the Gestapo to his burgeoning portfolio of security agencies in the Third Reich.

Turmoil in Bushell's private life overshadowed these successes, however, though his private papers shed little light on the issue. Whether he had simply run out of money or there were problems with affairs of the heart – the two areas of his life in which Roger was always vulnerable – he turned to his mother for help.

Dorothe was in bed in Springs, recovering from flu, when she received a cable from Roger:

PLEASE COME HOME, I NEED YOU.

Dorothe sailed for Britain five days later.

> *We knew there had been trouble and the kind of trouble, but
> not how serious it was,* she confided in her journal. At the
> end of 1933, *Ben had sent Roger a large sum of money to
> invest, thinking it would steady him and interest him to
> increase it even in a small way. Had he told me, I would have
> begged him to wait until Roger's skiing holiday was over.*

But Ben Bushell did not consult his wife, who feared the skiing
world 'and how the lookiest and smartest women' would do all
they could to spoil their son.

> *The temptation to take some at least of that money to a
> place where money counted would be enormous, and when
> a young man has money in his pocket a certain type of
> woman can tell it a mile off.*

Dorothe's son invested a portion of the money in shares that he
was convinced would have risen sufficiently by the time of his
return to cover any money he had spent on the Continent.

> *It was wrong of him,* wrote Dorothe, *but from a human
> point of view it was understandable. The temptation
> should not have been put in his way. However, it's no good
> thinking of that now – the soul finds itself in all sorts of
> queer ways and possibly being lowered in his own
> estimation and realising his weakness may do much good
> for Roger – that harm will have been done also is
> something I must realise and face up to.*

At Southampton:

> [Roger came] *running up the companionway and out onto
> the deck without seeing me or hearing me call – so that I*

*saw him for a moment before I was enveloped in a bearlike
hug and emotion clouded my vision. There was a change as
I knew there must be. The light was dimmed . . .*

*He put his arms right round me, his cheek against mine
in his old way and he said: 'Mummie, thank God you've
come, I've wanted you so much. How I love you.' Then
more hugs, our kisses oblivious of passers-by . . . did a
mother ever have a warmer welcome?*

Roger spoke briefly to his mother of his troubles on the journey to
Ascot, where he left her with the North-Lewises. Harry North-
Lewis was Roger's guardian in England. He was a lawyer who
loved mischief; his wife, Eleanor, Dorothe's sister-in-law, loved
laughter. They lived in a large, red-brick house called Grey Friars,
with rolling lawns edged by trees. Rosemary was there, too.

It was not until some days later that Roger and his mother
found themselves alone in the flat in Tite Street.

*First of all Roger and I had dinner and then went to see
'King Kong', for the cold hours between 8 and 12 are no
time for dressing the wound or spirit and I know this is the
night he has chosen to tell me why he brought me home.*

King Kong tugged at their hearts. 'It is perhaps the greatest fantasy
of the decade. Often crude but enthralling – a modern fairy story
with the same pathos surrounding the monster.'

Afterwards, they returned to the flat in the car he had recently
bought for £6 and which Dorothe said 'resembled an ancient
kitchen utensil'. The fire was still burning and then it was blazing
– Roger started to talk.

*There was a woman in it of course and money spending –
but no evil – we all do wrong at times in our lives but evil is
another matter. It had been a bitter experience for my son
and I think and hope I was some comfort to him. I know I*

was; but such experiences leave the young with but one desire, to harden themselves to [achieve] invulnerability. There is something within him which has been so hurt that he will never allow it to be hurt again. I only hope it does not cloud his vision when real love comes.

Dorothe was far too discreet, even in her journal, to reveal what it was that distressed her son so much that he asked her to make the 5,000-mile journey from South Africa at such short notice. But it clearly involved money and women and must have gone far beyond a mere dalliance. Was he having an affair with someone who was married? Was a pregnancy involved? Neither Roger's nor Dorothe's papers provide the truth. What is clear is that, no matter how badly Roger had behaved or how much trouble he faced, his doting mother was not willing to condemn his actions.

Within a short time, Dorothe felt that there was no doubt that either his confession, or what she had said to him regarding life and his parents' unshakeable love for him, had dissolved the cloud.

He is more his old self, she wrote, *full of nonsense, wanting his own way, critical of me, all good signs and sometimes the cracks are quite hard to take; but the fact that he does talk to me is a wonderful salve.*

He would go out many a night, and not return until two or three in the morning, but then he would open her door, sit on her bed and talk for an hour or so.

One night, we talked until the maid brought us tea – very bad for bodies but good for our spirits. As long as he gives me this adorable companionship, I can take any crack – besides which, they do me good and enlarge my vision. If only I could give him a few back, but I am not quick

56

enough and I love him too dearly. Besides, there are such secret places in the hearts of the young.

As it turned out, real love was not far away, and this time Roger would not share it with his mother, which was perhaps a sign of its seriousness.

Lady Georgiana Curzon had a public face as well as a private one. Apart from appearing regularly on the court and social pages of national newspapers, and in London magazines, Georgie was used as a model by the cosmetics firm Pond's to advertise its cold cream and tissues in the United States, and across the British Empire. The advertisers thought she would turns heads; she certainly turned Roger's.

Her father, Earl Howe, knew his place in the world. As well as holding one of the grandest titles in the aristocracy, he became aide-de-camp to King George V. He had other interests, too. He was a motor-racing fanatic who founded the British Racing Drivers' Club and won the Le Mans 24-hour race, driving an Alfa Romeo, in 1931.

Photographs taken by Georgie suggest that her affair with Roger started in the summer of 1934, and letters written later confirm that it was both romantic and serious. Pages of a photograph album paint a picture of a joyous summer: on the beach, picnicking, and in each other's arms. One in particular shows a couple sitting on a lawn against a backdrop of trees and bushes, Georgie's left arm hanging round Roger's shoulder, the two of them smiling gently but happily, at ease in each other's company. It is a picture of a couple in love.

By the early summer of the following year, when Peter Clive, a fellow pilot whose father was Britain's ambassador to Japan, asked Bushell to be godfather to his daughter Caroline, Roger was a firmly established member of 601 Squadron and just beginning to make a serious name for himself as a barrister.

On 10 July 1935, he joined the Clive family at the christening at the great, Doric-pillared church of St Peter in Eaton Square, Belgravia. Behind the pillars and huge wooden doors, St Peter's is a simple but beautiful church, decorated in pastels and full of light. It was a beautiful day. According to weather reports, the sky was blue and temperatures were in the high eighties from London right across central Europe. The godmother, Lady Tollemache, was unable to attend, but she was represented by the delicate beauty of Lady Georgiana Curzon.

At about the same time, Hitler was also taking part in a religious ceremony, but there was little romance about the events in East Prussia. *Pathé News* released footage of the Führer in attendance as Paul von Hindenburg, the former president of Germany, was laid to rest in a new, granite-like mausoleum at East Tannenberg, scene of the great general's victory over the Russians during the First World War. Hitler was cementing his hold on power as the country started its march towards another conflict.

Just a week later, Roger was at the wedding of Earl Howe's only son, Edward, the Viscount Curzon, to Priscilla Weighall, an heiress of great wealth, at the chapel of St Michael and St George in St Paul's Cathedral. A photograph of him shows an impressive man in a morning suit, sun-tanned and smart, cigarette in hand, striding ahead of two bridesmaids: Miss Livia Paravicini on his left, and Georgie in the centre. They were clearly enjoying themselves.

Perhaps, just for a moment, Roger allowed himself to dream of his own wedding in equally grand surroundings. But Earl Howe was having none of it: Bushell had come too close, and he was not going to allow 'that penniless, South African barrister' to marry his daughter.

Within three months, an announcement in *The Times* listed the forthcoming marriage of Lieutenant H. Kidston RN, youngest son of the late Captain Glen Kidston and Lady Windham, of 25 Berkeley Square, and Lady Georgiana Curzon.

They were married less than a month later, on 27 November 1935, at Holy Trinity Church in Penn Street, near Amersham, Buckinghamshire.

Home Kidston was the brother of a powerful motor-racing figure who, like his father, was also named Glen Kidston and a friend of Earl Howe. Steeped in money from Clyde shipping, Glen Kidston had made a name for himself as a naval officer in the First World War, but acquired celebrity status as a member of the glamorous Bentley Boys, a group of wealthy racing drivers who drove the famous British marque in the 1920s, and as the reputed lover of Barbara Cartland, the romantic novelist. He was killed in an air crash in 1931.

His son had met Georgie two years previously when they were both twenty-three, just before he left Britain for New Zealand. Writing some years later, Kidston admitted that he had not known Georgie well when he left Britain, but he had written to her frequently, encouraged by a few weeks' happy memories, and that he had thought this had nurtured love on both sides.

He would later confess to Georgie that he had felt that almost everyone had assumed they would marry and that he had considered he had little option but to do so. He did admit that he had found Georgie lively company and was swayed by the fact that she had waited for him throughout the time he was abroad.

In 1941, Kidston acknowledged the doubts he had felt about marriage to Georgie at the time. He had confided in his friend Pat Drysdale, who was helping with all the arrangements, that he feared he might be making a terrible mistake and perhaps it would be better to call the whole thing off. However, he set his doubts on one side and went through with the occasion.

In his ceremonial uniform, stiff collar and golden epaulettes, a ceremonial sword in his hand, Home Kidston cuts a dashing figure in the wedding photographs that appeared in the national press. Georgie looks a little less certain.

Nothing is known of Roger Bushell's whereabouts on this day, but it was not the first time he had been thwarted in love, and it would not be the last.

6

Chelsea Boys

The red-brick flat at No. 1 Shelley Court in Tite Street became a formidable bastion from which Roger emerged to face the world, striding confidently and embracing the friendship with Michael Peacock, his South African alter ego.

Peacock had arrived in London from Brasenose College, Oxford, with a similarly undistinguished degree. The two men had known each other for more than ten years and they had always been close but, with Georgie's exit, the friendship appears to have taken on a new vitality. As they pursued legal careers in the same chambers at 1 Temple Gardens, and Peacock joined the ranks of 601 Squadron, their lives almost took on a surreal quality. They did everything together.

With two bedrooms, a kitchen and living room, the flat was not exactly a home with aristocratic pretensions, but they could claim Oscar Wilde as a former neighbour in the terraced street, which leads down to the Thames. Many years later, Bushell's younger sister, Lis, recalled this 'hysterically funny' couple who shared a car and clothing, even legal briefs on occasions. 'If one had the tailcoat, the other could not go out that night,' she said.

Looking pretty chipper in her eighties, with bright eyes, an occasional mischievous smile, and wearing a red scarf pinned by a diamond brooch cut in the shape of a flying sword – the emblem of 601 Squadron – Lis Carter vividly remembered this period in the lives of her brother and Peacock. 'They were priceless, those two. And they had an old girl called Mrs Robinson who was their char who must have been an absolute saint the way she coped with them. The two men adored her, but what she put up with was unbelievable.

'Half the time she didn't get paid until they'd got some money and then she'd have to go without for a week or two. She was a real Cockney, a scream of a woman, but trust them to find her.

'They were full of fun and led a wonderful, carefree sort of existence. They would get home late and be back in court for 9 a.m. They did the job and they did the job well, but they played hard, too. Thank God they did.'

Bushell still had an eye for women. 'There were very few people who had the experience that Roger had of the female sex, I can assure you,' said his sister. 'Roger always had a girlfriend and very often a married one and a rich one. He had many, many girlfriends.'

But the only romantic drama at this time involved Bushell's guardian, Harry North-Lewis, who found himself at the heart of the divorce case that would allow Wallis Simpson to marry King Edward VIII. The affair triggered a constitutional crisis. The monarch was forbidden from marrying a divorcée, let alone an American divorcée who had been married twice and was suspected of sympathising with the Nazis.

On 27 October 1936, Mrs Simpson was granted a decree nisi. She had married Ernest Simpson, an Anglo-American shipping executive, at Chelsea and Kensington Register Office, eight years earlier. According to one member of the family, the King sent 'Uncle Harry' a pair of diamond cuff-links as a mark of gratitude for his legal services, but this seems unlikely, as North-Lewis represented Mr Simpson and apparently drove a hard bargain. The King abdicated on 10 December.

Bushell had started work as a junior barrister at 1 Temple Gardens in the chambers of Sir Henry Curtis-Bennett, a fashionable silk who was employed by the War Office during the First World War to cross-examine suspected spies, including Mata Hari. When he died in 1936, Bushell joined Peacock at the same address in the chambers of G. D. 'Khaki' Roberts, a big, ebullient man, who embraced his two young juniors almost as if they were his sons.

Hailed as a lawyer with a bright future, Bushell practised on the South Eastern Circuit, and at the Central Criminal Court.

Interesting days, these, in legal circles, *said a reporter in the* Empire News, with expert observers in the Temple making argument as to the likely candidates succeeding the F. E. Smiths, Carsons, Marshall Halls [eminent lawyers] of yesterday.

One frequently named is young Roger Bushell, whom I heard make an eloquent and successful plea at the Old Bailey the other day.

'A fledgeling to watch,' the newspaper reporter concluded.

In the years running up to the Second World War, Bushell's cases made headlines in the national newspapers on many occasions as he defended and prosecuted murderers, thieves and rapists. One trial that caught the public imagination was the case of 'The Kissing Cafe', in which the owner was accused of profiting from waitresses who were offering clients something a little more exciting than sugar for their tea or coffee, and charging five shillings rather than the usual sixpence. Peacock defended the café owner and Roger the two waitresses, whose behaviour had been witnessed by two undercover policemen.

Bushell's methods of cross-examination were as 'unconventional as his slalom technique', according to Arnold Lunn, the skiing pioneer.

The *Daily Mail* reported on Bushell's cross-examination of the policemen:

You, Detective Spink, *Bushell said*, with your remarkable hearing, heard cuddling. How do you hear cuddling?

When two persons have their arms round each other they make most peculiar noises, *the police officer responded.*

Was this a smacking kiss? *asked Bushell.*

It was a very good kiss.

An affectionate kiss that rang out across the room? *inquired Bushell.*

I could not say that, *said Spink.*

Have you ever tried to detect the noise in Puzzle Corner [radio show] of the B.B.C.? *asked Bushell.*

Spink said he had not, and on this occasion Bushell's 'white-hot belligerence' did not pay off. The café owner and her waitresses were all fined for disorderly conduct.

Tributes to his ability piled up among Roger's personal letters.

Congratulations on a very admirable defence, wrote one interested party about another case. *If it had not been for your excellent speech to the jury this morning, I am properly certain they would have found him guilty of the greater offence.*

The writer then added what was probably the ultimate compliment for a junior barrister: 'An American attorney from New York sitting next to me asked if you were a King's Counsel?'

In another role, illustrating further contrast in his character, Bushell was welcomed into the East End. With Peacock, he took on charity work, offering legal advice free of charge. 'They got on frightfully well,' recalled Lis Carter, 'and came back with hysterical stories.'

Bushell and Peacock also offered their services to any members of 601, whatever their background or class – pilots or ground crew – who found themselves at odds with the authorities.

If an airman was charged with negligently failing to secure bombs properly beneath an aircraft, or a pilot court-martialled for stunting over his girl-friend's house, one of them would, if asked, act as counsel for the defence, *wrote Tom Moulson, the chronicler of 601's history.* They won more than their share of cases and became something of a legend. The authorities were continually embarrassed.

On one occasion, Bushell was briefed to defend a fitter at North Coates aerodrome. Moulson writes: 'He flew a squadron aircraft to North Coates in uniform, but appeared at the court in wig and gown as though in the High Court. Having driven the key prosecution witness to anger – a favourite ruse – and then demolished him with polite ease, he changed back into uniform and took tea in the mess.'

The only other person in the mess was the 'humiliated' prosecution witness, who complained that he had just been 'bloody well subverted by some young charlatan of a lawyer from London'.

Mike Peacock reversed the costume touch when he flew to defend an officer at Kenley in one of the latest fighters, wearing his gown and changing his flying helmet for a wig while taxiing in to dispersal. The ground crew and reception party were so bewildered they could not at first believe their eyes, *wrote Moulson.*

For the Air Ministry, the 'last straw' came when Peacock demolished the evidence of a vicar who accused a pilot of low flying.

Bushell and Peacock saw law as conflict, *wrote Moulson.* The air force saw law as discipline. In challenging this concept with such verve and repeated success, they strained the patience of Authority to breaking point.

The commanding officer of 601 Squadron, Brian Thynne, was informed that Flight Lieutenants Bushell and Peacock were no longer to act as defence counsel in courts-martial. The order was subsequently withdrawn, but the message was clear.

Bushell was joined at 601 Squadron by Max Aitken, his friend from Cambridge who, by 1936, was general manager of the *Sunday Express.* G. W. S. 'Mouse' Cleaver and Paddy Green, who were both international skiers, were also recruited, as well as aristocrats such as Robert Forbes-Leeth, Henry St Valery Norman, Richard Demetriadi and William Drogo Sturges Montagu.

The Honorary Commodore of 601 Squadron was Sir Philip Sassoon, Conservative MP for Hythe, Under Secretary of State for Air, art collector and socialite. He was a cousin of Siegfried Sassoon, the First World War poet, and had been private secretary to Field Marshal Haig, the British commander on the Western Front.

Sir Philip entertained the pilots of 601 at his country house at Port Lympne in Kent once a year, locking up the more fragile of his art treasures before their arrival. The success of these parties was often put down to 'Roger Bushell's hearty good spirits and exuberance'. Lunn, who had watched him at work, said he was a 'brilliant after-dinner speaker, and master of the technique of making a party go'.

Photographs and film of Bushell from this period show him by a pool wearing dark glasses and a striped robe, possibly at Port Lympne. He is smoking rakishly, as if in a scene from *The Great Gatsby*.

According to Moulson:

> Bushell lived explosively happily. He was in his element. One day a scarlet ear-ring was found in his aircraft. The air officer commanding somehow learned of this and commented, 'I suppose he swallowed the other one!' When the squadron was converted to Demons, and equipped with radio telephone, Bushell's forceful language shook the wireless amateurs for miles around London.

Summer camp was considered to be the highlight of the auxiliary officer's life: two weeks of constant flying and camaraderie, and it was on these occasions that the rivalry between 601 and 600 (City of London) Squadron found full expression. On 15 August 1936, the *Daily Sketch* reported on an intensive 'war' not in the schedule of operations:

> An officer of the 600th Squadron was invited to Lympne, where he was taken prisoner, bound and gagged, and then flown to

Hawkinge [airfield], where he was dumped on the parade ground.

Members of his squadron rushed out to see the mysterious bundle left by the machine when they were attacked by a dozen aeroplanes carrying bombs of soot and flour and balloons filled with ink and milk.

Just after 4 a.m. on Friday, No. 600 Squadron retaliated with an attack on 601 Squadron at Lympne. Bombs of soot, yellow ochre, inks, eggs, old fruit and treacle were dropped from 15 machines.

But the high jinks could not last. Within a few weeks, the new German air force, the Luftwaffe, was in action for the first time, dropping real bombs on Madrid: Hitler had sent a volunteer force known as the Condor Legion to support General Francisco Franco's nationalist forces in the Spanish Civil War. As Hermann Göring, head of the Luftwaffe, testified during his trial in 1945, the Spanish Civil War gave him an opportunity to put his young air force to the test, and a means by which his men could gain experience.

The Condor Legion, experimenting with aircraft such as the Heinkel He 111 bomber and the Messerschmitt Bf 109 fighter, was modern and fast. Among its next targets was Guernica, the town immortalised in Pablo Picasso's depiction of suffering. On a market day, Monday, 26 April 1937, Göring's pilots committed the first major atrocity of the Nazi era. Guernica was undefended. Hundreds were killed by the German bombers: the Basque authorities put the number at 1,654.

In Britain, the government of Stanley Baldwin had already responded by expanding the Royal Air Force, commissioning new fighters and ordering the development of radar, which would give early warning of the approach of hostile aircraft. For all their revelry, the pilots of 601 Squadron were aware of events on the Continent and took their flying seriously.

The next jolt came with the *Anschluss*, Hitler's takeover of Austria. The German army invaded on the morning of 12 March 1938, without meeting any organised resistance. Reinhard Heydrich moved in with elements of the SS and Gestapo to organise the arrest of those opposed to Nazi rule – more than 22,000 people in all.

In May 1938, Bushell was selected to perform aerobatics at the Empire Air Display, 'a tremendous compliment to the Auxiliaries and his squadron'. He was the most outstanding of 601's officers, probably one of the best in the air force. 'His piloting, of course, was exceptional from the start,' wrote Brian Thynne, his commanding officer, in a letter to Bushell's parents, 'and this in a Squadron where everyone was so enthusiastic, and where the normal level was so high, that to be outstanding in that crowd was a difficult feat . . .

'When I took command of the Squadron, and Roger commanded B Flight, he soon proved himself to be the almost perfect Flight Commander, and incidentally, of the greatest assistance to me, always ready with help and advice, and could be relied on to back me up.'

Then came Czechoslovakia. During the summer of 1938, tensions rose as the Nazis made strident territorial demands on the Czech government of Edvard Beneš, a distinguished politician who had been instrumental in gaining independence for his country after 1918. Hitler insisted that the 3 million people of German origin living in areas along the Czech border known as the Sudetenland must be allowed to unite with Germany. Beneš stood firm and the two countries mobilised their forces.

Thousands of miles away, on the veldt east of Johannesburg, Ben and Dorothe Bushell received a telegram, dated 27 September 1938, from their son in London.

WAR NOW CERTAIN. VERY WELL. DONT WORRY ABOUT ME.
LOVE YOU ALL ALWAYS – ROGER

A coded message had ordered 601 Squadron to move from Hendon in north London to Biggin Hill in west Kent. The entire squadron was in position within 24 hours.

Two days later, Britain and France, which had pledged to support the Czechs, appeased Hitler to avoid war: they allowed Nazi Germany to occupy the Sudetenland after receiving assurances from Hitler that Germany would go no further. As the *Wehrmacht* – the German armed forces – moved in, nearly 200,000 people – Czechs, Jews and anti-fascists – fled to the heartlands of Bohemia and Moravia. Beneš resigned.

Hailed by Neville Chamberlain, the British prime minister, as 'Peace for our time', the Munich Agreement horrified the Czech people and is regarded by many as a day of shame for Western diplomacy. Nevertheless, it bought the RAF an extra year.

The Hawker Demon that Bushell had flown to Biggin Hill was no match for the new Heinkels and Messerschmitts of the Luftwaffe. It was obsolete. His squadron was short of gunnery practice and had virtually no night flying experience. The RAF was tactically naïve, and radar was not yet fully developed.

In the House of Commons, Chamberlain told MPs: 'Ever since I assumed my present office, my main purpose has been to work for the pacification of Europe, for the removal of those suspicions and those animosities which have so long poisoned the air. The path which leads to appeasement is long and bristles with obstacles. The question of Czechoslovakia is the latest and perhaps the most dangerous. Now that we have got past it, I feel that it may be possible to make further progress along the road to sanity.'

It was not a road down which Adolf Hitler wished to travel, however. The Slovaks, probably encouraged by the Germans, gave him an alternative route by declaring independence from the Czechs. At a meeting in Berlin, Hitler bullied Emil Hácha, the much-diminished president of Czechoslovakia who was left with a rump state, into agreeing to the establishment of a German protectorate over his country.

Only two hours later, at six in the morning of 15 March, German troops crossed the Czech border and reached Prague by nine, despite heavy snowfalls, *wrote the historian Robert Gerwarth in* Hitler's Hangman. The Czech army, demoralised and under orders not to interfere, remained in its barracks. On the evening of the invasion, Hitler arrived in Prague. Heydrich was with him when the swastika was raised over Hradschin [Hradčany in Czech] Castle. The following morning, Joachim von Ribbentrop announced on Prague radio a decree drafted by the State Secretary of the Ministry of the Interior, Dr Wilhelm Stuckart, which declared that the newly conquered Czech lands were henceforth to be known as the Reich Protectorate of Bohemia and Moravia.

The invasion gave the *Wehrmacht* bases from which to attack Poland later in the year, and new resources, including a sophisticated arms industry. Political terror was introduced immediately. Heydrich mobilised two *Einsatzgruppen*, the SS action groups that would murder millions in Poland and Russia, as well as the SD, the intelligence arm of Heinrich Himmler's SS, and the Gestapo, the German secret police. Thousands of Czechs were detained. Prague was put under curfew.

Watching from the American Embassy that night, the diplomat George Kennan witnessed the change in the Czech capital.

Kennan described the streets of Prague, which were usually so full of life, as completely deserted. He felt that, even when people returned, the streets of the ancient city would never be the same again. The curfew had marked the end of a long and tragic day.

Several weeks after Heydrich had repressed the many Czech opponents of the Nazis, Ben and Dorothe Bushell boarded a ship in Cape Town destined for London. Elizabeth, their youngest child, was with them. In a year or so, she would go to the University of Cape Town, but, for the time being, Lis could concentrate on celebrating her seventeenth birthday among family and friends in London.

'It's my most vivid memory of him [Roger],' she said. 'Going to dinner at the Savoy and dancing, which was my seventeenth birthday; he was twenty-nine, perhaps twenty-eight turning twenty-nine, and we all went to dinner at the Savoy.

'Roger was full of beans. As the clock struck twelve, and I turned seventeen, he said, "Right, I'm going to show you how people really kiss." He went down the drain and we came up for air two minutes later. "There you are, now you know," he said, thinking I was sweet seventeen and never been kissed, which wasn't exactly true. But it made him happy.

'He was everything to me,' said Lis, who was warned by friends that she would never find a husband if she measured every other boy against her brother. 'I didn't see much of him so he was sort of glamorised. Tods [Rosemary] had a much more realistic view because she'd lived with him.'

Dorothe, writing in her journal for the last time, found that:

My children are detached from me and this enables me to detach myself also. To look at them, appraise them as an outsider, is a very salutary thing for a parent to do. I watch them and listen to them as if they were not mine, as if I had no claim on them and no responsibility with regard to their upbringing.

I cannot keep it up for long, but half an hour will balance and steady my judgement. Unconsciously, Roger taught me to do it, for he saw me one day. 'Mamma, you worry about our behaviour not because it's really bad

71

behaviour but because it will reflect on you as our parent.'

Like so many of his remarks, it was damnably true. So looking at them from outside, imaging them as the children of my friends, I realised their charm, their brightness, their intelligence. Their response, their gaiety, their smiles for the outside world are delightful and that is their true, un-hampered selves. With such weapons they will face life and win through.

The other side which they sometimes show me is because they are on the defensive against my shibboleths, which do not fit their generation. I also realise that the very things that upset me I would not even notice in other young people and that therefore I am being very unfair to them.

In her son, she found a man of purpose:

Roger has matured early and only by bearing that in mind can one attempt to understand him and be the friend which a parent should try to be even if they never accomplish it, Dorothe wrote. *Behind his gaiety and nonsense . . . is an unswerving sense of purpose and a will to carry it out.*

Loving as he is fundamentally, he will never let his heart completely control his head and so he will grow into a fine man. He is egotistical, he does not attempt to disguise it, but relies on his undoubted charm to make it palatable to others. Were his goal solely a material one, I would be anxious, but material things only appeal to him as they aid his pilgrimage.

Something of greater value beckons him and the knowledge of it shines in his curiously dilated pupils – at times a rim of brilliant blue shines over them. In this way he casts almost a spell and others are caught up and follow

his call. As when he was a child I felt I must never grasp or
try to possess, so now I feel he is a man of fate.

As the Bushells sailed back to South Africa – a journey that they
would not make again for many years – the pilots of 601 Squadron
prepared for war.

7

On the Brink

Hitler's next target was Poland. Just as with Czechoslovakia the previous summer, he made territorial demands, only on this occasion it was for the return of the 'Danzig Corridor', which was surrendered after Germany's defeat in the First World War. As early as June 1939, the *Wehrmacht* started to move troops towards its eastern border.

Poland's fate was decided in Moscow on 23 August 1939 when the Nazi foreign minister, Joachim von Ribbentrop, met the Russian leader, Josef Stalin. Germany would take Lithuania; Russia would take Latvia, Estonia, Finland and parts of Romania. Both countries would invade Poland.

Hitler was jubilant. He had secured his Eastern Front.

Roger Bushell was appalled. A day later, he wrote to his parents from Marseilles, where he had just boarded the flying boat *Cambria*. 'It's that silly ass Hitler again!' he told them in a letter addressed to 'My darlings'. He continued on the first of twelve sheets of Imperial Airways writing paper, decorated with a palm tree in the top left corner and headed, 'Flying in the Cambria'.

Can you beat it – it's becoming such a bore too – sort of annual affair – and what is much worse, it's mucked up my holiday this time.

But let me begin at the beginning. First and foremost, I know I am a rotten son and a worse letter writer but there it is. It's done now and these times are such that it is no good entering into long explanations. I can't explain anyway and all I can say is sorry.

Written in pencil in a bold, confident hand, the letter started with a confessional – often the trait of a soldier about to go to war – and continued with an explanation of how he came to be on the flying boat.

He had driven to the south of France with Max Aitken and Aitken's girlfriend after the squadron's summer camp, to stay with Duncan Orr-Lewis, a Canadian baronet, in Antibes. 'We had a great party on Wednesday night,' wrote Roger, who had stayed up until breakfast. At lunch on the Thursday, a telegram had arrived, recalling him at once: he was due to take over the command of 601 Squadron from Brian Thynne.

Willie Rhodes-Moorhouse, another of the squadron's pilots, was with him. 'We packed our things and off we went by car,' wrote Bushell. 'Cannes was in a complete flat spin and everyone was packing their things.'

Four years younger than Bushell, Rhodes-Moorhouse was the son of the first British pilot to receive the Victoria Cross for operations in the air. His father, also named William, had bombed the railway junction at Courtrai in May 1915 as the Germans tried to reinforce troops engaged in fierce fighting around the Belgian town of Ypres. He attacked his target with a single bomb from just 300 feet, but was hit by heavy ground fire and died twenty-four hours after coaxing his aircraft back to the aerodrome at Merville.

With the help of Orr-Lewis, the two 601 pilots arranged a transfer of money at the Carlton Hotel in Cannes, and Roger had a letter from the French Embassy, emphasising that he should be 'helped in all matters' in an emergency. The British consul also gave him a note and suggested he try Air France in Marseilles.

They left that afternoon, Bushell and Rhodes-Moorhouse, and his wife, Amalia Demetriadi, a beautiful woman with classic looks who was reported to have turned down a screen test to play Scarlett O'Hara in the Hollywood film *Gone With The Wind*. She was the sister of another 601 pilot, Dick Demetriadi.

Well, we set out, wrote Bushell, *Willy and his wife and I about 4 o'clock and motored to Marseilles. It took us just on four hours instead of two! The road was crammed with cars all going back, to say nothing of troops and lorries.*

In an interesting aside from a man brought up in South Africa, he added, 'Incidentally, they've got black troops stationed all the way along the coast at Cannes.'

Returning to the journey, he said:

We went straight to the aerodrome at Marignane and found only a boy and a goat there. I produced my letter and note and explained I had to get back at once.

They were absolutely grand – in spite of the fact that the boats aren't allowed to carry passengers from Marseilles, they said they'd take me and so here I am. We left at eight this morning and get to Southampton at 12.30 with luck.

Willy, I left to get home with Muggins [otherwise known as Amalia Rhodes-Moorhouse] by car as best he could because it isn't so important for him to be there as for me, wrote Bushell. *There wasn't a room to be had at Marseilles and one of the Imperial chaps put me up at his flat for the night. Was at Wellington with me too, oddly enough. So there the whole sad story is.*

Bushell wired ahead and asked for 601 to send an aircraft to take him from Southampton to Hendon.

He did not know at this moment whether the squadron, which was flying the fighter version of the twin-engine Bristol Blenheim, had been officially declared operational or whether it had been sent to its front-line airfield, but it was, he said, 'no good flapping'. Whatever the future held, and however bleak the news, Bushell was confident in his own prospects.

By the time this reaches you, we'll all know one way or another, he told his parents, *and it's no use trying to tell what will happen. Things are pretty black though just at this moment. But don't worry yourselves, my darlings. I was born lucky and if it [war] does come, I've no doubt I'll get lots of medals and end up on the general staff.*

He promised to cable them when he got back to London, and to keep an eye on Rosemary, who was in Britain with her husband, Roy Serrurier, a businessman whom she had married in 1938. In the meantime, he told them, 'hold your thumbs for me'.

Bushell's parents had left West Springs and were living in Hermanus, the town where, as a boy, Roger had fished from the rocks, and where the family had spent so many holidays over the previous twenty-five years. Ben had bought a plot of land there and built a house, which they lived in after his retirement that April. It was called 'Broadmerston', which harked back to the Gloucestershire village settled by his ancestors in the 13th century.

The house stood alone on a slope several hundred yards from the sea, which in August 1939 it overlooked. Behind it, mountains rise quite steeply. Built with grey stone on two storeys, the house sat within a couple of acres. The building had a thatched roof, big windows with beautiful views at every point, and stairs, wood panelling, doors and bookshelves made from teak, one of the hallmarks of wealth in pre-war South Africa.

In the sitting room there is a bay window; flower-patterned curtains made by Tods still hang there. To the right, a brick fireplace – very English – and, further round, another door that leads to the room that was Ben's study. In here was a lovely old desk and a big armchair, and a wall covered from top to bottom with photographs of Roger.

Outside, Dorothe cultivated a shady garden, ideal for picnics; verdant, but full of striking colours: yellows, purples and reds. Ben, who could have been the model for Mr McGregor in Beatrix Potter's *The Tale of Peter Rabbit*, tended a vegetable garden where he spent much of his time. He kept his fishing rods in a storeroom under the stairs.

Roger's telegram was received at the Mossel River post office in Hermanus, on Saturday, 26 August, the same day that he disembarked at Southampton.

JUST BACK BY FLYING-BOAT FROM SOUTH OF FRANCE. EMBODIED YESTERDAY. ADDRESS 601 HENDON. DON'T WORRY. AM FIGHTING FIT. ALL LOVE. ROGER

For more than four years, Roger's letters and cards would be delivered to the post office on the Mossel River – a rather nondescript, single-storey building that still stands, looking like a scout hut, facing the southern seas on the road east out of Hermanus.

A week after Roger's parents received his telegram, the waiting ended: Germany invaded Poland by land, sea and air. The city of Wieluń was bombed by Junkers Ju 87 'Stuka' dive-bombers on 1 September 1939, at 4.45 a.m. A few minutes later, the battleship *Schleswig Holstein*, which had been on a courtesy visit to Danzig, opened fire on the Polish garrison on the Westerplatte, the peninsula covering the harbour. Around 1.5 million men led by five tank divisions with 1,500 Panzers crossed the border. The Poles fought bravely but were outgunned and outmanoeuvred by the German generals.

In the wake of the German armies came Heydrich's SS action squads, the *Einsatzgruppen*, and the SD and the Gestapo, which unleashed terror on the civilian population caught up in the invasion. Professionals, intellectuals, communists and other 'undesirables' – all those considered to be enemies of the German state – were shot or sent to concentration camps. Thousands of civilians are thought to have been executed in the first weeks.

The day after the German invasion, 601 Squadron was posted to Biggin Hill, where Brian Thynne remained in command. He told Bushell that, with the onset of hostilities, he had changed his mind about handing over to his flight commander. Bushell's reaction is not recorded. That evening, Winston Churchill visited the officers' mess on his way to Chartwell.

The British ultimatum to Germany, demanding an immediate cessation of hostilities, expired at 11 a.m. on 3 September 1939. A few minutes later, Chamberlain announced that a state of war existed between the two countries.

Airmen were gathered round wireless sets and mess speakers at Biggin Hill as the prime minister concluded his address to the nation: 'May God bless you all,' he said. 'May He defend the right. It is the evil things that we shall be fighters against – brute force, bad faith, injustice, oppression and persecution – and against these the right will prevail.'

Afterwards, Bushell told his mother, 'The world has gone mad.'

The aerodrome was ready for action. Fuelled and armed, the Hurricanes of 32 and 79 Squadrons and the Blenheims of 601 were dispersed around the perimeter of the airfield, which was near Westerham in Kent. Plotters and controllers waited in the operations room for the first signs of the Luftwaffe. Three Hurricanes were scrambled, but it was a false alarm.

In the warm September sunshine, pilots could be seen 'drinking beer and playing backgammon, or on the airfield grass, eating splendid lunches delivered by Fortnum and Mason'. To many, it seemed like an extension of their summer camp.

One of the issues that most concerned 'the Millionaires' at this time was the impact of petrol rationing – on their private transport. Rhodes-Moorhouse was assigned the task of buying petrol;

he returned to the aerodrome having purchased a nearby service station, but he announced that the pumps were not full. This was remedied when another pilot, Loel Guinness, a member of the brewing family, remembered he was a director of Shell and organised a delivery.

But the mood changed quickly. Training was stepped up and the crews started to live in a permanent state of readiness.

On 5 September, in a letter that opened, 'Dearest Father', Bushell said:

> *The squadron is grand and I know they'll follow me anywhere. I am a damn good pilot and I've years of experience and therefore I ought to stand a better chance than most . . .*
>
> *As for everything else in service – it's all on the top line now. We're here, we've got what we want and we're prepared. That is all there is to it. Everyone is absolutely calm.*

He wrote a separate letter on the same day to Dorothe, opening, 'My darling, darling Mummy', and telling her about the change of airfields.

> *There was a tremendous lot to do at Hendon getting the whole squadron mobilised and as we did night flying all one night and were duty squadron (getting up at 4.30 a.m.) as well, there was not much sleep going.*

Tods and her husband, Roy, and their baby were now safe in Yorkshire. Roger had seen them at a cocktail party at Hendon before they left.

Bushell said Hendon was entirely 'unsuitable' as an operational station. He spent his birthday – 30 August – there and was flying all night, but he celebrated with a 'cracking party' the next day, and then they moved to Biggin Hill. 'It's difficult to believe there is a war on. It's all so very peaceful – gorgeous weather and everything working perfectly smoothly.'

But the war was very definitely changing their lives.

We were night duty squadron last night and slept up at our end with our machines and though they expected a raid nothing happened and we all slept like logs.

From Biggin Hill, the crews could see the barrage balloons, which were intended to impede enemy aircraft flying low over London. 'Very impressive they look,' wrote Bushell. 'Whether they are any good or not I don't know but at any rate we avoid London like the plague! We counted 453 the evening before last.'

As he was writing the letter to his father, South Africa's decision to fight alongside Britain was announced on the wireless. 'Great news,' he wrote. 'The Union is coming in. I was very frightened that bloody Dutchman [the South African leader, Jan Smuts] might keep her out.'

In lines that are both poignant and probably important to Ben Bushell, Roger finally brought himself to apologise to his father for his past behaviour, but still finished with a quip: 'Please forgive me for all my delinquencies in the past,' he wrote. 'I'll try to make up for them by getting lots of Germans for you!'

He put pen to paper again on 11 September.

I started to write this yesterday and no sooner had I sat down than the phone went and they wanted me to go up and shoot a balloon down that had broken away from the barrage. I found it at 22,000 ft and I and my air-gunner amused ourselves filling it full of lead. I left [it] at 9,000ft sinking rapidly and it must have fallen in the sea.

We had our first take-off in anger . . . the sirens went and we were ordered into the air. We patrolled about for an hour and a bit and saw nothing and then landed. It was the most beautiful morning and you could see for a hundred miles. I don't believe there were any Germans!

Bushell's writing at this time is prolific. He probably wrote to his parents on more occasions during these few weeks than he had done through much of the past decade, and he was happy to indulge in small talk: 'I have a dear little house which I share with Whitney Straight, McMullen who is the C.O. of 70 Squadron, and a funny little Irishman called Bill Igo.' Unsurprisingly, the women on the base attracted his attention. 'They look very sweet in their air force uniforms and I am afraid there will be a heavy mortality among the NCOs.' He also passed on Air Vice-Marshal Nicholl's best wishes. 'You took him down the mine about two years ago when he was out there. Nice old chap. He is the administrative chief at Fighter Command.'

Bushell had forthright views on developments in Eastern Europe. When the Red Army crossed Poland's eastern border in mid-September, he told his parents:

The Russian business seems very odd. I see he [Stalin] says he is doing a bit of 'peaceful penetration' in Poland. I should think it is evens that he fights with or against Germany inside a month. It's goodbye to poor Poland anyhow. Why we do nothing I simply don't understand. Bar pamphlets and the Kiel raid [when the RAF attacked ships in the German port], we appear to have done damn all.

I think it's madness myself and I think it is Chamberlain who is holding back. Unless we do something soon the Germans will have finished with Poland and can then concentrate on us.

Roger's first combat of the war was not, in fact, over the skies of Britain, France or Germany: it was at a court-martial at RAF Stanmore, which highlighted shortcomings in Britain's air defences, particularly over the issue of aircraft recognition.

The war had begun with false alarms: air-raid sirens heralded only empty skies. The Luftwaffe stayed at home: its single-engine fighter aircraft, principally the Messerschmitt Bf 109, could not reach Britain from German bases. But on 6 September 1939, an observation post on Mersea Island in the Blackwater estuary had reported what it thought was enemy aircraft crossing the Channel. Hurricanes from 56 Squadron at North Weald were scrambled.

The Hurricanes in turn were picked up by a radar station at Canewdon on the Thames estuary. More fighters, including twelve Spitfires from 74 Squadron at Hornchurch, were alerted. The first flight of three Spitfires was commanded by Flight Lieutenant Adolph 'Sailor' Malan, a South African who was to become the RAF's top ace during the Battle of Britain, with twenty-seven confirmed kills. Another section of three aircraft was led by Pilot Officer Vincent 'Paddy' Byrne, with Pilot Officer John Freeborn right behind him.

The Spitfires ran into the Hurricanes. Malan ordered Byrne and Freeborn to attack. They shot down two of the Hurricanes, killing Pilot Officer Montague Hulton-Harrop. Freeborn was about to attack another aircraft when he realised it was an RAF Blenheim. When they landed, the two pilots were arrested.

Bushell was withdrawn from his squadron at Biggin Hill after agreeing to defend Byrne and Freeborn in a case dubbed 'the Battle of Barking Creek'. Sir Patrick Hastings, an RAF intelligence officer who had been a prominent KC, led the defence. His contention at the hearing on 7 October was that the case should never have been brought, while Bushell argued that the affair was a tragic accident. The four-man tribunal agreed and the two pilots were acquitted.

The case led to the introduction of a new identification system in time for the Battle of Britain the following summer. It also marked the end of Roger Bushell's legal career; his time was taken up with more pressing concerns.

He never mentioned the case to his parents – 'There is very little news and what there is of the war I'm not allowed to tell you'

– but, in a letter to his mother on 3 October, he hinted that changes might be afoot:

> *All the boys are well but we are all fretting about the inaction. I doubt if we stay together much longer. There are too many experienced people in the squadron for them not to split us up . . . you had better send all your letters in future c/o The Air Ministry, London, because who knows where I shall be in a few weeks' time.*

Six days later, Bushell was on the verge of being promoted to squadron leader. He told his mother and father:

> *There is only one thing of importance to tell you and it is somewhat ironic in view of your latest letters which ask whether I have been promoted yet.*
>
> *I have not actually been promoted yet but I am going to be. I am going to form a new squadron – where and what it is called I cannot tell you, of course. The news only came through last night and it came as a great shock because naturally the idea of leaving the squadron hits one pretty hard. But looking at things broadly it won't be too bad and it will be very interesting getting a new squadron together and in addition – for what it is worth – it is a great honour to be the first auxiliary to be asked to form a new squadron. I am hoping to be able to take a couple of the boys with me as flight commanders . . . I do not yet know when I go but almost any moment.*

No. 92 Squadron's service logbook recorded Bushell's arrival two days later at Tangmere aerodrome in Sussex:

> *F/Lt Bushell was posted to command the squadron with effect from 10/10/39. This officer came from No. 601 Fighter Squadron Auxiliary Air Force and is the first AAF*

officer to be posted to command and form a new squadron. As a result of various conversations with those in higher authority, he was able to persuade No. 11 (F) Group to allow him to take two Officers ['Paddy' Green and Jack Munro-Hinds] from his old squadron with him.

As the new squadron commander, Bushell was already pulling strings. He would need to: on 15 October, a note in the squadron's operations record book, henceforth known as the 'log', said: 'There is no equipment.'

Bushell was not downhearted, however. The squadron log recorded that 'the commanding officer of this squadron was tonight very hospitably entertained at Tangmere Cottage by Lord and Lady Willoughby de Broke and other members of No. 605 Squadron and retired to his bed at a late hour, feeling that Tangmere was the best station to be found in the best country in the best of all possible wars'.

8

Flying High

Michael Peacock was the first of the barristers from 1 Temple Gardens to exchange fire with German forces: while Bushell was struggling to put together an operational squadron at Tangmere, Peacock was winning 601 Squadron's first medal for gallantry, in a daring raid on the German seaplane base at Borkum in the Frisian Islands.

Six of the squadron's pilots were ordered to RAF Northolt in west London, where they were joined for the sortie by navigators from Coastal Command and gunners from Bomber Command. Peacock led the three Blenheims from A Flight, which had been Bushell's responsibility, and Max Aitken led the three from B Flight. Six more Blenheims with regular RAF crews from No. 125 Squadron joined them at Northolt.

The pilots were briefed by Group Captain Augustus Orlebar, who told the crews they would be flying to Germany the next day.

There was a cool silence, a gentle murmur of uneasy laughs, a sarcastic comment or two, silence again, *wrote Tom Moulson.*

Seaplanes from Borkum had been laying magnetic mines in the approaches to East Anglian harbours and the Thames estuary. The plan was to tackle the problem at its root and attack the seaplane base in daylight.

After the raid the next day, 28 November 1939, an Air Ministry statement said the Blenheim fighters had launched their attack at dusk and taken the German defenders by surprise.

Five German seaplanes were machine-gunned, and two of them are believed to have been seriously damaged; three out of four machine-gun posts on the Borkum Mole were probably put out of action; German coastal patrol boats were riddled with bullets; and valuable information of the enemy's fortifications was collected.

None of the British pilots had been in action before they took part in this raid. They all returned safely to great acclaim, making headlines in newspapers across the English-speaking world. Peacock was awarded the Distinguished Flying Cross.

Squadron Leader Bushell would have to wait a further seven months before he led 92 Squadron into battle.

Bushell's squadron had last seen action during the First World War. It was formed in 1917 and sent to France, where it flew almost continually, destroying thirty-seven enemy aircraft, until the Armistice. The squadron was disbanded in 1919.

Twenty years later, Bushell found there were many obstacles in the way of resurrecting No. 92 as a front-line squadron. Its operations record book, which survives in the National Archives at Kew, was written by someone who added colour and wit to the detail of daily life. It is a contemporaneous account of Bushell's labours as he built a squadron from nothing and prepared it for war.

Having persuaded the Air Ministry to transfer two senior pilots from 601 Squadron to be his senior officers, Bushell spoke to the station commander at Tangmere and arranged to report for duty on Sunday, 15 October. Tangmere was a thoroughly modern aerodrome, part of 11 Fighter Group, with barrack blocks, workshops, an armoury and a mechanical transport facility. New runways, blast protection pens and a perimeter track were all added in the first months of the war.

The entry for 10 October in the squadron log read as follows:

No 92 FIGHTER SQUADRON was on this date re-formed as a night Fighter Squadron at R.A.F. Station Tangmere.

It is to be equipped with Blenheim aircraft, firing 5 guns forward, and one gun in the rear turret, powered by two MERCURY VIII engines. The establishment will be 21 Officer and Airmen Pilots, 2 non-flying Officers and 209 other ranks.

Five days later, the log stated:

F/Lt BUSHELL reported for duty and discovered that the squadron consisted of himself, 3 airmen pilots (565197 Sgt Pratt, 741920 Sgt Pearce, 740822 Sgt Allen), the latter two coming from the Volunteer Reserve, and 98 other ranks. The senior N.C.Os are 314109 F/Sgt BENNETT, Disciplinarian, 355016 F/Sgt HUGHES, Fitter 1, who has come from No 43 (F) SQUADRON stationed here, and 362993 F/Sgt LEECH. There is no office equipment, no aeroplanes and indeed no equipment of any sort.

Hangars and offices vacated by No. 1 Squadron, which had been dispatched to France, were made available to Bushell. Two other fighter squadrons were stationed at Tangmere at this time: No. 43, commanded by Squadron Leader R. Baine, and No. 605 County of Warwick Squadron AAF, commanded by Squadron Leader Lord Willoughby de Broke. Both of these squadrons were equipped with Hurricanes.

Having been entertained by the Willoughby de Brokeses – otherwise known as John Verney and his beautiful wife, the former Rachel Wrey – at Tangmere Cottage, a pretty red-brick house in Tangmere village, close to the aerodrome, Bushell emerged the next morning with no obvious sign of a hangover or lack of sleep. He constituted himself as his own adjutant, flight commander, engineer officer, parachute officer and map officer, enabling him to deal with all ranks at whatever level he found the most effective to do business.

As a result, 92 Squadron was airborne before the end of the day.

In his combined capacity of Adjutant and Flight Commander, the log report said, *he visited the adjutant of No 605 Squadron, P/O Longsden, who was extremely helpful and lent him a Hind aircraft to give the three Sgt Pilots some flying . . . None of these pilots has any experience at all on twin-engine aircraft and efforts are being made to have them sent on a conversion course.*

Bushell also flew to RAF Debden in north Essex to recruit a former member of 601.

The squadron log recorded that its commanding officer borrowed and scavenged at every opportunity. Bushell persuaded a unit at Thorney Island, a Coastal Command base in Hampshire, to allow his pilots to inspect their Avro Ansons. 'This will at least show them what a twin looks like,' said the wit writing the log. On the same day, 18 October, he secured a pledge from 11 Group to supply some sort of twin-engine aircraft for training, but there were still no signs of the squadron's Blenheims or its equipment.

Two days later, Paddy Green and Jack Munro-Hinds reported for duty, which allowed Bushell to relieve himself of the posts of flight commander and adjutant. Charles Patrick Green, known as 'Paddy', was close to Bushell. They had similar backgrounds: Green was brought up in South Africa, had graduated from Cambridge and was elected a Fellow of the Royal Geographical Society. He won a bronze medal at the 1936 Olympics as part of Britain's four-man bobsleigh team.

The three men took over rooms in No. 7 Officers' Married Quarters.

Indeed the Commanding Officer and his first two officers repaired there in the evening and celebrated with

*considerable élan the re-birth of 92 Squadron of the
Auxiliary Air Force,* said the log entry. *It is devoutly to be
hoped that 601 will be proud of her offspring and that the
said offspring will grow up in that spirit of hardy
independence so characteristic of its parent.*

One cannot help but wonder whether Bushell wrote the log
himself.

When, on 21 October, they were told that thirteen pilots from
two flying training schools were being posted to the squadron,
the logbook remained in great form: 'Children though they may
be, it is hoped by some divine providence they will have flown
twins.'

The first four pilots reported the next day. All of them had
flown twin-engine aircraft for between 80 and 100 hours. 'Divine
providence has intervened,' rejoiced the log report. It was also
announced that Pilot Officer Vincent 'Paddy' Byrne, one of the
74 Squadron pilots defended by Bushell after the Battle of
Barking Creek, would join him as a second flight commander.
With the help of his usual contacts, Bushell took a short cut and
arranged for Byrne to be attached to 601 while he was trained on
Blenheims.

The log, however, was not satisfied: 'Still no news of any aeroplanes,' it read.

Next day, Bushell confronted Wing Commander Mulholland
from Fighter Command, who promised that Blenheims, including
a dual-control aircraft for training, would be allotted to the
squadron 'immediately'.

A signal received on 24 October said six aircraft were on their
way.

Things seem to be moving, said the log. *The squadron is,
however, still without any equipment and it is feared that a
situation may well arise where the Squadron is in
possession of aircraft with nothing to maintain them.*

The next problem concerned a Gloster Gauntlet biplane that had been loaned to the squadron. In an unusual entry in the log, dated 25 October – one that seems to sit with the cavalier spirit of 601 Squadron then being injected into No. 92 – it is recorded that the Gauntlet developed a major fault while Paddy Green was flying to Lady Willoughby de Broke's Warwickshire home to collect her furs. Later the same day, the commanding officer dined 'extremely well' with the station commander before the party went on to one of Lady Willoughby de Broke's soirées at Tangmere Cottage, where 'a good and rough time was had by all'.

Quite what the very lovely Lady Willoughby de Broke made of a 'rough time' is a mystery, but at least she was in possession of her furs.

Bushell's work now began to pay off handsomely. Over the next few days, eight more Blenheims were allotted to the squadron, and its pilots were sent to Hendon for training. More pilots arrived, too. 'This brings us up to our full establishment,' said the log report without comment. Green and Munro-Hinds collected the first of the Blenheims, Nos. L6726 and L6727, from RAF Aston Down in Gloucestershire, and a guard was put on the hangars at Tangmere.

At the beginning of November, Bushell went on leave. It is not known where he went, or what he did with this break from the squadron, but when he returned he drove on relentlessly with the job of preparing the squadron for war, in spite of bad weather and mechanical problems.

A page from the log bears witness to Bushell's endeavours, and sheds light on the lives of airmen during what came to be known as the 'Phoney War' – those few months of uncertainty and frenetic activity as the RAF worked up its squadrons before Hitler attacked in the West.

Nov 8: S/LDR BUSHELL, F/LT GREEN and P/O
MUNRO-HINDS take three Blenheims to Hendon. After
leaving two Blenheims there, they proceed to Aston Down

in the remaining aircraft. At Aston Down they collect one new Blenheim, No. L2624 and return to Tangmere. During local Flying later in the day F/LT GREEN in this new aircraft, broke the starboard flap control, and will be unserviceable until new rods can be obtained. We succeeded in borrowing some tools from FORD to replace three broken valve springs in another Blenheim engine.

Nov 9: Torrential rain and South-westerly Gale. No flying possible in forenoon, but weather improved later, and local flying practice became possible in the afternoon.

Nov 10, 11 and 12: The weather continued very poor and it was impossible to fetch any new aircraft from Aston Down or Tern Hill, and only local flying practice was possible.

Nov 13: P/O MUNRO-HINDS did some local flying practice, but on Landing had difficulty lowering undercarriage and flaps owing to a leak in the hydraulic system. S/LDR BUSHELL & F/LT GREEN went to Aston Down in one Blenheim, and picked up the last new one from there. F/LT GREEN returned at once, and S/Ldr BUSHELL landed at Filton on the return journey to see the Bristol Engine people. They were kind enough to promise to send two engineers with a full set of Mercury tools here for a fortnight to give our men some Mercury experience. On landing at Tangmere, S/Ldr BUSHELL discovered all the rods on his Starboard flap, broken.

Nov 14: S/LDR BUSHELL, F/LT GREEN and P/O MUNRO-HINDS attempted to collect two Blenheims from Tern Hill, but were forced by bad weather to return to Tangmere. In the afternoon the weather closed right in and flying became impossible. The two Mercury Experts from Bristols arrived.

A week later, the squadron suffered its first casualties. Jack Munro-Hinds, flying a new Blenheim just picked up from RAF

Tern Hill in Shropshire, crashed on the north-east boundary of Tangmere aerodrome. Two other airmen died with him. 'The cause of the accident is at present under review,' recorded the log. 'The aircraft is a total wreck. The weather at the time was, for once, fine and clear.'

Munro-Hinds was buried at Windsor five days later. No. 92 Squadron gave the salute.

Bushell pressed on. His pilots became familiar with their new aircraft and flying practice increased whenever weather permitted, and sometimes when it did not: 'P/O Fraser lost himself in a local blizzard, and forced landed in a turnip field near Wantage,' the log report said on 5 December 1939.

Flying at dusk then started, as a prelude to intensive night flying in preparation for their role as a night-fighter squadron. 'The COMMANDING OFFICER and F/LT GREEN each did one hour Night Flying in very dark conditions,' reported the log for 11 December. The next day, two more crew were killed in a low-flying accident.

In the week before Christmas, Bushell led formation flying, flew weather tests and took his fledgeling pilots on dual-control training flights. Many of the new pilots began to go solo.

Having finally taken delivery of all their aircraft and equipment, the crews were dismayed to hear on 23 December that they were to move to Croydon, south of London.

Christmas Day, the log noted. *As this squadron is not yet Operational, today was observed as a holiday. We learned today that our move to Croydon is fixed for 29/12/39 by 1800 hours. In spite of this news, a pleasant time was had by all.*

Bushell's rank of squadron leader was confirmed on 1 January 1940, and, shortly afterwards, he took another period of leave.

For the squadron, night flying became a priority, but there were more casualties as they struggled with the conditions.

P/O Whitmarsh who had completed about one hour's night dual took off on his first night solo, said the squadron log for 24 February. *For some reason – not yet determined – he crashed from a low altitude into houses on the West boundary of the Aerodrome. The machine disintegrated, exploded and burst into flames. P/O Whitmarsh was thrown clear and killed instantly. Damage by fire and impact was done to 5 dwelling houses, 3 cars and garages. Two civilians died in hospital, a third is seriously injured and 8 more have shock. P/O Whitmarsh was the sole occupant of the aircraft, BLENHEIM L6724. Night flying ceased.*

The war was already taking its toll on Bushell's night-fighter squadron, but then their prospects changed. They were told they would be equipped with Spitfires, the most modern fighter plane in the world at this time, flying predominantly in daylight. On 5 March 1940:

F/LT BYRNE took some pilots to Northolt to examine a Spitfire, as this day our Allotment for 21 Spitfires was received. The next day, Squadron Leader Bushell flew to RAF Cosford to collect the first batch of this 'sleek, strong and incredibly high-powered fighter'.

More than forty years later, another 92 Squadron fighter pilot wrote about Bushell's first experience of the Spitfire. The author was Simon Morris, who flew English Electric Lightnings from Britain's forward bases in Germany in the 1970s – and who found 92 Squadron's notes from the Second World War in a rubbish skip on his base.

There were no two-seater versions of the Spitfire, which meant that a fighter pilot's first flight in the aircraft was always his first solo flight. A more experienced pilot simply explained the cockpit drills, wrote Morris in his history of No. 92, *Cobra in the Sky* (a reference to the squadron's insignia).

For over an hour, Bushell sat in the aircraft while the chap standing on the wing ordered him to place his hands on the various controls. When he had memorised the position of each knob, lever, switch and dial, they went over the various drills for pre-take-off and landing checks, which took the best part of another hour. When he was happy and ready to put it all into practice, they called the ground crew, started the engine and, with one last shout above the roar of the powerful Merlin: 'Don't forget, be careful not to get her nose too far forward on take-off. Once the tail's up you've only a few inches clearance between the prop tips and the deck!' Then his instructor was gone.

Left alone, Bushell felt uneasy as he looked through the tiny windscreen at the slender shark's head cowling covering the only engine – after he had been so used to having two. He realised the Spitfire bore no relation to any aircraft he had flown before.

He signalled 'Chocks away', eased the throttle forward, opened the radiator wide to prevent overheating, eased off the brakes and taxied carefully to the downwind end of the field. There, he turned her into wind, stopped and began his pre-take-off checks. As soon as he became involved in this mental task he became more relaxed, then he lined her up on the runway.

He eased the throttle open and she seemed to leap forward. At first he couldn't see anything ahead because of the long cowling, but as the speed built up rapidly, the controls took effect and the tail came up, giving him a clear view ahead. Gently, he checked the stick, keeping the prop tips clear of the ground. The aircraft had a strong inclination to swing to the right due to the torque of the air from the prop striking the fin, so a strong boot of left rudder was needed to keep her straight. Then suddenly she leapt airborne.

At this point he had the hazardous task of raising the undercarriage. First he throttled back to climbing revs, then tightened the large friction nut to keep the throttle steady. He had to change hands and hold the stick with his left. Here was the moment of danger. He had to keep a careful eye on the air speed and keep it constant by raising or lowering the nose very gently with his left hand and at the same time with his right he had to pump vigorously for several seconds. Even the best of beginners couldn't be expected to hold her steady in a climb at this point. A gentle 'porpoising' movement was inevitable. Then the thump under his feet told him the wheels were in their belly housings and he began to fly this new creature. He found it a gentle and sensitive machine that responded to the most delicate, suggestive pressures from its master's hands and feet.

On the way back to Croydon, he spent twenty minutes looping, rolling, spinning and stalling, while generally getting the feel of the aircraft. Then he descended in a long, gentle dive and touched 360mph, levelled out near the aerodrome and concentrated on the difficult task of landing a new aircraft for the first time.

He throttled back, opened the radiator wide, slid back his hood and began the approach. As he turned across wind he lowered the undercarriage and flaps, then he turned into the wind, put the prop to fine pitch and eased the stick back. He couldn't see a thing as the long nose obscured everything ahead of him, so he had to put her into a gentle side slip and then straighten her out just before the wheels touched. Stick back, gently but firmly into the pit of the stomach, a soft jolt and she was rolling bumpily over the grass. He kept her straight with the brakes, slowed her down to taxiing speed and trundled leisurely to dispersal.

Roger Bushell had just delivered the first Spitfire to No. 92 – a momentous occasion, joyous for pilots and ground crew alike. For four years, the squadron would fly Spitfires in almost uninterrupted combat, through the conflagration to come.

Two other relationships appear to have developed in the first months of 1940 that would have profound effects on the life of Squadron Leader Bushell. One was a proposal of marriage; the other, which is not documented but seems likely from post-war papers, is his introduction to British military intelligence.

Bushell had known Peggy Hamilton – formally known as Marguerite – for some time. Unlike many of his previous girlfriends, she was neither wealthy, nor married, but it appears that, like him, she had serious social ambitions.

One of three sisters, Peggy was born in 1916, the daughter of Ion Wentworth Hamilton and his wife, Lavinia, from Nettlebed, Henley-on-Thames. Her father had been killed in a car crash when she was a child.

Like Georgiana Curzon, she was an elegant woman, with fine features. She appears from photographs to have been strong-willed and confident. With big, dark eyes, Peggy had the poise of a woman who knew that she was good looking.

She was a familiar figure to 'the Millionaires' of 601 Squadron and would join the fighter pilots for drinks at the Berkeley Hotel in Knightsbridge. One man who met Bushell and Hamilton as a couple at this time was Wing Commander Reginald Piff, who later married Peggy's younger sister, Frances. She 'had just returned from a skiing holiday in Arosa with her elder sister Marguerite and Roger Bushell, a barrister and Royal Auxiliary Air Force pilot, with whom Peggy apparently shared a bon vivant lifestyle,' wrote Piff in his memoirs.

Peggy lived in a flat at Wellesley House just off Sloane Square in Chelsea, a short walk from his flat in Tite Street. Bushell and Hamilton, it seems, were well-suited and, during the time that he was learning to master the Spitfire, he proposed to her. She accepted.

It was also at this time – the date and location is not known – that Bushell is likely to have met members of MI9 (Military Intelligence 9) to discuss the issues of escape and evasion in the event of him being shot down, as well as the potential for gathering information behind enemy lines and the use of codes to communicate with the intelligence services in London.

MI9 was born out of the experience of the First World War when the War Office realised only late in the day that prisoners of war – both British servicemen held in German camps, and Germans held in Britain and France – were a potential intelligence asset that, with the right handling, could provide information on the enemy. A small new sub-branch of the War Office intelligence directorate was established towards the end of the First World War. It was called MI1a.

The new unit started to organise secret communication with officer camps by coded letter. 'No startling results were obtained,' wrote M. R. D. Foot and J. M. Langley in their history of MI9, 'but enough was done to suggest that the still rudimentary system might be worth following up.'

As the likelihood of another war with Germany grew, British military intelligence held conferences involving former prisoners and escapers from the 1914–18 conflict. The Air Ministry also took part and, in November 1939, the British Expeditionary Force, which had been sent to France after the declaration of war, called for the setting up of an agency 'to facilitate escapes of British prisoners of war from enemy prison camps'.

On 23 December 1939, a day on which propitious dense fog descended over the south of England, 'a new section of the Intelligence Directorate at the War Office' was formed, according to documents distributed to a handful of people in British intelligence, including MI5, responsible for domestic security, and MI6, the foreign intelligence service.

'It will be called M.I.9,' said the founding charter.

The new section would operate from Room 424 at the Metropole Hotel, a few hundred yards from the War Office. The man in charge was Norman Crockatt, a forty-five-year-old former regular soldier who had been highly decorated and badly wounded on the Western Front during the First World War.

Crockatt's natural grace of bearing, set off by a tall, well-proportioned figure and piercing greenish eyes, made him a noticeable figure in any company; in an age of drab clothes and battledress, he wore at every opportunity the colourful gear of his regiment, the Royal Scots, *wrote Foot and Langley, who both served with Crockatt*. He was also clear headed, quick witted, a good organiser, a good judge of men, and no respecter of red tape: excellent qualities for his early struggles with the War Office.

In assessing MI9's role after the war, Crockatt wrote that its objectives had been:

a) To facilitate escapes of British prisoners of war, thereby getting back service personnel and containing additional enemy manpower on guard duties
b) To facilitate the return to the United Kingdom of those who succeeded in evading capture in enemy-occupied territory
c) To collect and distribute information
d) To assist in the denial of information to the enemy
e) To maintain the morale of British prisoners of war in enemy prison camps.

The head of MI9 also outlined the methods used, which included lectures to sailors, soldiers and airmen; instruction in the use of code; the publication of regular bulletins; the preparation of plans for escape and evasion; and the commissioning of technical research for escape aids, and their production and distribution.

According to Foot and Langley:

One of Crockatt's principal aims at this early stage in the war was to inculcate and foster in the armed services the quality to which he had to give the cumbrous name of 'escape-mindedness': the constant readiness, if caught in enemy hands, to work for and seize on every conceivable chance of getting out of them. His lectures preached escape-mindedness all over the BEF (British

Expeditionary Force), the AEAF (Allied Expeditionary Air Force), home forces, Bomber Command, Fighter Command, the fleet, anyone who would hear, and preached it with success. To such an extent indeed did they succeed that the phrase, 'It is an officer's duty to escape' has now become more or less proverbial; and the duty to escape applied to all ranks.

Crockatt believed that prisoners remained an active force; that a 'fighting man remained a fighting man, whether he was in enemy hands or not', according to Foot and Langley, and that a soldier's duty 'to continue fighting' overrode everything else.

Information was to be obtained from prisoners through code correspondence with the various prisoner-of-war camps and through the interrogation of escapers and evaders.

In his post-war report on MI9, Crockatt included a section on 'Special Instruction'. It read:

This was a lecture of a Top Secret character and dealt with a system of code communication which could be used in normal correspondence. For reasons of security it was sometimes given the title of 'Camp Conditions' and was always restricted to a very limited number of officers and W.O.s [warrant officers]. A small number of staff officers and all Intelligence officers on H.Qs of formations received this instruction.

It was recommended that no attempt should be made to instruct more than ten persons at a time and only those capable of grasping details readily . . .

Lecturers were instructed to satisfy themselves by checking practice letters that personnel who attended the lecture understood the system, and their capabilities were further checked by M.I.9 before their registration with I.S.9 [Intelligence School 9] as potential 'users'.

According to official papers in the National Archive, Bushell was registered with IS9, known officially as Intelligence School 9 but also used as cover for MI9. It is not known for certain whether this registration took place while he was in command of 92 Squadron, but it is known that the RAF's fighter squadrons and their commanders were targeted by the new intelligence agency in the weeks after it started work.

Armed with a Spitfire squadron, supported by British intelligence, and with a stunning new fiancée at his side, Roger Bushell was ready to go to war.

9

First Combat

At Croydon aerodrome, where Neville Chamberlain had landed after signing the Munich Agreement eighteen months previously, the pilots of 92 Squadron were still learning how to fly Spitfires. Bushell gave them dual instruction on a single-engine training aircraft and then, one by one, sent them solo.

As he did so, the war erupted again, this time closer to home.

It was clear to the Nazi leadership that Britain would not respect Norway's neutrality. For some weeks, Winston Churchill, First Lord of the Admiralty, had been agitating for action to stop the supply of Swedish iron ore to German industry through Norwegian ports. The Royal Navy gathered a task force in Scotland and embarked 14,000 British and French troops. Destroyers laid mines in Norwegian waters on 8 April 1940.

Hitler knew of the plans in advance because the German navy's signal intelligence agency, B-Dienst, had broken British naval codes. He ordered the invasion of Norway and Denmark on 9 April. During the following month, the Germans suffered crippling losses to their surface fleet: thirteen major warships were sunk and three others badly damaged, which did not augur well for the invasion of Britain planned later that year.

But the campaign was disastrous for the British, too; they suffered heavy losses, including an aircraft carrier, the HMS *Glorious*, and were forced to withdraw their ground forces after a muddled campaign blighted by a lack of air cover.

When Chamberlain resigned, Churchill became prime minister on the afternoon of 10 May, after the start of what the historian A. J. P. Taylor called a 'real war' in the West. The German armies had invaded Belgium and the Netherlands, and would soon attack France.

Four days later, the pilots of 92 Squadron read reports of Churchill's first prime ministerial address to the House of Commons: 'I have nothing to offer but blood, toil, tears and sweat,' he said. 'We have before us an ordeal of the most grievous kind. We have before us many long months of struggle and suffering. You ask, what is our policy? I will say: it is to wage war, by sea, land and air, with all our might and with all the strength that God can give us; to wage war on a monstrous tyranny . . . You ask, what is our aim? I can answer in one word: victory – victory at all costs, victory in spite of all terror; victory, however long and hard the road may be.'

Bushell's squadron had been declared operational on 9 May 1940 and moved to Northolt in West London. Notes in the log for 10 May reflected the change in mood:

Six Spitfires are kept at the different dispersal points in Readiness. At about 1500 hours, a practice operational movement was made and after the firing of a white rocket, three of the Readiness section went up. Owing to the progress of the War today everyone was recalled from leave and all leave has been stopped.

On 12 May, the log report stated:

At about noon today a warning came through and nine Spitfires were put at Readiness till the All Clear was given. And on 14 May: *The usual operational duties were carried out, both 'A' and 'B' Flights now being available and at Readiness from 0830 till 1700 . . . the weather remains bright and clear. Night flying took place at dusk.*

As the pilots prepared for combat, time was short, and Bushell knew it. Flying Officer Robert Stanford Tuck, who would become one of the RAF's greatest aces, joined 92 from 65 Squadron at Hornchurch at about this time. He was an experienced pilot, who had been in the RAF since 1935. Bushell immediately promoted him to flight lieutenant and gave him command of a flight.

According to Tuck's biography, written after the war by Larry Forrester, Bushell told his new flight commander:

> We'll be getting a crack at them soon, don't worry. You're just the sort of bloke I need, and I'm bloody well going to work you till you're on your knees. We've got to lick this squadron into top shape in double-quick time. Go and dump your kit. I'll meet you at dispersal in ten minutes.

Tuck was 'astounded and delighted' to find that the atmosphere of the Croydon mess was even 'wilder and woollier' than that of his old squadron from the regular RAF. 'In some mysterious way, these war-time chaps had managed to learn the entire range of RAF slang and idiom, all the rude songs, all the traditional nicknames and, most surprising of all, they had the same cynical approach to anything that savoured even faintly of militarism, rhetoric or red tape.' Even the youngest of 92's officers had acquired the 'languid arrogance' of experienced pilots.

Bushell had:

> . . . engendered a fine squadron spirit with his overwhelming, enveloping aura of personality and strength. [His] voice was strong and cultured, and his diction was like an actor's, yet there was no false, courtroom pomp about him and he could bellow cheerful vulgarities and roar the bawdiest choruses with the rest of them.
>
> He was never one to stand on ceremony, but [was] a candid and open character, ready to joke or play the fool with all, *Tuck told his biographer*. Yet when there was serious talk, the affability and humour fell away and he became direct, shrewd, commanding.

At 1.38 p.m. on 15 May, Bushell snatched time to send a telegram from Ruislip in west London to his parents, saying:

AM VERY FIT AND WELL. LOVE ROGER BUSHELL.

It was received at the Mossel River post office on the morning of 16 May.

Flying practice started at RAF Northolt at about noon that day after heavy overnight rain and poor visibility during the morning.

> *At 1400 hours,* said the log, *THREE SPITFIRES did firing practice with a Blenheim flown by F/O Barry-Smith who is attached to the STATION temporarily with a BEAUFORT bomber. THREE SPITFIRES left for France this afternoon to escort a FLAMINGO, under the command of F/O TUCK. Night flying took place. The night was clear with a three-quarter moon.*

Tuck's personal logbook for the same day said: 'Escorting Prime Minister to Le Bourget.'

They left Hendon for Paris at 1.30 p.m., flying at 2,000ft. The Germans had broken through at Sedan and the road to Paris was clear. General Heinz Guderian, commander of the German army's XIX Panzer Corps, swept forward, according to A. J. P. Taylor, 'disregarding orders to halt from his army commander and even evading similar orders from Hitler who for a moment lost his nerve. The German tanks drove unimpeded along the open road'.

The French prime minister, Paul Reynaud, called for further assistance, more troops, more British fighter squadrons. However, Air Marshal Hugh Dowding, the head of Fighter Command, was adamant that no more British planes should be deployed in this way. He told the chiefs of staff that the remaining squadrons should be saved for the defence of Britain.

In Paris, the French High Command made their own entreaties for greater RAF support, both from bomber and fighter squadrons, as they were all too aware of their own inferiority in the skies. The prime minister asked the War Cabinet to meet the French request. More fighters were sent to France, some operating in the morning, some in the afternoon, but the survivors returned each day to their bases in Kent.

Tuck's logbook for 17 May said, very simply: 'Escorting prime minister back' and stated that they flew at just 1,000ft.

Two days later, Bushell took three Spitfires to Hendon for another escort flight to Paris, but they were stood down.

One of the casualties of Britain's commitment to France was Bushell's closest friend. In a tragic denouement to the parallel lives of the two barristers who had emerged from childhood in South Africa, shared victory and defeat as teenagers at Wellington, and a morning suit and a flat in Tite Street, Michael Peacock was killed while trying to halt the German advance.

Like Bushell, Peacock had been promoted to squadron leader, but transferred to No. 85 Squadron, flying Hawker Hurricanes. He was shot down by Messerschmitt Bf 109 fighters while strafing German troops near Arras on 20 May. It was his first day in command.

'Poor Mike, I am afraid, is dead,' wrote Bushell to his head of chambers, 'Khaki' Roberts, a month later.

Roberts paid tribute to Peacock: 'He had a genius for friendship, the most lovable nature, and a quaint, almost scholarly, sense of the whimsical, which made him a charming companion.'

At Northolt, on 21 May, an eighteen-year-old pilot officer, Geoffrey Wellum, reported for flying duties. He met his commanding officer twenty-four hours later. 'I only saw Roger for a very short time,' said Wellum, during an interview in 2012. 'I suppose about ten minutes. I was eighteen years and nine months and a little bit in awe of joining an operational fighter squadron at that age. They were flying Spitfires and I'd never seen a Spitfire, let alone flown one.

'Roger gave me the impression of being a rather tough cookie. He was, I think now, a little bit rough with me for being a youngster, saying I wasn't very bright and all the rest of it.'

Sitting behind his desk, Bushell had looked down at the new pilot's logbook. Wellum recalls him saying something like, 'Well, it's got above average but that doesn't mean anything to me. Not after only 120 hours.'

'He was severe, dominating, obviously intelligent, but the first impression was of a rather unfriendly chap,' said Wellum. 'I remember him saying, "So, you've flown a Harvard [single-engine trainer], have you? Something that folds up, undercarriage flaps and that sort of thing?" and he nodded his head, and I said, "Yes." And he said, "Well, at least you've flown something that folds up . . ." And I said "Yes" again . . . and then it changed, like that, and he said, "Well, if you break a bloody Spitfire, there will be hell to pay."'

It was clear to Wellum that Bushell thought the squadron would struggle to cope with untrained pilots at this time; he believed Wellum should have been sent to an operational training unit instead.

The squadron was waiting for its first action, probably over the French port of Dunkirk, where tens of thousands of British troops were gathering in the hope of evacuation. Bushell wanted Wellum to understand the point he was making.

'I can still see his face, quite clearly,' said Wellum, more than seventy years later. 'We weren't made terribly welcome, but I think the squadron worshipped him. He inspired a very aggressive, attacking "Let's get at 'em" attitude. They never lost it, that atmosphere, the feeling that Bushell put into 92 Squadron.

'I was introduced to the other pilots in the officers' mess that evening, but Roger never came up and said "Welcome", or anything like that, he remained with close friends, old skiing friends like Paddy Green; it was a bit of a club. A chap called Pat Learmond looked after us, and Pat did just that. He never left us all night long.

'Roger had too much on his mind, I think, at that time, because they went off to Dunkirk the next morning. They couldn't wait to go to Dunkirk, they just couldn't wait . . . they were all getting excited and all the rest of it, knocking back drinks.

'There was a kind of madness.'

The frenzied nature of the squadron's first day of combat is described in several books that were published after the war, drawing on interviews with pilots involved in the fighting. The accounts are dramatic.

In the early morning of 23 May, Bushell met Tuck. They drove in a black Humber to a dispersal hut before flying from Northolt to a forward aerodrome: Hornchurch in Essex.

Once there, they have breakfast: bacon and eggs. At this point, the reports vary, but sometime between eight o'clock and ten thirty, the phone rings. The pilots strap themselves into their Spitfires.

Tuck looks towards Bushell's fighter; the squadron leader taxies into position. He signals to his flight, releases the brakes, and pushes the throttle forward. Five Spitfires follow him.

Bushell's voice is heard over the radio: 'Taking off,' he says.

The squadron rises in two flights of six, each broken down further into formations of three. Bushell leads them towards the French coast.

Below them, Boulogne, then Calais and Dunkirk. Black smoke rising from the beaches; above, blue sky and the sun, very bright. Twelve pairs of eyes scan the horizon for enemy planes.

Suddenly, over the intercom, a voice cries out. Then the Messerschmitts arrive. And Pat Learmond dies. A woofing explosion. His machine is gone. Just a pulsating ball of flame, which keeps position, flies on, then sinks.

Bushell raps out orders.

Tuck attacks a Bf 109, and Bushell chases another, but loses his prey in cloud.

They return to Hornchurch, mourn the loss of Learmond, and eat sandwiches. The planes are re-armed and refuelled.

At 1.45 p.m., but it might have been later, the phone rings again. They receive orders to fly another 'offensive' patrol over France. The Spitfires climb to 12,000ft – Tuck's logbook says 15,000ft, while the official combat report suggests they were flying too low, at 4,000ft – as they patrol twelve miles inland from Calais and Dunkirk.

Bushell sees the enemy first and orders his squadron to climb steeply. They enter a defensive circle of forty, perhaps more, twin-engined Messerschmitt Me 110 fighters covering each other's tails. There are German bombers too, and other fighters.

One pilot wonders how Bushell proposes to attack this 'armada' with his twelve Spitfires. He thinks of Henry V at Agincourt, another battlefield not far below in the French countryside.

Bushell's voice breaks radio silence. He is heard swearing as he chases an Me 110 inland. Against a sky full of bullets, full of smoke trails, Tuck sees another German fighter attack Bushell from above. It scores several hits. 'It looks like the chopper,' says Tuck, who later records the day's events in his logbook. His first report for the morning: 'Offensive patrol. Shot down 1 Messerschmitt 109. Lost Pat Learmond.' The second is for the afternoon: 'Offensive patrol. Shot down 2 ME 110. Lost Roger, John Gillies, Paddy Green, and Sgt Klipsch.'

The squadron's log is remarkably emotive:

The whole squadron left at dawn for HORNCHURCH where they commenced Patrol flying over the FRENCH COAST. At about 8.30 hours they ran into six MESSERSCHMITTS and a dogfight ensued. The result was a great victory for 92 Squadron and all six GERMAN machines Me's 109 were brought down with only one loss to us. It is with the greatest regret that we lost PILOT

OFFICER P. A. G. LEARMOND in this fight. He was seen to come down in flames over DUNKERQUE. In the afternoon, the Squadron went out again on Patrol and this time encountered at least FORTY MESSERSCHMITTS flying in close formation. The result of this fight was that another seventeen GERMAN machines, Me's 110 were brought down and 92 SQUADRON LEADER R. J. BUSHELL – the COMMANDING OFFICER – FLYING OFFICER J. GILLIES and SGT PILOT P. KLIPSCH (566457). FLIGHT LIEUTENANT C. P. GREEN was wounded in the leg and is now in hospital at SHORNCLIFFE. The remainder of the Squadron returned to Hornchurch badly 'shot-up' with SEVEN SPITFIRES unserviceable. It has been a glorious day for the SQUADRON, with TWENTY-THREE GERMAN MACHINES brought down, but the loss of the COMMANDING OFFICER and the THREE OTHERS has been a very severe blow to us all, and to the SQUADRON which was created and trained last October by our late SQUADRON LEADER.

The official combat report filed by 92 Squadron's intelligence officer is a more measured document and probably sheds greater light on the events of the day:

No 92 Squadron while on patrol Boulogne-Calais-Dunkirk from 17.20 to 19.20 hours sighted a large formation of enemy aircraft over Calais at 8–10,000 feet. About thirty enemy aircraft, mostly Me 110s, were ahead, and behind them a further group of fifteen to twenty aircraft of types not identified, but including Ju 87s and Ju 88s. Some aircraft started dive bombing attacks on Boulogne harbour, with others circling in the vicinity. No. 92 Squadron at 4,000 feet climbed to engage and a series of dogfights ensued, mainly with Me 110s. Blue 1 states that he saw some Hurricanes already engaging the enemy, but as the sky was so full of aircraft a clear statement of the situation is impossible. As a result of the dogfight, seven Me 110s were definitely shot down and five Me 110s and two Junkers 88s were probably shot down. Most of our aircraft were hit many times.

Pilots state that the Me 110s' evasive tactics are a steep turn towards the Spitfire's tail, to enable the rear gunner to open fire. About twenty Me 110s were seen flying in line astern in a tight circle around the bombers, which was very difficult to attack. The Me 110 is not so fast as the Spitfire on the level, but very good in a fast turn and a steep dive, though the Spitfire can hold it on a turn. They appear to use the stall turn a great deal.

Pilot Officer Wellum was shocked by the day's events and distressed by the death of Pat Learmond, the only pilot to have befriended him in the bar at Northolt the night before. He questioned the squadron's 'gung-ho' tactics: 'There are the black cross aeroplanes, there are the Germans, "Go at 'em!" All very good,' said Wellum, 'but I soon came to realise that you had to think about this. The end of the first day when four of them didn't come back, I thought, "Hold on a minute, this is a bit serious." It never entered my mind, I enjoyed my training, I was, as I say, eighteen years old, but then I thought, "Hold on, this is bloody dangerous." The idea of being shot down didn't appeal to me one little bit.

'And so I sort of took myself for a little walk around – and what was left of the squadron – and I thought, "Well, what do you do to prevent yourself from being shot down?" Answer: Make yourself a difficult target. How do you go about that? Answer: Don't present yourself as an easy target. That's the two answers.

Right, how do we go about that? Never stay still for more than twenty seconds. In the combat area never stay still. Even if you can't see your antagonist, don't stay still, chuck it about.'

Wellum flew in combat almost continuously for the next three years as No. 92 Squadron combined Bushell's aggression with new, refined tactics that would take a toll on Luftwaffe pilots. By the end of 23 May 1940, badly mauled as they were, the pilots of 92 had already hit the enemy hard – and their 'late' squadron leader was very much alive.

It would be some weeks before the Air Ministry finally confirmed that Roger Bushell had survived and was a prisoner of war – a period of terrible anxiety for Ben and Dorothe Bushell, living thousands of miles away in Hermanus on the South African coast.

The first telegram from the Under Secretary of State at the Air Ministry was sent on 24 May.

IMMEDIATE: DEEPLY REGRET TO INFORM YOU THAT YOUR SON SQUADRON LEADER ROGER JOYCE BUSHELL IS REPORTED MISSING AND BELIEVED TO HAVE LOST HIS LIFE AS THE RESULT OF AIR OPERATIONS ON 23 MAY 1940. LETTER FOLLOWS. ANY FURTHER INFORMATION WILL BE IMMEDIATELY COMMUNICATED TO YOU.

On 25 May, Group Captain Stanley Vincent, the station commander at RAF Northolt, wrote to Ben Bushell, saying:

Your Son was only at Northolt with me for a comparatively short time, but in that time I had formed the very highest opinion of him, particularly as regards his real gift of leadership. From an entirely impersonal point of view, his loss is very great to the Royal Air Force in general and to his

*Squadron in particular. His Squadron would have followed
him anywhere and in fact did so in the operation in which
he was lost. He was last seen by members of his formation
going straight in to a large formation of enemy bombers in
France.*

*I hope of course most sincerely that he may yet turn up.
We have had two or three others from here who have been
reported as missing and who have subsequently turned up
again. The odds were, however, terrifically in favour of the
enemy and I fear that we must face the probability that he
was killed in the engagement.*

Three days later, Brian Thynne, the former commander of 601
Squadron who had been posted to RAF headquarters at Bentley
Priory, also wrote to the Bushells:

*I do hope that by the time you will get this, he has turned
up again. I can promise you that any number of people
have either baled out or had to force land, and have turned
up safe and sound days later, and full of good stories – but
of course I know it must be terribly anxious work waiting
for news . . . .*

*Roger was over ground occupied by the French and may
therefore easily turn up again. Indeed, I feel sure he will as
one cannot conceive of all the colossal work he had put
into building that squadron up from its infancy being
whacked out in the first action.*

Then, on 14 June, the Bushells received another telegram from the
Air Ministry.

INFORMATION NOW RECEIVED FROM THE INTERNATIONAL
RED CROSS STATES THAT YOUR SON SQDN/LEADER ROGER
JOYCE BUSHELL IS A PRISONER OF WAR IN GERMANY.
LETTER FOLLOWS.

A letter from the Air Ministry followed in which it advised the Bushells that Roger was being held at a camp known as Dulag Luft, and enclosed a pamphlet regarding communications with prisoners of war.

'It is understood that the treatment and general conditions in the German prisoner of war camp is [sic] good,' said the Air Ministry, 'and there is no immediate cause for anxiety.' It was signed by the Director of Personal Services.

Group Captain Vincent wrote again, on 15 June, saying, 'It is with the very greatest pleasure that I write to offer our hearty congratulations upon the splendid news that your son is a prisoner of war and not, as we had come to think inevitable, killed in action.'

Vincent continued, writing a paragraph that would be tellingly prophetic: 'We have no details, so we hope most sincerely that he has not been wounded, and that he is well, and making such a nuisance of himself to the Hun that they will deeply regret having taken him a prisoner!'

He finished by saying, 'It [the news] has done us all a lot of good here and we are looking forward to beating the Germans and fetching him back as soon as possible.'

Another letter, written by George Irvin, a friend of Ben's who was in England, tried to put into context what his imprisoned son had achieved:

I learned a little of what the Air Force had done in the evacuation from Dunkirk. Roger, and other Squadron leaders, worked like super-men, and naturally their losses were heaviest.

I always felt sure that the navy would take away any man who was alive on Dunkirk beach, but the fact that so many were alive and were evacuated, with all that that implied, was due to the Air Force, and especially to the Squadron leaders.

When therefore you and Dorothy [sic] worry about Roger's imprisonment, you will know it was very much worthwhile.

Finally, probably in August, Ben and Dorothe received a letter from Germany dated 31 July:

> *My darling Mummy and Daddy,* it read. *You must know by now that I am a prisoner of war and alive and well, which for you I imagine is the chief thing . . . I was shot down near Boulogne on May 23rd in a big battle with Messerschmitts. I got two of them first so I have done something to win the war . . .*
> *I have a letter from Uncle Harry in which he says I was reported 'Missing believed killed' so I am afraid you must have had a bad time.*

And, he added, probably with a wry smile as he was writing: 'I understand I had some very flattering obituary notices, which will make amusing reading!!'

10

Prisoner of War

Exhausted by the tension of flying and fighting, probably disorientated by his violent crash landing, Bushell sat in a field just outside Boulogne and inhaled smoke from a cigarette. 'I suppose I can count myself lucky,' he wrote later.

Burning fiercely, his Spitfire was split in two pieces, broken just behind the cockpit. The aircraft had been hit by cannon fire from an Me 110, almost certainly flown by Karl Langenberg, a twenty-six-year-old from Augsburg who was attached to the Luftwaffe unit ZG76.

Langenberg claimed to have shot down two of the three Spitfires lost by 92 Squadron on the evening of 23 May. Paul Klipsch's aircraft dived vertically into farmland at Wierre-Effroy, north-east of Boulogne at 6.05 p.m. Another pilot, John Gillies, was hit at 6.07 p.m. but survived and was taken prisoner. Bushell's Spitfire was forced down at 6.20 p.m.

In those first few minutes on the ground, Bushell ignored the advice of MI9 that the potential for escape is often greatest immediately after being shot down. There was no cover and, besides, it was a lovely evening and he thought he was behind Allied lines.

My engine was badly shot up and caught fire, he wrote later in a letter to his parents. *I turned everything off. The fire went out and I glided down. There was a lot of glycol [anti-freeze used in aero engines] and I couldn't see very much. I turned the engine on again and it ran for a little while, then the engine seized and a lot of smoke and fumes came into the cockpit.*

116

*So I prepared to land, undercarriage up. This I did
successfully only to get a knock on the nose, which bled like
a pig. The old girl burst into flames and, as you can
imagine, I moved pretty quickly. I'd landed just east of
Boulogne. I thought, of course, that I was well behind our
lines and then, to my rage and astonishment, a German
motorcycle came round the corner and I was taken prisoner.*

Bushell was trapped by the most advanced elements of General
Guderian's XIX Panzer Corps, part of the *Wehrmacht*'s Army
Group A, which was racing towards the Channel ports. Guderian
was an expert in tank warfare who made his name during the
French campaign. His forces had taken the towns of Amiens and
Abbeville on 20 May and then, after covering 200 miles in ten
days, reached the coast at Noyelles, south of Boulogne, which fell
forty-eight hours later.

Bushell was assembled with other prisoners, including John
Gillies, who could barely contain his joy at seeing him. 'I had
great admiration for Roger as a Squadron Commander and,
sorry though I was to see him in the same plight as myself, I must
admit it was one of the best moments of my life to see him
coming into the same field in France 3 days after I was captured,'
wrote Gillies.

He would accompany Bushell on the march into Germany;
their destination was Dulag Luft, the air force interrogation
centre just outside the town of Oberursel near Frankfurt, more
than 350 miles from the French coast. 'A long journey,' wrote
Bushell.

Gillies, the son of a prominent surgeon, added: 'During the
year that followed, the march through France and the time at
Dulag Luft, he became a personal friend as well. And my admiration for him there increased, as it was under such very difficult
conditions.'

It is not known for certain whether they walked all the way, or
whether they were among hundreds of other prisoners or

thousands, but the washing facilities at Dulag Luft would have been a welcome sight once they arrived.

As they marched, possibly through the Pas de Calais, then south of Lille, Bushell and Gillies would have witnessed signs of the *Wehrmacht*'s superiority in the field – a land littered with the debris of the defeated Allied armies.

I wrote to you twice when I was on the way to this camp, Bushell told his parents, *but I very much doubt whether you got the letters as they were written from places in France and everything was such a shambles that they probably never got through.*

A degree of order replaced the chaos of the northern battlefields as they headed east, and a new landscape emerged, peopled by purposeful men and women, energised by the momentous German victory in the Battle of France. At some stage, the RAF prisoners would have left the main column and, towards the end of their journey, they may well have boarded a tram or train in Frankfurt.

At nearly fifteen stone, Bushell had been one of the biggest fighter pilots in the RAF. He shed many pounds during the march into captivity. He had not washed properly for many days and was probably still wearing the clothes in which he had been shot down.

Built on the site of a government poultry farm, Dulag Luft lay about four miles north-west of Frankfurt on the outskirts of Oberursel, 300 yards to the north of the main road between Frankfurt and Bad Homburg. When it opened in December 1939, the camp comprised just one white stone building, with a large steep roof, and housed a handful of the first RAF officers to be captured. In 1940, three wooden barracks were added and the stone house was used only for interrogating prisoners and holding individuals in solitary confinement. Nearby farm buildings were turned into a command centre. To the north and west were woods; to the east, a market garden; and to the south, a sports field.

The commandant was Major Theo Rumpel, a veteran intelligence officer who had worked with the British, trading in the Far East, during the 1920s. He was a charming, cultured man who would have been very much at home in the dining room at Pembroke College, Cambridge, or with the aristocrats of 601 Squadron. He was an Anglophile who admired the British ruling classes; he appreciated good manners and liked men who were well-educated. With a long angular face, blue-grey eyes, uneven teeth but a friendly smile, Major Rumpel spoke perfect English and used charm and guile as weapons of interrogation. He was good at his job.

After the German armed forces had conquered France and the Low Countries, supplies – often the spoils of war – were plentiful. Prisoners also received regular Red Cross parcels containing food and clothing. The regime appeared to be relatively relaxed: Rumpel was more concerned with intelligence than security, and prisoners were even taken to one of three local beer gardens. Many British and German officers remained relatively courteous to each other, too, but the reality was more complex.

Among the millions of documents in the National Archives at Kew, there is a file on Dulag Luft marked 'Top Secret'. Covering the period of Bushell's internment there, it is a history of the camp, written after the war, from its opening in December 1939 until June 1941. The file is important because it documents the birth of resistance among captured Royal Air Force officers, who would become one of the most belligerent groups of anti-Nazis in the Third Reich.

When they arrived at Dulag Luft, prisoners were stripped and given overalls while their uniforms were searched for escape aids such as compasses and maps. Soon afterwards, they were put in solitary confinement.

German interrogators visited the new prisoners within twenty-four hours and presented them with bogus Red Cross forms, requiring them to answer many questions: their name, surname, service number, rank, trade and service; their date and place of birth; their profession; their religion; whether married or single and if they had children; their home address and the address of their next of kin; their rate of pay; when, where and by whom they were shot down; where and by whom they were taken prisoner; their squadron, group, command, station and station number; the letters and numbers of their aircraft, and the type of aircraft; their state of health and whether they were wounded; the names and surnames of members of their crew and whether they were wounded, killed or taken prisoner.

It wasn't very subtle, but while most airmen refused to give information other than their name, rank and number, as laid down in service regulations, some filled in the forms, answered questions or were duped into doing so, enabling Luftwaffe intelligence officers to build up files on RAF squadrons and crew. From some prisoners, they even extracted more sensitive information.

Prisoners whom the Germans did not consider valuable as potential sources of information were usually moved within a few days to permanent camps elsewhere in Germany or Occupied Europe. But prisoners the Germans suspected of withholding useful information would remain at Dulag Luft for further interrogation, involving perhaps thirty days' solitary confinement without tobacco or books, or, in extreme cases, some form of physical ill-treatment.

Solitary confinement was an alarming prospect for many men. Aidan Crawley, who flew with 601 Squadron but was shot down over Italy in 1941, gives a graphic analysis in his post-war assessment of RAF escapes.

We are so much creatures of our environment that it requires a great effort of will to retain our personalities when that environment is removed; solitary confinement in a cell ten feet long by four feet wide is about as near to living in a vacuum as a man has been able to contrive, *he wrote in Escape from Germany.* When the society of his fellow human beings is taken away from a man, when there is no certainty that it will be restored, when there are no books or writing materials to remind him of it or to keep the mind busy, he is left face to face with the bare bones of himself. The prospect is often terrifying.

Bushell was better equipped than most to deal with the threat posed by the German interrogators: as a barrister, he was well versed in the art of cross-examination, as well as dealing quickly with point and counter-point. He also spoke fluent German.

No record appears to have survived of Bushell's interrogation by Luftwaffe intelligence officers, but he was highly regarded by both his British and German peers: Major Rumpel allowed him to join the twenty or so officers on the Permanent Staff who looked after the interests of Allied prisoners passing through the camp and liaised with the German commandant and his senior officers. Another man who had a high opinion of Bushell was Wing Commander Harry 'Wings' Day, the Senior British Officer at the camp. Bushell and Day would spend much of the next four years working together in an attempt to make life as difficult as possible for their captors.

Born in Sarawak, Borneo, in 1898, Harry Melville Arbuthnot Day started military life in the navy. A descendant of George Miller Bligh who served in HMS *Victory* at Trafalgar, he joined the Royal Marines in 1916 and was in the battleship HMS *Britannia* when she was torpedoed just two days before the cessation of hostilities in November 1918. He was awarded the Albert Medal, one of the highest awards for bravery, after repeatedly returning below deck to rescue other members of the crew.

Day joined the Fleet Air Arm in 1924, but switched to the Royal Air Force in 1930. He was promoted to wing commander in July

1939 and put in command of No. 57 Squadron, flying Blenheims. He volunteered for the squadron's first operational mission of the war, a reconnaissance flight over Kaiserslautern, western Germany, on 25 October 1939, when the aircraft was shot down by a German fighter. He suffered burns to his hands and face but baled out and was taken prisoner. The other two members of his crew were killed.

Within a few days of Bushell's arrival at Dulag Luft, Day, a tall, lean man with narrow eyes, asked the mercurial South African to take over responsibility for all escape activity.

I had already been a prisoner for 9 months when Roger first arrived at Dulag Luft, wrote Day in a letter to Bushell's parents five years later. *I was the Senior British Officer there and I quickly recognised the high qualities of Roger. Usually newcomers only stayed there a short time but I was on good terms with the German Commandant and I managed to obtain his consent to allow Roger to stay; which suited Roger very well. He was very keen to escape and did not wish to be sent into the middle or Eastern Germany if it were possible to avoid it. He quickly show[ed] his outstanding qualities and we began to get things moving for an escape.*

Bushell started work by using the first letters in his monthly allowance to establish contact with Britain and Switzerland, rather than South Africa. On 8 June 1940, long before he posted his first letter from the camp to Ben and Dorothe, he wrote to John Brinton, the former adjutant of 92 Squadron, who, according to the log, returned to 'civilian life' on 14 May, but remained an important contact. The letter is remarkable in that it was passed by the Dulag Luft censors without being touched.

Giving his address as Dulag Luft Deutschland (Allemagne), Bushell provided Brinton with detailed information about the dogfight in which he was shot down and the performance of the Me 110s. The letter was precise, and it was typed:

> *As soon as the battle started, about 4 or 5 of them fell on me and oh boy did I start dodging. My first (Me 110) I got with a deflection shot from underneath. He went down in a long glide with his port engine pouring smoke, and I went into a spin as two others were firing at me from my aft quarter. I only did one turn of the spin and pulled out left and up. I then saw an Me [110] below me trying to fire up at me so I went head on at him and he went head on at me. We were both firing and everything was red flashes. I killed the pilot because suddenly he pulled right up at me and missed by inches. I went over the top of him and as I turned saw him rear right up in a stall and go down with his engine smoking. I hadn't got long to watch, but he was out of control and half on his back. My machine by then was pouring glycol and was on fire.*

He went on to give Brinton a list of RAF officers held at Dulag Luft.

> *I did most of the journey here with F/O Gillies who used to be in 604 and who was shot down much the same time. Amongst others here are W/C Day, P/O Falkus, Lt Thurston, S/L Stephenson, F/O Cazenove, Lt Wood, S/L Lockett. Vincent Byrne is also here and has had some great adventures. The little man is full of beans.*

Bushell also had information about the death of Pat Learmond:

> *I was told by some soldiers from Calais that a machine flown by P/O Learmond crashed on the beach. The pilot was already dead. He had a bullet through his head. You might pass this on to the Air Ministry.*

He was subtle enough to put in a few kind words about the Germans, a constant trait in his letters at this time.

The censors were meant to be a rigorous section of the Dulag Luft intelligence organisation. The head of it was *Hauptmann* Günther von Massow, whose step-brother, Gerd, was a high-ranking Luftwaffe officer in charge of the Fuhrer's personal flight. Gunther von Massow was in his mid-thirties, but unfit for military service.

Day told his biographer, Eric Sydney Smith, that:

> . . . von Massow's staff were all girls and pretty ones too, whom the prisoners knew by sight as they saw them passing the camp. Each girl, so Wings found out, had the care of certain prisoners' mail, thereby gaining a personal interest and knowledge of a prisoner's affairs. They sometimes used this knowledge unofficially to pass through letters quickly when there was some crisis in the recipient's affairs.

On the same day as he wrote to John Brinton, Bushell sent a postcard to 'Khaki' Roberts, telling him:

> We are very well treated . . . we can receive as many letters as we like so please write and ask others to as well.
>
> Please tell Hollis to send me the standard law books like Salmond etc and also all the quarterlies so I can keep my hand in. He can find out the regulations from the Red Cross or a Bookseller and they can be paid for out of any fees he receives on my behalf. Any balance of fees is please to be kept until after the war. Perhaps he can open an account for me & pay them into it.

He clearly regarded his incarceration at this time as a very temporary matter.

Prisoners could receive from home almost as many books as they wanted. 'A cheap set of Shakespeare would be grand. Please write, and remember me to everyone,' wrote Bushell.

With an eye over his shoulder at neutral Switzerland, Bushell wrote to his skiing friends and, among other things, asked them to contact his parents in South Africa.

Tony Page wrote to Ben and Dorothe from Zurich on 6 September, saying:

> *I and other friends Roger has in Switzerland have received several letters from him since he was shot down . . . communication with England is still pretty bad and at times impossible, so that Roger does not receive many letters or any parcels from there. He has, however, half a dozen friends in Switzerland who write to him fairly often and send him a few things . . . some clothes and underwear and chocolate. I am also making arrangements to send him some money, for there is a canteen where he can buy various things.*

Bushell's networking produced results. He received 'Springbok' cigarettes from South Africa and 'Players' cigarettes from Harrods; food parcels from Switzerland and Madeira; and books and puzzles and games. He wrote to Harry North-Lewis, his childhood guardian, to sort out his finances, and he tried constantly to reassure his parents that he was safe and well and that they had nothing to worry about.

On 31 July, in his first letter to the family in Hermanus, Bushell wrote:

> *The camp is run by the German Air Force and we are very well treated. We live in army huts two to a room or sometimes three – I share mine with John Gillies, another auxiliary. We go for walks twice a week and swim once a week and the commandant here does everything he can to make life reasonable for us. All our food and clothing needs are catered for by the Red Cross so don't worry on that score. We get paid a certain amount every ten days, which*

keeps us in cigarettes, and we are allowed to buy a certain amount of drink, which means we have a party every now and then . . .

My darlings, there is so much I have to tell you but most of it will have to wait until after the war. Give Eliza and Tods a big kiss and please don't worry. I have nothing to complain of here and we live a very peaceful if uneventful existence.

He concluded by saying, *After the war I'll soon get back into my stride and thanks heavens I'm not married.*

Perhaps Bushell was trying to reassure himself as well as his parents, but in the eight weeks between his first letter to Ben and Dorothe – just as the Battle of Britain was reaching its climax – and his next on 30 September, the very attractive figure of Peggy Hamilton suddenly appears to have loomed large in all their lives.

I am so glad that Peggy wrote to you, he told his parents. She is, I am quite sure, the only person in the world for me and I know that you will adore her. We had known each other for a long time but it was only in the last months before I was shot down that we really discovered each other and then, alas, my other activities prevented me seeing a great deal of her. I have never stopped cursing myself for not marrying her while I had the chance but that error will be remedied the moment I get back, I can assure you.

I have written to my bank and Uncle Harry and told them I wish my pay [to be] made over to her and I want you to see that that is carried out and indeed, as I know you will, I want you to help her in any way you can. It drives me almost frantic with London being bombed to feel that she is there nursing in the middle of it and the lack of news is simply maddening. I have had two wonderful letters from her but nothing since the 11th July, which arrived in August. However, one must be patient and no doubt in the end more letters will come in.

There is one other thing I want you to do if you can and that is to buy a really lovely diamond off Oppy [Ernest Oppenheimer, Ben Bushell's employer], which I will arrange to pay for out of my pay and to send it to her and tell her to have it made into a ring. While I am a prisoner is probably the only time that I will have enough money to buy her something really good.

In a sudden change of mood, Bushell becomes rather truculent.

I have written to Uncle Harry about the flat. Mike [Peacock] and I had shut it up to all intents and purposes and there is some rent owing as after the war started our circumstances were very much altered but the landlords can sing for that after the war. I told Uncle Harry to sell the furniture unless Peggy wants to have it and to have my clothes sent to Khaki [Roberts, his head of legal chambers]. Anyway, for all I know it is probably now in ruins so what the hell!

Probably frustrated, Bushell tries to change the tone again.

My page is almost at an end and it's time to go to bed. Oh, I almost forgot to tell you, I had an elegant birthday party on whisky supplied by the [German] commandant. He came over and joined in and we had a most friendly and delightful evening. In fact, we solved Europe's problems in the most amicable manner.

A little later, Bushell wrote to Uncle Harry:

I would be very grateful if you would get in touch with Miss Peggy Hamilton, 9, Wellesley House, Sloane Square. Sloane 8649. We were going to get married if I had not ended up here and we are going to as soon as this bloody war is over! I naturally want to see that she is provided for and I have written to Cox and Kings and told them that I wish my pay to be made over to her. In case they have not received any letter, would you please see that they do this.

My account at Barclay's Bank, 160 Piccadilly is overdrawn but I have a Life Insurance to cover it and I want the premiums continued. You might get them reduced as they cover flying risks and I will not be doing any more flying until the war is over!

Love and escape were two passions that ran strongly through the entire period of Bushell's captivity, sometimes driving him forward, sometimes distracting him. For the most part, however, it seems that the most destructive currents were held in check by his sense of duty.

'Roger was the organising genius of all our escaping exploits,' wrote Peter Cazenove, another 92 Squadron pilot who was taken prisoner and sent to Dulag Luft, 'and with his barrister's training, knowledge of German and the German people, a better man could not have been found.'

In October 1940, however, Wings Day replaced him as head of the escape organisation: the job was given to Lieutenant Commander Jimmy Buckley, a Fleet Air Arm pilot who outranked Bushell and had already tried to escape during the march from Calais. He had been shot down a few days after Bushell while strafing German positions on the French coast.

Tempting as it may be to suggest that Bushell, distracted and frustrated by his increasingly distant relationship with Peggy, was sacked, the evidence suggests that Buckley used his senior rank to muscle in on the job. 'Although Roger handed over the main organisation and direction to a Lt. Comdr Buckley,' wrote Day, 'he still did invaluable work in obtaining supplies etc, due to his great knowledge of German.'

According to the official history of Dulag Luft, Bushell acted as Buckley's deputy, devoting himself mainly to acquiring escape intelligence and equipment. But he also dealt with military intelligence, 'all military information was passed to 90120 S/Ldr R. BUSHELL, R.A.F. who collated it and passed it to the Senior British Officer, who decided what messages were to be sent to I.S.9'.

Day, Buckley and Bushell formed themselves into an escape committee and most discussions were held in a barracks room that was known to be free of listening devices. These three men would, according to Aidan Crawley, author of *Escape from Germany*, be the 'mainsprings of escape' for most of the camps where RAF prisoners were held throughout the war.

Bushell and Day also turned their attention to developing MI9's coding system, which would lead to communication between the camps and London, and start the flow of military intelligence from Germany.

While it is possible that Bushell was already registered with IS9 and may have been trained in the principles of writing code when he arrived at Dulag Luft, he does not appear to have known an operational code. All this changed in the summer of 1940 with the arrival of Pilot Officer W. H. C. 'Clem' Hunkin, who had been shot down on the night of 18 July 1940 while flying a Wellington bomber from RAF Marham in Norfolk, against a target in Bremen.

Hunkin was only at Dulag Luft for four days – from 20 July to

23 July – but it was enough time for him to pass on details of an official code called 'Amy', one of several given to MI9 by the Foreign Office's code experts, which enabled messages to be hidden in routine letters to friends and family. The key to 'Amy' was a pocket edition of *Hugo's French Dictionary*.

Kriegsgefangenenpost

An _Mrs M B Hunkin_
"Llancayo".

Dulag-Luft
3 Geprüft

Gebührenfrei

Empfangsort: _Llewellyn Ave_
Straße: _Neath S Wales_
Land: _England_
Landesteil (Provinz usw.)

—1.10.40 17-18

P.C. 66

OPENED BY
CENSOR
2181

Absender:
Vor- und Zuname: _Pilot Officer W.H.C Hunkin_
Gefangenennummer: _British Prisoner of War_
Lager-Bezeichnung: _Stalag Luft, Germany_

Deutschland (Allemagne)

Pilot Officer W.H. 'Clem' Hunkin provided the key to an operational code at Dulag Luft in July 1940. He wrote coded letters for British Intelligence throughout the war. This letter addressed to his mother in Wales was sent from Stalag Luft I at Barth on the Baltic coast, on 1 October, 1940.

26

CHAPTER V

CODE-LETTER MAIL.

1. **INTRODUCTION.**

The existence of an official code was not known until the Spring of 1940. The first P/W to arrive in this Camp who could operate the code and had been registered before he became a P/W was:-

42231 F/Lt. N.H. HENKIN, R.A.F.

who reported to the Senior British Officer that he knew the code. The Senior British Officer had a Hugo's French pocket dictionary and with the aid of this HENKIN taught the code to several other P's/W.

2. **ORGANISATION**

Military information was passed to:-

90120 S/Ldr. R. BUSHELL, R.A.F.

who collated it and passed it to the Senior British Officer, who decided what messages were to be sent to I.S.9. and divided the work between HENKIN, himself, and BUSHELL, all having been registered with I.S.9. as code users.

(a) <u>Sources of information</u>

    (i)   <u>'Contacts'</u>

        Information was acquired from 'contacts' by the method described in Chapter II, Section 10, sub-Section (a) of this history. The type of information acquired is fully described in the history of STALAG LUFT III (SAGAN) Part 1, Chapter V, Section 2 sub-Section (a) (i).

    (ii) <u>New P's/W</u>

        New P's/W were interrogated by the Senior British Officer and BUSHELL in the manner described in the history of STALAG LUFT III,(SAGAN), Part 1, Chapter V, Section 2, sub-Section a (iii).

(b) <u>Collation</u>

Collation of information from the above sources was done by BUSHELL and DAY.

(c) <u>Coding Staff</u>

The coding staff consisted of BUSHELL, DAY and HENKIN.

/(d)

Roger Bushell's role in collating military intelligence while a prisoner-of-war at the Luftwaffe transit camp, Dulag Luft, and his involvement in establishing contact with London through coded letters is documented in the Camp History, written after the war and marked Top Secret. The National Archive: AIR 40/1909, Chapter V, p26–27.

(d) <u>Code-Letter Writers</u>

All code letters were written by the Coding Staff.

(e) <u>Despatch of Messages</u>

The despatch of messages was organised by BUSHELL, DAY and RUMKIN.

3. <u>SECURITY.</u>

It was considered best from a security viewpoint that as few P's/W as possible should operate the code, and for that reason the number was kept down to three.

Encoding and letter writing were done in the morning before roll-call, or late in the evening, those times being free from visits by German interpreters. The number of messages was kept as small as possible because of the frequent visits of German interpreters.

4. <u>DURATION OF EACH CODE-USERS ACTIVITY</u>

BUSHELL, DAY and RUMKIN used the code from July, 1940 until the end of the period under review in this history.

5. <u>COMMENT</u>

It was considered that if P's/W had been properly briefed about the existence and operation of the code there would not have been so much delay before they got into touch with I.S.9.

Certain pre-arranged signals were used in this type of coded letter. The style of the date, perhaps written in Roman numerals, and the signature, perhaps underlined, or with an agreed word such as 'very' in the sign-off – 'Very best wishes' or 'Very kind regards' – alerted the recipient to the presence of a secret message, while the number of letters in the first two words after the initial greeting denoted the length of the message. Everyone registered by IS9 was given a code number that could be used to denote which words in the letter were part of the message and which pages of the dictionary had been used. There were several variants, however, and systems were changed, but the dictionary code remained the bedrock of communication throughout the war.

In the beginning, MI9 struggled to find any messages in letters from PoWs. After all, the prisoners could not exactly write directly to the intelligence agency in Room 424 at the Metropole Hotel, or, indeed, to any other single address that might come to the notice of the German censors.

As Norman Crockatt, head of MI9, explained in a post-war report:

Censorship was asked to send us for examination any letters received from prisoners of war suspected of secondary meaning or of containing a private means of communication. They were asked also to send us other types of letters – those giving information about conditions in camps, about morale, treatment, location etc. so that we could obtain a general picture. We examined these letters carefully and got in touch with the addressees in likely cases. By this method we discovered a few workable private codes, arranged by the prisoners of war before capture. We, therefore, wrote to the prisoners concerned, using the means they had employed and sending the letters from fictitious people and addresses.

Whenever a prisoner of war's mail was utilised
in this way we instructed Censorship to place
his name on our Watch List, which was supplied
to their sorters, whose duty it was to pick out
all letters coming from those on the List and to
send them to us for examination. We kept these
letters for 24 hours only and then returned them
to Censorship for forwarding to the addressees.
In the case of our letters to prisoners of war,
by arrangement with the G.P.O. [Post Office] we
had the correct place and date stamp franked on
each envelope. The letters were then sent to
Censorship who slit the envelopes in the same
way as they slit all letters going to prisoners
of war, stuck on the 'Passed by censor' labels
and mixed them with the thousands of other
letters being dispatched. It was essential that
these details should be strictly carried out, so
that letters, when reaching the German censors,
were no different from the thousands of genuine
ones.

Crockatt added: In this way we managed to obtain
contact with three Oflags [officer camps] in the
early months of 1941.

After the war, Day told his biographer, Sydney Smith, that the
first messages to MI9 were based on interrogation of new prisoners, explaining briefly the circumstances in which they had been
shot down.

Even though the messages took a month to six weeks, this was
valuable Intelligence material which helped the RAF at home to
take measures based on methods and tactics of German fighters,
and the positioning and strength of German anti-aircraft
defences.

135

Sydney Smith added: In those early days, the German censors probably had an idea that certain individual prisoners had some kind of code, but they took very little defensive action beyond occasionally delaying or losing prisoners' mail or expunging parts of a letter.

The precise chronology of coding at Dulag Luft is not clear, with conflicting records of how it all began, but the different reports illustrate the difficulty in establishing clear facts and shed light on the struggle facing the prisoners.

As the squadron leader of a fighter squadron flying operationally over France, Bushell had been an obvious target for MI9 in early 1940. 'Code users at this time amounted to about one per cent of the Army and Navy, most fighter pilots and about six per cent of other aircrew,' wrote Charles Rollings, author of several books on the camps. The official history of Dulag Luft suggests that Day was also registered for codework with IS9, but he was shot down before MI9 was established. He was certainly registered later. Another report suggests that code was first introduced at Dulag Luft by a man called Neil Prendergast, a sergeant pilot from No. 61 Squadron, but he appears to have arrived shortly after Clem Hunkin, and seems to have been influential in establishing code at another camp, Stalag Luft 1, afterwards.

The Dulag Luft file says Bushell and Day used code from July 1940 and were responsible for all coded letters and the dispatch of messages.

According to Rollings, three of the Permanents – Wings Day, John Gillies and the navy pilot, John Casson – were all equipped with MI9 codes, but Day told his biographer that he did not have a clue about codes until the second half of 1940. In his post-war report, Crockatt says MI9 received its first official code letter from an RAF prisoner of war in December 1940, almost a year after MI9 was formed. Perhaps the 'Permanents' at Dulag Luft made contact through unofficial codes. Whatever the truth, it was a slow and muddled start.

But the work gathered pace: all new prisoners at Dulag Luft were interrogated by Bushell and Day, and the Escape Committee passed on its new skills to key prisoners who would use them in other camps.

'The snowball was now assuming large proportions,' wrote Crockatt in his appraisal of MI9's work at this time.

While resistance was starting to flourish in the camps for officers, MI9 was not as successful in the camps for other ranks (OR) and had to resort to alternative means in influencing escape activity.

We had failed to discover a single private code amongst the hundreds of letters from [other Ranks] prisoners of war passed to us by Censorship to examine. We suggested, therefore, to the Oflags, that they should approach suitable padres and doctors and teach them an official code with the idea that they should volunteer for service in the Stalags [for other ranks]. This suggestion was carried out and both padres and doctors did excellent work in picking out the most reliable ORs in the Stalags, teaching them an official code, notifying us of their names, etc. and getting Code and Escape Committees organised.

Sydney Smith went on to note: As the prisoner population rose later to several thousands, all entitled to send home three postcards and two letters monthly, the code communication system was organised with several hundred operators in various camps. It proved enormously valuable.

Anyone reading Bushell's letters, including the German censors, are unlikely to have found any evidence of secret messages. Indeed, they are likely to have come to the opinion that here was a man who, far from stoking resistance to the authorities, was relatively content with his lot in life. On a postcard to his parents, dated 28 October 1940, Bushell wrote:

Am very well and have lots of parcels from both England and Switzerland. Nothing to worry over and we are very comfortable. Lots of books to pass the winter and will try to improve my mind.

He continues: The BEF stock of whisky seems to be inexhaustible and the commandant pushes it out on the smallest excuse ... arguments of all kinds wax fast and furious and considering all things we are a very happy family.

Behind the scenes, in fact, the 'family' was working on the first major escape of the war. It would turn the camps into a battleground into which the Germans would be forced to pour resources, and turn the ever-courteous, but rather ruthless, Theo Rumpel into the first German casualty of an unconventional war.

11

Man of Letters

By the end of November 1940, it was clear even to those men incarcerated in German prisoner-of-war camps that the conflict would be prolonged. Any prospect of Hitler launching a seaborne invasion was doomed by the Luftwaffe's failure to establish air superiority over England. The German air force lost 1,733 aircraft, more than half its front-line strength, during the Battle of Britain, which ended Hitler's run of victories in Europe.

The night bombing campaign that grew out of the battle and became known as the Blitz was ferocious at times, and terrifying for the millions being attacked in the streets of Britain. More than 30,000 people were killed in cities and towns across the country – Birmingham, Southampton, Sheffield, Manchester, Liverpool, Hull and Glasgow – but mainly in London. Millions were made homeless. Buckingham Palace was bombed, the City of London and large tracts of the East End were devastated. The House of Commons was destroyed.

But the Blitz posed no strategic threat. The Luftwaffe was not equipped or trained for strategic night bombing. Its impact on British industry was minimal. Even in Coventry, which became a symbol of suffering after a devastating raid on 14 November, most factories were working again within a week.

After a moment of panic, the British people pulled together again, their morale largely unshaken, in the face of the Nazi threat. But although it had survived, the country was still not in a position to carry the war to the Germans. Its own bomber force was just as impotent as the Luftwaffe in terms of hitting important targets at night, and it quickly became apparent that daylight raids were out of the question without long-range fighter escort. This was not available.

Hitler's military planners started to look eastwards, to Russia, and a second front that Hitler himself had warned against in his autobiography, *Mein Kampf*. At the same time, the British were looking westwards for help from the United States.

For the British airmen held in Dulag Luft, there was no prospect of liberation as winter approached in 1940. Unless, of course, it was engineered by the prisoners themselves.

Six months after being shot down, Roger Bushell wrote two letters twenty-four hours apart that provide insights into his changing state of mind and the issues that concerned him. The first was written on 29 November to John Brinton, his former adjutant with 92 Squadron. Whether it includes messages, coded or otherwise, or allusions that only Brinton would understand, is not known for certain but, once again, it passed the German censors untouched. The typed letter is certainly worthy of further consideration:

Dulag Luft, Germany
29.11.40.

My dear old John,
Many thanks for your letter of Sept. 3rd; it arrived on the 4th [of November]. News is the salt of life, and good news, however old it is, is about the best tonic one could have. Complete balls up of all communications has perforce been our lot, and one just waits and indeed lives for news from Home. As you can guess, it makes correspondence a bit tricky as the tittle-tattle of the camp is really hardly worth writing about. So you'll have to excuse me if this letter is dull, shallow and boring, compared to the quite crazy life you must be leading. The stress and strain of bombing during the winter, or indeed at any time, is difficult to visualise sitting here, and of course each one

of us is so very liable to let imagination run riot and fill gaps with the most unpleasant thoughts about what has happened to any or all of our friends and whether they are alive, wounded or dead.

Captivity I can assure you would be less hard to endure if only letter conditions improved. Do not think though that because I write in this way I cherish any doubts about the outcome, however indescribable the carnage before it is achieved. My mentality, as you know, is extremely impatient of any inactivity, and being completely out of things is the hardest part. Ultimately I know it is of no consequence – that is poor consolation to the victim though! In actual fact I cannot complain. The camp is good and very efficiently run – I have all that is necessary to bodily comfort, and only that devil the human mind makes one go crazy at times. Enough of this! I owe you an apology already. However, try please to understand, and when we both celebrate after the war, we'll make a night of it. Drink simply buckets of whisky and laugh like hell.

I was astonished that the boys were ALL alright – very best wishes to them. Our greatest pastime is talking about them and no detail is too small to miss. They constituted a great chapter in my life, galling though it is to sit here while they go on. It may sound rubbish, nevertheless I am sure the squadron'll do their stuff and do even more brilliant things in the future, no matter who is in it. Tell them I particularly expect them to get a few nice ones for me.

So far as parcels are concerned, individual firms seem to have been much more successful than the Red Cross. My entire library consists of book parcels sent off by friends from Smith's, Dent's, etc. Over and above that, several parcels of popular games like backgammon, chess and those absurd puzzles have arrived from Harrods. Anyone wishing to send anything to help to banish boredom for poor prisoners has only just got to go round, to Harrods preferably, therefore and do their stuff! My parcel position actually is excellent, few friends who I knew skiing in Switzerland have cashed in magnificently. They have been simply charming, and how I'm to pay them back God alone knows. I was simply delighted you were good enough to send duplicates of my letter to other friends. Splendid of you, old boy. Letters are bread and butter these days to all who love us, and what with the mail being what it is, it is possible many of them got lost. The Christmas letters will turn up in March assuming communications remain what they are! However, when you do get this, send copies especially to those who think they would be jollified by a lot of chat and who will realise that my tail is up in spite of everything. We may stagnate and as you can imagine we moan a lot nevertheless I can assure you we laugh a lot too.

That child of the Irish bogs, Vincent Byrne, affords us a lot of amusement. I despair of him at times – I've tried in vain to clothe him – I've given him vests, socks, shirts, slippers etc. The whole outfit is sold within a few hours, generally, for tobacco and he thinks I'm cuckoo when I curse him roundly. Of course there is no changing the leopard's spots. But I live in hopes.

Dear Old John [Gillies] is frightfully efficient – he runs hissing, flaps a lot and gets ragged a great deal but I don't know what we [would] do without him. He, Hugh Rowe – another auxiliary – and I share a room and we get on very well together – my page is coming to an end. I seem to have got a lot on it though and hope it hasn't bored you too much, eh. My best love to Mike and God bless you. Roger

It seems possible that Brinton was an intelligence contact, or at least a facilitator, who passed his letters to RAF intelligence or to M19, the British intelligence agency dealing with prisoners of war, and that the phrase, 'when you do get this send copies especially to those who think they would be jollified by a lot of chat and who will realise that my tail is up', is possibly significant.

For Bushell to tell Brinton about Byrne and Gillies, who had both been with No. 92 Squadron, is natural enough, but there appears to be good reasons why he would have wanted the specific information in this letter to be passed on.

Byrne was, as has been noted, one of the men defended by Bushell in the court-martial after the Battle of Barking Creek, and he would appear in cameo roles throughout the drama of Bushell's war. At this time, he was involved in an escapade that would ostensibly see him change sides in the hope of being landed on the coast of Ireland as a Nazi agent. At Dulag Luft, the Germans interviewed several Irish prisoners with the aim of recruiting them. Byrne decided to play along as it might provide him with a way out of the camp. He put his plan to Wings Day, the Senior British Officer, who was said to have checked out the plan with London through coded letters, and gained approval eight weeks later.

Day told Bushell, whose references in this letter to 'the child of the Irish bog' and 'no changing the leopard's spots' were almost certainly written in an attempt to help wrong-foot the Germans, while still informing London.

The reference to Gillies being 'frightfully efficient' is more straightforward. Gillies had become one of the leading figures in the coding operation and, as a result, was ordered by MI9 not to take part in any escape attempts. According to Day, he had 'a tidy mind and immaculate script'.

The second letter, written in pencil on 30 November, started with the usual complaints about the vagaries of the post, but was full of affection. It covered the gamut of Bushell family life, including the long-running battle with his father over finances, which was full of wit and gibes, and the unquestioning love for his mother. He signed off, 'God bless you, Roger', but not before finishing with the most telling paragraph of any letter he wrote from Dulag Luft, or possibly anywhere else during the time of his captivity.

Dulag Luft
Germany
30.11.40.

My Darlings,

Since I last wrote at the end of last month I have received letters from you all as follows: from father letters Nos 7 and 9 received on the 31st October and letters No 6 and 5 received on 2.11.40 and 8.11.40 respectively. From Mummy three letters undated, which arrived on 2.11.40 and from Eliza one letter dated 31.7.40 which arrived on the 8th. As you can see from these dates the mail is still hardly what one would expect in the 20th century! However we live in hope and the latest news is that letters can be sent air mail to Lisbon now from England so one hopes for an improvement.

I have not had a letter from Peggy dated later than September 1st and as you can imagine it is very worrying. In fact to all intents and purposes there has been no mail in since the big batch at the beginning of the month.

I get regular letters from Switzerland though and I can't begin to tell you how kind all my friends have been. Tony Page told me you had called him about clothes but I can assure you I am absolutely o.k. so far as that is concerned. I have had the clothes parcels from home and both Tony and Mme Paraviciere have sent me clothing as well so I have lots of warm clothes for the winter. But in any case our rooms are beautifully warm as we have a stove in each. No need to worry therefore.

My dearest father, your information and lecture about my bill from your tailor was particularly refreshing reading! Tell the old boy he can jolly well extend me credit until after the war. I imagine that your remark, 'It was at least a friendly action to give you of all people so much credit' referred obviously to the fact that I was in a

*somewhat hazardous job and was no reflection on my
financial standing! You will be delighted to hear that in
this place I am living well within my income and indeed
owing to the fact admittedly that our pay was cut in half
for some time and then restored I have saved over 200
marks. We get paid – or rather I do as a squadron leader
– 36 marks every ten days and it is paid in the form of
camp money of which the enclosed is an example and may
amuse you.*

*I am delighted that little Diana has done her stuff. Give
her my love. I have had no letter from Tods. You might tell
the wicked old girl to write and give her a big kiss.*

*It was very kind of you to arrange for the continuance of
life policy premiums but I have already arranged that
myself and also to pay off some of the overdraft. The main
bulk of my pay though I have made over to Peggy to use if
she needs it, and my overdraft can wait until the end of the
war. The Bank has the security of my life policy and they'll
have to put up with that. I consider that her needs are more
important than the bank's!*

*My darling Mummy, your letters are the greatest joy
and please don't think they are boring. I was delighted
with the story about the dogs and can well imagine
father's rage. Letters are wonderful things when you are a
prisoner. It isn't so much what is in them – news when it
does come is often depressing in so far as individuals are
concerned – as the way they are written and yours my
darling are so full of freshness and the country that they
are a great comfort.*

*Our life here pursues the even tenor of its ways. There is
ample to do as I now have many books that have been sent
from home and I have read a great deal. All the old classics
that one never had time to read since leaving school. I have
a whole set of Shakespeare which is a great joy – Ivanhoe,
Kim, Pride and Prejudice and many more. I have just been*

sent some by Barbara, which include two about Tahiti and Hawaii. They'll I hope take the mind away to better places for a few hours.

John Casson – [the actress] Sybil Thorndyke's [sic] son – entertains us with the most priceless shows about once a month, and bridge and arguments pass the time very quickly. The photographs I hope will amuse you. I have put a short description on the back of each. They will give you an idea of the camp and make it easier for you to realise how and where we live.

The first snow has fallen and we are being treated to a spell of beautiful weather – clear, crisp days and starry nights. The air is like wine and the snow has that squeaky crunch that makes me so homesick for Switzerland and a pair of skis. The line of hills that I can see from my window are pine-covered and in the evenings one can see the snow glistening on the trees. Furious football matches take place on the 'Sportplatz' in which I participated in goal for a while until I strained a muscle in my leg. I never did like soccer anyway!

There are so many things I would like to say and talk to you about but which are obviously taboo that you will have to use your imagination and guess them. The great thing to remember is that we are all very much where you would have us mentally if not geographically! However that is the best we can do in the circumstances.

So far as our treatment is concerned and lest you should be in doubt about it, I can assure you that our treatment is absolutely correct and what one would expect from one air force to another. You know me well enough to know that I would not write this if it were not true and I hope it will put your mind at rest once and for all.

My darlings my page is coming to an end and there is just about room enough left to tell you all how much I love you and how much I think of you.

He concluded the letter with the following paragraph:

Do you remember how I told you at the beginning of the war that I knew I would get through it. Well admittedly I never thought it would be this way but I am convinced now that there is some destiny which shapes our ends and that all my energies bottled up for the time being are meant to be used later on. God bless you. Roger

12

In Pursuit of Peggy

Grappling with an overwhelming sense of frustration, Bushell may well have been confined to Occupied Europe geographically, but mentally he was very much on his way to Switzerland as 1940 gave way to 1941.

He told Erik Hvalsoe, a skiing friend at the Derby Hotel in Davos Dorf, that he would be seeing him again 'one of these days'. In a postcard dated 10 December 1940, he wrote:

The first snow has come and the view of the hills from my window gives me many a heartache . . . best of luck for the season, old boy. The great day will come and then we'll all meet again.

Bushell was not dreaming: the letter was a declaration of intent backed by work on the ground. Wings Day's escape committee had been busy. Three tunnels were built by the Permanent Staff at Dulag Luft between July 1940 and June 1941, and kept secret both from their fellow prisoners and the Germans.

Digging was filthy work, and dangerous too. With the water table just four feet below the surface, it was often wet and icy cold. Using stolen shovels, the men dug through the unforgiving clay, which contained gravel and rock, and were cut and bruised as they inched their way forwards by the dim light of fat lamps. Day suffered blood poisoning, and complained that the tunnel smelt like a morgue.

While the prisoners of war were confronted by remorseless conditions underground, this was not yet the case on the surface. Under Major Rumpel's administration, there was no security section searching for signs of illegal activity; everything was, instead, geared to the gathering of information about the Royal Air Force and its operations. The barracks were surrounded by barbed wire, which was lit. Two sentry boxes, which were manned day and night, contained floodlights and machine guns. Guards from a contingent of about forty patrolled inside the fence. But there were no searches, no dedicated German 'ferrets' as they came to be called, looking for holes in the ground and escape equipment. Earth removed from the tunnels was dumped under the huts without fear of discovery.

Roll calls conducted twice a day, one at 9 a.m., the other one hour before sunset, were not always rigorous. Wings Day posted 'watchers' at strategic points whenever escape activity was in progress, according to the history of the camp, which was written by the RAF in 1945. All the 'new arrivals were warned of the microphones' and 'Day made an order that conversations of a confidential nature were to be held in the open, or, if that were impracticable, owing to the weather or the time, in wash-rooms', where the water could be turned on to drown out the speakers' voices. A German guard let it be known later that listening devices were monitored only between 6 p.m. and lock-up.

In a letter to Bushell's parents written after the war, Day described the digging of the three tunnels during 1940–41 when it seems that Roger conquered, temporarily at least, the claustrophobia that had dogged him in earlier years.

> *Two [tunnels] became unusable due to water coming into them, but finally in the end of May 1941, the third one was completed. We only allowed a few into the secret of the tunnel construction and the few had to work hard – often in icy cold water, darkness and bad air and with always the possibility of the tunnel collapsing and burying them – your son was one of the most indefatigable and enthusiastic workers, even though he decided later not to use the tunnel, but he did not stop working.*

The target for the tunnellers was a ditch, which would provide cover, running from east to west, lying on the far side of a road known as the Siedlungsstrasse, running south to north past the sports field and the barracks. A stream ran through the ditch, which was forded by a wooden bridge.

According to the camp history, 'the first tunnel to be started began from the central barrack and was continued in a southerly direction until it reached the ditch, at which point it became water-logged'.

The other two tunnels were built from the most westerly barrack block and were shallower than the first. 'One ran in a southerly direction and was not completed. The third ran South-west under the sentry box in the corner of the wire and changed its direction to due West and ran under the road to its exit in the ditch, at the only point where the ditch provided any protection from the sentry box in the South-west corner.'

Stove shovels from the barracks were used as spades for digging; wooden boards were taken from beds to make roof supports for the tunnels; lamps were made out of tins filled with margarine, which had been boiled and strained to create pure fat, with a wick made of pyjama cord. Tools such as small chisels, pliers, gimlets and a plane were 'borrowed' from the shoemaker's shop.

By the winter of 1940, conditions underground had deteriorated, and Jimmy Buckley suspended work on the tunnel, which ran from Day's own room. But planning for the escape, which would involve up to twenty men, continued.

Civilian clothes such as mackintoshes, shirts and woollen garments were collected from clothing parcels sent to the prisoners by their families. 'All civilian clothing sent in these parcels was supposed to be confiscated by the German N.C.O. in charge of the clothing store, but he could usually be persuaded to overlook such articles,' says the camp history.

Attempts were made at forging official German documents. 'Some very primitively forged Ausweiss [identity cards] were made by various Ps/W who realised that they would never pass a close scrutiny but would do if merely glanced at in bad light. The photographs for these Ausweiss were cut out of various illustrated papers, and bore some resemblance to the P/W whom they were supposed to represent. An ink pad was acquired and stamps were cut out of soft wood to give an outline of the Nazi emblem.'

Supplies of food were saved for escape rations.

Small-scale maps of Germany and Europe were, quite remarkably, purchased from the camp canteen, but 'a local, large-scale map' was obtained, probably by Bushell, from 'a contact', and 'a number of silk and rice-paper escape maps were smuggled into the camp'. New prisoners also brought in several compasses made by MI9, while a 'very good French compass was given by a French P/W and was most useful for tunnel construction.'

Apart from Bushell, Day and Buckley, the triumvirate driving the RAF's escape campaign in Germany, others who would play a prominent part were beginning to join them on the Permanent Staff.

Flight Lieutenant Michael Casey, a deeply committed Roman Catholic, was another expatriate. Born in Allahabad, northern India, in 1918, he was the son of the inspector-general of the Indian police, who sent him to Stonyhurst College in England. Casey joined the RAF in 1936 and was married just two weeks after the outbreak of war in September 1939. He was shot down on 16 October, flying a Blenheim on a reconnaissance mission near Emden, after a piece of flying described by the German pilot involved as 'an aerial steeplechase'.

The Stonyhurst magazine, quoting the Luftwaffe pilot, 'Lieutenant K', from an interview in a German newspaper, gave a 'vivid' account of the action:

> The enemy swung round to westward, seeking a cloud in which to escape, *said the German airman.* He swerved sharply, lessening considerably my chances of hitting him. I followed close at his heels and, seeing that he could not shake me off, he went into a spin dive into a cloudbank about 200 metres in depth . . .

He dived again and then there began a mad pursuit which almost beggars description. The Englishman was a good, adroit and skilful airman. He utilised every unevenness in the ground, every hedge, every ditch as cover. He slipped between trees and skimmed over the houses. As I raced on I could see the smashed tree tops silhouetted against the sky and the broken bushes flying through the air. Now and again I expected to see him remove a roof, but with his speed of 300 kilometres an hour he jumped over every obstacle. At times we were barely six feet from the ground, and even eye-witnesses thought he was down. But he went on, though escape was now out of the question.

At last, after another volley, I saw the pilot lay his machine on the ground, and the three occupants jumped out. They had not had time to release the landing gear of the aeroplane, which was already in flames, and it simply crashed in a potato field. I circled above them and they greeted me with clasped hands, as if to say that they would like to shake hands with me after a chivalrous fight.

Major John Dodge was another of the spirited characters who joined Bushell on the Permanent Staff at this time. Related by marriage to Winston Churchill, Dodge was born into a wealthy New York family in 1894. Naturalised as a British citizen in 1915, he served with the Royal Naval Division and the army during the First World War, distinguishing himself during the Allied landings at Gallipoli in Turkey.

After the war, he trekked through China and Russia, where he was arrested by the Cheka, the Soviet secret service, on suspicion of spying. Returning to Britain at the end of the 1920s, he became a member of the London Stock Exchange, a director of an American bank and represented Mile End on the London County Council. He also married an American debutante. They had two sons.

When hostilities broke out again, Dodge, aged forty-five, joined the Middlesex Regiment. He was 'transferred' to the RAF by

Major Rumpel when he was sent to Dulag Luft in error after he was found emerging from the Scheldt estuary between Belgium and Holland. Dodge had jumped from a prison ship after being captured on the French coast.

Casey and Dodge and the other 'Permanents' were instructed by the Escape Committee to foster 'friendly' relations with Rumpel's staff, while encouraging British airmen passing through Dulag Luft to work against the German regime once they had moved to other camps.

This policy towards the Germans, which created 'a high degree of friendliness', seems to have yielded benefits. No escape activity was suspected at this time, and Bushell and the other German speakers were able to garner information about the nearby town of Oberursel, the surrounding countryside, and local railways, not to mention the listening devices.

The 'Permanents' tried to embrace the hundreds of prisoners passing through the camp. They pooled their food parcels, arranged the communal messing of officers of all ranks, and provided them with as much new clothing as was available. Day even 'taxed' the Permanents to pay for new toiletries for other airmen. He thought this 'comradeship' would enable veterans like Bushell to train new ones in how to organise escapes, gather intelligence and set up MI9 coding stations in other camps.

'It is considered that this amounted to highly valuable pioneer work,' says the camp history, 'since it was from the veteran Ps/W at this camp that new Ps/W got their first impressions of P/W life, and a bad impression would have been most detrimental to morale and consequently to escape and intelligence work.'

In reality, it did not always work out quite so well. Some British airmen passing through the camp thought Day, Bushell and Buckley were far too friendly with the Germans and, noting Rumpel's whisky and wine, were living rather high on the hog. The Senior British Officer at another camp, Stalag Luft I at Barth, complained through official channels to both the German and British authorities, which Day resented deeply.

Even Rumpel came under fire from locals about the privileges enjoyed by the British prisoners: to whisky and wine could be added women.

The head of the agricultural college that used the nearby farmhouses and outhouses for its hens and cows complained about the 'shocking' sight of male nudity on the sports field, where the prisoners stripped to their underpants on sunny days. At tea with the female students of the college, Rumpel told them to 'look the other way' as they walked past, but one of them apparently responded: 'All the German men between eighteen and fifty are called up. But here are more than half-naked young men, good-looking men. And we do look at them. And they look at us, too.'

Rumpel reportedly blamed the young women, but was then put on the spot when one of the older students said: 'We never realised before that Englishmen were so lovely. They have beautiful bodies.'

While the women were not exactly consorting with the enemy, Rumpel certainly didn't want to foster any closer relationships than he was already doing. The guards were alerted.

Bushell still had women problems of his own. 'I have had at last another letter from Peggy dated end of October but nothing since,' he wrote to his parents on 31 January 1941. 'I can't believe she isn't writing and now with the air mail some people are getting letters from England in three weeks!'

In a ruse obviously geared to increase postal exchanges, Bushell asked Peggy to ignore the British Red Cross, which was failing to get parcels through to Dulag Luft, and send him tobacco and cigarettes straight from a firm with an export licence. 'I have also told her that it is my wish that SHE send my personal parcels. All this damned rubbish about next of kin.'

He thanked his parents for depositing money in his bank account, which was overdrawn, and paying off his tailor's bill, but added, probably to the despair of his long-suffering father: 'I have written to Peggy about money as all my pay is going to her and I have no doubt things will straighten themselves out eventually.'

A month later, on 27 February, in another letter to his parents, Bushell wrote:

I still have not heard from Peggy. My last letter from her was dated October 25th and I have only had five from her in all. There MUST be some explanation and I'll have to be patient I suppose. I am certainly being paid out for my past sins about letter-writing though! I never realised how important letters can be till I got stuck here. The only other news I've had of Peggy is a telegram she sent Mme Paraviciere who cabled from Switzerland for me and in which she said she'd been quite ill but was now recovered and that a letter was following. As you can imagine, that has not added to my peace of mind!

Then again, on 26 March 1941, he told his parents:

I'm gloomy about Peggy though. I suppose I ought not to worry but only one more letter from her has come in which was dated December 1st . . . since I started writing this another bunch of letters have come in, including one from John Brinton and one from Peggy's youngest sister but none from herself, alas.

Although he often hid his true feelings, Bushell continued to use his letters to reassure his parents:

There is nothing to worry about. Our latest diversion believe it or not is skiing! We bought skis through the canteen and use Red Cross boots and go out on the local hills with the German officers. You can imagine what it does to me! We went out today in beautiful powder snow, crisp frosty air, a blue sky and all the trees loaded with snow. It was too beautiful for words. And then of course one gets outside the damned barbed wire.

He also continued to use his letters to put his captors at ease.

Both sides hope like hell their side will win and naturally they don't get any information out of us though they try as it is their job to try, wrote Bushell in another letter. *However apart from the war and politics we find lots to talk about and I personally think it is rather a fine thing that a camp can be run on those lines. I have no doubt a lot of armchair patriots would think it was wrong, but after all those of us who are here have given practical proof of our patriotism and therefore we are probably the better judges.*

But the Germans were getting better at extracting information from downed crewmen. Rumpel and his senior interrogators gathered details of a device that helped British radar plotters to establish the identity of approaching aircraft. It was called Identification Friend or Foe (IFF), which the Germans then copied. Rumpel also discovered critical information about Rolls-Royce engines. He helped to set up an interceptor service at Wissant on the coast near Wimereux, south of Calais, which eavesdropped on British aircraft. As a result, Rumpel knew the call signs, numbers and bases of every RAF squadron; the Luftwaffe could also predict the RAF's targets and intercept its bombers.

During his own interrogation in London after the war, Erich Killinger, who succeeded Rumpel as commandant of Dulag Luft in 1941, gave details of the methods used by the Germans to gain information, which became increasingly sophisticated. Killinger knew one or two things about being a prisoner: he had been a pilot during the First World War and had escaped from Russian captivity in 1915.

The notes from Killinger's interrogation suggest that questioning of individuals at Dulag Luft 'could be carried out by the friendly approach, or one of a dozen methods, and might last up to three weeks. The main object was to establish gradually a personal relationship to the prisoner, who should come to regard the IO (Intelligence Officer) as an agreeable conversationalist.'

But the Germans also used 'bawling out and threats, usually vague. Threats to treat prisoners as saboteurs or parachutists etc. especially if some article of clothing was missing. Threats that he would be handed over to the Gestapo and shot. Bluff of all kinds.'

Crews were usually interrogated individually, but occasionally in pairs, with 'the usual game of saying that one of the crew had already talked'.

Women were sometimes used to question prisoners casually in the hospital and, occasionally, they were introduced into the formal interrogation process: 'She would come in as the IO was talking to the prisoner, smile at him in a friendly manner and then ask the IO some administrative question or other,' Killinger told his British interrogators. 'The IO would turn to the prisoner and say: "I am so sorry, but Fraulein X wants to have just a few details for Orderly Room records – purely routine. I am afraid they have got your particulars wrong."'

Sometimes a particularly technical approach was used with some officers, particularly engineers later in the war, who had 'an inveterate habit of boasting', according to Killinger. 'It was very easy to irritate prisoners and then let them boast of their machines.'

Drinking parties were also used to garner information, but 'were considered more of an excuse for the IOs to get drunk than anything else. The IOs were usually under the table before the prisoners'.

Killinger, a 'keen student of psychology' who was fifty-two in 1945, told his interrogators that listening devices were installed through the camp, and that his staff made 'extensive' use of informers recruited among the prisoners. This, he claimed, remained 'effective' until 1943, when it was 'evident Germany had lost the war'. The British report on Dulag Luft says the Germans also introduced 'agents' into the camp in the guise of British or Allied air force personnel.

By the start of 1941, Day and Bushell were becoming increasingly familiar with German techniques and had started their own manoeuvres in the shadows of the intelligence world as well as cranking up escape activity.

The third tunnel at Dulag Luft was reopened at the end of March, but the diggers were unable to make much progress until after the snow had melted in April. The digging was slow.

Buckley and his team had to carry out a great deal of maintenance because the stream had broken its banks and flooded the tunnel and much of the trench, *wrote Rollings*. Cave-ins had also occurred. It took a month for the tunnel to dry out and to fill in the holes left by falls. As digging progressed, the clay from the tunnel was dispersed under the other two huts. In mid-May, the diggers put up a probe made from a one-inch diameter metal water pipe painted white for the top two inches so that watchers inside the compound could see it. The probe broke through the road surface for six or seven inches just as a supply lorry was grinding its way along the Siedlungsstrasse. Word got back to the diggers, who hastily withdrew it.

Towards the end of the month, there was another crisis when builders began to construct a brick support to the culvert under the Siedlungsstrasse. The water in the stream rose to such a level that it was seeping into the tunnel. Day and Bushell spent days persuading the [German] adjutant, Fiergutt, that the dammed water would create a breeding ground for mosquitoes and all manner of disease-carrying flies and bugs that would threaten the health of the camp. Finally, Fiergutt sent an orderly to kick down the bricks, the prisoners watching gleefully as he ruined his highly polished jackboots.

At the end of May 1941, the tunnel was completed. The escape was planned for the evening of Sunday, 1 June, the Whitsun holiday, when many German staff at Dulag Luft would be away on leave and the moon would not rise until midnight.

The 'phoney war' between officers from rival air forces – a chivalric relationship at first glance involving smart, educated men with essentially shared values – had but a short time left to run. Soon they would be engulfed in a remorseless war with little room for mischief or manners.

In a letter to his parents dated 29 April 1941 – the last letter sent to the Mossel River post office from Dulag Luft – Bushell tackled familiar themes. He took his father to task over finance:

I'll deal with father's [letter] first as his is the latest in date and charges me with inefficiency in my attempted solution of my financial affairs! I'm paying off my overdraft slowly (though it hurts me!) as I agree it wouldn't be profitable to go on paying interest especially as Peggy doesn't need the money and we obviously don't want to have any more debts than can be helped. It's galling though sitting here feeling one is actually filling some ruddy bank's coffers and certainly will never get anything but a paltry overdraft by comparison in the future!

Bushell's pay was clearly the material evidence of his commitment to Peggy Hamilton, from a man confined hundreds of miles away with no freedom of action, and it was incredibly important to him.

Joking apart though I wrote to Uncle Harry last January and asked him to get particulars from Peggy as to how much we had in my account that accumulated out of my pay and if possible to try and persuade the bank to forego the interest provided that I brought my account back to them. I loathe doing it because my pay's some security for Peggy and though she doesn't seem to need it now it worries me to think it isn't there for her to use just in case of accidents.

He spelt out his frustration and sense of isolation:

> *You can imagine how absolutely helpless one feels*
> *especially with the delay in the post and I merely obeyed*
> *my natural instincts when I first fixed things up on my*
> *arrival here . . . it makes me simply livid to think of my pay*
> *going in to that nasty old bank to pay off a loan contracted*
> *long before the war.*

Having got his obvious frustrations off his chest, Bushell became
rather reflective:

> *Now that matter's dealt with, though, I have not made*
> *much sense over it and it seems pretty vague reading it*
> *through. One is very liable to become vague I find – one*
> *might be on a desert island so shut away from the world are*
> *we – papers and the wireless bring the war into perspective*
> *for a moment but the contact is an artificial one and we*
> *carry on in our little community in splendid isolation from*
> *the struggle and tragedy of it all.*

But then he got back to business, putting the Germans censors
back to sleep:

> *Now I've got myself completely resigned to being out of*
> *things completely, I find it not unpleasant. I'm sure that*
> *one's being in this camp goes a long way towards making*
> *an unsatisfactory interlude in life into something that'll do*
> *a lot towards destroying all the misunderstanding between*
> *our two people. It'd be rare to find a man with greater*
> *understanding than Major Rumpel, the commandant here,*
> *whose personality seems to've been transmitted to each*
> *and every one of his subordinates, combining to produce*
> *an atmosphere not of custody but rather of comradeship in*
> *spite of locks and barbed wire.*

Perhaps not surprisingly, Bushell was among a group of officers from the Permanent Staff, including Buckley, Day, Casson and Dodge, who were invited to have supper at Rumpel's private cottage not far from the camp. Sydney Smith described it as 'a hilarious evening'. When conversation turned briefly to escape, Rumpel dismissed their chances of getting out of Germany.

Bushell had been working hard on his German, talking to camp staff whenever he could, until his fellow prisoners jokingly referred to him as 'von Bushell'. He joined the discussion. 'Look, Major Rumpel,' he is reported to have said. 'I've escaped and I'm just on the Swiss border, and you are a German policeman. Now start talking to me just as a policeman would do.'

'A fast, noisy exchange followed, at the end of which Rumpel switched back into English, laughing: "Roger, that third or fourth word was so absolutely English that even a stupid policeman would see through you."'

Roger tried this once or twice more with the major and each time listened patiently while Rumpel pointed out his errors in German. 'Only a man like Roger Bushell could have tricked a man like Rumpel into giving him tips on how to argue his way across the Swiss frontier,' wrote Sydney Smith.

Bushell would soon be able to put Rumpel's tips to the test: back in the camp, fourteen members of the Permanent Staff and four other senior officers were ready to make the first major breakout of the war.

At the end of his last letter from Dulag Luft, Bushell said to his parents: 'My darlings, this really is the end of the page. Lots and lots of love to you and keep your fingers crossed!'

13

The Goat Shed

In the weeks before the breakout from Dulag Luft, Roger Bushell turned his back on the collective escape plan. Whether it was because he could not face going underground, one more time, after suppressing his fear of confined spaces while digging the tunnel, or whether it was down to a more opportunistic, some might say selfish, trait – highlighted so often in the Wellington College rugby reports – he decided to go it alone.

Bushell announced that he intended to hide on the sports field on the afternoon of the planned escape and get away several hours before the other seventeen escapers. His plan was to catch a train that evening. Some of the other prisoners protested: if he were caught, it would jeopardise the escape through the tunnel, they argued. But Wings Day backed Bushell.

The reason he did not use the tunnel was that his clever brain had conceived another plan which would get him clear of the camp earlier and thus allow him to catch a train at Frankfurt before the alarm of the tunnel escape had been given, Day wrote in a letter to Bushell's parents years later. *The method Roger used to escape, I am sure that Paddy Byrne must have told you, because I think he helped to hide Roger in the goat shed in the playing field.*

By the end of May 1941, the Escape Committee had a stash of German currency worth £15; they had mapped out the roads and paths in the vicinity of the camp; and they knew the local train times. MI9 had turned down Bushell's request via a coded letter for passports and other papers and the names of contacts, but it had provided information on how to enter Switzerland through the Schaffhausen salient, which bulges into south-west Germany and was reputedly less well-guarded than many areas of the frontier.

The official history of Dulag Luft has nothing to say about Bushell's individual escape, but it is described in three books: Paul Brickhill's *The Great Escape* (1951), Aidan Crawley's *Escape from Germany* (1956), and *Wings Day* by Sydney Smith (1968). All three authors had been prisoners of war and knew Bushell. Crawley had also served with him in 601 Squadron.

In the playing field, which was just outside the compound, there lived a goat, the memory of which will be fresh in the minds of all early RAF prisoners, *wrote Crawley*. The goat possessed character. Prisoners were constantly playing with it and at the least provocation, and sometimes without, the goat would attack them and butt them in the stomach. Some hardy spirits used to consider this a better game than football, with the result that the goat was seldom without company.

But the most important thing about the goat was that it had a kennel. From the beginning those prisoners who took an interest in the goat were constantly in and out of the kennel cleaning it or giving the goat food. But the kennel was also a place in which a man could sit unobserved by German guards, and to Bushell this suggested a means of escape.

While the tunnel was being built, Bushell and a colleague dug a hole in the kennel just large enough to conceal a man, and covered it with a firm trap so that the goat should not fall through. They carried the earth away gradually during their many visits to the goat. Bushell planned to hide himself in the kennel on the evening before the tunnel was due to break, and when it was dark to climb over the single strand of wire that surrounded the football field.

Brickhill picked up the story: On the day of the escape, a 'mock bullfight between the goat and the prisoners drew the guards' eyes (as it was meant to), and Roger crawled into the shed. There had been a lot of debate as to how he would get on in the shed. Buckley started the old gag by saying, "What about the smell?" and Paddy [Byrne] gave the stock reply: "Oh, the goat won't mind that." And as it happened, the goat didn't mind at all.'

Sydney Smith added that, after Bushell had stowed himself away, '[Squadron Leader] Nick Tindall led the "burial party" for him and reported brightly back to Wings: "He's tucked away all right, under the straw and droppings. I put a wad of goat dung over his face."'

Soon after dark, Bushell was off, well ahead of the others, and both plans went smoothly. At about 9 p.m., some of the prisoners not involved in the escape organised a noisy diversion in one of the barracks – it sounded like a party. Buckley opened the tunnel, and Byrne, who would stay behind, hid in the ditch to help the escapers on their way. Seventeen prisoners crawled out unobserved and were not missed until roll call the next morning.

The date of the escape is disputed. Some of the prisoners put it in the last week of May, others in the first weekend of June, the Whitsun bank holiday, some later in the month. It is an example of the vagaries of memory, even after only a few years, when the testimonies were recorded. What is beyond dispute is that, whenever it was, most of the escapers who used the tunnel were arrested in the Frankfurt area.

Bushell travelled much further than most and was, indeed, within sight of neutral Switzerland when he ran into trouble.

Dressed in a good civilian suit, which he had bought from one of the German guards, *wrote Crawley,* he travelled by express train to Tuttlingen and from there along the secondary line to Bonndorf, where he began to walk. He had maps and was also able to buy guide books en route.

The weather was perfect, and confident of being able to sustain a casual conversation without giving himself away, he walked by day across country. As it turned out he met no one,

and reached a point about five miles from the frontier without
difficulty.

According to a biographical documentary film made by Bushell's
niece, Lindy Wilson, for which she drew on her uncle's private
papers, Bushell said: 'I reached Bonndorf and went on foot to the
point I was making for, just a few kilometres from the Swiss
border. Things had gone almost too well, so I sat down for two
hours and made myself generate caution for the last, decisive
stage. I had the alternative of waiting for nightfall with all its
problems or bluffing it by daylight, and I chose the latter.'

Bushell was just 100 yards from the Swiss frontier – 'I could
have taken a girls' school across' – when he stopped to consider
his options.

Day described what Bushell had told him of his escape attempt
in a letter to Ben and Dorothe Bushell in July 1945.

> *It is now a long time ago,* wrote Day, *but I think he
> [Bushell] was arrested by a German frontier guard as he
> was walking down a road, still thinking that he was some
> distance from the actual frontier and line of guards. He was
> taken to a guardhouse but as it was getting dark, he decided
> to break away from his guards, which he did as they were
> turning into the door, and ran down the street – the guard
> first shot at him but did not hit him; however, he ran into
> another guard, who recaptured him again.*
>
> *So ended Roger's first attempt. I had also escaped at that
> time, but through the tunnel, and after recapture I was
> taken back to Frankfurt jail where I met Roger and some of
> the others.*

Despite the difficulties that the Allied escape attempt must have
caused the Dulag Luft staff, Bushell told his parents in a letter
some time later that Major Rumpel's staff had been remarkably
tolerant.

A chivalrous and sporting attitude was adopted towards us by all and sundry in the camp, wrote Bushell, *but orders came that the black sheep were to be moved. I was singularly impressed when invited out to dinner somewhere in the large town which I suppose I mustn't name, but which is seven or eight miles away from Dulag, by the security officer [Günther von Massow]. It was on the night before our departure and was very entertaining!*

Bushell's first letter to his parents after his thwarted escape attempt arrived at the Mossel River post office in the late summer of 1941. It was sent from Stalag Luft I, a Luftwaffe camp on the Baltic in northern Germany, and clearly showed that their son's spirit had not been broken.

My darlings, Bushell declared, *apologies for not writing at all last month . . . calculations went astray – you won't be surprised to learn why. It merely so happened that I'd left the camp without asking, having decided it was so long since I'd seen any of my friends!*
  Ghastly bad luck stopped me literally right at the last moment from seeing Tony Page again and as you've no doubt observed, I've changed my address. As almost all the old crowd from Dulag have collected here too, you will no doubt understand what I'm getting at. I'm rather dubious as to exactly how much of my adventures I can tell you without exciting the censor so I will leave the greater part until after the war.

The 'old crowd from Dulag' had split up after emerging from the Dulag Luft tunnel a few hours after Bushell had made his own dash for freedom. Most of them provided the authorities with reports of their own escape attempts after the war.

Day walked to the east 'because I thought this was the direction in which search parties were least likely to cover thoroughly', but he later changed direction. 'I had my own rations with me, sufficient, I thought, for fourteen days, and I walked north-west for five nights, hiding up in woods and coppices during the intervening days.'

He was discovered by two woodsmen who found his kit while he was looking for water. He spent three days in Frankfurt jail before being sent to Stalag Luft I, where he was sentenced to ten days' solitary confinement as punishment for the escape.

Major John Dodge, known to everyone as Johnny but nicknamed the 'Dodger', was the eleventh man out of the tunnel and teamed up with Wing Commander Noel 'Hetty' Hyde. 'After leaving the exit of the tunnel, we crawled along the bank of a stream outside the fence and removed the overalls which we had worn over our converted uniform,' said Dodge.

The two men had walked across fields to the main road, through the town of Oberursel to the autobahn that bypassed Frankfurt-am-Main. They kept walking until dawn when they hid in a thicket. As darkness fell, they moved off again, but were stopped by a policeman at a control point who shone a light on Dodge as they walked under a bridge. Pedestrians were not allowed on the autobahn. Neither of them could speak German.

Another of the escapers was a navy pilot, Sub-Lieutenant W. S. 'Peter' Butterworth, one of the last men out of the tunnel. He headed south with Mike Casey. 'I was wearing a civilian suit and cap and had plenty of food with me,' said Butterworth. They walked by day and slept in woods at night, but were eventually stopped outside a village south-east of Frankfurt by a German policeman who asked for their papers. They had none.

Frustrated as an escaper, Butterworth would go on to find more promising roles in the theatre at Stalag Luft III, making his name after the war as one of the stars of the *Carry On* films.

The testimony of Captain C. B. Griffiths, a member of the Royal Marines who teamed up with Flight Lieutenant J. B.

Boardman, probably comes closest to a script that might have inspired the scenes for the Hollywood film, *The Great Escape*, in which Steve McQueen makes for the Swiss border in a memorable, but entirely fictitious, motorcycle chase.

'We left the camp in civilian clothes, which we had made, at about 23.30 hours and walked to a farm a short distance from the camp,' said Griffiths. 'I had obtained information from a German *Unterofizzier* to the effect that a German Army motorcycle was kept at this farm and it was our intention to steal it. On arrival at the farm we discovered that a dog had been chained to the motor cycle.'

Griffiths and Boardman then made a wise decision. They abandoned their plans to steal the motorcycle and started walking south-east in the direction of Darmstadt. Unfortunately, they were stopped by a police patrol while approaching the town's railway yards. They were sentenced to fourteen days' solitary confinement for their part in the escape.

Squadron Leader Tindall, who had taken such delight in placing dung on Bushell's face as he hid in the goat hut on the day of the escape, and Flight Lieutenant D. E. Pinchbeck, were arrested in Mannheim, more than a hundred miles south of Dulag Luft, after boarding a goods train in Frankfurt. 'We tried to bluff our way out,' said Tindall. It didn't work. They were interrogated by the Gestapo.

Having walked into a 'prohibited area' south of Frankfurt, Flight Lieutenant R. D. Baughan and Flight Lieutenant A. B. Corbett were quickly recaptured and sent to the jail in Frankfurt.

Of the German speakers among the escapers, Flight Lieutenant F. H. Vivian was thought to have the best chance of success – Major Rumpel considered his grasp of the German language to be outstanding. Vivian certainly travelled far, reaching the Austrian town of Imst in the Tyrolean Alps, but was then recaptured by two members of the Hitler Youth.

Vivian's testimony, illustrating, as it does, the difficulties faced by even the most imaginative and best-equipped escaper, makes depressing reading.

I was wearing a blue sports coat, made out of a blanket, and knickerbockers of a bright green, made out of a Norwegian infantryman's trousers, and a hat of the same material, *he said*. I had a small amount of money – mostly given to me by Wing Commander Day – some food and a sketch map of the valley of the River Inn at the Swiss border, for which point I intended to make.

On emerging from the tunnel, I went down to the main road, it being daylight by then, and caught a train into Frankfurt, where I went to the station, bought a ticket and boarded a train. I continued travelling on slow trains for three or four days, sleeping at nights in fields and woods, having come to the end of my money when I reached the area of Kempten, in southern Bavaria.

I walked through the Fern Pass [in the Tyrolean Alps] and reached Imst. Just after I had passed Imst, two German youths in the *Volkssturm* came along in a truck and asked me for my papers. I tried to bluff my way out, but was unsuccessful and was taken to the town jail. From there I was taken by Luftwaffe personnel to Frankfurt jail, where I remained for three or four days. I was then taken to Stalag Luft I (Barth).

He was sentenced to fourteen days' solitary confinement.

The escape took the Germans at Dulag Luft by surprise, but one of Rumpel's officers realised that they had missed all of the obvious clues: they should have known what was happening simply because of the number of showers and baths taken by the prisoners, who were washing themselves after digging in the tunnel.

Triggering a *Kriegsfahndung* – a national manhunt involving the *Wehrmacht*, Reinhard Heydrich's security services, the frontier police, Hitler Youth, and a rural group known as *Landwatch* – the escape from Dulag Luft shocked the German authorities and led to change. The Führer himself was told of the breakout, the first mass escape by RAF officers.

From this moment, the conflict in most RAF prison camps would mirror the war in the air, with both sides seeking technological advantages and more effective intelligence with which to combat the other side in an ever-more challenging environment.

Rumpel was highly regarded as an intelligence officer. He had a fine military record, having distinguished himself in the First World War as a cavalry officer and as a fighter pilot in a squadron commanded by Hermann Göring. But he was a known Anglophile and politically suspect: he had only accepted an invitation in the 1930s to rejoin the German air force, as a member of the British section of Luftwaffe intelligence, on condition that he did not have to become a member of the Nazi party.

Holding on to his pronounced sense of chivalry, Rumpel went to Frankfurt jail to visit all the British prisoners who had been rounded up after the escape attempt. Day apologised for causing him so much trouble, but Rumpel replied that he would have done the same had their positions been reversed. 'To escape is a prisoner's job,' he said.

According to Sydney Smith, they shook hands. Rumpel wished him good luck, 'even if I'm not supposed to say so'.

As the RAF prisoners left Frankfurt prison and boarded a Luftwaffe coach, which would take them to the railway station, they found a case of champagne on which lay a note: 'With the compliments of Major Rumpel.'

It was a noble gesture from an honourable man.

Hitler wanted the Dulag Luft commandant sacked, apparently complaining that he could not win the war with 'defeatists' like Rumpel in key positions. Heinrich Himmler, head of the SS, attempted to take control of the prison camps, showing Hitler a selection of letters written by prisoners complaining about conditions in other camps after their favourable experiences of Dulag Luft.

Göring, however, defended his former comrade and Hitler backed down, but he insisted on all the escapers being moved to other camps. He did not have long to wait for Rumpel's departure, either. Erich Killinger was made commandant of Dulag Luft in November, when he ushered in a harsher regime: regular searches were introduced; the sports field was guarded. In future, escape would be more difficult.

Rumpel was 'promoted' and put in charge of a network of Luftwaffe training airfields near Görlitz, a town not far from Sagan, close to the Polish border.

Dulag Luft was not the only place to experience a harsher regime in a world bristling with conflict. Britain was still alone and still on the defensive. The Germans occupied Yugoslavia and Greece and took thousands of British prisoners after an airborne invasion of the Mediterranean island of Crete. German U-boats sank millions of tons of British shipping in the Atlantic. Hitler sent General Erwin Rommel to North Africa, where the British had enjoyed some success against the Italians. But against Rommel's Afrika Korps, they were forced on to the defensive again.

In Poland, Reinhard Heydrich had experimented with mass murder, but his forces – primarily the death squads of the SS *Einsatzgruppen* – were held back by the *Wehrmacht* during the campaigns in Norway and western Europe. By March 1941, Heydrich had been negotiating with the same generals about the SS's role in the forthcoming invasion of Russia, Operation Barbarossa.

The *Wehrmacht* had been uncomfortable with the scale of the SS's atrocities in Poland, where Heydrich's forces 'swept up' behind the advancing German armies, killing members of the Polish aristocracy, the intelligentsia, communists and Jews: all regarded as enemies of the Nazi state. In Russia, the generals would be less squeamish, and Heydrich would have what amounted almost to a free hand.

He was 'well aware that Operation Barbarossa was to be fought as a war of destruction,' wrote Robert Gerwarth in his biography of Heydrich.

When, on 30th March, Hitler assembled the supreme commanders of the armed forces in the New Reich Chancellery, he emphasised that the impending war with the Soviet Union would be a fight to the death between two irreconcilable ideologies, a war that left no room for outdated notions of chivalry.

By the time Bushell had joined the other recaptured escapers from Dulag Luft in Frankfurt jail, the Germans had already assembled millions of men for Operation Barbarossa, the onslaught on the Soviet Union.

14

Journey to Prague

At the bottom of a farm track near the town of Barth in rural Pomerania, almost overlooking the Baltic Sea, the Luftwaffe erected the first purpose-built prison camp of the war, Stalag Luft I. Set in a bleak landscape, it was a desolate place in winter, with big wooden huts built close to the salt marsh and sand dunes. 'The fences appeared stronger than the ones we had left at Dulag Luft', wrote Harry Crease of the Royal Canadian Air Force, and 'the guard towers looked uglier and more heavily armed'.

When the Dulag Luft escapers arrived, they also faced hostility from their own side; men who thought that Wings Day and Roger Bushell and the other Permanent Staff had been too cosy with the Germans.

Among the prisoners at Barth was Bertram 'Jimmy' James, a twenty-five-year-old with bright eyes, a gentle voice and an open face. Years later, he told the Bushell family that the prisoners had 'booed' the Permanent Staff from Dulag Luft. 'They were identified with soft living,' he said. 'They had been enjoying the fruits of the German occupation of France and captured British stock and so on. They had regular walks, went skiing on parole, and had plenty of booze and cigarettes. It led to a lot of resentment.

'Then we found out they had been sent to Barth for escaping from a tunnel they had been digging for over a year. Our attitude changed. They had deceived the Germans while they dug the first successful RAF tunnel of the war,' said James.

The Senior British Officer at Stalag Luft I, who had made an official complaint about Day and his colleagues, is believed to have been Squadron Leader Brian Paddon, who was transferred to Colditz before the Dulag Luft escapers arrived at the Barth camp.

Paddon left Stalag Luft I without leadership. The British prisoners were disorganised and ill-disciplined. Generally anarchic, many of them were dishevelled and lived in various states of undress. Rations had been poor, with the Germans spending about half a penny a week on food for each prisoner. They had been allowed a cup of artificial coffee made from acorns every morning; shredded cabbage and a few potatoes at lunch; and a slice of black bread of dubious origin with a piece of sausage or cheese in the evening.

Bushell lost weight. But he struck an optimistic note in the early letters from the camp to his parents in South Africa.

The weather at the moment is scorching hot and we lie outside getting marvellously sunburnt, and there is reason to think that bathing in the sea, which we are very near, will shortly be permitted, he wrote on 21 June 1941, the day before the Germans launched their invasion of Russia. *The Red Cross parcel position at the moment is good and Canadian parcels of late have been arriving as well. We are therefore full of food and healthy and there's nothing to worry about.*

News from Peggy Hamilton appeared to be encouraging as well:

At last I've heard by air mail. I've nothing later than April and she seems no better than me at letters. She will write oftener though now she can send letters air mail and has received my voluble complaints about her not writing!

He signs off, 'Your loving son, <u>Roger</u>'. Unusually, his name is underlined. This was, according to the post-war report by MI9, one of the signs of a coded letter.

On 31 July, Bushell appeared to be irritated, writing:

The mail still seems irregular. One can pick examples by the dozen – air mail letters come in dated May, June, July on

*the same day for instance, and post going home also seems
to suffer much the same fate. It's all very infuriating
especially as letters are our only link with the real world.
However I suppose it's childish to grumble as it serves no
useful purpose. After all, the war involves slightly bigger
issues than the erratic behaviour of Kriegies' [short for
Kriegsgefangener, meaning prisoner of war] mail.*

For all the benefits of Red Cross and Canadian parcels, and the
plentiful food described in the previous letter, he told his parents:

*You'll be speechless with amazement to hear I tip the scale
at 12st 4lbs – only very slightly under two stone lighter than
on arrival. I'm as fit as a fiddle and though my stomach still
has a suspicious bulge unless held in, I really hope that in
the not too distant future even that will disappear.*

The reason for this admission becomes clear:

*Somewhere about the middle of last week I sent a striking
portrait of myself to you, which critics would barely call a
masterpiece or people rave about, but which I thought
nevertheless would amuse you. I think it's too young-looking
and quite unlike me but you may not agree. It was done by
the Jugoslav who shared our room at Dulag . . .*
    *Damn! This letter is over. All my love to you. Am well
mentally and physically. <u>Roger</u>.*

Once again, his signature is underlined. And it is the first letter to
his parents in more than a year in which he had not mentioned
Peggy. Perhaps he was finally beginning to feel at ease about the
relationship; or perhaps he had given up on it entirely.
    Day took over as Senior British Officer at Stalag Luft I and
instilled a new sense of purpose among the prisoners. Many
tunnels had been started over the previous year, but the camp

at Barth was built on sand over a high water table: tunnels had to be shallow, no more than four feet deep. The Germans collapsed most of them by driving heavy wagons around the compound. They also placed sound detectors around the camp to pick up early evidence of tunnelling, and they introduced 'ferrets', German staff who roamed at will in search of escape activity.

Eventually, Day established a new escape committee, which was referred to as the 'X' organisation. Jimmy Buckley was put in charge and, slowly, they began to pose a challenge to the German security operation.

Bushell is not mentioned in official files on Stalag Luft I but he seems, nevertheless, to have made his presence felt. The Germans were referred to as 'goons' after a *Daily Mirror* cartoon strip that depicted them as low-browed ape-men of great strength and stupidity (the Germans were told it stood for 'German Officer or Non-Com'). The watchtowers were therefore known as 'goon boxes'. Bushell soon gained a reputation as a goon-baiter.

Looking back on this period, M. R. D. Foot, who wrote the history of MI9, emphasised the importance of goon-baiting during an interview about Bushell's life.

> The Germans began by saying to everybody – they said it to me – 'For you the war is over', but it isn't, it's still going on, *said Foot*. You must never forget you're on the winning side, and you must remind the Germans of that. If they know you speak German – and do it as often as you can – you take an air of convinced superiority to them. This could annoy some of the rear-area Germans looking after the prisoner-of-war camps, very much indeed, and, of course, was deliberately harped on by men as clever as Roger, who were good at it.

Jimmy James remembered Bushell's tactics and his powerful voice, which made an impact on the camp staff. 'If you didn't meet him,' said James, 'you heard him talking around the compound, expressing his views of the Germans.'

If Bushell was trying to gain the upper hand in Stalag Luft I with his goon-baiting, he clearly felt the need to do so in his missives home, too. The tone and structure of his next letter home were dramatically different from the first two from Barth. He was clearly irked by something his parents had written, not about the state of the post, nor of his finances, nor Peggy's inability to write regularly, but something much more compelling. 'My letters to you are personal and on no account are extracts to be sent to the Press,' he wrote on 13 August 1941. 'Very naïve of you.'

They were probably the harshest words he directed at his parents in all the years he was a prisoner, but it was a reflection of the importance he put on the content of his post. This unusual criticism of his parents underlines the fact that some of Bushell's letters contained sensitive or coded information.

His letter continued, in a somewhat less vexed tone.

> *Harry North-Lewis is sending me cigarettes at last. Do*
> *hope you've had further letters by now. I write every*
> *month. We live in huts here. I share a room with Squadron*
> *Leader Tindall from Dulag . . . there is no need to worry*
> *and our spirits are all sky high and really we have some*
> *very amusing times. Descriptions of life in the camp are*
> *difficult to write and satisfy everyone at the same time.*
> *Love. R.*

On this occasion, perhaps not surprisingly considering its content, the signature was not underlined.

The letter was significant for one other reason: a reference to Peggy Hamilton. 'Heard from P,' he wrote. 'She has the ring. You are a darling and she loves it.' At that moment, Bushell must have felt the relationship with Peggy was secure. For more than a year, he had committed his pay to her, and now she had his diamond ring.

177

Unbeknown to him, though, the woman from 9 Wellesley House, Sloane Square – who had partied with the pilots of 601 Squadron, skied with him in the Swiss resort of Arosa and had accepted his proposal of marriage – had also turned her back on the fiancé of 1940. Miss Marguerite Hamilton was moving up in the world.

The day after Bushell's letter of 13 August 1941, in which he passed on the good news that he had heard from Peggy, an announcement was published in *The Times* to reveal the forthcoming marriage of Captain Lord Petre and Miss M. Hamilton:

> A marriage has been arranged, and will shortly take place, between Captain Lord Petre (The Essex Regiment) of Ingatestone Hall, Essex, and Marguerite, daughter of the late Mr Ion Wentworth Hamilton and Mrs Hamilton, of Westwood, Nettlebed, Oxon.

Bushell received one more letter from Peggy that summer. Written on 24 July, three weeks before the announcement of her engagement to Lord Petre, the letter commiserated with him over his recapture so close to the Swiss border. But he would not know the truth about his fiancée until the autumn of 1942, more than a year later.

Joseph William Lionel Petre, the 17th Lord Petre, born on 5 June 1914, was head of an ancient Catholic dynasty that still wielded influence in a Protestant land and inhabited a fine country house in south-east England.

Harry North-Lewis or his wife, Eleanor, might have seen the notice of engagement, but the name of Marguerite Hamilton might not have registered with them as being the same Peggy Hamilton who had a 'bon vivant' relationship with their nephew. Bushell remained in the dark.

On 30 August, Bushell reached his 31st birthday, his second as an 'unwilling guest' in Nazi Germany.

The day was the same as all other days, not that it matters for I have always regarded birthdays as somewhat boring anniversaries anyway, he told his parents the next day. *As far as I can see I am likely to spend at least one more here before the war is over. Not that that matters either for it would be well worth spending another five here as long as at the end of it we win.*

You will be amused to hear that we've all put a fiver into a pool on the date of the end of the war. The popular idea is October or November '42 but my date is July 23rd 1943. The winner takes all – over £800!

With parcels from the Blandys in Madeira; Mrs Hummold, his godmother, in the United States; and plenty of new books, Bushell appeared to be relatively philosophical about a longer war. 'I think I shall learn Spanish this winter – always useful and languages come easily to me as you know,' he wrote.

He concluded by telling Ben and Dorothe about an escape attempt, which was unusual in a prisoner's letter, but the German censor let it go.

Another tunnel has just been discovered which involved the usual search, he wrote. *When we returned to the compound we found a cross over where the tunnel had been, with the epitaph, 'Olim meminisse iuvabit!'*

It is a line from the first book of Virgil's Aeneid, which, translated, means, *Perhaps it will be pleasing to remember these things one day!* The quote refers to periods of trial and tribulation, which often seem insurmountable, but which, years later, appear to have been a turning point.

So true, wrote Bushell. *The security officer is a school master and a classical scholar and the classics no doubt will supply the reply. All my love. R.*

As it turned out, Bushell would not see any more birthdays at Stalag Luft I.

> In September, wrote Day, the German Camp Authorities had what we used to call a 'purge'. That is to say, the Germans used to select all the chaps who they thought were keen escapees or made a nuisance of themselves, and send them away. Roger naturally was already a marked man, but I think it was chiefly that he had a row with a German, who had tried to be insolent to him, but who unfortunately had some influence in the German Anti-escape Department (Abwehr Department). So Roger went with 50 others . . . to Lübeck and [they] were interned with about 2,000 British Officers captured in Greece and who were living under very bad conditions.

Seventy miles to the west of Stalag Luft I, Oflag XC at Lübeck was run by the *Wehrmacht*. Its commandant, *Oberst Freiheirr* von Wachtmeister 'was a real bastard', according to Lieutenant Hugo Bracken RN. The guards bullied the prisoners at every opportunity, and they also ignored the provisions of the Geneva Convention – the treaty agreed in 1929 that defined the 'rules' of war under international law.

What was a 'very bad camp' deteriorated still further after a British bomber dropped a stick of incendiary bombs just outside the perimeter fence, destroying the German officers' mess, including, it seems, the commandant's wine cellar. The incident generated 'extreme personal hostility', wrote Michael Roth, another prisoner at Lübeck.

Rations were worse than at Barth, and there were no parcels

with which to supplement their diet because Wachtmeister refused to register the camp with the Red Cross. He even confiscated all books as a reprisal for the RAF attack on his wine cellar.

Bushell managed to send one postcard to his parents from Lübeck. He alluded to the new hardships, but tried to avoid alarming his family.

I have moved again, *he wrote*. This is an army camp and very different from Dulag. There are, besides us, all the Crete prisoners. At the moment no parcels have shown up but we live in hope. I share a room with four others – all RAF and we are very well and cheerful . . . no letters since I arrived here, except one from Mildred Blandy. When you write, tell her I like the cheese and sausages best and to send more. All my books left at last camp but they may be sent on. Am very fit so nothing to worry about. Roger.

Bushell may well have appreciated the contents of the parcels that he received, but Mildred Blandy placed herself at some risk to send them. She lived on Madeira, the Portuguese Atlantic island that was the first port of call for Union-Castle steamers sailing from Cape Town to Britain. Born in South Africa, she was one of Bushell's childhood friends, and had married Graham Blandy of the port-making family. She could often be found putting aside material for Bushell. A prime ingredient of her parcels would have been the island speciality, Bolo de Mel, a honey cake packed with fruit.

Her second son, John, recalled the excitement surrounding the packing of Bushell's parcels and his name being mentioned. 'I was too young to understand their significance,' he said. 'And there was a certain caginess from my parents about the parcels. Perhaps they didn't want me to know too much.'

Portugal was officially neutral during the war but there were elements in the government that were pro-Nazi. The highly efficient secret police, who had been trained by the Gestapo, were a constant reminder that you had to tread carefully. A general climate of unease on Madeira, where car headlights were painted over and windows were taped, as well as specific warnings issued by the local Red Cross about maintaining contact with Bushell, may go some way to explain why there are no records on the island of the British airman's friendship with Mildred Blandy.

Bushell remained at Lübeck for only about a month, but he was remarkably active during this time. The first few days were spent in solitary confinement, his punishment for the escape from Dulag Luft, which should have been served at Stalag Luft I.

'Roger, being an old PoW and knowing the ropes was, I heard, of inestimable help to the Senior British Officer in his efforts to obtain better conditions,' Day told Bushell's parents after the war. The SBO was Wing Commander 'Hetty' Hyde, one of the eighteen who escaped from Dulag Luft in June. He was criticised by some prisoners for not standing up to Wachtmeister's unpleasant regime, but he made Bushell his adjutant.

Apart from fighting for prisoners' rights, Bushell gathered together a small group of prisoners, including Hugo Bracken, to dig a tunnel, starting under one of the bunk beds in his own barrack block. The tunnel was kept secret from the other prisoners as well as the Germans. According to Charles Rollings, the PoW historian, Bracken was trained in code and wrote to MI9, asking for escape equipment.

The intelligence organisation in London was making a real impact towards the end of 1941. 'Our codework grew to such an extent,' wrote Norman Crockatt, the head of MI9, 'that it was obvious a special section had to be formed to deal with the volume of work.' MI9 set up IS9(Y) (Codes and Communications) with extra staff.

The agency solved the problems of identifying and addressing coded letters and made improvements to its code-writing craftwork to keep correspondence secret from the Germans.

> With the increase of our code correspondents we took certain carefully selected relatives of prisoners of war into our confidence and asked them to help us, *wrote Crockatt*. The response was magnificent and, although it meant a great deal of trouble for them, we never received a complaint of any description. Our method was to receive from the selected relative the letter he (or she) intended to send. We would then paraphrase it, so as to include our code message, using the same wording as far as possible, and return the amended letter for copying. The amended letter was then returned to us for checking and despatch. This system and our own methods of sending code letters from fictitious people enabled us to cover all our correspondents satisfactorily.

Crockatt assumed that the German censors used the same system as the British censors, whereby each prisoner's letters were checked against his previous mail.

> We were very careful, therefore, to have continuity in the text of our fictitious letters, so that the German Censor responsible for examining the mail of an individual prisoner of war would see that the style and contents were constant and unvaried.
>
> Everything possible was done by us to avoid suspicion being cast on the genuineness of one of our letters. This made every code letter a most exacting and painstaking job, but it was essential for the sake of security. We do not know of a single case where any fictitious code letter emanating from IS9 (Y) was ever suspected by the Germans and our ex-prisoners-of-war correspondents, whom we have interviewed on their return, are unanimous in their opinion that the enemy had never suspected code messages in any of our letters. They suspected that information was being received from England, but they did not know by what means.

Bracken would not receive a carefully crafted reply from MI9 to his plea for help: while the tunnel was making good progress, reaching more than sixty feet from Bushell's barrack, the prisoners discovered that they were to be moved again.

The news coincided with a surprise visit by diplomats from the American Embassy in Berlin. 'We were able to sneak them a written statement of our complaints and the many violations of the Geneva Convention,' wrote Flying Officer Michael Roth, according to Rollings, in his book, *Wire and Worse*. Very briefly, there was an improvement in conditions, with a promise of Red Cross parcels. At almost the same moment, however, Wachtmeister told the RAF prisoners that they would be sent to Oflag VIB at Warburg in central Germany.

It left enough time for one major confrontation between the British airmen and the repressive German regime.

Wachtmeister and his gang didn't let us go without a 'last squeeze', however, *recorded Michael Roth*. On 7 October they called a special *Appell* with orders that we were to bring all our blankets on parade with us. At pistol-point they then took two blankets away from all who had two. They insisted that we'd been issued with two blankets, but the fact is they'd only issued one blanket per man in the first place, and the ones they took belonging to us were clearly Red Cross issue from Geneva.

Our Wing Commander – not having himself an extra blanket – told us to give up our blankets without making a 'fuss'. Asinine creature. Squadron Leader Roger Bushell, a great goon-hater and superb linguist, got into a terrific shouting match with Wachtmeister's loathsome adjutant, who yelled out that all Englishmen were liars and told 70,000 lies. Bushell replied we were not liars and demanded that the adjutant produce the papers we had signed on our arrival for the original issue of one blanket per man. The adjutant refused. I believe that some kriegies forestalled the adjutant's plan by tearing a single blanket in half, folding it, and then handing in two halves as two whole blankets. It was a very unpleasant fracas, and our hatred for everything German became written on our faces.

Bushell was ready for the move; he had another escape in mind. He had teamed up with Flying Officer Jaroslav Zafouk, who had served in the Czechoslovak air force, but left his homeland after the German occupation and joined the RAF. He had been shot down over Hamburg in July 1941.

In his imperfect English, Zafouk gave a graphic account of what happened next in a letter to Ben Bushell, dated 12 November 1946.

As you can imagine, every one of the prisoners tried to escape and get back to England. The same was true with Roger and me and that's how we met and made friends, he wrote. *I was a new prisoner comparing to Roger . . . and I did not know and did not have things Roger had, which one decidedly needed in order to make one's escape a success. Well, Roger managed to get some German money and all sorts of things necessary for escape; [while] I had a good plan for escaping route, which seemed to both of us the best one.*

The two men decided to share all their resources and make the break together at the first opportunity.

We did not have to wait long. We got known that the Germans are going to move the whole camp and transport all of us by train to 'somewhere in Germany'. Roger and me got busy and we managed to make some sort of civilian clothes out of blankets, one of us using from naval uniform trousers, the other the jacket. Both of us looked more like two masqueraders than anything else. But we had no choice, we chosed rather this than to get out in a uniform.

The day came. Up to now we were quite short of food but we still managed to save a bit to take with us as our iron reserve. Roger had some German food coupons, which he got out of the German guard in the camp for some cigarettes, but we did not know what it is going to be like outside the barbed wire and maybe we shall not be able to use them. The Germans put us 30 in one cattle truck with two guards and we were ready for move and escape too.

The train started at about 9 o'clock PM. It was quite dark inside and we took out saws and started sawing the board on one end of the truck. Of this team there were another four boys and everybody took his part. After about an hour and a half of sawing we managed to loosen the board and took it inside. The first party, consisting of two people, was to go. It was past eleven. They managed to get out on one of the few stops our train made and Roger and me were the next.

Similar activity was going on in other trucks – and it was a dangerous undertaking. One man died when he mistimed his exit and went under the wheels of the truck.

Round about midnight the train came to a large goods station where it slowed down a bit and we decided to go, wrote Zafouk. *We crawled out of the hole and after having a look right and left, we jumped. After we got to our feet, both of us ran across about three rails and hid underneath a stationary train, waiting till our train passes and to see whether it is all clear for us to get up and dash for freedom.*

According to hearsay, the guards in the truck were court-martialled and sent to the Eastern Front, which almost amounted to a death sentence.

Everything seemed quiet, wrote Zafouk, *so we got up, ran back again across the rails, jumped the fence and stood on a road. Then we went into a field and layed down. After we rested from the excitement we just came through, we changed into our home-made civi-clothes and dug the uniform. We stayed in the field till the day broke out. Then we found in the vicinity a stream, where we washed ourselves and made ready for our next move.*

From now on everything went according to our plan we made, that is to go by train to the Czech border, to find my brother who would help us across, then to take the train again, to get to Prague, to get in connection with Czech underground people, who would help us to get either to Switzerland or to some place, other neutral country from where it would be only easy to get back to England again . . .

We did not know the name of the place we jumped out of the train, but we knew roughly that we are somewhere near Hanover, we went to the station and Roger bought two tickets for Hanover. We were rather lucky and did not have to wait too long for the train. It arrived in about half an hour, we got in, and in another 50 minutes we were in the main Hanover station.

There were plenty of people, mainly soldiers and all sorts of different uniforms. We tried to look like two foreign workmen. We succeeded to get out of the platform without any harm and went to gain some information about our next train to Dresden. We just missed one and we had to wait for the next one till four in the afternoon. Till then we tried to deal somehow with the spare time. We went to the restaurant and had lunch, in the station building, there was plenty of people and soldiers again.

We did not stay there longer than to finish the meal and went out into the streets. There we found an open cinema, so we bought tickets and went in, in order to hide ourselves, till comes the time for us to go and catch the train for Dresden. Then we went back to the station, bought tickets and looking out for the control of the Germans (the Germans used to control from time to time the identity cards of people who were travelling on the train, either on the station or during the travel of the train), we got luckily on the train.

The two men had no papers. They were remarkably fortunate to have travelled so far.

The train was not overcrowded, wrote Zafouk, and there was no control, so we got round about 9pm to Dresden. From there we took a slow train at about midnight to Brodenbach, this place was primely in Czechoslovakia, but after the occupation in 1939 the border was moved beyond this town. There we bought tickets to another border town called Bilwa. There we got out of the train about four in the morning and as I know this region very well, we took the shortest way to my brother's place, about four miles from the border outside the Protectorat Bohmer und Mahren [the German Protectorate of Bohemia and Moravia].

We still had to cross the border and that's where I hoped my brother still will be there and give us some sort of help, which he really did. Well, from the time we got out of the train, we walked about two-and-a-half hours till we got to the village where my brother stayed. He had a farmhouse there and about ten months later the Germans made him to leave it because he was a Czech and to go behind the border into Protectorate. Lucky for us he was at home and he was the first and only person who saw us.

He recognised me right away and without my questioning he rushed us inside, so nobody could see us,

*because he knew immediately here comes a dangerous
game, and it would be safe for neither of us if anybody
would see us with him. He gave us plenty to eat as we were
quite hungry and made us rest for the day.*

*Meanwhile he went out and found us a man who would
take us during the night across the border. Behind the
border is a town called Louny and from there we were to
take a train at 1.30am to Prague. The guide came to fetch us
at about 11pm. My brother gave us proper civilian clothes
so we would look respectably and not like two vagabonds
which we really looked like before. We crossed the border
safely and got to the station, bought tickets (my brother
provided us with some money) and at about six o'clock we
arrived in Prague.*

Bushell and Zafouk disembarked at the city's main railway
station, Hlavní Nádraží, which would have been starting to fill up
even at six in the morning. It is likely to have been Friday, 10
October 1941.

Barely four months after the escape from Dulag Luft, Bushell
was a free man again. He must have been filled with hope as he
walked through the Czech station, still one of the finest examples
of Art Nouveau architecture in central Europe, and out through
the Fantova Kavárna, with its grilled ticket booths, cafés and shops.
Perhaps drawing on a cigarette, perhaps even allowing himself
what his sister Lis would have described as a 'brief, fat chuckle', he
would have walked past the magnificently decorated walls, which
were painted a rich ochre, yellow and light blue, and through colonnaded passages. He would have noticed the figures of animals,
floral motifs and heraldry, and the semi-erotic marble sculptures
looking up at the domed ceiling. He might even have noticed the
time on the great clock hanging below a sign that says 'Praha'.

On the street outside, he would have seen the turrets that
flanked the building's central section, which rest on the shoulders
of two, giant nude youths (and caused controversy at one time).

189

He would have strode out onto Wilsonova, the great boulevard named after the American president who delivered the Treaty of Versailles, which led to the founding of the Czechoslovak state after the First World War.

At that moment, the Czech capital must have seemed like an El Dorado to the ebullient, cultured Bushell, who had travelled hundreds of miles unchallenged in just 48 hours. Unbeknown to Bushell, another man had arrived in Prague just a few days before him: Reinhard Heydrich.

15

Reinhard Heydrich

By any standard, Reinhard Tristan Eugen Heydrich was an extreme Nazi. He was born into a musical family in the city of Halle, where his father, Bruno, aspired to be a composer, and his mother, Elizabeth, taught piano. The family ran a music school, which thrived in the 1920s. The young Heydrich played the violin and was good at sport.

At the age of fifteen, Reinhard joined the *Freikorps*, the group of former soldiers on the paramilitary right who were bent on opposing revolution and restoring order. In 1922, aged eighteen, he joined the navy, a bastion of German military ambition in the years immediately following Germany's defeat in the First World War.

After six years at sea, Heydrich was promoted to first lieutenant and transferred to the communications section of the naval staff. But in a service that imposed a rigorous code of personal behaviour, he was court-martialled and dismissed in 1931 for proposing to his future wife, Lina von Osten, while conducting an affair with another woman. Unfortunately for Heydrich, the other woman was the daughter of a senior naval officer. The incident fostered in him a distrust of the German officer class.

Von Osten was an early supporter of the Nazis and urged Heydrich to apply for a job in Heinrich Himmler's fledgeling SS, the black-uniformed paramilitary organisation that provided personal security for Hitler and which would go on to bear responsibility for some of the greatest atrocities in human history.

Himmler was looking for an intelligence chief. Heydrich, a great fan of detective novels, claimed to have been involved with

191

intelligence work for the navy and outlined a plan for the organisation of a new intelligence service, the SD. He got the job.

Distinctly Nordic, Heydrich was tall, athletic and blond with high cheek bones, almost the opposite of Himmler and an exemplar of the Nazis' Aryan ideal. He was an educated man who was driven by demons that demanded revenge for Germany's defeat in the First World War; murderous satisfaction for his anti-Semitism; and a reckoning with a German officer class that, he believed, had turned its back on him as a young man.

Heydrich liked to give the impression that he was an aesthete who led a virtuous life; a man who exercised twice a day, ate sparingly, did not smoke or drink, at least in public, and was a loyal husband and father. In private, however, he was a binge drinker who had a voracious appetite for aggressive sexual encounters with prostitutes.

Drawing on his public image – rather than that witnessed in the brothels of Europe – Heydrich laid down the rules of recruitment for the SS. He ensured that a majority of his senior officers were from middle-class backgrounds similar to his own: he wanted graduates with ideas; he was not interested in promoting thugs.

Working for Himmler, Heydrich found enemies of the Nazi state where there were none, and created terror where there was no need, to accumulate power for himself and extend the influence of the SS.

He organised the murder of Ernst Röhm, the leader of the SA, the Nazi storm-troopers, and his leading lieutenants during the 'Night of the Long Knives' in April 1934. Rohm's 'brownshirts' had secured the streets for the Nazis during their battles for power, but his thugs had become an embarrassment to Hitler. The killings cleared the way for the unfettered rise of the SS, which had been subordinate to the SA. Shot by firing squad, Röhm had been godfather to Heydrich's first child.

Heydrich also orchestrated *Kristallnacht* – the 'Night of Broken Glass' – when 'spontaneous' attacks on Germany's Jewish community, its businesses and synagogues, occurred across the country in November 1938. The world was stunned and appalled.

By the time he was thirty-eight – just six years older than Bushell – Heydrich controlled much of the Nazi terror machine: the SS security service, the secret police known as the Gestapo, and the criminal police known as the Kripo. Thomas Mann, the German author who had been awarded the Nobel Prize for Literature but who had fled to the United States, called him the 'Hangman'.

In Russia, Heydrich was responsible for the killing squads known as the *Einsatzgruppen*, which were murdering tens of thousands of people. 'Himmler, Heydrich and other senior SS officers frequently visited their men in the field and their inspection tours usually preceded or coincided with an increase in the number of atrocities,' wrote the historian, Robert Gerwarth. 'Himmler and Heydrich's mere presence appears to have led to an upsurge in the mass murders of Jewish civilians in the formerly Soviet-occupied territories. By approving what had happened already and by encouraging their men to show more initiative, they made a contribution to the swift escalation of mass murder.'

Heydrich's imprint was also on plans for the Holocaust, the 'Final Solution' of the Jews, which would be confirmed in January 1942 at a conference chaired by Heydrich in the Berlin suburb of Wannsee.

In dealing with the Czechs, Hitler faced a number of dilemmas that differed from those presented by the peoples of the other conquered countries of central and eastern Europe. The Czechs were regarded as Germanic rather than Slav, while the Protectorate, inhabited by more than 7 million people, was seen as a natural part of Greater Germany that, in due time, would be incorporated in the Third Reich.

At a practical level, the Czechs had developed a first-class arms industry, which was regarded as being essential to the German war effort. The population also included thousands of highly trained engineers. Both elements needed to be kept working at the highest pitch.

From a military perspective, the Nazis could not allow any form of effective resistance to grow in Bohemia and Moravia. As the *Wehrmacht* advanced in Russia after the launch of Operation Barbarossa in June 1941, through eastern Poland, the Baltic states, Belorussia and Ukraine, it became increasingly dependent on supply lines in central Europe.

Since the German occupation of Bohemia and Moravia, the regime in Prague had been run by Konstantin von Neurath, a former German ambassador to Britain who was not seen as being close to the Nazis. In 1939, it was regarded as a relatively liberal regime, which aimed to give the Czechs a semblance of independence. The main purpose was to keep the people at work and to maintain arms production. The majority of Czechs tried to get on with their lives.

After the advent of war in September 1939, von Neurath took harsher measures, but disparate resistance groups unified under a central leadership, while sports associations such as Sokol provided new recruits. Once Russia had been invaded, resistance in Prague intensified: the distribution of anti-Nazi pamphlets became widespread; strikes threatened output in the arms factories; communists joined the fight; the official press was boycotted. The railways were targeted, too, while sabotage increased and attacks on German soldiers rose dramatically.

As challenges to German rule continued to increase, Hitler acted. On 28 September 1941 – just before Roger Bushell left Lübeck – Hitler dismissed von Neurath and made Heydrich acting Reich Protector of Bohemia and Moravia, with unlimited powers.

Heydrich had pressed for the most draconian measures to be taken against any opposition in the Occupied lands, and he now had free rein to carry out murder and torture on whatever scale was necessary to deal with the 'problem'. Even the Führer described Heydrich as a man with an 'iron heart'.

The impact of his appointment was immediate. Eight days before Bushell and Zafouk arrived in Prague, Heydrich told Nazi party officials gathered at the Czernin Palace that the restoration of order was a ruthless mission for the SS. In a chilling speech, delivered in secret, he told his audience: 'I must unambiguously and with unflinching hardness bring the citizens of this country, Czech or otherwise, to the understanding that there is no avoiding the fact they are members of the Reich and as such they owe allegiance to the Reich ... this is a task of priority required by the war. I must have peace of mind that every Czech worker works at his maximum for the German war effort ... this includes feeding the Czech worker, to put it frankly, so that he can do his work.'

He also addressed the issue of race, and emphasised the need for Bohemia and Moravia to be settled by people of German stock.

We have all kinds of people here, *he said*. Some of them are showing racial quality and good judgment. It's going to be simple to work on them – we can Germanise them. On the other hand, we have racially inferior elements and, what's worse, they demonstrate wrong judgment. These we must get out. There is a lot of space eastwards.

Between these two extremes, there are those in the middle that we have to examine thoroughly. We have racially inferior people but with good judgment, then we have racially unacceptable people with bad judgment. As to the first kind, we must resettle them in the Reich or somewhere else, but we have to make sure they no longer breed, because we don't care to develop them in this area ...

One group remains, though, these people are racially acceptable, but hostile in their thinking – that is the most dangerous group, because it is a racially pure class of leaders. We have to think through carefully what to do with them. We can relocate some of them into the Reich, put them in a purely German environment, and then Germanise and re-educate them. If this cannot be done, we must put them against the wall.

Heydrich took action as soon as he arrived in Prague: martial law was declared throughout Bohemia and Moravia while the

Czech prime minister, Alois Eliáš, who was known to be in contact with London, was arrested and put on trial. Heydrich established summary courts that were free to impose the harshest sentences. During the next two months, hundreds of Czechs were executed and thousands sent to concentration camps. New security sweeps uncovered dozens of illegal wireless transmitters, and radio links between the exiled Czech government in London, British intelligence and the Czech underground were severed. Meaningful resistance virtually ceased.

Heydrich's measures generated panic in London where President Beneš, leader of the Czech government in exile, feared that failure to resist Nazi rule would have serious implications for Czech independence after the war. The Special Operations Executive (SOE), the British secret service charged by Churchill with fomenting resistance inside the Occupied territories, also struggled to assert itself, particularly in Bohemia and Moravia.

Together, the Czech government in London and SOE began to plan the assassination of Heydrich, using Czech and Slovak volunteers who were already serving with British forces. The secret mission would be called Operation Anthropoid.

Plans for Anthropoid were agreed at almost the exact moment that Bushell and Zafouk arrived at Hlavní Nádraží, the main railway station.

Bohemians and Moravians were beginning to live in a state of serious nervous tension, in fear of a distrustful neighbour, a treacherous friend, a knock on the door. Everyone seemed to have a motive for betrayal even if the driving force was often self-preservation. 'There were so many spies at this time,' said Vlasta Christova, Zafouk's girlfriend, who would later become his wife.

The two fugitives also faced a change in the weather. The first snow fell in October, much earlier than usual, heralding an 'ice age' that lasted months.

In western Russia, where temperatures dropped to −40C, the weather played a major part in halting the advance of Hitler's armies on Moscow and Leningrad. Tens of thousands of unpre-

pared German troops died on the Eastern Front from hypother-
mia, malnutrition and frostbite.

The first priority for Roger Bushell and Jaroslav Zafouk was to
find shelter in Prague.

'I went to see a friend of mine, who let us stay in his lodging for
about four days,' wrote Zafouk in his letter to Ben Bushell after
the war. The man who helped them lived with his mother, but
managed to find them a single room with a separate entrance
elsewhere.

*My brother provided food for us. He came the next day
with full suitcase of it. We settled down after few days and
got used to the situation. Roger mainly stayed at home,
because we found it rather dangerous for him to go out not
knowing the language and I used to do the necessary
shopping. Meanwhile, I tried to get in touch with the
underground people.*

*My married cousin's husband worked on this
[underground] line, so I went to see her and talked about
the possibilities of us getting out. I was promised help from
him, but before he could really do something for us, the
Gestapo got hold of him, because they found out that he
works in the organisation and that door was closed for us
for some time.*

*After about a month, the friend of mine who gave us the
lodging asked me if we could not find for us some other
place as he had to hand over the room back to his friend
from whom he had borrowed it for us. As we had no other
place, he took us again to his own lodging for a few days.*

*Meanwhile, I found an old acquaintance, we used to go
to school together, who offered me to take us. Well, we
moved then there. It was a flat of two rooms and kitchen.
The family was father with the son and daughter. They gave
us one room to live in.*

The father and daughter worked in the office, the son

was in the Protectorate Police, said Zafouk, whose older brother – he was one of three – and father were the only members of his family who knew about his presence in Prague. *My brother brought us food from his farmhouse and my father supplied us with necessary money from my account I had in the bank before the war.*

As the people were not very well off and we realised quite well in what kind of danger they were, in case the Gestapo would discover us, we tried to help them with food, which was very difficult to get then. We made a family of five and lived and planned together.

According to documents in the Czech National Archive in Prague, the childhood friend who took Bushell and Zafouk into the family home was Blažena Zeithammelová, a former student of fine art who was 26 at the time. Known as Blaža, she looked slightly wistful. With blonde hair tied at the back, green-grey eyes, and full lips that turned up a little, she was certainly attractive – intelligent too, but perhaps also a little mysterious.

Blaža was well connected. She was a member of Sokol, the Slav sports association linked to the underground movement, active within the Red Cross, and she also worked for the resistance – having done so almost from the moment the Germans occupied Czechoslovakia in 1939. Her offer of shelter to Bushell and Zafouk was testimony to the courage of the Zeithammel family.

16

Family at War

As Heydrich prosecuted his onslaught against the Czech resistance, Roger Bushell's fate in Prague became entwined with a romantic affair that would have profound consequences.

After more than a year as a prisoner living in increasingly difficult conditions, and several weeks as a fugitive in a strange land where he did not speak the language, it is perhaps not surprising that he should have become involved with his host, Blažena Zeithammelová. Desire seems to have run strongly on both sides. 'Blaža was a very good-looking girl,' said Vlasta Christová, Zafouk's future wife, who met her several times during the winter of 1941–42. 'Blonde, voluptuous, she was a lot of fun to talk to.'

Bushell was unlikely to have known a woman intimately for some time. Their chemistry was probably irresistible, but it was careless of them both. The story of Blaža mirrors the courage, betrayal and suffering of the Czechs under German occupation, and with it Bushell's growing awareness of the true nature of Nazi tyranny.

The Zeithammels were important: they were members of a group led by Josef Mašín, one of the 'Three Kings' – 'Tři králové' – an underground network run by former army officers who were at the heart of the Czech Home Resistance movement (UVOD). After the disbandment of Czech forces in 1939, the Three Kings – Mašín, Josef Balabán and Václav Morávek, who had all been officers in the artillery – are said to have plundered the Czech barracks at Ruzyně, removing machine guns, rifles and ammunition, and established a secret arms factory making hundreds of bombs disguised as coal briquettes. They stole documents, official papers and stamps, and smuggled people out of the Protectorate.

With Edvard Beneš, the leader of the Czech exiles, crying out for information of any kind, Mašín organised the gathering of intelligence, and relayed it to London through one of two radio transmitters known as Sparta I and Sparta II. The group even penetrated the Skoda works at Pilsen and provided information on German weaponry including, it is claimed, a blueprint for the Tiger Tank.

In Bohemia and Moravia, they sabotaged telephone lines, railway bridges and fuel depots, and attacked German soldiers. They also struck further afield: they planted explosives in Berlin, targeting the Air Ministry and Police Directorate, and attempted to kill Heinrich Himmler with an attack on the Berlin-Anhalt railway station in January 1941 (the bomb went off as planned, but Himmler's train was either diverted or late). The attacks were noted by the American broadcaster, William Shirer, in his *Berlin Diary*. At this stage of the war, the Czech Home Resistance appeared to be one of the more formidable forces among the underground organisations in Occupied Europe.

In June 1940, the Three Kings were given responsibility for liaising with a senior German intelligence officer, Paul Thummel, who had been giving the Czechs high-calibre information about military planning, including details of the invasions of Poland and Norway. Known to the British secret services by his code name, A-54, Thummel had been posted from the *Abwehr* (military intelligence) office in Dresden to Prague.

Mašín recruited men and women from across Czech society, but he relied heavily on three groups of people: former soldiers from the artillery regiments; members of Sokol, the Slav sports association; and employees of the state railway company. With roots in all three groups, the Zeithammels were natural recruits.

Otto, the father, was a sixty-one-year-old construction engineer, a technical director of Czech state railways. Wearing a pinstripe suit, a neat moustache across the full width of his lips and with his dark brown hair brushed back high on his forehead, he looked rather severe in his passport photograph. He was a widower and had looked after his son and daughter since the death of his wife, Julie Vinopalová, in the mid-1930s. Born in Germany, but essentially a child of the Austro-Hungarian Empire, he travelled widely. He had a Czechoslovak passport that allowed him to visit any country in Europe, including the Soviet Union.

His son, Otokar, was born in 1917 in a town called Devente in what had become Yugoslavia after the First World War. He had a big open face, with brown-green eyes, blond hair, and a distinctive mouth similar to that of his sister. He failed to get into the sixth grade at secondary school and volunteered for the army. A letter from the Prague police department states that he had no political or cultural affiliations. In 1941, he was a member of the token Protectorate army, based in Prague with the 1st battalion – *Regierungstruppe des Protektorats Bohmen and Mahren* – providing a ceremonial guard for Emil Hácha, the Czech president of a puppet regime that ostensibly ran the Protectorate. Until the German occupation, Otokar Zeithammel had served with the artillery in the city of Pilsen.

More than four years younger than Bushell, Blaža was born in the Prague district of Smíchov on 17 November 1914. She graduated successfully from secondary school and pursued her studies at the Academy of Fine Art, which included a visit in 1935 to galleries and studios in Yugoslavia. Although her passport applications stated that she was single, Blaža had met an artillery officer called Miloslav Kraus in 1934 and had apparently agreed to marry him. Her father, however, hesitated, because of debts that had built up while his sick wife was treated in a sanatorium. The relationship between his daughter and Kraus then faltered.

In late 1939, Blaža took part in student demonstrations against the Nazis in Prague. The student leaders were executed and universities were closed. A few months later, on 12 February 1940, she applied for a job as a clerk with the Milk and Fat Union. The police declared her to be a woman of good character – single, Roman Catholic and Aryan.

But she was also a member of Sokol, the sports association that fostered a strong Slav identity, and she had three addresses in Prague: the family flat at 1 Přístavní Street, now Strakonická 23/1564 in Smíchov; a second address at Štefánikova 15/246, which was an office of the Red Cross; and a third registered at Desk Two of the Sokol office at Vrázova 6/1163.

The Zeithammel family home was a flat on the third floor of an imposing six-storey building overlooking the Vltava river in the district of Smíchov. Built from elegant orange-grey stone, the building would have been a respectable place to live in the thirties and forties, just a couple of miles south of the Old Town in central Prague. It stands on a Y-shaped junction where two roads from central Prague meet by the banks of the Vltava. Big wooden doors, with glass panels above them, mark entrances at the front and the back, where there is a path through a yard to another major road. Inside, there is an oval stairway, with twenty broad steps separating each floor. On every level there are two flats, each with double doors. Trees surround the building on three sides. Flower pots sit on the window sills.

By the time Bushell and Zafouk arrived at the Zeithammel flat, probably in November 1941, two of the Three Kings had been caught by the Gestapo. Josef Balabán had been arrested in April; Josif Mašín had been captured after a gun battle in May, but not before alerting London to German plans for the invasion of Russia. Both men were tortured and Balabán had been executed in October. The third 'King', Václav Morávek was still in touch with the German traitor, A-54, but time was running out.

Reinhard Heydrich, who had been sent to Prague to quash resistance and keep the arms industry running smoothly, was turning the territories of Bohemia and Moravia not into an occupied state simply subjugated by the Germans, which was bad enough, but into an SS state run by gangsters for whom no rules applied. In this environment, the Czechs became increasingly suspicious of each other.

Within twenty-four hours of arriving in Prague, Heydrich had taken measures against Czech Jews in mixed marriages and against Czechs who were friends of Jews. He had closed the synagogues. Thousands of Jews had started to be moved out of Prague.

Petr Ginz, a Jewish schoolboy with foppish brown hair and rather English looks, kept a diary. On 28 November he wrote:

> The Mautners, who live on our floor, have to leave for Theresienstadt [Terezín transit camp], together with thousands of other people. Among others that are leaving is Reach, Ervin Mautner, and many others. Mr Mautner went to the Community (Jewish) to ask if it wasn't a mistake (he is over fifty years old and ill). In the later afternoon we went for a walk through town over the Charles bridge.

Then, the next day,

> . . . Mr Mautner has already been to the Community; they said it was not an error. So he has to leave for the exhibition grounds on Monday, November 1. In a month the whole Mautner family will join him.

As tragedy unfolded at this time for so many people in Prague, the Zeithammels worked hard to prevent the SS terror from enveloping their own family. They were familiar with the street-craft of the resistance and certainly instilled it in Jaroslav Zafouk, one of the two fugitives living in their midst.

Vlasta Christová had known Jaroslav, whom she called Jarka, before the war. 'He saw my picture in 1938, then told his friend, "I've got to meet her," and came to Prague,' she said in an interview filmed by Bushell's niece, Lindy Wilson, in 2007.

After the German occupation, Zafouk told her he was going to England, 'probably through Poland and Sweden' and gave her a wedding ring. He asked her to wait for him, but they lost touch.

She did not see Zafouk again until more than two years later. 'I thought I saw him in 1941,' she said. 'I was coming back from a date, and there was this man standing in a street car [tram]. He had a moustache, I looked at him, "Oh my God, it must be him," but he didn't pay any attention to me at all. I was 90 per cent sure, but I didn't want to say anything to him. I got off, but he went on. My curiosity got hold of me. I wrote to his parents, telling them I knew him before the war, asking what happened to him, asking if he is fine?'

Vlasta heard nothing for a long time, but then she received several visits from Zafouk's brother and from Otokar Zeithammel. Eventually, Otokar arranged to meet Vlasta at a café near the place where she worked. He said he had some important news. 'After half an hour in the café he changed his mind, saying it was "too light". They needed a "much darker" place,' said Vlasta. 'I went for the meeting somewhere else. It was very dark, like a blackout, and he said, "Now I'm going to tell you something. Do you promise you're not going to scream?" And then Jarka walked in.'

For a while afterwards, the couple continued to meet in the city. 'We went to café houses, took long walks, and I asked, "Where do you live?" He said, "Don't ask, you will find out eventually."'

In December, Jarka finally invited Vlasta to the flat in Smíchov. 'He said, "We're having party where we live so we would like your mother and you to come." He said there would be another couple: Otokar's sister, and her "boyfriend". I asked, "What boy? Who's the boyfriend?" and Jaroslav said he was okay. "He's a Swiss friend, you'll meet him."'

When Blaža and her so-called boyfriend walked into the room, they were all introduced. 'He couldn't obviously speak Czech,' said Vlasta, 'but he spoke broken German. Most of our conversation was in German. Everything was going fine, the evening was progressing very nicely, but I could see him watching me – there was drinking, everyone was getting merrier. All of a sudden, he charged across the room, sat down next to me, and said, "So, what did they tell you about me?" I told him that he was a Swiss who used to ski with Jarka before the war. He started to imitate a shot-down plane. "I am not Swiss," he said. "I am British; I am RAF." And that's how I found out the whole story, what they were doing there. They were trying to get back to England. They had already tried twice. That was Roger, Roger Bushell – a very sweet man.'

Although Vlasta had not previously been invited to the flat in Smíchov – presumably until Jarka was confident that he could trust her completely – Bushell's decision to reveal his true identity to her at this first meeting revealed an astonishing lack of judgment. Perhaps his impetuosity had been fuelled by alcohol.

Bushell had rarely shown restraint. While with 601 Squadron, a senior officer is reported to have quipped: 'The trouble with Bushell is he's always hiding his light under himself.' Sitting in the flat in Smíchov, he wasn't going to be passed off as a neutral Swiss, however reckless it might have been to assert that he was British and RAF to boot. It was typical of him.

So was his decision to have an affair with Blaža. It was another example of Bushell's crushing need for a woman's love. He still seemed unable to make wise decisions about the suitability of the women in his life, their motives and circumstances. Perhaps his mother's all-embracing affection had impaired his judgment. Time and again there was a price to pay, whether it was the call to South Africa after his difficulties with women and money; the outright hostility of an aristocrat who circled the wagons to fend off Bushell's interest in his daughter; or the void apparently left by Peggy Hamilton.

Shortly before Christmas 1941, as the German armies retreated before Moscow and Hitler declared war on the United States after the Japanese attack on the American fleet at Pearl Harbor, Roger Bushell and Blažena Zeithammelová became lovers.

Vlasta did not learn about the affair until Jaroslav told her after the war. 'I got rather mad,' said Vlasta. 'I asked him, "Why didn't you tell me? I could have been more observant." He didn't want to talk about it – "It was their affair" – but I don't think he really agreed with it because he felt Blaža was playing a no-good game. He knew Roger would never have married her.'

But, even in hindsight, Vlasta felt there was an inevitability about Roger and Blaža's relationship. 'It was natural, when you think of it, two people together day after day for six months, so it happened . . . Blaža looking so good, you know, they got involved together, there was a war going on and lots of things happen in war which normally probably wouldn't happen . . . How could they help it? He was a man . . . It was natural.'

The twenty-seven-year-old sculptress who had embraced the resistance and given the fugitives shelter even took Bushell out into the city of Prague. 'They seemed pretty relaxed together,' said Vlasta, 'but I never thought anything serious was going on; they never acted like some lovers do. I never saw them kiss.'

Only a guess can be made at their daily routine, but it seems Blaža went to work at the Milk and Fat Union, bought Bushell cigarettes and taught him Czech. According to documents in the national achive in Prague, the Zeithammels were involved with several resistance cells, each with their own code name.

It is not clear whether Bushell became involved with the Czech resistance or whether he used his knowledge of MI9 codes to contact London, which Blaža might have been able to arrange through her contacts with Home Resistance. Josef Mašín's group had specialised in intelligence and communications with London.

Vlasta was unsure about his movements: she rarely saw him when she brought food to the flat in Smíchov. 'I don't know what he did all day. He told me he read, listened to the radio, but whatever he did, I don't know.'

Bushell was not confined to the Zeithammels' flat. He spoke German and was learning Czech, which he probably picked up quickly, bearing in mind the ease with which he learnt languages. According to Vlasta, he went for walks with Zafouk, and got lost on at least one occasion. He had a ration card and Czech papers supplied by a man called Sigmund Neudorfer. He is also known to have spent several days with another couple, Vojtěch Přidal and his wife, Ludmila, at their flat in Dušková, another road in Smíchov.

Born in 1909, a year before the British fugitive, Přidal was a highly qualified teacher. The Přidals had a son, Stanislav, who was just a few months old. Ludmila was registered at the same addresses as Blaža for the Red Cross and for membership of Sokol.

In his letter to Bushell's parents on 12 November 1946, Zafouk wrote:

After three months of staying with them [the Zeithammels], Roger and me offered them that we shall change the place, as they lived in the danger for long enough by now, but we were refused and they did not want us to leave their place, saying their flat is quite safe.

He continued: *The daughter knew some people who worked in the underground organisation, and they tried to find some way for us. Once, we actually got on our way to Turkey, but were sent back from the Slovakian border, because the chain of people who were to take us over, was broken by Gestapo. It was just before Christmas 1941. We came back to the family and there we waited for the next word go, which we were to get from the organisation. But that never came.*

Zafouk did not mention Bushell's relationship with Blažena in his letter to Bushell's parents after the war.

With a distance of more than seventy years, it might seem as though Bushell was in no hurry to leave Prague. Vlasta's testimony suggests he agitated for a way out, but it was not a straightforward issue. Heydrich's crackdown on Czech resistance meant that all movement was closely monitored, while a harsh winter made Bushell and Zafouk's predicament even more difficult.

Bushell told Wings Day that they had been waiting for better weather.

Day, the man who had been Senior British Officer at Dulag Luft, probably got to know Bushell better than anyone else over the course of the war: he also wrote to Roger's parents about the months that their son spent in the Czech capital. In his letter, dated 15 July 1945, Day said:

> *The reason Roger remained in Prague was that he hoped to get in touch with some kind of organisation, which could get him out of German occupied territory; also he wished to wait for summer before he hazarded a journey on his own account. I understood that he and his companion moved about in Prague quite freely and led a fairly normal existence.*

Again, there is no mention of the relationship with Blažena, which was at the heart of everything that happened to Bushell in Prague. But it is unsurprising that the affair was never mentioned to Bushell's parents – it would not have cast him in a particularly honourable light, and Day is unlikely to have wanted to add to the burdens of the Bushell family after the war – or, perhaps, Roger just never told Day about his Czech lover.

On the evening of 28 December 1941, events were set in motion hundreds of miles away that would have a profound effect on the lives of Roger Bushell and Blažena Zeithammelová. Two men, one a Czech called Jan Kubiš, the other a Slovak called Jozef Gabčik, almost certainly sat in the room where Bushell had celebrated his arrival as the commander of No. 92 Squadron in 1939.

Tangmere Cottage had been taken over by the Special Operations Executive (known to many as the Ministry of Ungentlemanly Warfare) just a few months after Bushell was shot down in 1940. Surrounded by trees and a high garden wall, the quaint red-brick cottage, with small white window frames and tidy lawns, was a discreet rendezvous, the point of departure for many agents heading for Occupied Europe.

Kubiš, with his kind, gentle face, and Gabčik, rough at the edges, but short and powerful, had volunteered for the most momentous mission ever undertaken by British secret services. Under the direction of Edvard Beneš's government-in-exile, the two men set out to kill Reinhard Heydrich.

A few hundred yards from the cottage, sitting on the runway at Tangmere aerodrome, was a four-engine Halifax bomber of No. 138 Special Duties Squadron. In the cockpit was Flight Lieutenant Ron Hockey, an experienced pilot who would make the perilous round trip to Czechoslovakia.

They took off from Tangmere at 10 p.m. On board the Halifax were nine agents: two communications teams known as Silver A and Silver B with new transmitters, and Gabčik and Kubiš.

For Hockey, the mission involved finding three different drop zones in difficult conditions. Snow was falling over Bohemia and Moravia, and visibility was poor. Hockey flew on in spite of night-fighter attacks. 'He was forced lower and lower by the weather,' reported the *Daily Telegraph* some years later, 'and obliged to make blind drops.'

The appalling weather had an immediate impact on the under-cover mission. Gabčik and Kubiš jumped from just 500 feet, land-ing near the village of Nehvizdy, east of Prague, rather than east of Pilsen in the west of the country, where their Czech contacts lived. Gabčik injured his ankle, but the Czech agents were helped by two local men, one a gamekeeper who found their parachutes and tracked them down in a quarry, and the local miller who was a member of the resistance. The two men had been incredibly fortunate.

Travelling with false papers that identified Gabčik as a lock-smith called Zedeněk Vyskočil, and Kubiš as a labourer called Otto Strnad, the two men reached Prague early in the new year.

According to Gerwarth, in *Hitler's Hangman*, they spent the next five months moving among various safe houses provided by the UVOD, the Home Resistance movement, and walking and cycling around Prague, looking for the right place to attack Heydrich.

Like Bushell, the two agents were careless. Both men broke the rules of secrecy laid down during their training in Britain by starting affairs with women they met through the families that helped them. They also left a trail that the Gestapo would later follow. But luck remained with them as they pursued their quarry, who was, in fact, aware of their presence.

Unbeknown to Gabčik and Kubiš, officers from *Flugmeldedienst* – the Luftwaffe monitoring service – had tracked Hockey's Halifax bomber as it entered Czech airspace and followed the descent of the parachutists. In his capacity as the acting Reich protector of Bohemia and Moravia, Heydrich was alerted.

The Germans continued their crackdown on the resistance. Paul Thummel, the German traitor known as A-54, was arrested on 20 March 1942. Václav Morávek, the last of the 'Three Kings', whose credo had been 'I believe in God and my pistols', died on 21 March; he shot himself rather than be captured after a gun battle with the Gestapo. He had remained in touch with Thummel and maintained contact with London while taunting the Gestapo officers who were looking for him.

In another move intended to hit the Czech underground, the Germans banned Sokol, the Slav sports association.

With a growing number of resistance families involved in preparations for the attack on Heydrich, word spread, and Home Resistance urged London to abandon Operation Anthropoid because of fears over the scale of reprisals. On 12 May, the Gestapo intercepted a warning transmitted by Silver A, one of the communications groups dropped on the same night as Gabčik and Kubiš:

```
From the preparations that Ota and Zdenek are
working on and the place where it is happening, we
guess, despite their silence, that they're
```

preparing to assassinate H. This assassination
would not help the allies and would bring immense
consequences upon our nation . . . we ask you to
give an order through SILVER not to carry out the
assassination. There is a danger of delay, issue
the order immediately. If necessary, for
international reasons, assassinate a local
Quisling [traitor] . . . the first choice would be
EM [Emanuel Moravec, the education minister].

Fears had grown in the Jewish community. On 13 April, the entry in Petr Ginz's diary reads:

> They announced the new transport. And it's all names with Lov-, Low-, Lev-, and so on. So we are worried about the Levituses, because I heard they are now taking mainly people with more property. I dropped by there in the afternoon, aunt was at the doctor's to have her bandages taken off, they are not leaving.

Another entry, on 16 April, states:

> We exercised in shirts, that's why we had to have the stars sewn on to them, too. So I had three stars on top of one another: on my overcoat, my coat and my shirt.

And on 17 May:

> Our teacher Mr Sommer is leaving with the transport for Theresienstadt [concentration camp].

For Bushell and Zafouk, Prague became an increasingly difficult place to live in the late spring of 1942. If ever there was a moment to lie low in the flat, perhaps to wait for an opportunity to get out of the Protectorate to Switzerland or Turkey, or to join the escape lines in France later in the year, this was it. Whatever popular literature might have said in the aftermath of the Second World War about evaders jumping on and off trains seemingly at will, the reality often involved a lot of hanging about, hours of boredom, and friction with the families who sheltered them.

Blažena Zeithammelová might have been aware of the plot to kill Heydrich and the implications it had for the people of the Protectorate, perhaps even her own family. One Czech source suggests that the Zeithammels knew the Khodols, one of the families sheltering Gabčik and Kubiš. In the Zeithammel apartment, there was certainly friction. According to Vlasta Christová, Blaža had asked Bushell for a promise that he would marry her after the war: she wanted some form of commitment that gave her a vision of the future. He refused.

In an interview with Bushell's niece, the film-maker Lindy Wilson, Vlasta maintained that Bushell told Blaža that he was 'committed to a woman in England', even though he was sleeping with his Czech hostess. He did not name the woman in question. It is a sign of his passion and his honesty, but also perhaps of his myopia, that he could not accommodate Blaža's wishes at this time.

Zafouk's wife later reflected on Blaža's position. 'She must have got so angry,' said Vlasta, 'because she truly believed this was going to be a nice happy marriage after the war . . . Roger must have been really firm about telling her, he didn't give her any hope whatever. So after that she probably thought it's no good anyway, so what's the saying? – "There's no fury like a woman scorned".' Roger's mother, Dorothe, writing in her journal about Roger's childhood, had noted that his honesty would at times get him into trouble – and, once again, the point was proved.

17

Love and Betrayal

Blažena Zeithammelová turned away and, in her distress, sought out her former boyfriend. Unbeknown to her, though, Miloslav Kraus had joined a Czech fascist organisation and become an informer, answering directly to the deputy head of the SD, the SS intelligence service.

Blaža told Kraus about the two airmen sheltering in the family apartment – the 'two birdies', as she called them – according to papers in the Czech National Archive in Prague, immediately endangering the fugitives she had fought so hard to protect during the previous six months.

When she had first met Kraus, at a party in the Vinohrady district of Prague in 1933, the nineteen-year-old Blaža had been studying sculpture at an arts-industrial high school before going to university. Kraus, eleven years older, was a soldier, serving with the artillery. He probably knew her brother. Born on 3 February 1902, Miloslav Kraus graduated at the age of twenty from the army academy at Hranice and then went to the artillery school. He was promoted to the rank of captain in 1936.

A black and white photograph taken after his graduation in 1922 portrays a rather delicate, even effeminate man. He had a high, sloping forehead, his brown hair brushed back, blue eyes, a classic aquiline nose and pursed lips. The couple were never officially engaged, but they wrote to each other and she apparently visited him often.

In 1937, with the Germans threatening the country, Kraus is said to have briefed Blaža about the ground rules of intelligence work. After the German occupation in 1939, Blaža told Kraus she was joining the underground movement. She introduced him to some of her colleagues in the resistance, or '*maffia*' as it was known in Prague, after the student demonstrations in November of that year.

Kraus tried to give the impression that he was working for the British, but he had already changed sides. At a bar frequented by Czech fascists in Louny, a small town on the Ohre river, north-west of Prague, he was persuaded by a man called Bedřich Husnik to join 'the Flag', an organisation synonymous with collaboration.

It is not known what Blaža was seeking from Kraus when she told him about Bushell and Zafouk: simply a shoulder to cry on, or perhaps help in trying to move the two fugitives. But it seems very unlikely that she would have done so had she known that her actions would also put at certain risk the lives of her father, brother and several friends, not to mention colleagues in the resistance.

As the historian M. R. D. Foot told Bushell's niece, Lindy Wilson, when asked about Bushell's predicament in Prague:

> It was against the law to be in the resistance and the penalty was a bullet in the back of the neck straight away or to be sent to a concentration camp and be worked to death . . . not only for you, but for all your family as well. You put not only yourself but all your relatives at risk if you went with the resistance.

Blaža would have known this, but what she seems to have been unaware of was her former boyfriend's change of allegiance.

From the moment she confided in Kraus, events moved quickly.

The harsh winter, one of the coldest of the twentieth century, had given way to a vibrant spring. Trees lining the riverbank were in bloom and the early mist rising off the Vltava had long gone by nine o'clock on the morning of Tuesday, 19 May 1942.

Roger Bushell was lying in bed when five Gestapo agents arrived at the Zeithammels' flat. He was probably smoking a Czech cigarette, casting a grey haze over the bright sunshine filling the lead-squared window frames. Jaroslav Zafouk was in the same bedroom.

One of the German police officers rang the doorbell repeatedly. When no one answered the big double door on the third floor, two Gestapo agents smashed it down – they carried long-handled hammers with iron heads weighing several pounds.

After more than six months living safely and undisturbed in the flat, this violent disturbance must have been shocking for Bushell and Zafouk. They had nowhere to hide. The Gestapo knew exactly who was inside the flat and where they would find them: they had been given very precise information.

Zafouk described the moment of their arrest in his letter to Ben Bushell:

> *Someone rang very violently the bell at the door and, as we were alone, Roger and me, nobody went to open and after little while we heard the front being forced and five men rushed into the flat. It was Gestapo. We were handcuffed and after a search we were taken to Gestapo headquarters in Prague.*

Vlasta, who heard the story second-hand from her husband after the war, was, nevertheless, a little more graphic. 'Jarka told me Roger got very angry at the Gestapo man and I think he hit him, so Roger was beaten quite a bit with his hot temper, and Jarka, he got more than he told me. He didn't like talking about it.'

The two Allied airmen were told to dress. Bushell put on a grey civilian suit given to him by Otto Zeithammel, Blaža's father, which he would use again later in the war. The two men were handcuffed and led outside.

As he was driven towards the Petschek Palace – Gestapo headquarters – on that Tuesday morning, sitting in the second row of a black Mercedes 260D limousine, Bushell probably had some sense of foreboding. The Mercedes, with its wood-lined tailboards and slit rear window, looked like something out of a Hollywood gangster movie.

Bushell clearly talked about his arrest to Wings Day.

> They were taken to the police headquarters, *wrote Day after the war,* where they found some of the families whom they knew, also under arrest. So I think it probable that an informer gave them away. Roger went through a very severe interrogation though he was not physically touched, however his companion was beaten up. Roger told me that the Gestapo seemed to think that he was a British Secret Service agent and that between the time of his escape and the time of his re-arrest he had been back in London and had recently returned to Czechoslovakia where he had been dropped by parachute in order to help foment and insurrection [sic].

Petschek Palace was a former Jewish bank at the top of Wenceslas Square, about three miles from the Zeithammels' flat in Smíchov on the opposite side of the Vltava river. The sombre and imposing five-storey building made from grey-black stone, which was taken over by the Gestapo in the summer of 1939, smacks of power and fear, and was well-suited to the mission of the Nazi secret police.

For the British airman, this was a defining moment in his life. Bushell had challenged established power wherever he found it during the previous twenty years of his life – whether it was the prefects in his house at Wellington; the porters at Pembroke College, Cambridge; the rules of skiing; the traditions of legal custom; the authority of the RAF; or, indeed, his father. As his sister Lis said years later, 'Being hidebound by regulations were [sic] not his scene at all. He cocked a snook at authority.'

All this was about to change. Bushell was looking at the real face of fascism for the first time.

Prisoners were taken into the basement of Petschek Palace by a back entrance and seated on wooden benches in a room they called the 'cinema' – which had nothing in common with the Odeon in Leicester Square. The 'cinema' was a waiting room for interrogation and torture, where suspects were forced to stare at a white wall. Pacing down the side of the room, an SS guard in black held a stick that he used to beat anyone whose gaze left the white wall.

While initially questioned in offices on the floors above, suspects were often returned to the basement, where further ordeals awaited them. The cells, which were approximately 12ft high, 8ft long and 4ft wide, had once been used as vaults for corporate clients of Mr Petschek's bank. Bolted behind solid brown doors with no window in them, the cells were lit by two bright circular lamps attached to the top of one wall, and contained a hard wooden bed. The only relief for a prisoner came from the privacy to be found in solitude. But the basement to this building also had a torture chamber, complete with a 'dentist's chair'. Clubs, sticks and whips were available to the Gestapo, as well as many other instruments of pain. Among the most destructive was a tunic that looked like a life jacket. Apparently innocuous on the outside, it was lined with metal strips that allowed the torturer to inflict grave internal damage without causing any sign of injury on the surface of the body.

Bushell underwent a long interrogation at the hands of a man called Bauer. Two years later, one of the 'Great Escapers' would be questioned by the same Gestapo officer. Like Zafouk, Flying Officer Ivo Tonder was Czech. He told British investigators after the war that Bauer was a tall, thin man with light blond hair who was probably in his mid- to late forties. 'There was also present a girl typist and an interpreter because Bauer spoke only German,' said Tonder. 'The interpreter was tall, slim and smartly dressed . . . there was a guard in a civilian suit beside me. The commissar [Bauer] had my military papers . . . I refused to answer any questions about my activities in England. Bauer at one point grew extremely angry and shouted that he would compel me to answer. At this stage he was foaming at the mouth but then calmed down, produced cigarettes and handed them round to everyone, including me. No violence was used against me. I think this was because when it seemed likely that violence would be used, I reminded them that I was a British prisoner of war. The interrogation lasted from 0900 hours to 1945 hours.'

Asked about Bushell's interrogation, the historian of M19, M. R. D. Foot, said: 'There was one rule about being interrogated, which was universal and which Roger will have picked up and applied, particularly in the secret services – you say nothing at all for the first 48 hours to give everyone who was in touch with you a chance to scarper.'

It is not known whether Bushell and Zafouk remained at the Petschek Palace overnight after their initial questioning, or whether they were taken later that day to Pankrác prison in south-east Prague.

'That was the last I've seen of Roger,' wrote Zafouk. 'We were interrogated separately.'

Blaža's father, Otto Zeithammel, was arrested on the same day while on a business trip to Louny, north-west of Prague, where Kraus's collaborators once gathered. He was driven to the Petschek Palace. Blaža's friend, Ludmila Přidalová, whose son, Stanislaw, was just ten months old, and her husband, the teacher Vojtěch, were also on the Gestapo's wanted list. They were arrested in Příkazy, a town in north-east Moravia, close to the Polish border, and taken to Gestapo headquarters. Another man, Sigmund Neudorfer, who had supplied Bushell with a ration card and Czech papers, could be found in the 'cinema' later in the day, staring at the white wall.

Zafouk's girlfriend, Vlasta, was also questioned by the Gestapo but freed. On 19 May, she had swapped shifts and was, unusually, at work in the morning. The switch probably saved her life; otherwise she would have been visiting the Zeithammel apartment when the Gestapo agents arrived.

Two Gestapo officers picked up Blaža at the offices of the Milk and Fat Union and took her away for questioning that lasted two hours, but she was not subjected to the full routine. After being released, she told Jaroslav Kvapil, her line manager at the union office, that the whole business with the pilots 'went to shit'. The whole issue had exploded, 'the pilots got arrested. We're screwed.'

More than three years later, Kvapil told the Czech court trying Kraus for collaborating with the Nazis, that he knew about the whole case. After her first meeting with the Gestapo, Kvapil said Blaža had called his office, and then she had called Kraus from Kvapil's office. She was, he said, 'acting like an intelligence officer'.

Kvapil said Kraus came to the Milk and Fat Union within fifteen minutes and he already appeared to know what was going on. 'In my opinion he was informed about the whole thing and was showing false interest in which people are involved in this case,' said Kvapil. 'If I remember rightly, she answered evasively . . . Miss Zeithammelová asked Kraus to help with freeing her father. I don't remember other details.'

Later that night, Vlasta took food to the Zeithammels' flat, but quickly moved to another floor when she saw that it had been smashed up. On the way out, she saw Blaža with Kraus. It was the last time Vlasta saw any member of the Zeithammel family.

Vlasta never came to terms with what Blaža had done even though she was undoubtedly betrayed by Kraus. 'It was inexcusable . . . she was in the resistance . . . but maybe she was so angry she just didn't think,' said Vlasta.

According to witnesses who testified against Kraus after the war, Blaža was interrogated several times over the next few days. She apparently tried to co-operate because she thought Kraus would help her. She also suspected that she was being followed and avoided her friends.

Kraus told her that, in the presence of the German police, she should pretend to be his fiancée. He would help her over difficulties with the Gestapo. He is said to have taken 10,000 crowns from her to bribe the Gestapo to free her father.

Zafouk was held in Prague for several weeks – much longer, it seems, than Bushell – and, according to Vlasta, he was tortured and beaten.

> *After the interrogation, which lasted over one month, I was handed over to a* Wehrmacht *prison, wrote Zafouk. There I found out that Roger left the same cell I was put in [at Pankrác prison in May] about two days before and was sent to war prison camp in Germany.*

It is difficult to establish the precise timetable of events, but it seems likely that, after being interrogated by the Gestapo, Bushell was sent to the Luftwaffe's new high-security camp, Stalag Luft III, at Sagan, about 120 miles south-east of Berlin, sometime between 20 May and 3 June 1942.

Vincent 'Paddy' Byrne, who had been one of the defendants at the Battle of Barking Creek in the autumn of 1939, was on hand again to witness events at Stalag Luft III, where he was doing time in the 'cooler' – the solitary confinement block where prisoners were sent for bad behaviour. Byrne told Roger's mother, Dorothe:

> *About June 1942 [it was May 1942, according to Ben Bushell's notes in the margin], I was doing a sentence in a prison in Lower Silesia, when one evening, I heard a voice speaking German, which sounded very like Roger's voice. On looking through the shutter, who should I see in the corridor but Roger, dressed in 'civvies' with a handbag, just back from Prague after being recaptured. I was amazed, but overjoyed to see him.*

The dramas that overtook Prague in May 1942 were not yet over. On the morning of Wednesday, 27 May 1942, Josef Gabčik and Jan Kubiš, the two agents sent from Britain to kill Reinhard Heydrich in Operation Anthropoid, were in position in the suburb of Liben. They were waiting on an uphill bend in the road on which they expected Heydrich to travel in his official car. The place for the attack had been chosen because Gabčik and Kubiš knew that the Reich Protector's driver would have to slow down at this point in the journey from Heydrich's summer residence in Panenské Břežany to Prague Castle. The timing of the attack was determined by information given to the resistance by an informer working for the Heydrich family: on that morning, Heydrich would leave home later than usual. After a brief stop at his office, he was due to fly to Berlin for a meeting with Hitler and might not return to Prague for some time.

Many people in Prague seem to have known that the attack was imminent. The senior members of the resistance who had tried to persuade Edvard Beneš, leader of the Czech government-in-exile, and his intelligence chief, František Moravec, to cancel the operation in view of their grave fears for the local population if it went ahead, had been ignored. Gabčik and Kubiš were determined to press on.

In London, the operation had been signed off by Sir Charles Hambro, the British banker who, in 1942, directed the Special Operations Executive (SOE).

The black Mercedes 320C, driven by SS *Oberscharführer* Johannes Klein, approached Kirchmayer Street from Kobylisy. The red standard of the Reich Protector flew from the right fender. The licence plate SS-3 indicated the identity of the man who sat in the front seat next to the driver. Arrogant to the end, Heydrich was travelling in an open-top car with no escort. At 10.35 a.m., the car braked on a sharp curve. Gabčik jumped in front of the vehicle, holding a Sten gun. The weapon jammed. Kubiš pulled a bomb out of his suitcase. Drawing on lessons learnt during his training by the SOE, it was fitted with a highly sensitive 'Always' fuse, and had been modified to maximise its effect on the target without endangering the thrower. But the bomb dropped short, just in front of the right rear fender. The explosion damaged the body of the vehicle and ripped off the right-hand door, and it also punctured the front passenger seat, wounding Heydrich.

As Gabčik and Kubiš escaped, they did not know whether they had harmed their target, but small particles of metal and upholstery from the car had penetrated his body. Heydrich was taken to a local hospital in a passing truck.

The results of his first operation were reported to Berlin by SS *Standartenführer* Horst Böhme, head of the SD in Prague, at 3.26 p.m. The message, sent by teleprinter, read:

A lacerated wound to the left of the back vertebrae without damage to the spinal cord. The projectile, a piece of sheet metal, shattered the 11th rib, punctured the stomach lining, and finally lodged in the spleen. The wound contains a number of horsehair and hair, probably material originating from the upholstery. The dangers: festering of the pleura due to pleurisy. During the operation the spleen was removed.

That night, the Nazis declared a state of emergency throughout Bohemia and Moravia. Himmler, head of the SS, ordered the arrest of the entire intelligentsia. 'The first 100 most important adversaries among the Czech intelligentsia must be shot tonight,' he said.

In his diary, Petr Ginz, the fourteen-year-old Jewish schoolboy, recorded events.

In the afternoon I went for a walk with Popper. There was a bomb assassination attempt against SS *Gruppenführer* Heydrich. That's why they ordered a state of emergency and people who will be seen today after 9 o'clock and tomorrow before 6 o'clock and won't stop immediately after being called will be shot dead. There is a reward of 10,000,000 crowns for whoever informs on those responsible for the assassination, and whoever knows about them and does not report it will be shot with his entire family.

The next day, 28 May, Petr added:

> This morning it was announced that Mr Heydrich's life is not in danger . . . In the evening they announced on loudspeakers that eight people have been shot for sheltering unregistered persons. Among them was a seventeen-year-old boy.

Another diarist, writing on the same day, voiced concerns for the future of the Nazi leadership. Joseph Goebbels, the propaganda minister and one of Hitler's oldest allies, noted that Heydrich was:

> . . . severely wounded . . . even if he is not in mortal danger at the moment, his condition is nevertheless worrisome . . . it is imperative that we get hold of the assassins. The background of the attack is not yet clear. But it is revealing that London reported on the attack very early on. We must be clear that such an attack could set a precedent if we do not counter it with the most brutal of means.

At that moment, Hitler's Nazi regime was at the peak of its powers. The *Wehrmacht* had overcome its difficulties of the previous winter and was once again on the move in Russia. As the snows melted, Leningrad was still under siege, and Moscow felt threatened again. General Friedrich von Paulus was preparing to order the Sixth Army southwards to the oilfields of the Caucasus and the city of Stalingrad. German submarines – the U-boats – continued to sink millions of tons of Allied shipping in the Atlantic and harry British convoys to Russia. The British armies in North Africa retreated once again. Germany's new ally, Japan, was advancing across the Pacific: Singapore, Malaya and Hong Kong had all fallen. The Nazis had also taken a new initiative in their drive to change the racial map of Europe. Engineered by Heydrich at the Wannsee conference in January, extermination camps such as Auschwitz and Treblinka were enabling the Nazis to murder tens of thousands of Jews and other so-called undesirables every day.

But the attack on Heydrich seems to have destabilised the Nazi regime; the sense of invulnerability felt by the Nazi leaders as they plundered vast tracts of Europe was broken. Like Goebbels, they demanded retribution, and in Bohemia and Moravia, thousands were arrested and a great terror unleashed on the population.

It was to prove a turning point both for Hitler and Bushell: for Hitler, there would be no more victories; for Bushell, only a burning hatred.

Heydrich's health rallied in the last days of May and it looked as though he might pull through. But then a fever took hold on 1 June and he slipped into a coma. Goebbels wrote in his diary that the loss of Heydrich would be disastrous, a thought echoed by British military intelligence in a report assessing the impact of the attack: 'If Heydrich should not survive the attempt or if he is invalided for some appreciable time, the loss for the Nazi regime would be very serious indeed. It can be safely said that next to Himmler, Heydrich is the soul of the terror machinery, which depends the fate of the inner front in Germany.'

On 3 June, *wrote the historian Robert Gerwarth*, Heydrich's condition deteriorated further. The doctors were unable to combat his septicaemia, his temperature soared and he was in great pain. The following morning, at nine o'clock, Heydrich succumbed to his blood infection. Hitler's 'hangman', as Thomas Mann famously called him in his BBC commentary the next day, was dead.

Heydrich's death had implications for all those who had lived and loved in the Zeithammel apartment in the Smíchov district of Prague.

Whether Bushell had known of or been implicated in the resistance plot to assassinate Heydrich when he lived with the Zeithammels is not known, but the Germans believed he knew enough to question him further. Bushell was taken to Berlin for questioning by the Gestapo.

Events developed in Prague, too. Forty-eight hours after Heydrich's death, two Gestapo agents visited the offices of the Milk and Fat Union. They searched Blaža's desk and took her away. Kraus was given a further 10,000 crowns – 5,000 by Vlasta Christová and 5,000 by Jaroslav Kvapil – to help to gain Blaža's release.

Her brother, Otokar Zeithammel, was arrested on the morning of 8 June. Kvapil was then taken to the Petschek Palace in the afternoon. Zafouk's father and brother were also arrested. More of Blaža's friends were questioned.

Miroslav Kraus disappeared, but made it known that he was being interrogated in Louny. The former captain in the Czech artillery had deceived and manipulated Blaža. Using other members of the Czech fascists, and reporting directly to the SD, he had gained enough information to destroy the Zeithammel family and their resistance contacts.

Kraus would ultimately emerge as a leading Czech collaborator, responsible for the deaths of many fellow citizens, including his landlady's son and colleagues in the registry of buildings in Louny, where he worked as a clerk after the Czechoslovak army was disbanded.

Vlasta lost her money, but although she had survived her own interrogation in the Petschek Palace, she knew what awaited the Zeithammels. 'The Gestapo was the same everywhere,' she said, 'specially trained people, really, really cruel people; torture, beaten up, get information out of you any possible way, I don't know what they did – terrible things.'

The Nazi regime took other measures against the Czech population. They called a public meeting in Prague's Old Town square to denounce the attack on Heydrich and to proclaim the Czech nation's allegiance to Hitler's Reich. Around 60,000 residents of the city took part in the demonstration; but there was no sign of Gabčik or Kubiš and the other Czechs and Slovaks sent by SOE to operate in Bohemia and Moravia.

Heydrich's coffin lay in state in Prague and was then taken by train to Berlin where he was given a martyr's funeral on Tuesday, 9 June, and buried with full military honours. Giving the eulogy, Himmler said that Heydrich was 'an ideal always to be emulated', while Hitler described him as one of 'bitterest foes of all enemies of the Reich'.

The funeral was barely over when the Nazis decided that the village of Lidice, which had wrongly come to be associated with the perpetrators of the assassination, would atone for Heydrich's death. Lidice had a population of 483 people living in 96 homes. A Baroque church, standing on high ground, dominated the village. Most of the houses were small, inhabited by the families of men who worked in the nearby mines and steel mills. The village had a school with two classrooms, a reading club called 'Motherland', a public library, a sports club and a volunteer firefighters' brigade.

During the night of 9 June, the inhabitants were rounded up and their homes set on fire. All the boys and men aged between fifteen and eighty-four were shot. The women were sent to Ravensbruck concentration camp, where many died, while eighty-one of the children were gassed in specially modified trucks at the extermination camp of Chełmno. Those children remaining, considered to be of the right racial stock, were sent for a 'proper upbringing' with German families. What remained of Lidice was levelled to the ground.

Gabčik and Kubiš and five other Czech and Slovak parachutists evaded the Gestapo and found sanctuary in the church of St Cyril and St Methodius in Resslova Street, but their luck was about to run out. Another agent sent from Britain, Karel Čurda, who had been hiding at his mother's house, walked into the Petschek Palace on 16 June and gave the Gestapo information about dozens of people who had helped the assassins. The Germans, armed with Čurda's information, raided the homes of all the Anthropoid families the next day and conducted a series of brutal interrogations. By 4.15 on the morning of 18 June, the Germans had surrounded the church in Resslova Street. The SOE agents resisted heroically, but were overwhelmed after the Germans flooded the crypt. Gabčik shot himself. Kubiš died in hospital from multiple wounds.

In his diary for Friday, 19 June 1942, Petr Ginz, the Jewish teenager, wrote:

> I heard they caught the assassins in Boromejsky [St Cyril and St Methodius] church. The chaplain hid them there. When Eva walked past it, she heard shooting and she saw shattered windows. Again they executed 153 people.

Several miles from the church of St Cyril and St Methodius, high in the northern suburbs of Prague, not far from the bend in the road where Heydrich had been attacked, is a windswept place called Kobylisy. Amid the lime trees, oaks and maples, perhaps less prevalent in 1942 than they are today, is the Kobylisy firing range, which was established as a training ground for the Austro-Hungarian Army between 1889 and 1891. The Nazis used it for executions.

Here, on a summer's evening – between seven and eight o'clock on Tuesday, 30 June – after weeks of interrogation and torture, Blažena Zeithammelová was shot. She stood next to her brother, Otokar, who was next to Vojtěch Přidal and his wife, Ludmila. Blaža's father, Otto, stood a couple of places further away. Sigmund Neudorfer, who had supplied Bushell with papers, was there too.

The Gestapo report on the executions, compiled by an officer called Jetrinke from the Police Regiment of Bohemia, said that sixty-two men and nine women had all been sentenced to death by the Prague court, sitting at Pankrác prison. Jetrinke said the firing squad was drawn from the 2nd Reserve Police Battalion. All those condemned to death were calm and composed before the executions were carried out. Death was instantaneous in all cases and certified by *Oberstabsarzt* Dr Stettner. The corpses were put in coffins and taken by lorry to the crematorium where, under police supervision, they were cremated.

Among the Czech patriots who died with the Zeithammels that evening was Josef Mašín, one of the Three Kings, who had been arrested more than a year before, and other members of his group. Just before he was killed, Mašín committed one last act of defiance, standing to attention and shouting, 'Long live the Czechoslovak Republic!' It probably gave them all a sense of courage, perhaps even, as they faced their executioners, a belief that their sacrifices would not be in vain.

18

Holding Out

Thousands of miles from Kobylisy, sitting in his study at home in Hermanus, with its wall covered in photographs of Roger, Ben Bushell must have wondered what, exactly, his only son was doing in Occupied Europe.

A series of letters, telegrams and cards received at the Mossel River post office in South Africa from correspondents in Europe, and a message from the Red Cross warning Ben not to try to contact his son, must have prompted questions about the nature of his son's 'contacts'; Ben Bushell may even have been concerned that the messages he received from people he had never heard of previously were simply a German ruse to track down the fugitive airman.

'It all began with the card from Countess Reichenbach,' wrote Ben Bushell. The first postcard was dated 15 March 1942, posted from San Materno, Switzerland, and addressed to: Bushell Esq, Springs, S. Africa. It was forwarded to him by his former secretary at the West Springs gold mine on 31 May – four days after the attack on Heydrich, while Roger was either in the custody of the Gestapo at Pankrác prison outside Prague, or in solitary confinement at Stalag Luft III.

> Dear Sir, *the postcard read,* I have been asked by Hans v. Held to tell you that your son Roger is well and full of humour. Another friend of Held is camp officer in charge of his camp. He tried once to escape but was caught near the Swiss border. His adventure caused him no subsequent difficulties. Yours very sincerely, Countess Reichenbach.

Notwithstanding any suspicions Ben Bushell may have had about the countess, he cabled a reply on 3 June:

DEEPLY GRATEFUL NEWS OF ROGER. PLEASE CABLE WHICH CAMP AND WHAT DATE HELD KNEW ROGER WAS WELL AS LAST LETTER DATED SEPTEMBER.

He also cabled Harry North-Lewis in London, Roger's erstwhile guardian, and the Red Cross.

Countess Reichenbach responded on 6 June.

NEWS FROM END OF FEBRUARY [1942]. CAMP IN THE BLACK FOREST. I TRY TO FIND OUT ADDRESS.

The information did not make sense. 'This was obviously quite wrong,' wrote Ben Bushell later in the margins of the family archive, 'as Roger was in Prague from October 1941, and it appeared to us that this was an attempt [by the Germans] to find out where he was, but I personally was doubtful. Roger escaped to the Swiss border in May 1941.'

Two days later, Ben Bushell responded to the countess for a second time.

VERY GRATEFUL CABLE ADDRESS. WHEN FOUND WAS ESCAPE REFERENCE YOUR POSTCARD RECENT.

Reichenbach replied:

GOING PORTUGAL NEXT WEEK. ADDRESS, CARE BARONESS FRIESEN, VILLA JEANINE, ESTORIL – ESCAPE ATTEMPTED AUTUMN. CABLING WHEN OBTAIN ADDRESS.

Even more confused, Ben Bushell wrote in the margin much later, 'Roger escaped in May '41 and again in Oct '41 so perhaps reference was to latter, but how could he be in camp as per postcard when he was then in Prague.'

On 10 June, Tony Page, one of Roger's friends in Switzerland, cabled South Africa.

RED CROSS INFORMS ME ROGER NOW AT OFLAG VIB [THE CAMP AT WARBURG IN CENTRAL GERMANY TO WHICH BUSHELL WAS TRAVELLING WHEN HE ESCAPED WITH JAROSLAV ZAFOUK] - PRISONER NO 621. FRIENDS HERE WITHOUT DIRECT NEWS SINCE OCTOBER. COMMUNICATION DIFFICULT. WILL CABLE FURTHER NEWS ON RECEIPT.

Twelve days later, on 22 June, Ben Bushell received a cable from the Red Cross, suggesting it was aware that Roger, held by the Gestapo in Berlin, was in difficulty.

VERY ANXIOUS YOU SHOULD NOT ATTEMPT TO GET IN TOUCH WITH ROGER AT PRESENT, IT SAID. HOPE BEFORE LONG TO RECEIVE NEWS OF HIM.

It seems likely that the Red Cross may have felt that any attempt by the family to contact Bushell at this time might jeopardise his position and his safety. Tony Page cabled again on 26 June.

ROGER WROTE JUNE 19TH FROM STALAG LUFT III BEING WELL.

Ben Bushell replied:

WARMEST THANKS FOR FINDING ADDRESS. GRATEFUL ANY FUTURE NEWS. PLEASE SEND ROGER OUR LOVING GREET-INGS FOR HIS BIRTHDAY 30TH AUGUST.

In a very confusing letter that seems to smack of subterfuge, dated 5 July but posted in Bathurst [now Banjul], capital of Gambia in West Africa, five days later, Countess Reichenbach wrote:

*I've just heard that Held has been killed in Russia. His
sister to whom I had written about your son has
discovered that he is healthy and in good spirits.
Latest news dates from June 20th . . . she was not
allowed to write the camp where he is interned. She
spoke to the officer commanding his camp who is a
friend of hers so that you can depend on the
reliability of the message.*

   *If you wish to write to your son I have arranged for you
to write direct to Baroness Friesen, Estoril, Ru a loa o das
Regres, Villa Jeanine. She will pass your message on to my
cousin, Held's sister, who will be in touch with the
officer . . . it is all rather complicated and one must be
careful not to compromise someone, but at least you will
be in touch with your son. I have left the matter in the
hands of friends as I am off to S. America. I much regret
not to be able to do more for you but you will realise the
difficulties. If Baroness Friesen leaves Portugal perhaps you
might find someone else who could get in touch with my
cousin Frau. V. Hippell, Berlin – Grunewald Salzbrunner
Strasse 42.*

Ben Bushell could have been forgiven for being perplexed by the
nature of this correspondence. His efforts to contact Roger
through Baroness Friesen proved to be fruitless. 'I tested this
avenue by cabling Baroness Friesen on 17/8/42. "Please send our
son our loving greetings for his birthday 30th August and say last
letter received dated September."'

'Roger never acknowledged either of my greetings sent per this
avenue and per Tony Page. Baroness Friesen sent me two evasive
letters saying she had forwarded my letter to the address Countess
Reichenbach gave me and that she had asked a Mrs Campbell to
send Roger food parcels but he received none.'

Nothing more was ever heard from Countess Reichenbach,
who 'disappeared' in South America, or Baroness Friesen. Who

were they – and what were their motives? The mystery has never been solved.

A cable from Harry North-Lewis on 29 August 1942 confirmed the information received earlier from Tony Page:

ROGER IS IN STALAG LUFT III. HAVE HEARD FROM THIS CAMP. SAYS HE WANTS FOR NOTHING.

But Bushell was in fact no longer at Stalag Luft III. He had been taken to Gestapo headquarters in Prinz-Albrecht-Strasse, Berlin, where he was being interrogated about his activities in Czechoslovakia. It is possible that he was in the custody of the *Abwehr*, the German military intelligence agency, and held at Tegel prison, but the Gestapo certainly had access to him.

Wings Day, who was a prisoner at Stalag Luft III at this time, admitted that Bushell was in a precarious position. After the war, he told Bushell's father:

Roger was soon removed from Prague [via Stalag Luft III] and placed in an Officers' Military jail in Berlin, where he remained for three months. It was during this period that von Marrow [Günther von Massow, who had worked at Dulag Luft but been transferred to Stalag Luft III] played – in my opinion – an important part. I had always been friendly with von Marrow and had often asked him if he had heard anything of Roger. He came to me one day and told me in great confidence – in fact he said he would be court-martialled and be put in prison in a fortress (fortress arrest he called it) if it was found out that he was giving secret information to me – that Roger had been arrested by the Gestapo in Prague with his companion and others. He continued that Roger was in a very serious situation, being mixed up with some kind of Resistance Movement, and he feared there was a possibility of Roger

233

*being 'made away with' by the Gestapo – you must
realise that the Gestapo held a much more terrible
reputation with the Germans than even with us. However,
he said that he was going to do everything he could in
soliciting of his General brother [Gerd von Massow] on
Roger's behalf and he knew that the commandant of
Stalag Luft III was already doing everything in his power
to get Roger back to the Camp and out of the clutches of
the Gestapo. He said he would keep me posted regarding
events, which he did. He told me when Roger was moved
to Berlin. This information I naturally used with the
Protecting Power (Swiss) Representatives when they
visited us.*

Bushell survived the summer of 1942 due to the (brief) time he
spent in Luftwaffe hands before the death of Heydrich: had he
still been in the hands of the Gestapo in Prague when Heydrich
died, it is likely that he would have met the same fate as the
Zeithammels. But the fact that the Luftwaffe, which detested the
SS, knew where Bushell was, and regarded him as their responsibility, saved his life. Not to mention Günther von Massow's decision to tell Day, who alerted the Swiss, that Bushell was being held
by the Gestapo.

As it was, the Nazis had every right to shoot Bushell. He was a
citizen of a country at war with Germany; he was not in uniform;
he had lived illegally with members of the underground for more
than six months; and he carried Protectorate papers. He could
have been condemned as a spy or an agent provocateur. If he had
been executed in Prague, it would have been difficult to prosecute
his killers under international law.

Jaroslav Zafouk received harsh treatment at the hands of the
Germans in Prague but, in the aftermath of Heydrich's death,
Bushell, the senior British officer, seems to have been regarded as
by far the more dangerous of the two RAF airmen. He was
known to be hostile to the Nazi regime, and it is no wonder that

von Massow feared he would be killed. Zafouk was sent to Colditz. Bushell found himself in Berlin at the heart of the SS empire.

Technically, Bushell was compelled by the rules of the Geneva Convention to give his name and rank or name and number. Beyond that, he was entitled to say nothing. But the reality was different.

Roger will have had a very difficult time in Berlin, *said M. R. D. Foot, the historian of MI9.* Probably being interrogated alternatively by the hard man and the soft man; the soft man giving him cigarettes and apologising for the dreadful manners of the hard man; the hard man bark-bark-barking at him all the time. He would have been threatened with physical torture, but probably not applying it. Not many prisoners of war were actually tortured. They were quite likely to take your boots off and trample on your toes, which will break up quite a lot of people quite fast, but if you're bloody-enough minded, and Roger was good at being bloody minded, you can stand up to that.

An intelligent prisoner, well aware of what was happening, could be cautious, even deviate from the questioning but, as Foot said, there was some information you kept very much to yourself. 'You never admit such things as what code you were using, if you were using a code, or who you were staying with, you simply don't admit that.'

If a prisoner showed any fear, he or she was usually finished. Once again, Bushell's legal training would have helped him to deal with the questioning and the type of men carrying out the interrogation, while his ability to speak German would have been useful. A touch of the 'suave belligerence' attributed to him by the author Paul Brickhill may even have unsettled his interrogators. Roger Bushell survived.

On 19 June 1942, he wrote to his parents. The letter was

stamped as having been sent from Stalag Luft III, which put him back in the custody of the Luftwaffe, but he was still in the hands of the Gestapo in Berlin.

> *My darlings,* the letter declared. *Here I am again! I escaped last October, was hidden in Prague during the intervening period, and was unfortunately recaptured last month. That explains everything I think. Further details I will tell you after the war. You will I know have had a very anxious and trying time, but I also know that you would not have expected me in the circumstances, to have done anything other than I did and we will therefore leave it at that.*
>
> *I am quite OK. And very well so you have nothing to worry about.*

The Gestapo forced Bushell to pretend he was in a prisoner-of-war camp so that no one knew he was being interrogated by them.

> *This is a Luftwaffe camp,* he wrote, *with old friends from Dulag of both nationalities here, so I am in excellent hands. At the moment, I am in the 'cooler' doing my stretch for my escape but I gather there are a number of parcels waiting for me and I have been fitted out with Red Cross clothes and a new uniform so at present want for nothing. There are lots of Red Cross parcels and cigarettes and so everything is fine.*

He finished by addressing the family and dealing with domestic issues:

> *There is little else that I can tell you except that I love you all very much and feel sure that it won't be very long now before the whole affair is over and we can all start over again with our normal lives. Am naturally bitterly*

disappointed at having been caught again, but my spirits
are sky high and you need have no fear that this life has got
me down yet or that it ever will, please God. Give
yourselves all a big hug and lots of love, Roger.

Written in hard pencil, the letter was neat, very precise, and untouched by the German censors in Berlin. The letter would also have been read by the Allied censors.

Bushell's second letter from Berlin revealed that he was receiving mail even though he was in Gestapo custody. The mood of the letter is subdued. Dated 29 July 1942, more than two months after his arrest in Prague, he wrote:

I do hope you have by now received my June letter
explaining why you hadn't heard from me. In case you
haven't, the reason was that I escaped last October and was
hidden in Prague until I was recaptured in May. I have now
had a letter from Tony Page telling me that he has cabled
you that I am O.K. which is a very great relief for I am
afraid you must have had a very anxious time. I have had a
number of letters from you, mainly old ones, the latest
being April 14th . . .

The next paragraph was of far greater significance:

I have had one or two letters from England – Khaki [his
head of chambers], and Georgie Curzon that was – she and
her husband have separated – I am not surprised. I never
did like the man. I have, however, heard nothing from either
Peggy or Harry North-Lewis.

Of the three women who defined Roger Bushell's war, this is the first letter to mention two of them – Peggy Hamilton and Lady Georgiana Curzon. The ashes of the third, a resistance fighter hopelessly mixed up in the heinous world of Nazi-occupied

Czechoslovakia, lay in a mass grave in a cemetery in northern Prague.

The Gestapo had informed Bushell that Blažena Zeithammelová and her family had been executed. His involvement with her remained a secret for many years. She was not mentioned in any letters written by Bushell or in any known correspondence between other people and his parents after the war. Even Zafouk kept quiet. It was his wife, Vlasta, who gave the secret away more than sixty years after the two airmen had hidden in Prague, and long after Jaroslav had died, in an interview with Bushell's niece, the South African film-maker Lindy Wilson, in 2007.

While Bushell had been Blaža's lover for several months in Prague, the root cause of her death was her inability to deal with Bushell's romantic loyalty to a woman in Britain to whom he had not been faithful, and whom he not seen for at least two years. At the time, this woman appeared to be Peggy Hamilton, the source of so much of Bushell's angst throughout 1940 and 1941.

But even in the month that Bushell reached Prague, Peggy had already abandoned him; it seems she was never going to save herself for an imprisoned fighter pilot who had proposed to her at the beginning of the war and who had never had an income to match the rest of 'the Millionaires' of 601 Squadron.

Having married Lord Petre in the private chapel at Ingatestone Hall, near Chelmsford, on 25 October 1941, she was, in the summer of 1942, pregnant with their only child. The *Essex Chronicle* reported the birth beneath a large front-page picture of Lady Petre in its edition of 7 August 1942.

A son and heir was born to Lord and Lady Petre, of Ingatestone Hall, at 8.30 p.m. on Tuesday at a nursing home at Windsor, *the story said*. Both mother and child were doing well.

The article also records an interesting change of name. Plain Peggy Hamilton, who had become Marguerite Hamilton in *The*

Times's engagement column only a few months before, had made another adjustment.

Lady Petre was Miss Marguerite Wentworth-Hamilton, *reported the* Chronicle, and her parents lived at Nettlebed, Oxfordshire.

Adding a touch of class to her identity, Peggy had used her late father's middle name to supplement her surname.

But, in another twist to the story, Vlasta revealed a further secret: seven years after being brushed aside by Earl Howe, Roger, it seems, might already have had his eye on a new relationship with Lady Georgiana Mary Curzon, a woman whose surname needed no embellishment. Whether they exchanged letters while he was a prisoner at Barth or Lübeck is not known, but Vlasta made it clear that, as far she and Jaroslav were concerned, the woman to whom Roger was committed in England when Blaža pleaded for his hand in marriage was Georgie. While the two men were hiding in Prague, Bushell must have revealed his true feelings for the debutante he had once loved in England, and Zafouk must have been left in no doubt that Bushell wanted to return to her, not Peggy.

After the war, the Zafouks searched for Georgie and had a meeting lasting two hours. 'I was very curious about her,' said Vlasta, 'because Roger wanted . . . or said he was engaged to her . . . I really don't know how Jarka found the address. I think she was in love with him, still.'

Bushell did not tell his parents about his affair with Georgie until late 1942. His sister, Rosemary, who lived with him for a while during the mid-1930s, might have known, but very few others would have done so. Among his fellow officers held captive in Germany at this time, Wings Day seems to have known – and he would hint at it in his biography years later. Day told the story of Bushell's desperation to be reunited with the young lady whom he had loved and lost, but who was waiting for him once more. Indeed, it seems that the only person who could have told Jaroslav and Vlasta about Roger's love for Georgie was Bushell himself.

Whatever the truth about Bushell's romantic attachments, Georgie's marriage to Home Kidston collapsed in scandal. Perhaps in fitting condemnation of Earl Howe's judgment over what was best for his daughter in terms of men and marriage, Home Kidston committed adultery with Joyce Mary McLean, otherwise known as Countess Howe – Georgiana's stepmother – at Southover House, Kidston's marital home, in Tolpuddle, Dorset, on Monday, 20 October 1941. The divorce papers suggest that his adultery continued during the weekend of 25 October and 26 October.

On an extraordinary day for Home Kidston, a naval officer serving in the destroyer HMS *Highlander*, he wrote to his wife on 30 October, having received a telegram from her the night before. She had confronted Kidston with an accusation of infidelity, saying that her stepmother, Joyce, had claimed that he loved her, not Georgie. Kidston's wife was intent on knowing the truth.

The naval officer's letter, written 'at sea', admitted that he had fallen in love with his mother-in-law during the previous ten days, but that he wished to tackle the situation with as much discretion as could be mustered. In his confession to Georgie, Kidston refused to take responsibility for his transgression, noting that neither he nor Joyce could have done anything to prevent such an outcome. Apart from acknowledging how cruel the whole situation must be to his wife, his main consideration seems to have been the realisation that her father might no longer like him.

If Georgie was hoping for any sign of remorse from her errant husband, she must have been somewhat disappointed. Kidston alluded to other difficulties, perhaps even other romantic liaisons, in the time since he and Georgie were married in November 1935, with an insouciance about married life that, to the contemporary reader, seems almost breathtaking.

He explained that this latest lapse in his behaviour followed a pattern that had been set when another guest, Audrey, had visited their marital home. He blamed his and Georgie's opposing attitudes to the issue of fidelity on their contrasting upbringings and acknowledged his responsibilities to their son Glen and to Georgie herself. However, although he apologised for the mess he had caused, Kidston made no attempt to apologise for his behaviour.

It is not known whether Kidston's ship was in action on 30 October before or after he wrote the letter to Georgie, but the destroyer, operating with her sister ship, HMS *Harvester*, sank the German submarine, U-32, north-west of Ireland on the same day. The action was a major success for the Royal Navy: U-32 was one of the most successful submarines in the German fleet. Under the command of Kapitleutenant Hans Jenisch, holder of the Knight's Cross – one of the highest awards for bravery in the German armed forces – the submarine had taken part in nine patrols, and sunk twenty ships, including the British liner *Empress of Britain*, the biggest ship to be sunk by a U-boat. Thirty-three member of the submarine's crew of forty-two, including Jenisch, were picked up by the British destroyers.

Kidston wrote to Georgie again on Sunday, 30 November but by now the focus of his correspondence had shifted. His main concern appeared to be what his domestic staff would think of him if he and Georgie met at home to discuss their marital difficulties. As this would be intolerable to him, Kidston agreed that Georgie's proposal to meet at the Berkeley Hotel would be a good idea if he could get leave from his ship. In the meantime, with an audacity that seems extraordinary to the modern reader, Kidston urged Georgie to keep his letters to her private as it was vital that their staff should not know about their private lives.

Having established his ground rules, Kidston made it clear that he felt it was an unsuitable marriage, which had featured many rows, including some in front of other people. With a breathtaking brutality, he described his initial attempts to cover up the mistake he had made in marrying Georgie as a tragic error, concluding that they should never have wed in the first place.

He did not spare his wife's feelings either when he explained to her that he and Joyce shared many of the same ideas about life and that, as a result, he would always love her, no matter what anyone might force him to say. With a final painful flourish, he assured Georgie that he was in fine health, and that his affair could not in any way be blamed on the war or any other excuse.

Nor was this the first occasion on which their marriage had reached some sort of crisis, as his remarks about Audrey perhaps indicate. Kidston was quick to remind Georgie that she had threatened to go away for a time after relatively trivial disagreements in the past. The conclusion Kidston reached, no doubt eradicating the need for any unwelcome sense of guilt, was that he believed his wife was not happy in their marriage either.

The Curzons, driven by Georgie's cuckolded father, moved quickly. Less than three months later, on 17 February 1942, Lady Georgiana petitioned for a dissolution of the marriage. She submitted a supplemental petition on 18 March. Kidston's privacy was stripped bare: his earnings from a substantial investment portfolio, including a Bugatti Owners' Club Debenture amounting to more than £21,000 a year, were listed in court documents.

Georgie and her father pushed for a harsh settlement. Kidston would not be allowed to see Glen, then aged seven, until the mid-1950s. He did not attend the hearings. His solicitor, Julian Lousada, told the court that he was serving abroad with the Royal Navy and there was 'no prospect' of him returning to England during the war 'and there is very great difficulty in communicating with him at all'.

Lady Georgiana Kidston was granted a decree nisi on 16 July 1942. Her father was awarded substantial damages against Kidston. But she had already started writing to the man she loved, who was in the custody of the security services in Berlin.

Bushell was also concerned about his private affairs, but more about his money than the future of any relationship with Peggy Hamilton. He was still unaware that she had married someone else. On 20 August 1942, a little more than two weeks after Lady Petre gave birth to a son, and perhaps four weeks after Lady Kidston had secured a divorce, Roger told his parents: 'I have also still not heard from either Peggy or Uncle Harry . . . I am becoming a little disturbed about what has and is happening to my pay. At the moment it all goes to P.'

After acknowledging a big improvement in the post from England, he restated the same concerns on 3 September:

I still have not heard from Peggy or Uncle Harry, which is rather disturbing me as I am beginning to be a little worried about my finances. As you know I made over all my pay to Peggy when I was shot down and I am now beginning to wonder whether I have not been had for a sucker!

By this time, the Luftwaffe had prised Bushell from the hands of the Gestapo. He was almost certainly in the 'cooler' at Stalag Luft III, serving his punishment for escaping from the PoW train carrying him to Warburg the previous year.

In another letter to his parents, dated 10 September 1942, he wrote:

The information you received from Countess R [on his whereabouts in Germany], whoever she may be, you will by now know to have been inaccurate. However, as it put an end to your worries it was probably a good thing.

Referring to the allegations made against him by the Gestapo, probably written more for the attention of the German censors than his parents, Bushell wrote:

There seems to have been a pretty good stock of rumours flying around on the subject of myself and as they were taken seriously in certain quarters, without a scrap of evidence to support them I might add, I have had quite an 'interesting' time the last three months. The whole affair is now I understand settled so that is that. Please do not worry about me. I am perfectly OK, have parcels, cigarettes and clothes and that is all one needs as a Krieg.

Roger also told his parents more about Georgie.

Have had a number of letters from Georgie Kidston – Georgie Curzon that was, an old flame of mine. She has been divorcing her husband who does not seem to have behaved very prettily, having gone off with her stepmother (sic!) and now poor G. is turning to her old love for comfort! It really is rather amusing because before this business I had not heard from her in years. I jolly nearly married her once. You didn't know that did you.

He signs off, *My love to you all darlings and a big hug for Eliza. Your loving son, Roger.*

The last act of the drama involving Peggy Hamilton was played out at Stalag Luft III, in which von Massow, who had openly supported or protected Bushell on three occasions, once again played a leading role. The story is best told by Wings Day in his letter to Dorothe Bushell after the war:

> *After about three months, Roger came back to the camp, which being a comparative short time showed that the efforts of all parties had had a good effect,* wrote Day. *Another thing he did which I think shows Von Marrow's delicacy of feelings and high regard for Roger. Amongst Von Marrow's duties was to be in charge of the German Censoring Department which dealt with all RAF PoW mail. While Roger was away in Prague and then in Gestapo hands, I understand Roger's fiancée got married and after the event wrote and told Roger. This letter of letters arrived and Von Marrow came to me as a friend of Roger's and told me that he was withholding the letters until Roger was allowed back into the compound amongst his friends. Von Marrow felt that if Roger received these letters while in solitary confinement, the shock would be harder to bear.*
>
> *I think this is the finest example of love and respect which Roger instilled in all who met and knew him, whether amongst his own people or in the ranks of his country's enemies.*

Of all the testimonies paid to Roger Bushell, this is hard currency. No opinion on the great saga of British prisoners in Germany during the Second World War carries more weight than that of Day, a sensitive man who turned every camp in which he held the rank of Senior British Officer into an 'operational base' from which to challenge the Germans.

However much Bushell was tormented by the pain of his private life, he seems to have earned the almost universal respect of men – Allied and German alike – who entered his orbit, and none more so than Day.

By the time Bushell became aware of Peggy's actions, she had been married almost a year, and was already a mother. He seems to have simply shrugged off the romantic debacle of his engagement, which was perhaps an indication that all was not what it had seemed.

The first letter that Bushell wrote to his parents from his new room, shared with an old friend, within the main prison compound at Stalag Luft III was both robust and philosophical. Dated 30 September 1942, it read:

> *There is some silly row going on about letters between our respective Govts. So we have been cut to one letter and one pc [postcard] per month and therefore God knows when you'll get this. We can only receive four letters a month too, which is a bore. However, keep on writing because the ban is bound to be lifted sooner or later and then we'll get them all in a lump.*
>
> *I am now sharing a room with Robert Tuck [Robert Stanford Tuck] whom you have no doubt heard of. He used to be one of the flight commanders in the old days but has now beaten me to it and is now a Wing Commander with a DSO [Distinguished Service Order] and three DFCs [Distinguished Flying Crosses]! He is a charming fellow and we have a lot of laughs.*

At this point in the letter, Ben Bushell wrote in the margin that it must have been a 'little trying' for Roger to find one of his own pilots turn up with a more senior rank to himself – not to mention the medals. 'His pride is touching,' wrote his father.

The letter from Stalag Luft III continued, 'John Gillies and most of the old lot from Dulag are here too. So there are lots of friends in the camp.'

Only then does he address the subject of his engagement, and very briefly. 'I only heard about Peggy a couple of weeks ago. Such is life but don't waste any false sympathy on me because I find I don't really care a damn about it.'

Bushell was clearly recovering from his ordeals.

*My friends have fitted me out with clothes and I am well
supplied with everything including cigarettes so you have
no need to worry. I received a cigarette parcel from the SA
[South Africa] Red Cross, presumably from you. Springbok
cigarettes. They were swell. Many thanks. We are still
getting lots of sun and I am good and brown again and full
of health and optimism once more.*

In a later letter, Bushell finally gives some clues as to what
happened to him in the German capital:

*The Germans kept me in Berlin for three months after I
was caught – a fact I did not tell you at the time
because a) I didn't wish to alarm you unnecessarily and
b) I wasn't allowed to. I don't expect it matters now
because it is all over with and if it does, no doubt
they'll censor it. I'll tell you why after the war, so don't
ask questions.*

The letter may also give the first indication of Bushell's move to
the Left. He seems a little less enamoured with aristocrats, perhaps
not surprisingly given his treatment by the Curzon family, but the
mood is clear.

*I've told Harry [North-Lewis] to do what he can to recover
the money [his service pay signed over to Peggy] but if P.
sticks her toes in there is nothing I can do I am afraid.
Legally that is. I haven't had an answer to my letters yet but
have no doubt he will do what he can. The whole business
is a bore and not worth discussing any more. A coronet
won't be worth much after this war anyway, which is not
unfunny.*

This was the last time Bushell ever mentioned Lady Petre, the former Peggy Hamilton. Once more, the world was changing. And Roger Bushell was about to go to war again.

19

Big X

The forest running south of Sagan – part of Germany in 1942, but handed to Poland after the Second World War – can be an eerie, deadening place.

For a prisoner of war, uncertain about his future as a guest of the Luftwaffe at Stalag Luft III, a high-security camp hewn out of the forest, Bushell's surroundings offered little hope. Only two things beckoned on the horizon: the constraints of captivity generated by a vast prison camp watched over by armed guards standing behind machine guns and searchlights; and a great vista of pine that cut the camp off from the nearby town and muffled virtually all sounds of the world outside.

No rivers or mountains here to conjure dreams; no farms nor fields; no steeples or spires. Just the seemingly endless forest, stretching outward and upward, rich in vegetation and wildlife, but a straitjacket for a man's soul.

The Gestapo in Berlin had released Roger Bushell so that he could return to Stalag Luft III – not to the relative comfort of his peers, but to the rigours of the camp prison known as the 'cooler'.

As he walked into the East Compound after his spell in solitary confinement, he must, physically at least, have struck those prisoners who had known him in 1939 or 1940 as a diminished figure. No longer looking like a well-built rugby player, he had lost the impressive muscular definition in his chest, neck and shoulders, as well as the ample cheeks that once danced to his fat chuckle. Now he looked gaunt.

Wings Day, the Senior British Officer in the East Compound, thought Bushell seemed 'shaken', which was not surprising given that he had been interrogated by the Gestapo for three months, and had been told the fate of the Zeithammel family.

'We all decided Roger must "sit back" anyway for some time and take no part in escape activities,' Day wrote in a letter to Dorothe Bushell after the war.

Contrary to the impression that Bushell had given his parents about events in Berlin, the Gestapo had not closed the case against him; it was merely on hold. While the interventions of Day and von Massow had thwarted the secret police in 1942, Bushell was left with no illusions about the future. If he fell into Gestapo hands again, he would be shot.

Whether or not he had in any way helped the resistance in Prague, the British officer had touched a number of German nerves. Believing that they were 'stabbed in the back' during the First World War, when many in the German military blamed the collapse of morale inside Germany for their country's defeat, the Gestapo usually dealt swiftly with anyone suspected of encouraging insurrection on the home front. As far as the Gestapo was concerned, this included the 'SS state' of Bohemia and Moravia.

The Gestapo interrogators would have known that Bushell was a German speaker who understood their culture and politics and had made friends in Germany before the war. He was a threatening presence by any measure.

Two other issues also complicated matters. The SS were concerned generally about British prisoners of war and wanted control of the camps. In racial terms, they regarded the British as being close to the Germans but, because of this, the SS fretted about the influence of British prisoners on the local population, such as the female agricultural students who had admired the inmates of Dulag Luft in 1940. At the same time, hostility was growing towards Churchill's 'terror flyers', the crews of the Royal Air Force.

By the autumn of 1942, when Bushell made the journey from Berlin back to Stalag Luft III, the Allied air offensive against Germany was gaining momentum. Any last vestiges of chivalry or honour in the air war had disappeared. Under the leadership of Sir Arthur 'Bomber' Harris, RAF Bomber Command had become the most ruthless arm of the British services, single-minded in its attempt to destroy the Nazi regime.

An increasing number of the RAF's new four-engine heavy bombers, the Halifax and Lancaster, were being used in the campaign. Bomb loads were bigger. Navigation was better. The city of Cologne was struck by 1,000 British bombers on one night in May. The Americans joined the offensive, with their own heavy bombers, the B24 Liberator and B17 Flying Fortress. By night, the RAF 'carpet-bombed' German cities; by day, the Americans attempted the precision bombing of industrial targets.

Whatever the method or strategy, whatever the moral arguments for and against the campaign, the casualty lists grew on both sides. While the Allied air forces pressed on to their targets night after night, day after day, the German defences improved, taking a heavier toll on the bombers. Tens of thousands of Allied aircrew died in the skies over Germany, while it was not unusual for Allied airmen who baled out of stricken aircraft to be lynched on the ground. Hundreds of thousands of German civilians – men, women and children – died in their own towns and cities as the British and American air forces tried to bomb Germany into defeat.

As a result, the number of Allied airmen taken prisoner increased rapidly. In 1939, Germany had just thirty-one prisoner-of-war camps. By the end, the number had increased to 248, with British and American prisoners held in 134 of them.

To cope with the influx, a new camp was developed on an existing site near Sagan, a town of 20,000 in Lower Silesia close to the Polish border. The Luftwaffe made thorough preparations.

Stalag Luft III, which held thousands of prisoners, was about as far from any neutral country as it was possible to be in the Third Reich, and the camp could be expanded at any time simply by cutting down more trees. Certain physical features made escape, particularly tunnelling, difficult; the sandy subsoil, for example, was bright yellow, so any sign of it on the surface, whether on prisoners' clothing, in their huts or elsewhere, would give away what was happening underground. The Germans also added obstacles of their own: the huts in which the men lived were raised several inches off the ground to make it easier to detect tunnel shafts and to search for evidence of tunnelling, while seismograph microphones were placed around the perimeter of the camp to detect the sounds of men working underground.

Hundreds of guards and security staff – the 'goons' – kept watch over the Allied officers. The compounds were surrounded by a double barbed-wire fence that was nine feet high. Watchtowers – the 'goon boxes' – rising six feet above the barbed wire, surrounded the camp, 100 to 150 yards apart. Standing behind their machine guns and searchlights, the guards had a clear view from their elevated platforms. Finally, a trip wire ran around the perimeter about thirty feet inside the camp to keep prisoners away from the main fence.

As part of a diverse strategy, the Germans encouraged prisoners to spend time on activities other than escape. Stalag Luft III became a centre of learning for many Allied airmen, with few of the usual distractions that beset male students as they tackle degrees and diplomas in their late teens and early twenties.

The Red Cross provided examination papers, while academics among the prisoners supervised their work. The camp also had extensive leisure facilities, some provided by the Germans, some created by imaginative prisoners.

A library grew out of the books posted to prisoners by their families, bookshops, educational institutions and other organisations from around the world. The inmates were allowed access to most of these, but the German censors balked at books about escape, interpretations of history that did not meet the Nazi view of the world, and works by Jewish authors.

According to Midge Gillies, author of *The Barbed-Wire University*, the first educational timetable at Stalag Luft III included fifty-five lectures a week in the summer of 1942.

'Eventually, 1,500 students were attending 220 classes each week and in the spring of 1943, one hundred students sat their City and Guilds of London Institute exams in the camp cinema, with the help of the Germans, who provided tables and chairs [paid for by the prisoners].'

Flight Lieutenant Alan Bryett, who was shot down in a Halifax bomber during a raid over Berlin in 1943, was among those prisoners who took up studies later in the war. At the age of ninety, he still had a clear recollection of life in Stalag Luft III. 'There were a great many things going on,' said Bryett, a dapper man dressed in a blue jacket and RAF tie, seated at home in Bromley, Kent. 'You could learn virtually any foreign language because there were nationalities of that language there. I specialised in French, which I'd done at school. There was plenty of activity. The academic side was very good . . . I did my banking exams after I found I could study banking accountancy. There was no shortage of things if you wanted to keep yourself occupied. If you wanted to do bugger all, you could do bugger all. If you wanted to occupy yourself, you could occupy yourself virtually all day.'

Sport of one sort or another was played by many inmates: football, rugby, basketball, volleyball, table tennis and athletics, even ice-hockey in winter, formed part of prison life. Members of the Sagan Golf Club played a 1,220-yard course, with a par 55, although the greens were called browns and the size of bunkers were restricted so that they were never deep enough to hide an escaper. Clubs were provided by the International Red Cross. A small reservoir in the middle of the camp was even used for model boats.

The prisoners built a theatre, seating 500 people, after the move to the North Compound and put on West End shows, often directed by Kenneth Mackintosh, one of the driving forces at Laurence Olivier's National Theatre in the 1970s, and John Casson and Peter Butterworth. The number of musicians in the camp increased with the length of the war, enabling the production of concerts, both classical and jazz, and music hall shows.

Among those who enriched the musical life of the camp was Cy Grant, an RAF navigator from Guyana who would later make his name as an actor, author and musician.

For me, being a prisoner of war for two years was equivalent to having a university education, *he wrote long after the end of hostilities.* Not only did I have an opportunity to reflect upon my life, about who I was, what I was doing there and what had brought me into that situation, but I was in the company of men who were officers, well-educated and above average intelligence. We were able to organise ourselves into a highly efficient community – escape committees, recreation facilities, libraries, theatre groups, a jazz band (in which I played) and music societies. I actually ran a music society for my block and in doing so increased my own knowledge of European classical music.

Games and gambling were widespread, with cigarettes the universal currency.

'If you wanted to spend the whole of your time playing bridge, you could – there were bridge teams that did nothing else,' said Bryett.

Squadron Leader John Barrett, who ended up in the East Compound of Stalag Luft III, was one of four British prisoners of war who cultivated an interest in ornithology and went on to play a major part in conservation after the war, running the Field Studies Centre at Dale in Pembrokeshire.

This was Stalag Luft III in all its growing diversity.

While the policies of the German regime did not appear to deter escape activity, it was all too often haphazard, spontaneous and unsuccessful. Many tunnels were dug but, one by one, they were discovered. The Germans were winning at Sagan, just as they seemed to be on almost every other front in the early autumn of 1942, but fortunes were about to change.

Many people witnessed a change in Bushell. One of those was Robert Stanford Tuck, the fighter ace who had flown with him on the day he was shot down in May 1940, and who now shared a room with him in the East Compound.

'Roger Bushell came back,' wrote Tuck's biographer, Larry Forrester, in his book, *Fly For Your Life*.

[He was] a very different Bushell from the one Tuck had known on 92 [Squadron]. No longer ready to play the fool, but grimly, quietly earnest. Still ringing in his ears were the screams of people being tortured by the Gestapo in adjoining cells . . . deep and cold ran his hatred for the Germans: he was obsessed with the desire to keep on fighting them.

Paul Brickhill, the Australian journalist who would later write the book, *The Great Escape*, recorded in his notes that Bushell was no longer the unrestrained man:

. . . who thought escape was good, risky sport like skiing . . . now he was moodier, and that gaze from that twisted eye was more foreboding. He cursed all Germans indiscriminately, but inside it was a clear, cool-headed hatred and it found sublimation in outwitting them.

Letters to his parents give more than a hint of the bitterness Bushell felt and the change in the way he saw the world.

The weather has been simply astonishing and I am writing this in shirtsleeves at my open window, he wrote on 31 October 1942. *Outside people are lying about in the sun and overhead the pale blue German sky, so like those pale blue Aryan eyes, looks down with stolid indifference on us. The winter having done its best for us last year [when it halted the German advance on the Eastern Front] looks at the moment as though it has forgotten all about turning up at all this year, though maybe it is just saving things up.*

As ever, he tried to reassure his parents, too.

> *You need have no fear for my personal needs. We have and will no doubt continue to receive sufficient fuel and I am well enough equipped with Red Cross clothes. I now sport an airman's tunic having lost all my belongings during my escape – [the words 'my escape' were blacked out by the German censor, but Ben Bushell 'read his words by strong light behind the blacked outs'] – but I fortunately found a greatcoat awaiting me when I returned so I am quite OK. Am dabbling in history at the moment and that together with my Czech [he had started studying the language in Prague with Blaža] makes the days pass reasonably quickly.*

The letter is notable for the fact that it was the first occasion on which the German censors deleted anything written by Bushell. Apart from the reference to his last escape, they blacked out a sentence that said, 'We are as usual full of optimism and good spirits', which would have passed the censors in Dulag Luft even a few months earlier without much thought, but the final clause, 'now at last with good reason', undoubtedly rankled with the authorities.

For the first time since September 1939, the Germans and Austrians guarding British and American air force officers in late 1942 were confronted by the reality that they may eventually have to answer to the men in their charge.

News from the front lines in Russia, North Africa, the North Atlantic and the Far East were not encouraging for supporters of the Third Reich: General Montgomery ground out a significant British victory at El Alamein, marking the beginning of the end for General Rommel's Afrika Korps, which was in full retreat after the battle in the last week of October; in an operation called

Torch, the Americans landed troops in Algeria and Morocco, the French colonies controlled by collaborators loyal to the Vichy government; in the Atlantic, the British, American and Canadian navies at last began to take a heavy toll of the U-boats; and at Stalingrad, the Russians were sucking the German Sixth Army into the city, which would become a graveyard for the *Wehrmacht*'s ambitions. Added to this, the Japanese advance was halted in New Guinea and Guadalcanal. It was, as the historian, A. J. P. Taylor wrote, the last year of victories for Germany and Japan, and the first of Allied ones.

Informed by the BBC, which was monitored on an illegal wireless by prisoners in the Centre Compound, Bushell probably knew about the change in mood and had no intention of being cowed by threats from the Gestapo or, for that matter, any other German. Bushell would tell his parents in a letter from Stalag Luft III that the BBC was doing its stuff 'magnificently'.

Day had told Bushell's parents that their son had agreed to take a back seat after his arrival at Stalag Luft III, 'but said that if later on the opportunity to make "a good getaway" offered, he was not going to sit back in the camp'.

There are no minutes of meetings at Stalag Luft III, no primary record of conversation apart from the memories of the prisoners themselves.

Paul Brickhill described the escape in a programme broadcast on the BBC on Sunday, 16 September 1945, which, according to *The Times*, was 'the first indication that Squadron Leader Bushell was the organising genius behind the escape from Stalag Luft III', and certainly the first occasion on which he came to the notice of the British public.

Six years later, on Sunday, 4 March 1951, the BBC broadcast a play adapted from Brickhill's book, *The Great Escape*, which had just been published. The original tapes have apparently been lost, but the script can be found in the files of the Imperial War Museum. At first glance, the play appears simplistic, but it conveys the feel of the period and rings with emotional truth.

'"The Great Escape",' the narrator would have announced, as millions of people listened. 'This is the story of the mass escape from Stalag Luft III in 1944 . . . in this programme we use the real names of these men. I need hardly say that we do so with the utmost respect and admiration.

'In 1942,' the script continued, 'Stalag Luft III was a new camp for Allied Air Force Officers, ironically known as "Göring's Luxury Camp". In fact, it was a desolate arrangement of huts and barbed wire at Sagan, in Germany's dust-bowl Silesia, up towards the Polish border. Paul Brickhill, who has written the history of the escape and whom I [the narrator] represent in this programme, found himself there after being shot down over the Mareth Line in Tunisia. His part in it was to run the Stooges who guarded the forger of tickets and passes. He describes himself as the "Boswell" [a reference to the celebrated biographer] of the show.

'The "Johnson" is a remarkable man called Roger Bushell, who had been a prisoner since his Spitfire was shot down over Dunkirk.'

A 'Friend' then joins the script: 'I had known Roger since his early twenties when he'd been British ski champion. He was a big, tempestuous fellow, and once, in an international race in Canada, the tip of one ski had caught the inner corner of his eye and gashed it wickedly so as to cause a permanent droop, giving him a strangely sinister look.

'Since his capture in 1940, Roger had made such a nuisance of himself that he'd ended up in the care of the Gestapo. His transfer to Stalag Luft III had been effected by a German who knew and liked him – von Masse [Günther von Massow] – the camp's chief censor officer, who got no thanks for his pains when Roger arrived.'

'Von Masse', according to the script, said: 'Ah, Squadron Leader – welcome to Stalag Luft III.'

Bushell responded: 'Ah, to hell with you. I've just been staying with some friends of yours in Prague.'

Von Masse: 'Ah, the Gestapo. They are no friends of ours.'

Bushell: 'Oh no? You're on the same side, aren't you? What did they do to the Czech family that looked after me? Shot them in the back. My God, I've seen things there – Lidice wasn't the only one.'

The narrator broke in at that moment: 'Von Masse was so upset that he forgot to search him, which was what Roger had banked on. He came into the compound with a smart grey suit, which he had been given by his Czech host and which he planned to use on his next escape. But we found him less boisterous than of old.'

The script then moves on to engage other prisoners. Wally Floody, an engineer and expert tunneller, says: 'Roger! How are you – where have you been?'

Bushell: 'I've been staying with some gentlemen I don't like – let's leave it at that. Well, now, tell me how you are fixed here.'

'Oh, we're keeping them busy, Roger,' says Peter Fanshawe. 'The night we arrived here Wings Day and a couple of others tried to walk out in fake Luftwaffe uniforms. But the guard wasn't fooled, and they got fourteen days in the cooler.'

Bushell responded: 'Oh. What about the tunnel situation?'

'Well, as you see,' said Floody, 'they've cleared the ground on the far side of the wire for over 100ft. And it's sandy soil which collapses easily. They've also got microphones buried all around the wire to pick up any tunnelling sound.'

'You've got to go deep then?' said Bushell.

Floody answered: 'Yes, and that raises the problem of ventilation. People get terribly ill.'

Another prisoner, Tim Walenn, joined the conversation. 'We've had some bad falls of sand. Floody nearly got suffocated only a week ago.'

'Oh, that's a risk we all take,' said Floody. 'The major problem, though, is hiding the sand when we dig it out. That's what gave away the last tunnel when it only had a hundred feet to go.'

Bushell: 'What about the commandant, is he all right?'

Fanshawe: 'Oh, not bad – service type, very correct.'

Bushell: 'And how about the factories, forging and that kind of thing?'

Floody: 'Oh, they're coming along. What we need is an overall control. We'd like you to do it, Roger. Will you take it on?'

Bushell: 'Mm – I'd love to. I'm in a dirty mood about these Germans now. Let's get on with it.'

In reality, Bushell apparently agonised for some time before taking on the role of 'X', but the play corresponds with most known reports of what happened after Bushell's return to Stalag Luft III. The story of von Massow, who had befriended Bushell at Dulag Luft and looked after his interests in so many ways at Stalag Luft III, was indeed correct in that he had been so upset by Bushell's attitude towards him, he had forgotten to remove the prisoner's civilian suit. And the German commandant, *Oberst* Friedrich von Lindeiner, was certainly 'very correct', but also an honourable man who took pride in his camp and its inmates.

The escape organisation, run once again by Wings Day and Jimmy Buckley – who had done the same at Dulag Luft and Stalag Luft I – faced apparently insuperable problems. Many tunnels had been started, but all of them were discovered. Day had himself already tried to escape and been sent to the cooler.

Floody, a big Canadian fighter pilot who had worked in the gold mining industry before the war; Peter Fanshawe, a naval airman known as 'Hornblower' who was shot down attacking the German battleship *Scharnhorst*; and Tim Walenn, an artist who founded the Midland Bank Flying Club, were all destined to be among Bushell's leading lieutenants at Stalag Luft III.

Bushell's chance to 'sit back', as Day had described it after ordering him to take a rest from escape activity, did not last long. Day and Buckley were transferred to another camp, Oflag XXIB at Schubin in Poland. 'He did lie low,' wrote Day, 'but owing to the purging of myself and Lieut. Comdr. Buckley to another camp in October 1942, Roger was the only one capable of running the

escape activities . . . his wide knowledge and outstanding qualities of mind and drive made him the only man suitable to take
over the job.'

Bushell took over the escape committee – the X organisation –
and, from that moment, was known as 'Big X'. He proceeded to
put the business of escaping on an industrial footing.

As the only man from Stalag Luft I who still had an interest in
the sweepstake predicting the date on which the war would end –
Bushell had taken a long view – it is not surprising perhaps that
he took a strategic approach to his new responsibilities. 'As head
of the Escape Committee, Roger went very warily and during the
Winter of 1942 till March 1943 he stopped all escape attempts in
order to put the Germans off their guard,' wrote Day.

Hardened by his experience of the Nazis in Prague and Berlin,
Bushell had a clear message for his fellow prisoners, nearly all of
whom had survived the traumatic experience of being shot down
– either by jumping from blazing aircraft or surviving in the
wreckage of crashed bombers and fighters: 'The only reason that
God allowed us this extra ration of life is so we can make life hell
for the Hun,' he said, reminding them that they were all still very
much at war.

More than sixty years later, Sydney Dowse, himself an indomitable escaper who was known as 'Laughing Boy' because of his
cheerful nature, explained why Bushell was a good choice for Big
X: 'He had a clear brain, he knew what he wanted and what he
didn't want. And what he expected of us – and that was very
important because sometimes we wouldn't necessarily know what
we should do and he would make it clear what we ought to do.'

Another prisoner, Walter Morison, who, like Bushell, had been
at Cambridge, said: 'He took charge and brought order and discipline into the whole process . . . escape became the principal
industry.'

He was a 'formidable figure', according to the historian, M. R. D.
Foot, the historian of MI9 who emphasised the importance of Big
X. 'It was a very responsible position,' he said.

In the autumn of 1942, the prisoners became aware that they were to be transferred to a new compound to the west of the East Compound, beyond the section of the camp known as the *Kommandantur*, where the German administrative buildings were sited. Russian prisoners had already cleared an area of the forest and were beginning to put up new wooden huts.

Big X intended to take advantage of the move. He outlined his plans at a meeting of the escape committee.

As the narrator told listeners to Brickhill's play on BBC radio, 'The conference lasted two hours, with all of them shooting ideas, some wild, some good. When it broke up, they had the basic points decided – three tunnels 30ft deep with underground railways, and workshops, mass-produced compasses and maps, and a huge intelligence and security operation. Roger took the details to Massey, the Senior British Officer, and the group captain listened, resting his game [gammy] leg on his bunk and drawing on a pipe.'

At the age of forty-four, Group Captain Herbert Massey was an unusual prisoner. He had been injured in the First World War, but remained in the air force and continued to fly. He was shot down in a four-engine Stirling bomber over the Dutch coast in 1942, and, due to his rank, had succeeded Day as Senior British Officer.

According to Brickhill's script, Massey commented that it was 'a very elaborate plan', and asked, 'Do you think you can carry it off?'

Bushell replied: 'I'm sure we can, sir. We've been learning the hard way.'

'All right, Bushell,' replied Massey, 'but look here, you've been out twice now and nearly made it. The Gestapo think you're a saboteur and would be happy to get something more on you. Why don't you lie low for a while and leave it to the others? I don't want you getting a bullet in the back of the head.'

'I won't, sir,' replied Bushell. 'This is going to be a long job, and if we get out they'll have forgotten about me. I'll worry about that when the time comes, if you don't mind.'

Big X had just told the camp leadership that he would try to get 200 men out in one night. But Bushell's ambition was not confined to getting valuable air force officers back to Britain. He also wanted to cause as much disruption to the German war effort as possible.

Breathtaking in its scope and ambition, the plan, which involved the work of up to 600 men, would only start to be implemented in earnest once the prisoners had moved to the new North Compound, which was scheduled for January but then delayed. In the meantime, just as Bushell directed, the inmates set about giving the Germans a false sense of security: escape activity was limited. Everyone started work instead on plans for the new campaign.

Bushell wanted to build three big tunnels, which were named 'Tom', 'Dick' and 'Harry' after the move to the North Compound. That way, if one was discovered, they could fall back on the other two. The tunnel shafts would be sunk to depths that would put them out of range of the seismograph microphones. They would be robust, shored up with wooden boards pillaged from beds and panelling, lit by electric lights and air-conditioned. The digging would involve teams of men working only when it was considered safe. Security was paramount.

The escape committee, driven by Bushell, would make use of every skill available within the camp. He appointed representatives in each hut, which were home to more than 100 men, to help with the running of this immensely complex and hazardous operation, while the intelligence operation would be ratcheted up to levels probably unimagined by MI9.

Nearly seventy years on, in an age of spreadsheets, computers and consultants, Bushell's leadership of the X organisation would be held up as a masterpiece of project management that ticked all the boxes in terms of cost, quality control, time management, risk, integration, communications and use of human resources. Just occasionally, Bushell would long for the advice of his father, Ben, the former mining engineer, but it could never be available.

Paddy Byrne told Bushell's parents:

He took over the escaping organisation of Luft III and worked day and night to build up an organisation, the like of which had never been equalled before . . . he knew the art of being a prisoner better than most of us . . . one would think he enjoyed being a prisoner, which of course was not so, but he would not let anything get him down.

While Bushell did not exactly radiate joy in a letter to his parents in late December 1942 – 'We had quite a comic Xmas, with lots of Red X food and home brewed booze, which had to be tasted to be believed, but which produced the desired oblivion, which is all that is required in a place like this' – he told John Brinton, his former adjutant at 92 Squadron, that 'we are all bubbling over with optimism at the moment, and I personally am quite certain we have at last had our last Xmas here.'

As 1942 gave way to 1943, Bushell devoted himself to three noble enterprises, the tunnels that would be known as 'Tom', 'Dick' and 'Harry'; and one great passion, Lady Georgiana Mary Curzon.

20

Going Underground

A significant shift in Bushell's political thinking appears to have occurred during 1943 as he took over the reins of the X committee and organised the mass breakout from Stalag Luft III.

Using the tools and language of the Left, the former alpine playboy banned private enterprise and embraced the collective endeavour – albeit very much his collective endeavour – nurturing every element of the great plan, demanding rigour from his colleagues and driving them on in a manner that would have delighted the Soviet leader, 'Uncle Joe' Stalin.

Sitting in a mock Parliament set up by the camp's debating society to discuss the future of the world, Bushell would take his place in the autumn of 1943 as 'deputy leader of the Labour Party' and advocate the nationalisation of all major industries after the war. He was not the only radical, which gives an insight into the nature of the camp leadership: Squadron Leader Tom Kirby-Green, one of Bushell's security chiefs who was born in modern Malawi, then known as Nyasaland, called for a new deal for Britain's colonies under which the rights of the native peoples should be recognised.

Whatever political ideals Bushell may have harboured – there are no mentions of any in his letters home, but post-war politics would have been an interesting challenge for the censor – he excelled at hammering out practical issues and pulling the many levers related to escape activity at Stalag Luft III. 'He had a mind like a filing cabinet, and that was one of the reasons he was so brilliant at organisation,' wrote Brickhill.

Big X challenged the Germans on two distinct fronts while trying to disguise his own involvement.

The first was the development of the tunnels – but with a new emphasis on the security of the project – and the provision of sophisticated equipment, both for construction and escape.

The second was the aggressive pursuit of all kinds of intelligence: information that would assist the 200 Allied airmen Bushell intended to get out of the camp, and any military intelligence that would help the Allies to win the war.

Although Bushell's ambition was stamped on this enterprise, the thirty-two-year-old squadron leader was not in a position of untrammelled power. He was answerable to Group Captain Massey, the Senior British Officer, and the nineteen other members of the escape committee, but they nonetheless seem to have followed where he led, and there is no record of serious disagreements.

According to the official history of the North Compound, which was written after the war by some of the men involved in the operation at Stalag Luft III and can be found in the National Archive at Kew:

The Escape Committee had been set up before the transfer from the East Compound, and had already done all preliminary planning and was ready to come into action as soon as the move took place. *The report said that*: the first Head of the Committee was 90120 [service number] S/Ldr. R. Bushell, R.A.F.

The Committee assumed a complete and strict control of all escape activities, and attempts. It had the support of the Senior British Officer, who was responsible for the appointment of Bushell. Plans had already been made for the construction of three large tunnels, and no other tunnels were allowed to be constructed.

Each of the nineteen members of the X organisation had different responsibilities as they moved to the North Compound in March 1943. Each was recorded in the official camp history. These ranged from being in charge of carpentry (Squadron Leader C. N. S.

Campbell, RAF) or compound security (Lieutenant Colonel A. P. Clark, United States Air Corps), to overseeing the collection of escape intelligence (Wing Commander A. Eyre, RAF), or forgery (Flight Lieutenant G. W. Walenn, RAF).

Three men, Flight Lieutenant C. W. Floody (RCAF), Flight Lieutenant R. G. Ker-Ramsey (RAF) and Flight Lieutenant H. C. Marshall (RAF) represented the tunnel committee; while Lieutenant Commander N. R. Quill (RN) was appointed Big X's personal adviser from late April.

Under Bushell's leadership, the men of the North Compound of Stalag Luft III would become one of the most belligerent, imaginative and mischievous forces ever to confront Hitler's 'monstrous tyranny', as Churchill once described it, embodying everything that Major Norman Crockatt had set out to achieve when he founded MI9, the British intelligence agency established in December 1939 to aid escape and evasion.

As a marked man, the third element of Bushell's policy was to convince the Germans that he had given up all escape activity and was pursuing other interests. He tried to fade into the background: he played rugby; read many books; started to learn Danish and Spanish to add to his other languages, and taught German. He also started to take an interest in amateur dramatics, though with Mackintosh, Butterworth and Casson among the directors and producers, it was hardly amateur.

In a letter to his parents dated 28 February 1943, Bushell wrote:

I have taken to the boards – in the camp theatre – as a fat and worried old stockbroker who gets the wind up about the world and his own affairs at 5 a.m. (in bed). It is an amusing playlet called 'Apprehensions' and the girls are played by fellow Kriegies – some of them are astonishingly good. It has been a great success and amused me no end. We go on tomorrow night for a second series. The acting, after my training at the Bar, I find not very difficult! Lots of love to you all.

Behind the scenes, it was very different. Bushell held daily conferences with his heads of department, thrashed out problems, and exhorted them to meet their production targets: Tim Walenn was told he would need to forge 200 official documents within three months; Tommy Guest, head of tailoring, was told to deliver 200 civilian outfits; and Des Plunkett was asked for 1,000 maps.

Bushell's decision to restrict escape activity paid off. Approaching the German administration in what appeared to be a co-operative spirit, Group Captain Massey, the SBO, offered to send parties of Allied prisoners from the East Compound to help with work on the new North Compound. Under the Geneva Convention, captured officers were forbidden from undertaking any kind of work for their captors, but *Oberst* von Lindeiner naïvely accepted the British offer. The commandant also made one other decision that would help the escapers. He allowed some of the trees growing in the North Compound to remain there.

Big X made the most of this opportunity.

For three months before the North Compound was opened, the three P.s/W who had been in charge of tunnelling operations in the East Compound, and were to continue in the North Compound, went over on working parties, ostensibly to help build the Compound theatre, and made themselves thoroughly familiar with the layout of the Compound, *the official history said*.

The three PoWs were engineers: the Canadian Wally Floody; Robert 'Crump' Ker-Ramsey, a short stocky man ideally built for working in tunnels; and Flight Lieutenant Henry Cuthbert Marshall, a Spitfire pilot known to everyone as Johnny.

Assisted by members of the escape organisation's mapping department, who surveyed the compound, the engineers decided that two of Bushell's three tunnels would run to the west and one to the north, and all three would have exits in the woods. If the Germans found one of the tunnels, the official history explained, the escape committee thought it unlikely that they would look for others, believing that the prisoners must have expended all their energies on the one tunnel due to its scale and sophistication.

On 27 March 1943, about 850 prisoners moved from the East Compound to the North. In scenes similar to the ones portrayed at the start of the Hollywood film, *The Great Escape*, released in 1963, lorries and carts carrying trees and rubbish were going in the opposite direction.

> Many prisoners of war took the opportunity of jumping onto these transports in the hope that they would, with luck, get outside the Camp, *reported the official history.* None of them were prepared or had any escape aids and all of them were apprehended.

But this indiscipline lasted only briefly: the X organisation took command and got to work. One of its first moves was to appeal for volunteers.

> Notices were posted in every barrack inviting those who wished to take part in various kinds of sport to put their names on a list, *wrote Aidan Crawley in his book Escape from Germany.* It had already been made known secretly that these lists were to register volunteers for the escape organisation, and about two-thirds of the camp applied. As there was no room for sport on such a scale and such long lists might have aroused suspicion, they were at once re-sorted by the camp adjutant in a special file under educational headings. Under 'History' came those who were to disperse the sand from tunnels, under 'German' those who were to be contacts [also known as traders], under 'Rugger' those who were to dig, and so on.

According to the official history, however, the escape committee already knew who were 'the leading spirits, the experts, the escapers, the self-effacing but thoroughly co-operative men, and the 'not-interested' class.

When the Germans had come up with their plan for Stalag Luft III, their intention had been to put most of the captured officers from the Allied air forces in one escape-proof camp. It was a mistake. In doing so, they created an exceptional pool of international talent from which Bushell and the X organisation could draw.

Among the American, Australian, Belgian, British, Canadian, Czech, Danish, Dutch, French, Greek, Lithuanian, New Zealand, Polish and South African airmen were millionaires, missionaries and miners, scientists, artists and photographers, journalists and cowboys. Bushell employed every skill available to him. Engineers and surveyors would join the tunnelling teams; tailors and clothiers would make German military uniforms, civilian suits and casual clothes; draughtsmen and artists would forge documents and papers provided by German 'contacts', and copy maps; and carpenters would make air pumps for the tunnels and secret cupboards where equipment could be hidden. Food would also be harvested for escape rations. And so the list went on.

After the move to the North Compound, the engineers searched for the best sites for the three tunnel traps – the entrances to the tunnels – taking into account the German guard placements and blind spots. The mapping team committed their surveys to paper. Metal workers started to produce shovels and the carpentry 'workshops' opened. Sound tests were also undertaken to find out how much noise could be made without alerting the Germans.

By 11th April, 1943, the sites for the three traps had been chosen and work began, *said the official history*. The traps were built in concrete parts of the barrack flooring because the huts were built off the ground, and only the concrete parts continued down into the ground . . . one of the tunnels running West was to begin from Barrack 123. The engineer in charge of this tunnel was Marshall. The tunnel was given the name of 'TOM'.

The official history explained that the trap was made in the concrete floor of a small annexe to one of the rooms, covering an area of two square feet. A removable concrete block of this size was made from cement that had been left lying around by German workers, and was put in place of the concrete flooring, which had been chipped out.

Tunnellers reporting for duty were unable to find this trap until shown where it was, *said the official history*. The first tunnel trap was completed on 15 April, and work began on sinking the shaft.

The second tunnel running West began in barrack 122. It was named 'DICK'. The engineer in charge of it was named Ker-Ramsey.

In the floor of the wash-room of barrack 122 there was an iron grating covering a concrete drain eighteen inches square and two feet deep. The grating was taken up, any water was baled out and one side was chipped away and replaced with a concrete slab that could be slid up and down.

The tunnel running north, 'HARRY', began in barrack 104 and the engineer in charge of it was Floody. According to the official camp history, in this room:

. . . there was a stove standing on a hundred tiles. These were taken up and the concrete scraped from them with a pick-axe acquired from Russian P.s/W. The tiles were reset into a wooden trap, the cement taking four days to set. When it was ready it did not satisfy the engineer or the trap-makers, so it was exchanged for one from the Compound kitchen, which had the tiles set in wood. These were taken up, cleaned, and reset. Another four days were allowed for the cement to harden. The trap was lifted by two strips of sheet metal which folded down sideways and could be hooked up with a knife. Within the next three days, the four inches of concrete and brick which lay under the trap were chipped away.

As the engineers worked on the traps and shafts, everyone waited anxiously, knowing that these were among the most critical moments if Bushell's plan was to have any chance of success. The noise of shattered concrete was camouflaged by the sounds of choirs and musicians, bashed pots and pans and other diversions organised by the escape committee, but they could work only between 12.30 p.m. and 2.30 p.m., when most of the noise was made, and between 10 p.m. and 11.50 p.m. at night. Such were the risks that nothing was done if more than one German 'ferret' or guard was in the compound.

The vertical shafts of each tunnel were built by the three engineers, *records the official history*. They were all about thirty feet deep and had ladders twenty-five feet long. Three chambers were built at the foot of each shaft. The pump chamber [for ventilation] was five feet long, five and a half feet high and two and a half feet wide. The general storage chamber for tools, shoring, lamps, tins etc was ten feet long, three feet nine inches high, two and a half feet wide for the first four feet, and then two feet square for the last six feet.

Power for lighting the tunnels was obtained by tapping the German wiring as it passed through the double wall of the barracks. Leads were conducted inside the double walls, then under the floor to the tunnel shafts. The power was cut off during the day and lamps filled with margarine instead. They burned for an hour at a time and were brought up every night for servicing.

As soon as the vertical shafts were finished, work began after morning roll-call and continued until a few minutes before evening roll-call, after which a second shift of tunnellers went down and worked till just before 'lock-up' time. A three-shift system was operated: 'A' shift working during one day, 'B' shift during the evening, 'C' shift the next day, and 'A' shift the next evening. The numbers of men in each shift were usually six: two men at the working face, one digging and the other loading the sand to be taken back to the shaft, one man to collect the sand at the shaft, one to operate the air pump, and two in the general chamber to prepare shoring and airline tins [a seamless row of powdered-milk cans down which air was pumped to the face of the tunnel], preparing lamps etc.

The shafts were completed by the end of May, and work on all three tunnels continued until July, when heavy falls of sand blocked both 'Dick' and 'Harry'. It took some time to get going again. An attempt to strengthen the tunnels was made by shoring them up with bed boards, the tongue of one board fitting into the groove of the next, after every six feet of tunnel had been excavated. The line of tins, enabling air to be pumped to the tunnel face, was also laid as the tunnellers pushed forward – hour after hour, day after day.

While the vertical shafts were under construction the excavated sand was hauled up in jugs, *said the official history*. As soon as the tunnels were long enough, rails were laid and a trolley hauled backwards and forwards between the working face and the dispersal chamber. The rails, which were made from strips of wooden beading, were nailed to the wood of the tunnel floor. The gauge was twelve and a half inches. The trolleys had wooden frames with edges to hold two wooden boxes which fitted into the frames. The axles and wheel rims were made of metal. The rope consisted of plaited string.

The trolleys and railway were a great improvement on the sledges used in previous tunnels of similar size, because the sledges had to be pulled along the floor and wore out quickly, also they caused falls of sand. They were very heavy to pull, and tunnellers could not ride to the working face and back on them because this made them too heavy. The trolleys, running on wheels and rails, required much less effort to pull and tunnellers could ride on them. There was much less strain on the ropes, which when pulling sledges, broke frequently.

Bushell was, however, vexed over how to dispose of the yellow sand. The problem was solved by Peter Fanshawe and described in the play for the BBC.

The chief 'ferret', an honest and incorruptible man with a sense of humour called Hermann Glemnitz, had apparently expressed the view that tunnelling would be limited because the prisoners would be unable to hide the sand.

'Glemnitz is right, curse him,' said Wally Floody. 'How are we going to hide the sand?'

'Now this is your problem, Fanshawe,' said Bushell. 'You're OC [officer commanding] sand dispersal.'

Fanshawe replied: 'Well, we could spread the yellow sand in the compound and cover it with the grey top soil.'

'Mm – sounds possible,' said Bushell. 'But how are you going to spread the stuff without being spotted? It'll look pretty obvious.'

Fanshawe seemed to have the answer. 'Ah – I've got a new invention, Roger – trouser bags.'

'What?' said Bushell.

'I've cut the legs off some of those long woollen underpants the Red Cross are so fond of sending us,' said Fanshawe, 'and tied them together by a string which you loop round your neck.'

Bushell responded: 'Go on.'

'Then the legs hang down inside your trousers,' said Fanshawe. 'Now each leg has a pin stuck in the bottom which leads up by a string into your trouser pocket. You fill the bags with sand at the trap doors and you wander round the various spots, and then you pull the string in your pocket. Out come the pins and the sand flows out the bottom of your trousers. If you're not a complete clot, the ferrets will never see a thing.'

'Well, I'll be damned,' said Bushell. 'For a conservative citizen like yourself, I call that indecently brilliant. We'll try it immediately.'

'I have,' said Fanshawe. 'It works.'

Like the tunnels themselves, the men dispersing the sand had a nickname – 'penguins'. Nicknames were used so that the words 'tunnel' and 'dispersers' were never heard in the compound.

Sand excavated from the tunnels was put into sacks in the dispersal chamber and hauled to the top of the vertical shafts, where it was poured through funnels made from tins into Fanshawe's trouser bags. Penguins picked up the bags from coat hooks in the trap-rooms. Whenever possible, the sand was dispersed over large sandy areas created by the digging of drains when the compound was built. Many of these patches were hidden from the view of guards and watchtowers by buildings.

More than 200 volunteers were used to disperse the sand over 'the circuit' – a well-trodden path around the perimeter of the camp, in the prisoners' gardens and twenty-odd other sites elsewhere. It cannot have been easy: the vertical shaft and three chambers produced twelve tons of sand from each of the three tunnels. A further ton of sand was excavated from just over every three feet of tunnel. This meant that 130 tons of sand were dispersed by the penguins on 18,000 journeys from the trap-rooms to the dispersal sites.

Bushell was also obsessed by security. A tall American colonel, A. P. 'Junior' Clark was appointed 'Big S' in charge of compound security, with George Harsh, another American, as his deputy. Kirby-Green monitored the movements of the German staff, who were logged in and out of the compound. Bushell also appointed a 'Little X' and a 'Little S' in every hut. The security operation included another 150 men.

The trap of each tunnel had its own security man who was responsible [for ensuring] that the coast was clear when the trap was opened and closed, and ascertaining that no traces of sand or any other suspicious sign was present near the trap, that it was properly closed and bore no suspicious marks of use, *said the official history.*

The purpose of the duty pilot system was to note in a logbook the time of entry and departure of every German in the compound, with his name or a description of him, and to make sure that the escape departments knew of the threat. The entire compound was warned when search parties approached. For the benefit of the tunnellers, the system in the North Compound was refined further with the site divided into a safe zone and a danger zone. Work stopped when any German entered the area in which the three tunnels were located. The Germans, meanwhile, were well aware that their movements were being monitored and, at times, some logged themselves in and out with the duty pilot. Kirby-Green also operated a night shift, which they managed to keep secret from the Germans.

Bushell briefed representatives from each hut every week on the progress of the three tunnels and heard proposals for any alternative means of escape. These would be considered by the relevant heads of department.

When a plan was approved, the escaper would be provided with clothing, papers, food, maps, any tools he needed and a cover story. Before making the attempt, he would be briefed by Bushell, who would take him through 'the fullest possible' details of his route, possible contacts and the greatest sources of danger.

He would learn by heart the story he was to tell, who he was, his business, his presence in every locality, etc, and would be warned how to behave in case of capture, how he must destroy all equipment, especially forged documents, deny that he had any equipment or was helped in any way by any other P/W, and generally to divert any suspicion of organisation of escape in the camp.

By this time, the organisation of the engineering had become a formidable operation. The official history of Stalag Luft III spells it out:

> The magnitude of these undertakings surpassed all other similar projects instituted in other Prisoner of War Camps in Germany. The ingenuity, skill, determination, team-spirit and leadership displayed by the personnel connected with all aspects of these undertakings is self-evident and further comment would be superfluous.

Bushell did not write to his family in South Africa at the end of March. 'We were all moving and I left it until too late,' he told them in his letter of 29 April, but that was the only indication he gave them of the burdens he was carrying as Big X.

> *We are now in a new camp built next door to the old one. It is a great improvement. Much bigger and with trees in it! In some places you can hardly see the wire. You've no idea what a difference that makes.*
>
> *I have a room to myself in the same hut as Bob [Stanford Tuck]. I expect I'll have to take in a partner though soon as the place is filling up rapidly and the other main RAF camp has now moved into our old quarters.*

Bushell told his parents that the Germans had stopped all parcels from Portugal, which meant he would no longer be receiving Mildred Blandy's cheese and sausages from Madeira. 'Don't worry though,' he wrote, 'we are very well off [for] food and, thanks to the Red X, are the best fed people in Europe to-day.'

He apologised that his own letters were 'pretty dull', but told Ben and Dorothe that he had had several letters from England, where the mood was very definitely changing. 'They are all full of optimism which this time I know is not misplaced,' he wrote.

He had heard from Tony Page in Zurich. 'My friend Lile is now married,' wrote Bushell. 'Flicky Taylor says Christopher is still in the Desert [North Africa] though very nearly at the end of the journey now. Jimmy Little also wrote. He is married now too.'

And then, a little wistfully perhaps, he added: 'I'll be the only bachelor left in England by the end of the war.'

21

Love of a Lady

Despite the unpredictable nature of the postal service between southern England and eastern Germany, Roger Bushell's relationship with Georgiana Curzon was blossoming. As letters were exchanged, it became increasingly clear that, contrary to Bushell's stated concern, he would not remain a bachelor for long if he survived the war.

He hinted at the burgeoning nature of his relationship with Georgie in a letter to his parents, who were complaining about the absence of post from Germany.

> *Please do not get upset about their non-arrival for I write regularly each month and the reason must be the chaotic state of the mail these days. The letters I receive from you are the best indication of that. Everybody is in the same boat and I, for example, have not had a single letter from England this month tho' I am quite certain Georgie, if no one else, has written me reams!*

Bushell's younger sister, Lis, went further when asked about the affair in 2004. 'It was this sort of passionate love scene through letters – then onward – and he was absolutely determined, he couldn't wait to get out, to marry her,' she said. He was 'fascinated' by her.

While Georgiana was writing 'reams' to Bushell, her father, Earl Howe, was taking to task his estranged wife, Joyce Mary McLean, Countess Howe, and her lover, Home Kidston – Georgiana's husband – in the Probate, Divorce and Admiralty Division of the High Court of Justice, where he was pushing for a settlement in his daughter's divorce. The countess, who denied adultery and was submitting her own applications, had delayed the case.

In legal documents dating from July 1943, Earl Howe, who was serving as a commodore in the Royal Navy, outlined his concerns about the health of his daughter, Georgie. He expressed his belief that the consistent tactics adopted by his wife, the Countess Howe, to hold up divorce proceedings were undertaken with the clear intention of adding to the strain suffered by his daughter. He pointed out that Georgie's doctor was also concerned about Georgie's well-being.

Earl Howe, who, of course, had issues of his own concerning Kidston's adultery, was adamant that his daughter and grandson, Glen, should be spared such anxiety and strain so that they could live quietly and try to rebuild their shattered lives after the destruction of their family life by Georgie's husband.

According to Wings Day, however, the former Senior British Officer at Stalag Luft III who was close to Bushell, Home Kidston may not have been the only guilty party in his marriage.

Day told his biographer, Sydney Smith, that in 1940, while he was at Dulag Luft, the Luftwaffe transit camp near Frankfurt, the commandant, Theo Rumpel, had told him the story of a young prisoner who was in love.

The officer had asked to see Rumpel and, in confidence, without Wings' knowledge, *wrote Sydney Smith*, he had told Rumpel the story of a love affair with a girl whose titled parents would not let her marry him. She had taken lodgings near his fighter base in Kent, and there they met in their spare moments, and spare nights. The officer told Rumpel that the pain of separation was more than he could bear. He begged to be liberated. He said to Rumpel. 'You could easily lend me a car to get to the Spanish frontier. Look' – he had pointed to the map of Europe – 'it's not very far really. You do not understand how we feel. It's, well, it's so much more important than war or anything. No one, nothing, should be allowed to separate people who feel as we do . . . will you please let me go home?'

He was not mad or even unbalanced, *wrote Sydney Smith*. He was in love, facing years of separation. Rumpel found himself saying 'No' reluctantly, even apologetically.

Wings knew who the officer was, though he never knew Wings knew his secret. He became a dedicated escaper . . .

Day does not name the man, but the similarities between the officer and Bushell are compelling: Bushell's attempt to marry Lady Georgiana Curzon had been thwarted by her parents; he flew from the Kent fighter base of Biggin Hill at the start of the war and, according to 92 Squadron's logbook, stayed there over-night on several occasions when he was based at other aero-dromes such as Tangmere and Croydon. Georgie's husband, Kidston, would have been at sea for much of this time. And who, but Bushell, would have had the audacity to request a private meeting with Rumpel to ask him for a car in which to drive to Spain?

If Bushell was the officer in question, the story gives weight to Vlasta Christova's assertion that the woman to whom he was committed in Britain – and for whom he spurned his Czech lover, Blaža Zeithammelová – was not his fiancée, Peggy Hamilton, but Georgiana Curzon.

The post from Stalag Luft III did not improve and remained a major subject of discussion with Bushell's parents. 'The mail is rotten these days,' he told them in a letter dated 26 May 1943, 'and it is quite clear it is being held up somewhere, probably due to insufficient censoring staff or perhaps just sheer laziness. Very exasperating.'

In the same letter, he referred to the compound filling up with prisoners. 'We are about 1,500-strong now,' he wrote, which was an indication of the growing strength of the air offensive against Germany – as well as the mounting losses suffered by the Allied air forces. On an ever-increasing scale,

Sir Arthur Harris continued the bombing of Germany at night, with the Americans hitting targets by day: the RAF attacked the Ruhr from March to June 1943, including Wing Commander Guy Gibson's attack on the great dams. Elsewhere, in May, German forces had surrendered in Tunisia, ending the fighting in North Africa.

Bushell continued: 'Newcomers very optimistic especially about effect of our particular efforts,' a reference perhaps to escape activity in the North Compound, but there were also signs that he retained an interest in South Africa: 'We had an SA party on Gen Smuts' [the South African prime minister's] birthday and sent him a telegram. Wonder if he ever gets it?'

With his thoughts still very much in the southern hemisphere, he added: 'Eliza's trip to Basutoland [modern Lesotho] sounds enchanting. Maybe I'll come out and run a skiing resort there after the war if all else fails!'

A month later, as the British and Americans gathered forces for the invasion of Sicily and the Russians prepared to face the *Wehrmacht* in the great tank battle at Kursk, Bushell confronted his mother over her undated mail.

> It is quite untrue that I never acknowledge Mummie's letters, he wrote on 28 June 1943. Whenever I receive one, I acknowledge it as well as I am able but as they are almost invariably undated – this is a complaint of some years' standing now! – it is sometimes difficult to be very explicit having regard to the limitations of space. Please don't fuss, darling. I love getting your letters very much indeed and I am sure that most of them get through sooner or later. If I do not refer to them in detail, that does not mean I do not read them through and through. But remember that with the dreadful time lag in our letters it's a little difficult to keep up an intelligent correspondence.

He adopted a teasing tone for his final flourish:

*I am a shocking letter-writer anyway. Some years of
experience should have taught you that by now. None of
our generation knows how to write letters. Too much rush
– long distance telephones, radio, aeroplanes and so on are
not the background for such a slow and wearisome
business as putting pen (pencil, if you must be exact) to
paper. If I had a dictaphone, an efficient and pretty typist
and a comfortable office, I'd write you wonderful letters. As
it is, I've got to the end of this niggardly page, and have
only time to tell you I am well, full of hope and love you all
very much.*

He continued to get letters from every member of the family,
including one from Tods that was undated – 'This seems to be
becoming a habit among the female Bushells!' wrote Roger.

For all the vagaries of life as a prisoner, the killings in Prague
and the shadow of the Gestapo, Bushell remained sensitive to the
fate of others. In the summer of 1943, news reached him of the
death of a friend who had been a pilot with 601 Squadron.

*James Little has been killed – flying accident – six weeks
before being made a Group Captain and therefore
grounded,* he wrote in a letter to his parents. *It is too
damnable. I still find it difficult to believe. All through the
Battle of B and then a further tour of ops and now a silly
bloody accident. I feel so desperately sorry for Sheila – she
was trying like hell to have a baby and couldn't manage it
in time – and his family. Of the three boys, there's only
Douglas left. The youngest one was killed over Dunkirk.*

He also remained sensitive to family affairs in South Africa. He
received a letter from Lis, now aged twenty-one, complaining
about her father's 'tantrums' over her relationship with a 'new
young man' who may, it seems, have been a member of the clergy.
Bushell stood up for his sister and put Ben in his place:

I personally see nothing to get fussed about, he told his father on 29 August 1943. *The whole thing is obviously absurd and she'll never marry him – anyway, he has now departed until the end of the war.*

With some regard for his father's feelings, he adds:

I said nothing of this in my letter to her, which I wrote with some care and I think will, together with natural causes, produce the right result. If she does not show it to you, I wouldn't bother to mention it.

Bushell's letter to Lis reveals a caring, loving brother – and perhaps gives a greater insight into his feelings about romance:

Have just read your long letter about your young man . . . I wasn't very surprised for I was pretty sure if it wasn't one it would be another of the young men hanging around you and it was only a question of time before you fell for one of them. I personally – and that's maybe why I've never married yet – think that it doesn't matter two pins who the other person is as long as it is really the right one. But – and it is a very big 'But' – there are an enormous number of possible 'right ones' and environment and the sort of life one likes living have a lot to do with making that 'right one' stay right. As you know, I don't go for parson's lunch [straitened domestic means] and I don't think you do and I doubt very much whether in the long run – when you get down to the prosaic side of living – you'd think a great deal of it . . .

Another thing. I have fallen in and out of love (seriously) more times than I like to remember so I should think you're quite likely the same. For we are very alike, aren't we? Therefore I should think it over pretty seriously and don't do anything silly till after the war. Uniforms are much more attractive than dog-collars!

Returning to the letter to his father, which took on something of the air of a lecture on parenthood, Roger continued with relish:

But, my dear old Father, please do not take her, at any rate to her face, so seriously. I remember so well that most of the wickedness I committed when young were [sic] at any rate partially due to your fierce lecturing. I suggest the most effective method of stopping her is to adopt a completely indifferent, maybe even benign, attitude and throw, at the same time, as many other attractive young men at her head as possible.

I personally was not in the slightest surprised and would have considered her somewhat abnormal if she had not fallen for someone sooner or later considering the circumstances. And I consider it very fortunate that the young man, who was almost bound to be unsuitable anyway, has departed so soon.

Responding to his father's concerns about a possible pregnancy, Roger reassures him that, 'as for the biological end, Eliza has far too much common sense and will know exactly what she's doing.'

The letter concluded with a nod to the passing years. 'Tomorrow I am 33. Heigh ho! Lots of love, Roger'.

With not a hint of the burdens he carried at Stalag Luft III, Bushell returned to the subject of Lis's boyfriends in his next letter at the conclusion of a remarkable piece of advice from son to father.

You have time on your side, and a policy of masterly inactivity is therefore obviously the right one. I suggest therefore you stop fussing . . . this is good advice and therefore don't ignore it or think it flippant for it is given from someone who, I suspect (unless you have misled me all my life!) has far more knowledge and experience of the opposite sex than you have. La y est! [There it is!]

Roger Bushell's letters bear testament to his growing confidence during the summer of 1943. Most things, it seemed, had gone his way: Georgie's divorce was finally settled – and his escape organisation had flourished.

22

Secret Agent

In the Silesian forest south of Sagan, perhaps only the birds, singing in the pine tops, felt in any way free from the burdens of war. Many Germans became nervous after their forces had been defeated by the Russians at Stalingrad and Kursk. Few realised that the country faced a catastrophe worse than 1918.

At Stalag Luft III, the prisoners found many Germans troubled by their future – and their past. The assertion by Günther von Massow, the officer in charge of the censors who had once befriended Bushell, that the Gestapo were 'no friends of ours' was a telling reminder that many Germans also hated the Nazi security agencies founded by Himmler and Heydrich.

But for the thousands of Allied prisoners incarcerated at Sagan, the war was far from won, even though it seemed clear that they were, at last, on the winning side. And for some inmates, waiting for life to begin again, as their wives and girlfriends took new lovers and other men took their jobs and positions at home, imprisonment became intolerable.

In this maelstrom of doubt and yearning, betrayal and frustration, Roger Bushell found redemption as a loyal soldier.

'He was a hard man – and a very just man,' said Alex Cassie, one of the PoW forgers who, years afterwards, retained a clear and precise recollection of Big X at this time. The men of Stalag Luft III felt they were in 'safe hands . . . things would be organised properly'.

'He was a barrister,' said Walter Morison, another prisoner, 'cool, logical and ruthless.'

Escapes involving large numbers of prisoners served two significant purposes – they rattled the enemy, including the Nazi leadership, which was a considerable feat for prisoners of war, and raised morale. But it was those who escaped in ones and twos, unhindered by national manhunts, who were most likely to reach the safety of a neutral country: in a car to the Spanish border, perhaps; or hidden in a goat shed in order to get a train to Switzerland without the hue and cry that would accompany a mass breakout. Whatever his passion for Lady Georgiana Curzon – and however desperately he felt the need to hold her again – Bushell chose to remain at Stalag Luft III to play his part in the fight against Nazism. And by the summer of 1943, the North Compound was not only the engine room of escaping in Germany: it was also an operational outpost of British Intelligence.

Under the direction of Wings Day, the Senior British Officer when the new camp opened in the spring of 1942, and then developed and refined by Bushell under Day's successor, Herbert Massey, the prisoners became a sophisticated source of information on Germany.

As the system of coded letters became more reliable, British intelligence was able to make greater demands, asking specific questions in relation to information on Germany – which was one of Bushell's prime areas of responsibility – while increasing the supply of equipment to the prisoners.

One of MI9's officers, Clayton Hutton, was the prototype for James Bond's 'Q', and specialised in providing the prisoners with escape material smuggled into PoW camps. German money and maps were hidden inside 'Monopoly' boards, gramophone records and playing cards; templates for civilian suits and coats were imprinted on blankets. According to the official history, MI9 also sent the X organisation parcels containing a radio receiver, radio parts, dyes, a typewriter, a camera, films and developing materials, stamps and documents, although many of these items did not arrive until after the mass escape.

Whether MI9 operated within the boundaries of international law is debatable. British Intelligence seems to have been prepared to contravene the Geneva Convention and compromise the Red Cross.

Major Norman Crockatt always insisted that he had forbidden the use of Red Cross parcels as a means for smuggling, as he feared that the prisoners would lose all these precious supplies if contraband were ever discovered in them. MI9, nevertheless, used a number of other covers associated with charitable organisations, albeit phoney ones, such as the British Local Ladies Comforts Society, the London Jigsaw Club and the Lancashire Penny Fund to supply the prisoners with illicit material.

The first bulk parcel containing nothing but unconcealed escape material was successfully received by prisoners at Colditz Castle (Oflag IV-C) at Christmas 1942.

We had been notified by a successful escaper from the camp that, if we sent a parcel with a specially marked label, described in advance in a code letter, our contacts would be able to break into the store room and abstract it, *wrote Major Crockatt in his post-war report on MI9's campaign.* Everything worked according to plan and we immediately suggested to other camps that they should adopt a similar method. Eventually 70% of the camps were receiving escape material by this means.

The most ambitious demand made by MI9 occurred in July 1943 when the X organisation at Stalag Luft III was told to seek information on the development of Hitler's new terror weapons, principally the VI flying bomb and V2 rocket. Day, who had returned to Stalag Luft III and was acting as Senior British Officer while Massey was in hospital, described the instructions as the most 'clearly defined' he had ever received. The information was shared with Bushell.

MI9 suggested in coded messages that some prisoners might escape with the sole intention of finding out more about the German rockets. Bushell's special adviser in the North Compound in Stalag Luft III, Lieutenant Commander Norman Quill, was, according to Day, ordered to recruit a 'commando' team that could use one of the tunnels to undertake an intelligence mission to the Baltic.

In this world, where German allegiances were beginning to shift, and more Germans were showing a willingness to collaborate with the prisoners, Bushell thrived. Every German who entered the camp was engaged in conversation. If they proved talkative, a German-speaking prisoner or 'trader' was assigned to them. Some Germans could be bribed with chocolate, cigarettes and coffee from Red Cross parcels, which were genuine riches in a land growing short of resources. Other Germans had such an antipathy towards the Nazis that they took considerable personal risks to pass on information.

According to another post-war file, the 'X report', compiled by members of the escape committee, much of the most valuable work carried out at Stalag Luft III would have been 'totally' impossible had it not been for the comparative ease with which it was possible to corrupt members of the German staff and Germans visiting the camp.

The great majority of Germans seem to be quite willing to sell information of both military and escape importance to Ps/W for a few cigarettes or some chocolate, coffee etc, *said the report*. This traitorous streak is not confined only to other ranks but is found just as frequently among the officers. It is amazing what risks German personnel still take in order to obtain a few extra luxuries. The stupidity of the lower ranking Germans has to be seen to be believed. They literally throw themselves into the power of the prisoners, by such

stupid actions as signing receipts for goods
received . . . the course of the war has a certain
effect on a number of corrupt Germans, but even in
the autumn of 1940, Germans could still be bought
over; later on after the failure of Stalingrad,
corruptibility increased very rapidly.

One prisoner, Sydney Dowse, the 'Laughing Boy', had already reported that new weapons were being developed on the Baltic island of Peenemünde. A second source then emerged. Dowse's contact was Corporal Eberhard Hesse, a former law student who disliked the Nazis, and who had heard from his brother, Dr Wolfgang Hesse, that the Germans were developing rocket-propelled weapons at the Peenemünde Army Research Centre.

'As usual we got this information back to England, and there is good reason to suppose that it helped to shorten the war by many months,' wrote Jimmy James, one of the prisoners who had given Day and Bushell such a lukewarm welcome at Stalag Luft I two years previously, in his autobiography, *Moonless Night*.

It has never been officially disclosed what role the prisoners of Stalag Luft III played in delaying the German rocket programme – information about Peenemünde is believed to have come from several sources – but the site was bombed on the night of 17 August 1943. Under a full moon, nearly 600 RAF heavy bombers, led by a specialist 'master bomber' and target-finding 'pathfinder' aircraft, attacked Peenemünde in a precision raid, which was only rarely attempted by night – forty of the bombers, with nearly 300 men on board, were shot down.

The official camp history, however, confirmed that information obtained from German contacts included 'experiments with new weapons, location of experimental sites and their defences'. It also made clear, without naming specific targets, that the prisoners provided details of troop movements; the locations of factories; airfields and their defences; bomb damage, economic data and the state of German morale.

Bushell and the leaders of the X organisation constituted a spy ring operating in breach of international law.

'It is recognised in customary international law that persons otherwise entitled to the status of prisoners of war may forfeit the right to such status by the commission of certain acts such as espionage . . .,' wrote William E. S. Flory in his book, *Prisoners of War: A Study in the Development of International Law*, published in 1942. 'The quality of a military spy is dependent on four conditions: 1) he must either be in search of or have obtained information; 2) he must intend to put the information in the hands of the enemy, 3) his mission must carry him into the zone of operations; and 4) he must be acting clandestinely or on false pretences.'

A post-war file, codenamed the 'Z report', concentrates on intelligence matters and makes clear the priorities of the day. This document is also filed in the National Archive at Kew.

It became apparent to the Senior British Officer [Wings Day] that the methods of communication with England should be developed from matters regarding Escaping to those of Military Intelligence which was considered as being of greater importance, *said the Z report.* From then on a system was developed which would allow the greatest use to be made of any military information which came into the camp, and through the use of coded letters could be despatched to England.

For this purpose, a chain of command was established that involved the SBO, his most senior intelligence officers, including Bushell at both Dulag Luft and Stalag Luft III, and a chief coding officer.

It cannot be stressed too much that the control of all messages lay completely in the hands of the

292

Senior British Officer, other than the Intelligence and Coding Officers who prepared and decoded all outgoing and incoming messages. It was seen very early that the success of the organisation would depend entirely upon secrecy. It was one of the aims of the organisation to withhold any knowledge from all prisoners in the camp that such an organisation existed.

The Senior British Officer approved of all messages despatched to England from June 1941 until the end of the war. He also saw all messages which came from England. He appointed to work under him Intelligence Officers whose duty it was to interrogate all new P/W, collate all the information which came from German sources, other prison camps, or any other information that reached the camp.

Neither Brickhill nor Crawley mentioned codes, or MI9, in their books, which were written in the late 1940s. Brickhill may not have known about either – the majority of prisoners were ignorant of such details – but Crawley, who was elected as a Labour MP in 1945 and became Under Secretary of State for Air in Clement Attlee's post-war government, had to suspend publication of his book (an edited version appeared in 1956) as officials were concerned that, with the outbreak of the Korean War, the disclosure of the secret campaign waged during the Second World War would harm the chances of British prisoners held in North Korea. Crawley, who had been one of the intelligence officers at Stalag Luft III, helped to write the official history and was aware of Bushell's activities. Day's biography was not published until the late Sixties.

Infiltration was the most significant concern.

The greatest care had to be taken to check the true identities of new arrivals in the camp in an endeavour to prevent the German authorities from placing German agents inside the camp, *continued the Z Report*. The Germans did attempt to do this when they placed an Egyptian Air Force officer in the North Compound, Stalag Luft III. This officer was immediately placed under close arrest and after some days broke down and admitted he had been placed there by the German authorities.

The chief coding officer worked with a handful of key coding staff, who dictated the contents of coded letters to 172 prisoners; they were, with one or two notable exceptions, unaware of the identity of other code writers or the scale of the operation at Stalag Luft III. Of those 172 officers, three names would have been familiar to MI9's agents in London – Bushell and Day, who were both privy to all the secret exchanges, and Pilot Officer W. H. C. 'Clem' Hunkin. They had been the original three code writers at Dulag Luft in the summer of 1940.

Bushell had already helped to set up an organisation known as 'Plug', which tried to create 'subtle and insidious propaganda' to undermine the morale of the Germans.

The German-speaking 'traders' who were each 'attached' to different members of the camp staff, met once a week.

The current news was studied closely, *says the official history,* and when German newspapers told stories of heroic action, a parallel was sought which had been similarly advertised and had then had results disastrous to the Germans, e.g. the propaganda about Stalingrad . . .

The similarity was suggested gently by 'traders' to their contacts. Extracts from German newspapers were put on a notice board in the Compound kitchen with the similarity pointed out. German newspaper extracts predicting success were put on the board when the result was failure, and when German newspapers had dropped the subject, fearing an adverse effect on morale.

Extracts from German and Italian papers which contradicted each other were put up together.

The campaign worked. In the summer of 1943, the camp received a visit from the Gestapo. One reason, suggested the official history, was that German morale was lower at Sagan than at other camps.

It was also a sign that Himmler's SS were encroaching on the Luftwaffe's areas of responsibility.

Voicing its concerns in a report on internal security dated 12 August 1943, the SS made clear its resentment of British prisoners of war in general:

We learn from many sources that the outward bearing of the British is not failing to make an impression on the local population, the document said. A report from Central Germany, for instance, states: 'Although a large proportion of British prisoners in Germany come from ordinary working classes, a large number of them speak impeccable and fluent German. Their attitude is self-possessed and, indeed, often borders on arrogance. Their bearing and their whole behaviour are doubtless intended as effective propaganda.'

From Klagenfurt, too, we hear: 'Of all the prisoners of war in this district, the British are the most respected and discussed by the local population. The reason for this lies in the smart appearance of individuals, as well as the smartness of organised units . . . their attitude is extraordinarily self-possessed, one could almost say arrogant and overbearing. This, combined with the good impression they give of their nation, influences the German people in a way that should not be under-estimated . . .

'The attitude of British prisoners to the Reich is absolutely hostile. They make fun of Germany, German institutions and leaders on all possible occasions. In Bayreuth, for instance, two British prisoners called themselves "Churchill" and "Roosevelt". As a foil they picked on a German worker who stuttered and called him "Hitler" as a joke. Some other British prisoners were singing a rude song to the tune of *Deutschland uber Alles* as they passed two high German officials in uniform. When one of these officials said, "That's going a little too far, my friends", one of the prisoners who understood German called back, "We're not your friends, we're British."

'The manner in which the British behave to the population leaves no doubt of their confidence in victory. They take every opportunity to show that Germany will lose the war, and that they will soon be masters in Germany. This assurance of victory and self-possession does not fail to impress the people, who think they see in these qualities the symbol of British strength.'

It concluded by stating that the presence of British prisoners of war in Germany was 'thoroughly demoralising'.

Von Lindeiner, the commandant at Stalag Luft III, warned senior Allied officers of the pressure being exerted by the SS, and that there were men in senior positions who did not care about the protection afforded to prisoners under the provisions of the Geneva Convention. According to Day, even Theo Rumpel, the former commandant of Dulag Luft who was now running a network of training airfields in the region, visited the camp to support von Lindeiner's warnings – and to confront Bushell himself over the dangers he would face if he escaped again.

But the Allied officers pursued their campaign on all fronts, with Bushell still involved in all aspects of the escape committee's work – including passing on its growing expertise to prisoners in other camps. Communication was, once again, organised through coded letters, between the various Senior British Officers, between British clergymen, between fathers, sons and brothers in different camps, and through the transfer of prisoners.

On one occasion, it was arranged for Sergeant J. N. Gibson, a member of the escape committee from the Centre Compound for other ranks – where there was very little escape activity – to switch identities in the sick quarters and move to the officers' compound where he could be briefed about escape activities. 'Gibson reported to Group Captain Massey and was introduced to Squadron Leader R. Bushell RAF, the Chief of the Officers' Organisation,' said the official camp history. Two weeks later, Gibson switched identities again in order to return to his own compound, where he started to reorganise the NCOs' escape activities.

By 1943, the 'contact' system, which exploited the readiness of Germans to collaborate, was working effectively in Stalag Luft III. The system involved engaging all individuals entering the compound, including German officers, interpreters, *Abwehr* staff, guards, administrative staff, German workers and foreign workers, with a view to extracting from them something useful by way of information or material.

Germans whose duties brought them into the compound regularly were always dealt with by the same individual contact, and at the same time all other camp personnel were forbidden to deal with Germans or have them in their rooms, *said the X report.* This point is of the greatest importance, and enabled a system to be built up whereby a German who was willing to co-operate was assured of a warm reception in the room of an officer whom he knew, who could speak his language, and to whom he could unburden his troubles in comparative safety. At the same time, should the presence of the German in question be a source of danger in the compound to the security of any particular operation, it was fairly certain that he would, sooner or later, gravitate to his contact's room to receive his coffee or cigarettes, and in many cases stay there for a considerable time.

In addition to contacts established inside the compound, [Allied] officers carrying out camp administrative duties such as Parcels, Clothing, Book Censoring, often had unique opportunities of extracting information from the German administrative staff of their particular departments, while working with them in offices in the *Vorlager* [the camp administrative section].

Extortion was sometimes used with the Germans who had signed receipts or compromised themselves in other ways, but sometimes it was simply the case that the prisoners found Germans who were anti-Nazi and turned against their own side on principle. One of the most remarkable collaborators was a fair-haired corporal called 'Harry', who worked in many different offices of the camp administration. According to Crawley,

Harry was a genuine Democrat and was prepared to take genuine risks to do anything which he considered might bring an end to the Nazi regime. Once his confidence had been gained, he supplied a great deal of information . . .

Within the camp itself there was little that Harry was not prepared to try to find out, and as he often had access to the German Adjutant's office or walked out with one of the girls who acted as typists, he kept the prisoners well informed about orders which came from Berlin and about camp administration generally. Changes in the regulations governing entrance to and exit from the compounds, alterations in passes and changes of German personnel were all reported accurately.

The German serviceman called 'Harry' in Crawley's account was in fact Sydney Dowse's contact, Corporal Hesse, who also put the prisoners in touch with other Germans who were prepared to help them.

Another German was asked to go to Paris to contact the French resistance movement, and to obtain from them certain passes for French workers in Germany. 'He arranged to go there,' said the X report. 'His fare was paid by the "X" organisation, and he brought back the documents required.'

Among the 'traders' who dealt with these men was none other than Bushell, and the effect of all this painstaking work revealed itself in the progress made by Big X's senior lieutenants in preparing for the escape. Listeners to the BBC play, which established Bushell's role as Big X, were given an insight into the scale of the great endeavour.

The forger, Tim Walenn, told the BBC audience: 'I'd started by faking gate passes and simple travel permits. We had an *Ausweis* for being on Reich property, two types of *Urlaubsschein* for crossing frontiers, about three different forms of travel permit, and a French worker's identity card. We also had our own camera for passport photos. We also used to fake letters for escapers to carry. If a man got out, say, as a French worker, we could give him a bundle of letters in French bearing loving bits of gossip from his wife back in Cherbourg or somewhere . . . Altogether we turned out about four hundred documents. We had fifty forgers and stooges on the job three to five hours a day for a year.'

Des Plunkett, a draughtsman who had undertaken aerial survey work before the war, outlined the work of the mapping department: 'We mapped the escape routes down through Czechoslovakia to Switzerland and France, and through the Baltic to Sweden. Tracing was too slow, so we got a contact to scrounge some invalid jellies through a German in the hospital block. From these we got the gelatine by extracting the sugar, and poured it into flat trays made from old food tins. When it was set there was our mimeograph [which enabled them to print multiple copies]. We drew the maps with ink made from the crushed lead of indelible pencils – strictly *verboten*, but the tame Germans supplied them.'

Tommy Guest, the tailor, told the BBC audience: 'Our main trouble was cloth. The only jackets and trousers ever issued in the compound came through the Red Cross, and they were either rough old Polish uniforms or the unlovely stuff they issued, and still do, to RAF other ranks, made of heavy serge. A couple of people shaved the serge nap off with razor blades, and then we dyed it – with beetroot juice, or a boot polish solution, and once or twice in dyes made from the covers of books soaked in water.'

Al Hake, an Australian with a talent for technical drawing and metalwork, was in charge of making compasses. 'We made the compass casings out of gramophone records, broken and heated and then pressed into a mould. The direction needle was a sewing needle which we'd rubbed against a magnet. Our compasses were finished jobs – if you'd turned them over you would have found the base was professionally engraved: "Made in Stalag Luft III".'

All of these men answered to Bushell. As the collaborator Corporal Eberhard Hesse told MI9's officers during his interrogation after the war: 'At times S/L Bushell was practically in charge of the German, British and American camps because nothing was done without his knowledge and approval.'

23

Treading the Boards

From the moment that Major Norman Crockatt established
MI9 in the first months of the war, it was clear that the agency
intended to treat British prisoners held in Occupied Europe as
'combatants'. Nearly four years later, under Roger Bushell's leadership, MI9's ambitions were reaching their apotheosis in the
North Compound of Stalag Luft III, in clear breach of the Geneva
Convention.

As the great drama took shape, Bushell still sought shelter on
the stage, where he rehearsed his roles in an attempt to avoid the
scrutiny of German security. As he told his parents, acting came
'naturally'.

'I have just finished playing Malcolm in "George and Margaret".
Great fun and a great success,' he told Ben and Dorothe. 'My
daughter – a young fighter boy – had to be seen to be believed he
was so good.'

According to Paul Brickhill, who was a prisoner in the North
Compound, Bushell took several parts – and was outstanding.
'One couldn't have a personality or ego as powerful as Bushell's
without being a good actor,' he wrote.

But his leading role was as Big X and by 1943, Bushell was at
the peak of his powers as an RAF officer. He 'commanded'
hundreds of Allied airmen in the North Compound, and influ-
enced many more further afield, with the escape industry gaining
momentum above and below ground.

In April 1943, Wings Day and Jimmy Buckley had engineered
the escape of thirty-four prisoners through a tunnel at Oflag
XXIB at Schubin in central Poland, where they had been transferred the previous autumn. The escapers included Aidan Crawley,

author of *Escape from Germany*. Their forged documents had withstood many tests, including several examinations by the Gestapo, which augured well for the men of the North Compound.

> Even better, *wrote Crawley,* was the commotion caused in the German High Command. According to the Germans themselves, three hundred thousand troops covering the whole of the province of Warthegau and all frontier areas were turned out for the search. More than one prisoner had the satisfaction of seeing lines of German soldiers combing the fields sixty or seventy miles from Schubin as he passed them comfortably in a train.

It was first-hand and very welcome evidence that the Germans had to divert manpower to look for the escapers.

But there were casualties. Buckley, who ran the escape committees at Dulag Luft in 1940, Stalag Luft I in 1941 and Stalag Luft III in 1942, and a Danish officer, Jorge Thalbitzer, were drowned while trying to cross from Denmark to Sweden in canoes. Buckley's body was never found – a reminder, if one were needed, of the dangers facing men trying to escape from Occupied Europe. Day and the other recaptured escapers were sent back to Stalag Luft III.

As the diggers pushed on with the three tunnels, Bushell organised the second mass escape of the year by RAF prisoners, but on this occasion it would be through the main gate of the North Compound.

Big X decided to orchestrate an outbreak of lice, which always galvanised the German authorities because of the dangers of typhus. The only delousing facilities at Stalag Luft III were among the German administrative buildings adjacent to the East Compound, where bedding and clothing could be heated in steam ovens while the prisoners washed in hot showers. It involved a short walk that took the prisoners along a path by the forest outside the wire surrounding the camp.

As genuine delousing parties were a familiar sight to the Germans guarding the entrance to the North Compound, Bushell created two extra parties of prisoners – escorted by Allied airmen dressed in German uniforms.

He dallied with the idea of joining the escape himself, but finally chose to remain behind in his role as Big X.

> *Roger did not take part, but was the organising genius*
> *behind it,* wrote Day in his letter to Dorothe Bushell after
> the war. *It took great organisation and preparatory work,*
> *because the right type of 'passes' had to be obtained,*
> *uniforms, rifles and equipment, to be good enough to pass*
> *the proper guards in daylight . . . all these things had to be*
> *kept hidden from the Germans till the right moment came*
> *to make the attempt. All this rested on Roger's shoulders.*

The escape took place on 11 June 1943, several weeks after the 'discovery' of lice, but it was very nearly scuppered at the last minute when the escape committee discovered that the German escorts had been ordered to carry pistols rather than rifles. In the end, Bushell's carpenters and tailors improvised pistol butts and leather holsters, and the escape attempt went ahead.

> Two of these [de-lousing parties], escorted by Prisoners of War
> disguised as German guards, were to march towards the East
> Compound *Vorlager*, and then make off into the woods border-
> ing the road, *recorded the official history.* The second party
> would occupy the attention of the guards and sentries while the
> first party got into the woods.
>
> The Compound Adjutant made an unofficial arrangement
> with the Camp Commandant, on the day in question, that after
> the morning parties had gone out, no further parties would leave
> until 14.30 hours. The guards usually were changed at 14.00

hours and it was unlikely that the new guards would know anything of this arrangement.

All the escapers, who had been selected by Bushell, assembled at the compound gate, where they were joined by two fluent German speakers – one of whom was Flight Lieutenant Roger de Wever – disguised as guards. Under their uniforms, the prisoners wore civilian clothes made by Tommy Guest's tailors and had forged documents, escape food, money, maps and compasses provided by the X organisation.

De Wever, at the front of the column, reached the first gate and we held our breath, *recalled one of the escapers, Walter Morison, in his memoirs, Flak and Ferrets*. There was a delay and some words were exchanged. Maybe the sentry was suspicious. But then one of the senior officers in the party waiting behind us shouted some abuse: 'What the hell is going on? We'll be late for the Commandant. Get a move on, there!'

That authoritative military voice did the trick and the guard let us through. Then came the second gate, but this time there was no hold up and suddenly we were out – out, but still in view, and the warning trumpet could still have sent us scurrying for cover . . .

A minute later an extraordinary scene unfolded in the woods as twenty-four prisoners were transformed into businessmen, commercial travellers and workmen, who vanished as quickly as they had come, leaving only piles of discarded clothing.

Some of the men headed for the railway station in the nearby town of Sagan, while others, including Morison and his travelling companion, Lorne Welch, set out on foot.

Back in the North Compound, the second party passed through the first gate but was halted at the second by a German guard who did not recognise one of their 'escorts', Bob van der Stok, a Dutch airman, and took him to the guardroom for questioning.

Bushell was watching from the compound as the escape unravelled: an *Abwehr* officer realised what had happened and raised the alarm.

At Sagan railway station, two of the prisoners from the first group were arrested after being recognised by the camp's medical officer. Most of the others were rounded up in the vicinity.

Three men were at large for longer. Morison and Welch, wearing Luftwaffe uniforms, were captured trying to steal a German aircraft at an aerodrome five miles away. 'Amazingly, we had in the camp detailed handling notes for the Junkers 87 and 88 bombers, that ubiquitous three-engined heavy transport, the Junkers 52, the front-line fighters Messerschmitt 109 and 110 and the Bucker Jungman and Jungmeister trainers,' wrote Morison, who had hoped to fly to Sweden.

The third man was John Stower, a sugar planter from Argentina who had been shot down in a Wellington bomber while laying mines in the North Sea the previous summer. Accounts of his escape differ, but it seems that he may have reached Swiss territory; then, quite unwittingly, walked back into Germany, where he was arrested.

After the escape, tension with the German authorities ratcheted up: the sight of Allied prisoners wandering around in German uniforms had struck a nerve. For the first time, von Lindeiner, the commandant at Stalag Luft IIII, was confronted with the sophisticated nature of Bushell's escape organisation – and the deep suspicion that the prisoners had received inside help, particularly with forged documents.

All the escapers were sent to 'the cooler' for two weeks' solitary confinement, but there were too many prisoners, which meant they had to share cells. Those who had worn German uniforms received longer sentences. After six weeks, Morison and Welch were sent to Colditz.

In the North Compound, the Luftwaffe increased security measures and suspended Red Cross parcels. They also cut down all the trees in the compound to give the guards a clearer line of sight. 'The Germans were pretty smart,' said Sydney Dowse. 'We might have thought of them as idiots – but they weren't.'

Like the prisoners, who were becoming increasingly sophisticated in planning their escapes, the Germans – and particularly the Luftwaffe – were becoming more adept with countermeasures. Staff accumulated critical experience by remaining in the same jobs for long periods of time, sometimes for the duration of the war. The 'ferrets' were chosen carefully and given special training. Von Lindeiner also opened an 'escape museum' at Stalag Luft III in order to help his officers to get the measure of the Allied airmen's ingenuity. Escape became more difficult.

Roll calls, usually held in the morning and evening, could be called at any time, particularly when the Germans suspected that a tunnel was being dug. The prisoners were counted carefully. Guards in the goon boxes – often men on leave from flak batteries on the Eastern Front – were briefed to look out for changes in the prisoners' routine such as a sudden increase in the number of men visiting one particular hut. They also tried using informers, electronic listening devices and placing 'spies' in the forest in an attempt to thwart the escapers.

Many of von Lindeiner's officers took pride in their expertise. When Hermann Glemnitz, the chief ferret, escorted a group of Allied airmen being transferred to Schubin, where the camp was run by the German Army, he tried to warn the commandant about the RAF officers' record in matters of escape. Glemnitz, a wise man who had seen much of the world and spoke several languages, was treated with contempt.

Showing signs of intense anger, he returned to address his charges before handing them over: 'I went in there just now, gentlemen, to warn these Army blockheads what a handful you are and to give them the benefit of my experience with you. They told me they would handle you themselves and to get the hell out of the office. I tell you they know nothing, nothing! So I say to you: escape, escape, escape!'

Glemnitz was cheered loudly by the Allied airmen. But for all his fine qualities, not least among them common decency and a sense of humour, Glemnitz had served on the Western Front during the First World War and was a loyal German soldier – as well as being a formidable opponent.

In the summer of 1943, Bushell told the X organisation to concentrate on 'Tom' and to shut down the two other tunnels, with 'Dick', which was 70ft long, used to hide the sand excavated from 'Tom', the most advanced of the tunnels. Whether this was because of Day's intelligence mission; the building of a new compound which would make it impossible to escape through either 'Tom' or 'Dick' because it would put the sanctuary of the woods out of reach; or Bushell's stated desire to involve the Americans before the Germans moved them in the autumn, is not known for certain.

Few men shared the secrets of Stalag Luft III. Day certainly knew the truth and Bushell would have maintained any cover required: the need to embark on an intelligence mission concerning the development of Germany's new rockets, as outlined in Day's biography, would seem to have justified the need to cut corners. With this, Bushell's alleged desire to reward the Americans who worked on the tunnels is unlikely to have justified further risks, and seems remarkably out of character for a man who was obsessed with security.

Predictably, the decision to press on with greater urgency had fateful consequences. Seismographic microphones started to pick up sounds of unusual activity along the western perimeter, which was bisected by two of the tunnels, 'Tom' and 'Dick', while German suspicions seem to have been confirmed by two other incidents. One report suggested that a 'penguin' was seen unloading sand while watching a volleyball match. Another recorded that Glemnitz noticed an increase in the amount of sand showing up in the prisoners' gardens.

Bushell was alerted to these alarming developments by his intelligence officers. More worryingly, Glemnitz increased the number of searches and concentrated on Hut 123, where the trap to 'Tom' was located, at the far end of the western perimeter.

In an attempt to divert Glemnitz's attention from Tom, Bushell sent a trail of prisoners carrying Red Cross boxes to huts on the eastern perimeter. He also tried to use his 'traders' to persuade their German contacts that no tunnel existed.

Like two chess players, Bushell and Glemnitz tried to counter each other's moves, while Big X battled to keep his options open. Glemnitz was not fooled, however, and he increased the pressure: the Germans virtually ransacked the three huts – 106, 107 and 123 – facing the western wire. Night searches were ordered. Nothing was found.

Ferrets started to hide in the huts in an attempt to glean information. Corporal Karl Griese, a dedicated but hateful ferret known as 'Rubberneck', was discovered in the kitchen block after the duty pilot noticed he had remained in the compound.

Rubberneck urged Glemnitz to shut down the duty pilots, but the senior ferret refused. He thought it better to have them in the open rather than operate in the shadows, as would undoubtedly be the case if he sent them to the cooler.

Bushell also pressed on. His tunnellers broke records, advancing more than ten feet a day. Soon they would start to dig upwards towards the edge of the woods.

The BBC play based on Brickhill's book caught the mood during exchanges between Bushell, the American George Harsh, who was one of Big X's security chiefs, and Wally Floody, the Canadian engineer.

The scene opened with Harsh commenting on the Germans' new security measures: 'Have you seen the guys in the goon boxes?' he asked Bushell. 'Every son of a gun has got his field glasses up watching all the time.'

Bushell answered: 'There's one thing we've got to keep in mind. Glemnitz has no idea of the scale on which we've got things organised. He mustn't get to thinking it's anything more than a little effort of a few blokes. If he does, he'll turn the whole camp inside out.'

At this point, the narrator added: 'About eleven o'clock the next morning, three heavy wagons careered around the compound, mostly along the sides of the huts, trying to collapse any tunnels by weight. Tunnels thirty feet deep were safe from that sort of thing. But a few days later, Roger called his committee together again.'

Bushell declared: 'We're in the big stuff now. You all saw the little bony-faced civilian von Lindeiner was driving round the camp this morning. I've learnt from the kitchen goon that he's second in command of Breslau Criminal Police. From now on, anything can happen.'

Floody answered. 'Well, it's just a race, then. We'll have to cut a few corners.'

Bushell replied: 'That's exactly what we can't do. If they get any more evidence they'll go crazy. You'll find yourself sleeping out in the dirt while they tear up all the floors.'

Another member of the escape organisation suggested that they close everything down until the fuss had blown over, but Bushell was adamant that they go on. 'It's too late to close up now, anyway,' he said. 'The goons will go on hunting till they find something, and the longer they go on, the more chance they'll have of finding Dick and Harry as well.'

But then Glemnitz had a stroke of good fortune.

The date on which the Germans discovered 'Tom' is disputed. Many sources record 8 September 1943 – and this seems to be the more likely – but the official history of Stalag Luft III says it was more than a month later. According to this document, which was written shortly after the end of the war by several of the men involved, 'Tom progressed until 10th October, when it was two-hundred and eighty-five feet long. It was discovered by accident by a ferret who was idly tapping with a pick axe, which caused a chip to fly off the trap.'

Sydney Smith wrote:

> The Germans were especially incensed by this tunnel. They had suspected its existence and had desperately searched for a clue to its beginning and direction. They had applied themselves tenaciously to every kind of ransack and probe prompted by ingenuity and experience. Yet here was a tunnel which for a good six months had beaten their heavy lorries, their seismographs, their searches, their forest binocular teams, and then been found only by accident.

Von Lindeiner, the German commandant, ordered the trap to be broken open. He sent for Karl Pilz, a ferret from the East Compound who was an expert on tunnels and one of the few members of the camp staff prepared to go underground. What he found stunned his German colleagues. The tunnel, one of the longest ever constructed in a prisoner of war camp, was an impressive piece of engineering both in terms of its scale and the quality of workmanship. Indeed, 'Tom' gained celebrity status and was even photographed by the German press.

But the tunnel also raised serious questions about German security. Around 1,500 bed boards and thirty-five bunk beds had been used in its construction, not to mention the ventilation system and electric lights. Equally remarkable was the fact that the prisoners had successfully disposed of more than 80 tons of yellow sand from 'Tom' – and probably another 80 tons from 'Dick' and 'Harry'.

After the discovery of the tunnel, Glemnitz made an unusual slip. He was overheard telling a fellow ferret that, in future, he would keep an eye on the beds. Bushell reacted immediately and ordered a vast collection of wood, which was hidden throughout the camp for use in the future.

When the Germans found a tunnel, they usually filled it with water, which collapsed the roof. 'Tom' was too solid a construction for this kind of treatment. Instead, the camp authorities decided to blow it up. A sapper is said to have laid 100lbs of dynamite – rather too much for the task – and succeeded in wrecking much of Hut 123 and part of the camp's drainage system, as well as raising the spirits of the Allied prisoners.

One other event raised morale, too – an ingenious escape from the East Compound. Three men – Eric Williams, Michael Codner and Oliver Philpot – reached England in what became famous as the 'Wooden Horse' escape. Over a period of more than three months, the prisoners used a wooden vaulting box to disguise a tunnel dug almost next to the wire. Two diggers would be carried out inside it. While they were tunnelling underground, other prisoners took turns in vaulting the 'horse'. The two tunnellers would then be carried back to the huts at the end of the day. By the end of October, the tunnel was more than 100 feet long. They broke out on 29 October. Williams and Codner reached the Polish port of Stettin. Philpot headed for Danzig. All three succeeded in boarding ships bound for Sweden, and from there to England.

In the North Compound, the digging teams switched their attentions to 'Harry', with its trap in Hut 104. But German security measures had increased to such an extent – including an influx of ferrets – that the prisoners were unable to disperse sand. Bushell called a halt and closed the tunnel until further notice. Morale among the prisoners sagged.

Shortly afterwards, most of the American prisoners in the North Compound were moved to the new South Compound, where they thought there would be new opportunities for escape. They were wrong – and the hand of Bushell was detected in events, which, if true, reveal the extent of his ruthlessness: Albert 'Bub' Clark, who had been Big S on the X organisation in the North Compound, suspected that Bushell had set up the Americans as fall guys.

The Germans had learnt the lessons of the previous year when hundreds of prisoners had been moved to the new North Compound, where they found tools and equipment left by German constructors, and trees still standing.

South Compound was neat and clean when it opened, *wrote Arthur Durand in his book, Stalag Luft III: The Secret Story.* The sand under the barracks was raked smooth, all the trees were cleared, and all loose articles were removed. As an extra security measure, the Germans put a shadow on Clark. For two weeks he could not even go to the latrine without somebody following him. Although Clark was never able to confirm his suspicions, he is convinced that Bushell was responsible, at least indirectly, for the Germans' precautions. Clark felt that, in an effort to divert the Germans' attention from the two tunnels still under construction in North, Bushell secretly gave them the impression that the British were happy to see the Americans go: that they, not the British, were the fanatic tunnellers who achieved the wonders underground that were revealed when tunnel Tom was discovered. The implication plainly was that the British would be causing no more trouble now that the bloody Yanks were gone, and the Germans would do well to concentrate on the South rather than the North Compound. The Germans apparently took the bait, for they sent their most diligent and successful anti-escape expert, Glemnitz, to South Compound, where he continued to be a keen opponent.

In the North Compound, Alan Bryett, who became involved with the X organisation while working for his banking qualifications, met Bushell for the only time.

'Squadron Leader Murray, the head of our hut, was there, and he said, "You're going to hear what's going on here and you're going to meet people. I'm going to introduce you to the man who's in charge of the whole thing." I'd been there a while then. I didn't know it was Roger Bushell. I just knew he was one of the important people.

'At the end of his little talk, Bushell said something like this: "Never show any respect to me. Never wink at me, never pay any attention to me at all. If I don't talk to you, that's the end of it, we don't talk. It doesn't matter what I'm doing – if you see me walking round the circuit with a tree growing out of my mouth, just ignore it. Don't acknowledge me in any way. Don't salute me, don't show any rank, never pick me out in any way at all."

'He was a very secretive person . . . that was the nearest I came to him talking to me.'

None of the drama of the autumn filtered into Bushell's letters home, but some of his feelings about the nature of leadership, which chime with Bryett's recollections, can be found in his writing:

> *Have just finished Duff Cooper's* Life of Talleyrand *[the veteran French diplomat who dominated European affairs during the French Revolution and the reign of Napoleon I],* he wrote to his parents on 30 October 1943. *What a wonderful man and how I admire him. He never lost control of his feelings no matter how trying the circumstances, and what a truly great disregard for public opinion.*

Bushell was struggling with his study of Russian but had mastered Danish:

> *It is so childishly easy and was ideal for the summer. I suspect what I speak is more like Norwegian than Danish for my teacher is the former. But no matter. I get a sort of absurd vanity out of having added the smatterings of another language to my list.*

In his letter of 30 November, Bushell returned to a familiar theme:

> *The mail gets worse and worse. I write every month but as*
> *there are obviously more important things to worry about*
> *than prisoners' mail, you'll just have to be patient and*
> *remember that it can't be very much longer before I'll be*
> *able to write you a real letter again.*

While hopes of an Allied victory clearly rose, Bushell continued
to study Russian and spend more time on stage: 'Torquemada's
cross-word puzzles are child's play compared to the grammar! . . . Am acting in some more plays, which help pass the
time and am going to do Professor Higgins which should make
you laugh.'

But he was also acutely aware of time passing him by:

> *My sergeant rigger from 601 has just arrived as a Squadron*
> *Leader! Such is life, but he is a very nice lad, has done damn*
> *well and had lot to tell me about people.*

Troubled by the failure of 'Tom' and driven by the need to
sustain the X organisation – neither of which he was able to
discuss with his parents – Bushell clearly worked hard on his
letters, trying to make them sound genuine and interesting, probably for the benefit of the censors as well as his parents. He
finished a letter on 30 November, as usual, by reassuring his
parents of his well-being:

> *Bless you all. I am very well and mentally as contented as it*
> *is possible to be in a place like this. Love, Roger.*

The truth was different.

Bushell carried enormous burdens on behalf of MI9. This
would have been clear to anyone who, in early 1944, saw the
photograph, probably taken in the North Compound in October

or November 1943, of Bushell standing beside Robert Stanford Tuck. The portrait is of a troubled man, his face drawn and dark, his mouth open, caught in mid-sentence. The picture was a source of concern for Bushell.

On 30 December 1943, he told his parents:

I wouldn't worry about the photograph by the way. It was taken on a bad day, in winter, was in a bad light and was overdeveloped. I was probably also in a bad temper! I don't look any younger these days but am very well, all things considered, and a month of decent, civilised life, will put me back to normal.

But if anything gave away his feelings – certainly those of a man with many regrets – Bushell made one more telling comment about his future as a civilian in the letter of 30 December: 'I will have one great advantage,' he wrote. 'I will be very much wiser!'

Dorothe Bushell would not have been fooled by his letter. 'Roger was one of those people whose face is the window of their spirit,' she had written in her journal ten years earlier. 'When all was well, there was a light in there. When he was troubled or wrongly judged, the light dimmed and he was thought to be morose when he was deeply perturbed and unhappy.'

24

Eve of Battle

Wings Day had no doubts about Bushell's state of mind, nor about one of his primary motives for escaping from Stalag Luft III.

> Tunnel Harry was almost ready and at the end of it, *wrote Day's biographer, Sydney Smith,* Wings knew there remained for Roger Bushell only two alternatives, besides the long-cherished victory of escape: the girl he loved and had once lost who was now waiting again, or the Gestapo.

Two other factors shaped his outlook.

For nearly four years Bushell, a man used to success, had been dogged by failure: he had been shot down on his first day of combat; on the two occasions he had escaped, he had been recaptured; and his second attempt had cost the lives of the Czech family who sheltered him. Even his fiancée had deserted him.

But Bushell was determined to play a role in the defeat of Hitler's Germany. He hated the Nazis. 'He'd seen the Gestapo torturing people and he did not tolerate Germans any more,' wrote Brickhill.

The other factor that determined his behaviour was a simple sense of duty. Having apparently been denied a car to the Spanish border by Theo Rumpel in the early months of captivity, Bushell engaged in two great endeavours that could only stand in the way of him being reunited with Lady Georgiana Curzon: the gathering of intelligence and its transmission to London, and the organisation of escape activity on such a scale that disruption of the German war effort rather than escape itself became the primary aim of the escapers. The scale of these activities clearly constrained his own opportunities for getting home – and reinforce the fact that he put duty first.

By December 1943, much of the optimistic good humour of the previous Christmas had disappeared. 'We have managed to get through Xmas in our own way though in a place like this it is a pretty average mockery,' Bushell told his parents in his letter of 30 December, which contained a declaration about the future. 'This time however it really is "a last Xmas" and no mistake,' he wrote.

Big X ordered 'Harry' to be opened up again on 10 January 1944, with the aim of getting the 200 men out of the camp once the weather improved in the spring. It took two hours to open the trapdoor, which had been sealed in October.

Aidan Crawley recalled the excitement as the small team of engineers and carpenters gathered once again:

> When digging had ceased, the tunnel was already 115 ft. long, and they longed to see how the wooden shoring had stood up to the winter and how solid the construction of the tunnel had been.

'It was in good condition,' recorded the official history of Stalag Luft III. 'The air-line had sand in it, some of the shoring was weak, and the kitbags of the air-pump needed changing', but after only four days of maintenance work, the digging teams started work once again at the face of the tunnel.

With snow covering the ground, the escape committee faced one major problem: it was impossible to disperse the bright yellow sand on the frozen surface of the compound: the ferrets would have picked up on every trace. 'It was necessary to have a permanently enclosed space which was not subject to German inspection,' recorded the camp history. Just such a place was found under the floor of the camp theatre, where the Germans presumed there was no space; but it had, after all, been built by the prisoners. An entrance to the space was cut under one of the theatre seats.

The decision to hide sand under the theatre, which had been built only on condition it would never be used for escape activity, was accompanied by protests from some of those most closely involved with the building, but the protests were ignored.

Teams of 'big men' carrying two sacks weighing seventeen and a half pounds each took the sand to the theatre in the hours of darkness before the prisoners were locked in their huts at 9 p.m. each night. The sacks were slung around the neck and hidden under greatcoats. Eight kitbags, each containing up to 100lb of sand, were kept in the dispersal chamber and hauled up when the trap was opened. The kitbags were taken to a neighbouring barrack, placed in a 'loading' room and then picked up by the carriers, who took a variety of routes to the theatre.

A pronounced sense of mischief appeared to accompany this operation. 'Traffic' controllers were stationed at various points on the journey from the loading room to the theatre.

> If there were no Germans at large in the Compound and 'contacts' were safely in the room of their traders, sand was carried in kit-bags straight from the trap-room to the theatre, a distance of 200 yards, *recorded the camp history*. The greatest amount of sand disposed of during this period January–March, 1944 was done by this method, when a trader kept his 'ferret contact' in his room, which was in the 'HARRY' barrack, for two hours, while four tons was taken to the theatre, representing thirteen feet of tunnel.

The smell of freshly dug sand noticeable in the loading room was masked by a tin of pungent tobacco, which was kept smouldering in the corridor every evening while, every morning, the dispersal routes were checked for traces of spilled sand. In this way, eighty tons were dispersed without the Germans even getting a sniff of it.

As the entire X organisation came to life once more, the spirits of the prisoners rose. 'Morale was closely bound up with escape attempts,' *recorded the camp history*, 'and would rise when these were successful, and drop at times of inactivity.'

Morale was also bound up in the content of daily news bulletins drawn from the BBC, which was monitored on clandestine wirelesses, and distributed throughout the camp.

By January 1944, the Germans were retreating on all fronts. Their submarines had lost the Battle of the Atlantic, enabling the British and Americans to start the build-up of men and supplies for the invasion of northern Europe virtually unhindered by German forces. In Italy, the Allies landed at Anzio and, briefly, threatened Rome. In the air, the introduction of the Mustang long-range fighter enabled the American bombers to begin daylight attacks on the German synthetic oil plants, with devastating effects. The Russians had liberated much of the Ukraine and reached the eastern borders of pre-war Poland and Romania. But the war was far from won. As the historian, A. J. P. Taylor, wrote:

> At the beginning of 1944 the German and Japanese empires were still largely intact, though somewhat clipped at the edges. Great buffers of conquered territory still warded off the Allied assaults.

Bushell's first letter of 1944 struck a philosophical note but, with references to the tedious nature of life in captivity and the desire to embark on a journey, real or imagined, it must have suggested to his parents that he was working on another escape.

> *Now, what am I to write to you about?* read the letter to Ben and Dorothe on 31 January 1944. *The weather? It's dull like the countryside and our existence. My fellow human beings? They're ordinary and alas somewhat dull, too.*

The war? But that's a topic worn threadbare in our daily lives and a letter should be like a holiday – New world and new people – like a cinema – artificial (but none the less effective) enchantment for a short hour or so. We Europeans know so little about it but it should and, I'm beginning to believe, can be possible to transfer yourself to another part of the world or even to other worlds 'with your mind'. The Indian philosophies practise it and, more important, appear to put it into practice. And all the older religions teach it. Ever read The New Immortality *by Dunne? He proves it mathematically or so he says. I'm no mathematician so I can't say.*

Bushell, who remained intellectually active throughout his captivity, concluded the letter:

Am reading Nietzsche's Zarathustra. *It's a relief from learning Russian! Bless you all. I am ever so well, Roger.*

Thirty feet below the North Compound, preparations for the only journey that really mattered to Bushell went smoothly until the end of January, when a full moon interrupted the dispersal of sand to the theatre.

The estimated distance to the edge of the wood was 220 feet, in addition to the 115 feet already dug when the tunnel was reopened. One of the diggers was a Welshman called Ken Rees who had been shot down in a Wellington bomber on his 56th operation of the war, a few days after he was married, in 1942. Rees was keen to get home. 'I found that as far as I was concerned the best place to be was at the face, either digging or as a digger's mate,' he wrote in his memoir, *Lie In The Dark and Listen.*

It could be a little unnerving when there was a sudden fall of sand and you were left in complete darkness until another fat lamp could be sent up, but generally you were kept far too busy to brood on any danger. If you were on Halfway House duties, though, you had a lot of spare time to consider your position. It could suddenly occur to you that you were actually in a two-foot square tunnel, twenty-five feet down under the Vorlager, and totally dependent for your survival there on basically only flimsy bed boards holding off the tons of earth above you.

The diggers pressed on, however, reaching the 200ft mark in mid-February, when they also started work on the second halfway house, an area of the tunnel that was widened so two men could pass. These two halfway houses were named 'Leicester Square' and 'Piccadilly'.

What Ken Rees did not know was that the Germans were no longer listening for evidence of tunnelling: the seismographic microphones had been turned off on 19 December to enable the extension of the system to two new compounds, and would not be used again for more than three months.

Bushell wrote to his family again on 28 February 1944. The letter, full of whimsy, love and humour, would appear to contradict observations that he was becoming tense and obsessive. It was to be the last letter written by Bushell from Stalag Luft III.

My darlings – The mail continues to be appalling and this month's crop has only produced one letter from Father 30/11/43 and one from Eliza in her own inimitable type-writing and dated Nov 11th. Whenever I get one of Eliza's letters a wave of sympathy for that unfortunate type writer sweeps over me. What a pounding it must get! The herculean force which has superimposed an e over a recalcitrant l or z that has got into the wrong place must shake its wretched bones like dice in a box. As for those dashing vertical dashes which constitute the polite fiction of erasure, they are a dagger's wounds that send the word 'to heaven or to hell' far more effectively than did ever Macbeth's end Duncan. And then there are the complicated

mental gymnastics (which have a charm all of their own)
required to decypher both the punctuation and the syntax. I
start by taking a mental cold plunge into the middle of it,
come up gasping, jump out and then wade in with deep
breathing exercises from the beginning. Brushing aside
obscurities in the text, I dash through, get the general sense
(sic) of the thing and then start over again. Next instalment
next month! Bless you all. I am very well and full of
confidence as usual! Roger.

At almost the same moment, Bushell had a stroke of good fortune, with the discovery that Corporal Griese – the hated 'Rubberneck', who had succeeded Glemnitz as senior ferret in the North Compound, and the prisoners' most dangerous adversary – would take two weeks' holiday from 1 March. Every effort would be made to finish the tunnel and seal it down before Rubberneck returned.

But on the day Corporal Griese was scheduled to start his leave, the Germans struck a blow that must have involved a considerable amount of luck: they removed about twenty men, including Wally Floody, the chief tunnel engineer; George Harsh, head of tunnel security; Peter Fanshawe, head of sand dispersal; and several other members of the escape organisation from the North Compound and sent them to another compound at Belaria, about three miles away.

Robert Stanford Tuck, who had been due to pair up with Bushell if the escape succeeded, was also among those men removed by the Germans from the North Compound. 'Even so, Tuck chuckled to think that the Germans hadn't taken Big X or several other key men!' wrote Larry Forrester in Tuck's biography, *Fly For Your Life*. 'Bushell's brainwave about producing *Pygmalion* [he had been rehearsing for the leading role of Henry Higgins] had provided a wonderful cover for most of the top organisers. Tuck had been offered a small part in the play, but he'd turned it down.'

With the departure of several key men, Big X lost a day of Rubberneck's leave while the escape committee reorganised key positions and new men took the places of those who had been taken away.

Instead of damping the spirits of those who remained, the loss of so many experts acted as a spur, *wrote Aidan Crawley*. For the next fortnight these men thought tunnels, dreamed tunnels and even, with caution, talked tunnels. There appeared to be no time to think or do anything else. The results surpassed expectations. On 3rd March, twelve feet of tunnel was dug, shored and the sand dispersed. Next day that record was beaten and fourteen feet of completed tunnel was constructed, a record that lasted until the end of the war.

Further afield, there were sinister developments that gave Himmler's SS a yet greater role in the affairs of recaptured Allied airmen.

Kugel Erlass – 'the Bullet Order' – changed the status of recaptured prisoners of war. In a document issued by Heinrich Müller, head of the Gestapo, on 4 March 1944, it laid down that all recaptured prisoners – other than British and American – were to be handed to the Gestapo and sent to Mauthausen concentration camp in Austria, where they would be shot. Müller's order stated that 'the recaptured P.W. are to be reported to the local army registration office as "Escaped and not recaptured". Their mail is to be appropriately dealt with. Enquiries from representatives of the Protecting Power and the International Red Cross and other auxiliary bodies will be given an identical reply.'

In other words, the air force officers from Czechoslovakia, Denmark, France, Greece, Norway and the many other nations represented in the North Compound would be made 'to disappear' if they were recaptured after escaping; British and American prisoners would be taken into police custody where the Gestapo would decide their fates on a case-by-case basis.

With these orders, the Germans turned their backs on the Geneva Convention.

At Stalag Luft III, some of the German officers, including the commandant, von Lindeiner, tried to persuade the prisoners that escaping had suddenly become a very dangerous game. According to documents in the National Archive: 'About the middle of February 1944 the Commandant of Stalag Luft 3 addressed the Senior Officer of each Compound in regard to escape penalties. During his address he stressed the fact that in future penalties would be much more severe than in the past. No comment on, or questions arising from, his address were permitted.'

Sydney Dowse's remarkable contact, Corporal Eberhard Hesse, who seemed to know that a tunnel was being constructed, raised the question of Bushell's involvement: he was convinced Bushell would be shot if he escaped and was recaptured. In an interview recorded by the Imperial War Museum, Dowse said he had passed on the warning and told Bushell not to join the escape: 'I've got it on very firm grounds from Hesse that, should you ever go out, there'll be no more of you,' Dowse said.

Whether Bushell and the other members of the X organisation thought the Germans were bluffing is not known, but the warnings were not heeded. The digging teams pressed on.

'When 'HARRY' was three hundred and forty-five feet long, a vertical shaft was constructed to within nine inches of the ground level,' recorded the camp history. 'The construction work was completed by 14th March.'

It was the day before Rubberneck returned from leave. 'The diggers knew that the unbelievable had been achieved,' wrote Crawley. The trap was sealed.

A few hours later, Corporal Griese returned from his holiday and ordered a search of Hut 104. 'It was obvious that the Germans thought, or were even certain, there was a tunnel there,' Wings

Day told his biographer, Sydney Smith. 'The break would have to be soon.'

Of the 600 men who had worked on the project in one role or another, 500 applied to take part in the escape, on which there would be only 200 places.

> The first thirty places were reserved for the Escape Committee's choice of whom they considered most likely to make a successful escape, *recorded the camp history*. These were fluent German speakers and were to go out first because they were to travel by train. Their names were put into a hat and drawn to give the order in which they were to go out.

Roger Bushell was number four.

The other names on the list of 200 potential escapers were drawn by a variety of ballots.

All the escapers were provided with civilian clothes, forged documents, money, food, maps and compasses. The first thirty, who were going by train, had attaché cases, but no Red Cross food and only a small map of the frontier section, because the discovery of maps or Red Cross food would have given them away. Every escaper had an identity card, ration cards, letters from German firms and an authority to travel by train. About forty men were scheduled to travel on workmen's trains for part of their journey; the remainder would go on foot, irrespective of the harsh weather.

Bushell interviewed every one of the other 199 men who had been selected for the escape, according to the camp history, briefing them on customs and travel, and checking their cover stories. Whatever his motives, he certainly kept himself busy.

The battle lines between the prisoners and their captors were drawn. Both sides seemed to have known that an 'offensive' was imminent.

Between 15 and 17 March, von Lindeiner held a conference involving the commandants of other camps, local police and his senior officers to discuss security. The agenda struck a realistic tone. Thousands of Allied airmen were falling into German hands every month, but the Luftwaffe had no time to train new staff. According to the minutes, one of the most intractable problems was the 'esprit de corps, prevailing in particular within the British Air Force'.

Bushell undoubtedly bore some of the responsibility for engendering this spirit in Stalag Luft III, particularly in the North Compound. Keith Mountfort, a major in the Parachute Regiment who was held in Stalag Luft III, witnessed Big X in action in the days before the escape. With the Senior British Officer standing at his side, Bushell explained the objects of the operation in his final briefing – an eve-of-battle speech – to the prisoners.

> *He said that apart from the value of getting some experienced officers back to England,* wrote Mountfort, in a letter to Bushell's parents after the war, *one vital factor was to cause alarm and inconvenience throughout a large part of Germany. Another was to cause extra precautionary measures to be taken by the Germans and necessitate extra guards and the replacement of certain camp staff.*

Mountfort quoted Bushell as telling the prisoners:

> *For those of you who have been unlucky enough not to draw a place in Harry, I can promise plenty of entertainment later. Because, irrespective of how we get on, once the Germans have discovered that a large number of officers have escaped from a tunnel which has been constructed under their very noses, for over a year, it will be a case of* après nous, le déluge.
>
> *At that moment, more than ever,* wrote Mountfort, *he had the camp behind him to a man.*

The mood in the North Compound is best described as electric. Such was the state of excitement, in fact, that some prisoners feared it would be detected by the Germans.

But there was still work to be done. In the tunnel, blankets had to be laid on the last fifty feet of railway to deaden the noise when the escapers were hauled to the exit, and the trolleys had to be fitted with platforms on which the escapers could lie. Strong ropes that could withstand the strain of pulling trolleys bearing escapers were stolen from a consignment scheduled to be used in the construction of a boxing ring. And more electric lights had to be fitted.

Alan Bryett, head of security in Hut 122, where 'Dick' was located, went down 'Harry' shortly before the escape. 'I was completely overwhelmed,' he said. 'I couldn't believe that such a wonderful thing had been done. Overwhelmed, yes.'

The escape committee faced a number of complicated manoeuvres before the escape could go ahead: the 200 escapers would have to be moved into Hut 104, where the trap for Harry was located, in such a way that it did not attract the attention of the Germans. The choreography was worked out in fine detail; clothing and other escape equipment had to be distributed; while the forgers had to wait until the timing of the escape was fixed before they could date all the papers that they hoped would allow the men to travel through Occupied Europe.

The BBC play based on the book by Paul Brickhill, who was a prisoner in the North Compound at the time, captured the language and mood as Bushell made the final decisions.

Confronted by Johnny Marshall, who asserted that they could not possibly make the break in such cold weather, Bushell replied that they certainly could.

'Doesn't give the cross-country boys much chance,' responded Marshall.

'Johnny, they haven't much chance anyway,' said Bushell. 'You know as well as I do they'll nearly all be caught. We can't lose "Harry" just because conditions are tough. It isn't only to get

327

people home. It's to muck the goons about too, and get them to divert troops to look for us.'

Robert 'Crump' Ker-Ramsey, who had taken over responsibility for the tunnelling after Wally Floody had been sent to Belaria, then asked: 'When do we go then?'

Bushell replied: 'Well, we want no moon; a wind to cover up noises; and reasonable weather. Now the three most moonless nights for the next five weeks are the 23rd, 24th and 25th of March. The 25th's no good, that's a Saturday. And that means Sunday timetables for most of the train travelling. We'll work towards the 23rd or 24th and see how the weather turns out.'

Snow still lay on the ground on Friday, 24 March, but there was mildness in the air. Having listened to the camp's weather expert, Bushell declared: 'All right, then. Tonight's the night. How about it?'

Marshall was still set against the break. 'What about the cross-country men?' he asked again. 'They'll freeze to death.'

Bushell said: 'No. We can't wait for the next no-moon period. We'd lose the tunnel. What do you say, Wings?'

Wings Day had no hesitations and, through Brickhill's pen, delivered the verdict of MI9: 'It's an operational war, chaps. It isn't just a question of getting a few people home. It's bigger than that. Most of the boys will be caught anyway, but if we get a good team out there'll be a flap all over Germany, and we'll have done something useful.'

The discussion was concluded by Bushell: 'Thanks, Wings,' he said. 'Well, that's it. Tonight.'

Within a few minutes, the entire camp seemed to know that the decision had been made.

Bushell left himself with just one more task. Albert 'Bub' Clark, the American who suspected Bushell's influence when the Germans put the squeeze on him after he moved from the North to the South Compound in the autumn of 1943, remembered the moment when he was called to the wire that separated the British and American compounds and held his last conversation with Big X.

'Somebody came to me and said Roger Bushell is over on the other side of the wire calling, wants to talk to you, so I immediately went out there and Roger very quietly said, "We go tonight, please don't do anything to screw us up" – or words to that effect. And I assured him we had no plans and would not mess anything up and wished him luck. And that was of course the last I ever saw of him.'

Wings Day saw Bushell later that night in Hut 104.

We escapees were all collected in the Barrack from which the tunnel opened, he told Bushell's parents after the war. *Roger was dressed in a well-cut grey tweed suit, with trilby hat, greatcoat and small attaché case. He looked exactly the part of a prosperous businessman. He was in very good spirits and convinced that he was going to get home.*

He left to go through the tunnel before me as he was catching a train to Breslau, which left about 9pm. My train for Berlin did not leave before 1am. It was the last I saw of him.

25

Goodbye, Harry

Roger Bushell was the one man among the escapers who gathered in Hut 104 on the night of Friday, 24 March 1944, who
knew that he would be killed if he were caught by the Germans.

Whether it was learning the role of Henry Higgins for the camp
theatre's production of *Pygmalion*, embracing the philosophies
of Indian mystics or wrestling with the difficulties of Russian
grammar, Bushell was clearly capable of rationalising his own
position. He was mentally alert and intellectually agile.

With his intelligence network, which gave him a comprehensive
overview of life in Stalag Luft III and the development of the war,
Bushell was better informed than most prisoners in the camp. The
warnings from friends and foes alike had been unambiguous: if
the men of the Gestapo had been determined to kill him in 1942,
they would, with their backs to the wall after years of torturing
and murdering opponents of the Third Reich, have no compunc-
tion about dealing with him in 1944.

Whether he analysed all the evidence in the same manner in
which he would have built a legal case, or whether he just decided
to 'go for it' in the way that he pointed his skis downhill or led his
vastly outnumbered Spitfires into battle, is not known. With 200
Allied aircrew – among them some of the most able men in the
British armed forces – destined at last to be at large in the heart of
Hitler's Germany, not to mention his intelligence activities,
Bushell had certainly done his military duty.

The decision to take part in the escape was by no means irra-
tional. Travelling as a French businessman, speaking fluent French,
as well as German, wearing a real civilian suit and carrying what
he believed to be very good papers, Bushell had reasons to be

confident of success. According to Peter Cazenove, a former 92 Squadron pilot who had been with Bushell for much of the past four years: 'All their passes and equipment were 100%.'

Bushell's partner on the escape, the Frenchman Bernard Scheidhauer, had been one of the key players in the intelligence operation. They hoped to get to Paris where they would link up with the French resistance.

For Big X, the war was approaching its climax.

As Bushell felt the blast of cold air from the tunnel's newly opened exit shaft, Johnny Bull climbed the last rungs of the ladder and stuck his head into the open air.

Bull was in open ground behind the nearest goon box. The surveyors had miscalculated. The tunnel's exit was about 10ft short of the pine forest.

Bushell and Bull briefly discussed whether to close up the tunnel and try again later, but quickly dismissed this option because of the dates on personal documents.

According to the camp history, the exit shaft had been finally opened at 10.15 p.m. – long after Bushell was scheduled to have caught the 9 p.m. train to Breslau, 120 miles south-east of Sagan – and Bull acted as traffic officer for the next 20 escapers.

Lying on a blanket at the top of the shaft, he had a clear view of the patrolling sentries and controlled every exit by pressing the escaper's head until it was safe for him to come out, when he tapped him on the head. The first Prisoner of War to crawl from the tunnel exit to the wood took a rope from the top of the ladder to a tree in the wood. Each succeeding escaper crawled to the wood keeping one hand on the rope, which was jerked if it was necessary for him to lie flat and keep still. The first man out in every ten was the marshalling officer of his party and detailed each man to hide behind a tree until all ten were assembled.

Bushell was among the first men to emerge from the tunnel and arrived in the forest breathless, but grinning. He took over the role of control officer. Minutes later, Scheidhauer arrived. They waited until Rupert Stevens, a South African bomber pilot, joined them and then exchanged roles.

'The first 20 out of the tunnel assembled at a point in the woods 200 yards from the exit,' said Johnny Marshall in a statement made to British authorities after the war. 'Bushell who was in this party said that there would be a train from Sagan Station at 11pm which we should all catch and that we should go to the station by twos and threes. He himself reached the station almost immediately but the rest of us had difficulty in finding the entrance to the station in the darkness.'

Back in Hut 104, the escape was dogged by mishaps. Two hours had already been lost while Bull and Marshall had wrestled with Harry's exit, which had been jammed by swollen timbers, and Bushell had taken more time to come up with a strategy once he had realised that the tunnel exit had fallen short of the forest. In the barrack, where nervous men waited, further errors cost more time: some men ignored the advice to travel light and restrict the size of cases, causing delays in the tunnel.

Air Marshal Sir Arthur 'Bomber' Harris also played a part in delaying the air force escapers: he had ordered the last major air raid of the war on Berlin, with his squadrons of heavy bombers – a force of 811 aircraft – drifting south of the German capital, which meant that the town of Sagan, the camp – and the prisoners' tunnel – were all blacked out.

Ken Rees recalled the chaos: 'More things began to go wrong,' he wrote. 'First, someone carrying a suitcase caused a fall which Cookie Long took ages to repair. Then the RAF stepped in and really put things back . . . the goons suddenly put out all the lights, causing mayhem down in the tunnel. Escapers who had never been down it before abruptly and without explanation found themselves in total darkness, trapped in a claustrophobic hole. Everything stopped until some oil lights were lit and passed down the tunnel.'

But most of the Great Escapers remained in strong spirits. Jimmy James recalled his sense of exhilaration as the word came for him to move from the barrack into the tunnel. 'Everyone was very excited,' he said, in an interview recorded with the Imperial War Museum. 'Climbing down the shaft was going thirty foot down, like down a ship's hold, then I was holding on to the trolley and being pulled up to the first halfway house. There I changed trolleys and was pulled up to the next one. Finally I was pulled up to the exit hole and I looked up and saw the stars. The RAF motto came to mind – *Per Ardua Ad Astra* [Through adversity to the stars].'

Bushell and Scheidhauer were almost two hours later than planned for the train to Breslau when they walked through the small hut-like entrance, which was almost hidden between houses, facing the pine forest at the back of the station. The two men descended the stairs before entering the subway that led to the ticket office and platforms. But they did arrive in time to catch the 11 p.m. train, just as the station was filling up with escaped prisoners.

Hannelore Zoller, a censor in the mailing office, was suspicious of the many men she saw in the station as she walked through it after visiting the cinema in Sagan.

'I shall never forget the night of the great escape,' recalled Zoller. 'We noticed two or three little groups of strange-looking men who seemed to be waiting for a train. They were extraordinarily dressed and looked somewhat nervous. Knowing that in our camp kriegies had self-made clothes from their variety shows, we had a fair idea that these men could have escaped from the camp. We waited for a moment and observed them and then some of them disappeared.'

Zoller's observations may have coincided with the moment that Bushell and Scheidhauer boarded their train.

'We went to see the station policeman and told him of our suspicion,' continued Zoller. 'He asked one group to identify themselves. They produced some documents to prove they were '*Fremdarbeiter*', which meant foreign labourers. My friend and I then continued on our way to the camp and at the gate asked the guard whether anything was going on in the camp – escape or so. "No, everything is quiet," he said.'

She considered phoning the commandant, and even discussed it with her friends, but it was past midnight. 'We thought we would probably make a fool of ourselves,' she said.

Des Plunkett, who had been responsible for producing the escapers' maps and was the thirteenth man out of the tunnel, also boarded the train to Breslau. He retained a vivid memory of the journey. Bushell passed him in the corridor, but as he was doing so, he slipped his hand into Plunkett's and gave it a slight squeeze. He didn't say anything and didn't look at him. Plunkett noticed that he was doing this to all the other escapers who were standing in the train.

Accompanied by cigarette smoke, sweat and nervous tension, the last of the escapers carrying suitcases left Hut 104 sometime after 1 a.m. They were followed by men who carried blankets, which should have been rolled up neatly to help get them down the tunnel, but several prisoners had ignored their instructions, while some were overloaded with food.

Eventually it was decided that because the blanket carriers were taking fourteen minutes to get through and already it was not going to be possible for more than one hundred to escape, no more blanket rolls must be carried, *recorded the camp history*. This was unfortunate because the weather was very cold, but by this time it was essential for emergency measures to be taken. This increased the rate of flow, but fifteen minutes later a frame was knocked out in the tunnel which caused a fall of sand. It took another half hour to repair this. As soon as this was done, the same thing happened further along the tunnel, and this took twenty minutes to repair.

The organisers in Hut 104 decided that the last escape would take place at 5 a.m. and that the 87th escaper into the tunnel would be the last man to make the break.

The escape was discovered when a German guard, veering fom his usual beat, noticed figures in the woods.

> A shot was heard, *recorded the camp history*. The escapers still in the tunnel were called back, men were put to watch at every window, and the remainder of the two hundred started burning all their forged papers, getting out of their civilian clothes and hiding their compasses and food. A report came back from the exit that there was a lot of shouting in the woods and a party of guards had just left the Guardroom and were making for the sentry-tower nearest the exit. Seven escapers who were in the tunnel came out quickly, the trap was replaced and the stove put back on top of it.

In the South Compound, the American Bub Clark could not sleep that night. 'I remember hearing the shot early in the morning, which I'm sure I knew would signal the end of the tunnel,' Clark said in an interview after the war. 'I went out kinda early and all of the ferrets . . . they were very agitated . . . and we casually asked them . . . and they said big tunnel break in the north camp, and I remember one of them, a little smart-arse ferret saying, "I knew it, I knew it was coming, I knew it was going to be." They just didn't know where, or exactly when.'

An hour later, Freddie Dvorak, one of the Czechs among the escapers, heard an announcement over the loud speaker at Breslau station calling for the station master, the chief of the security police and the chief of the ordinary police.

Dvorak saw Bushell. 'We had to wait on the station at Breslau until about 0600 hours,' he told British investigators after the war. 'We also met S/L Bushell and talked to him about the progress of the escape.'

At Breslau, it was possible for Bushell and Scheidhauer to buy tickets direct to the Gare de l'Est in Paris via Dresden, Leipzig, Frankfurt, Mainz, Saarbrücken and Metz.

At Stalag Luft III, the Germans mounted four machine guns near Hut 104 and trained them on the barracks. The commandant, von Lindeiner, arrived and turned the prisoners out into the snow. They waited twenty minutes while the barrack hut was searched. More guards arrived.

According to the camp history, the commandant threatened to shoot if there were any disturbances. 'Von Lindeiner was himself red with controlled anger,' recalled Rees.

As Bushell had predicted, *Après moi, le déluge.*

One of the ferrets entered the tunnel from the exit and eventually surfaced in Hut 104 after the prisoners were urged to let him out. The Germans feared he would suffocate.

All the prisoners who had come out of Hut 104 were ordered to strip in the intense cold while they were searched. Four prisoners were sent to the cooler, two for resisting attempts to take away their clothes, one for mocking the Germans and one for laughing. At 8.30 a.m., they were all marched off to be checked against their photographs. Roll call was held at 11 a.m.

Seventy-six prisoners had escaped through the tunnel; far fewer than the 200 that Bushell envisaged would get out, but it was still the biggest British escape of the war.

Hitler was informed within hours, according to Field Marshal Wilhelm Keitel, the chief of the German High Command. Some reports suggest that Hitler was not told until the Sunday but, either way, he reacted badly.

With Nazi Germany in increasing disarray, its forces retreating on all fronts and an Allied invasion of north-west Europe considered imminent, it is perhaps surprising that Hitler's leading lieutenants – Hermann Göring, head of the Luftwaffe; Heinrich Himmler, head of the security apparatus including the SS and Gestapo; and Keitel – should put Bushell and his escapers at the top of their agenda. But if Bushell had set out to make life 'hell for the Hun', he succeeded beyond his ambitions: what became known as the 'Great Escape' went right to the top.

At the Berghof, Hitler's mountain headquarters above the town of Berchtesgaden in Bavaria, on Saturday, 25 March or Sunday, 26 March, the leaders of Nazi Germany decided the fate of Big X.

In his memoirs, written in the weeks before he was executed by the Allies after the war, Keitel wrote:

> The SS *Reichsführer* [Himmler] zealously reported the escape of eighty British officers from Camp Sagan, and willingly depicted the consequences: the *Landwacht*, a paramilitary auxiliary police formation, would have to be alerted and that would cost millions of manhours and so on.
>
> Hitler's reaction was immediate: the escapees were to be turned over to the police, and he added the outrageous afterthought that they were to be shot. Even those who had already been picked up were to be handed over to Himmler.

Keitel, who used his memoirs to justify his own actions, claimed that he had protested that the action would constitute a violation of the Geneva Convention. Himmler and Göring bickered and blamed Keitel – who was responsible for the inspection of prisoner-of-war camps – for the escape.

Hitler was persuaded to limit the executions to fifty – the Nazis liked nice round numbers – of the escaped airmen, but otherwise stuck 'stubbornly' to his decision to exact a price.

As Hitler spelt out his orders, Bushell was heading for France, travelling further and faster than any of the other escapers.

After the meeting at the Berghof, Keitel summoned two senior officers, General Hans von Graevenitz, head of the prisoner of war camps, and his deputy, General Adolf Westhoff, a veteran of the Eastern Front.

Keitel said: 'Gentlemen, this must stop. We cannot allow this to happen again. The officers who have escaped will be shot . . . you will publish a notice in the prison camps where PWs are held telling PWs what action had been taken in this case in order that it will be a deterrent to other escapes.'

The two generals objected, but Keitel said, 'That was his order and it will have to be carried out.'

The SS took matters into its own hands. Himmler sent a top-secret document known as the 'Sagan Order' to SS *Obergruppenführer* Ernst Kaltenbrunner, who had succeeded Reinhard Heydrich as head of the Nazi security apparatus.

It said:

```
The increase of escapes by officer POWs is a menace
to internal security. I am disappointed and
indignant about the inefficient security measures.
As a deterrent, the Führer has ordered that more
than half of the escaped officers are to be shot.
Therefore I order that Department V [the
Kriminalpolizei, or 'Kripo'] hand over for
interrogation to Department IV [the Gestapo] more
than half of the recaptured officers. After
interrogation the officers are to be returned to
their original camp and to be shot en route. The
shootings will be explained by the fact that the
recaptured officers were shot whilst trying to
escape, or because they offered resistance, so
that nothing can be proved later.
```

The fifty escapers who would be executed were chosen by SS *Gruppenführer* Arthur Nebe, the head of the Kripo. He was a career detective who had risen through the Nazi ranks and had commanded one of Heydrich's killing squads, the *Einsatzgruppen*, in Russia. By what criteria he chose the fifty men who were to be murdered, is not known, but his orders were followed to the letter. No nationality was spared. Young and old perished. Some of the most troublesome prisoners survived.

As the train on which Bushell and Scheidhauer continued towards Saarbrücken on the French border on Sunday, March 26, the two men had successfully put 500 miles between themselves and Stalag Luft III. Paris beckoned. But then they ran into trouble.

A policeman appeared to be uncertain about the authenticity of their papers. Some reports suggest an official stamp was missing. It was the beginning of the end.

Bushell and Scheidhauer were taken off the train at Saarbrücken and interviewed by the criminal police. Documents in the National Archive, prepared by British officers investigating German crimes after the war ended, tell the story of their arrest.

The confidential report states:

```
Kripo-Sekretar KRAUS and/or Kripo official BENDER
of Saarbrücken, on duty at the railway station,
arrested two men, in civilian clothing and
bearing papers of French labourers, after one of
them had inadvertently replied to a question of
KRAUS or BENDER in English . . . and took them to
the Kripo office. At the Kripo office, it was
determined that the two men were (Major RAF)
ROGER BUSHELL and (Lt) BERNHARD SCHEIDHAUER
(possibly a Free Frenchman serving with British
forces) and that they were among the escaped
officers being sought.
```

Bushell was undoubtedly aware of his precarious position; Scheidhauer perhaps less so. The two men were separated. Both admitted their true identities and the fact that they had escaped from Stalag Luft III in Lower Silesia.

The document gives no hint as to which officer slipped up, but for either to have been wrong-footed after so many months of meticulous preparation and their work in intelligence, seems a cruel outcome. Only two days earlier, Bushell had been briefing all the other prisoners on how to deal with questioning by German police.

The British officer accepted food and cigarettes and talked about his life as a student at Cambridge, his training as a barrister, and the fact that he had travelled in Germany during the 1930s. He expressed gratitude for the considerate treatment he had received, which he had not expected. Indeed, he must have retained some sense of hope.

Then everything changed. Bushell and Scheidhauer had been at large for less than two days, and now Hitler's rage caught up with them. They were transferred to Lerchesflur prison, where their case was taken up by the Saarbrücken Gestapo. A few hours later, they were removed on the pretence of being taken to Berlin for further interrogation.

Emil Schulz, a Gestapo officer, told British investigators after the war that Dr Leopold Spann, head of the Saarbrücken Gestapo, ordered him to attend a meeting in his office.

'Dr Spann asked me first whether I had been in action,' said Schulz. 'I replied in the negative. Hereupon he said words to the effect, "What I am telling you now, remains between us. There are two English RAF officers in the Lerchesflur prison at Saarbrucken, who had escaped. These are to be shot on orders . . ."'

Spann asked Schulz whether he knew a suitable place to kill them. Schulz suggested the motorway.

Walter Breithaupt, a Gestapo driver, said that Schulz collected the prisoners and their luggage and signed the forms authorising their release into Gestapo custody. 'It all went very quickly,' said Breithaupt.

After driving to Gestapo headquarters, Schulz told the two RAF officers to wait in the lobby on the ground floor. Bushell and Scheidhauer put down their luggage and spoke in English.

Schulz returned from Dr Spann's office. 'We went out through the door and Schulz made the two sit in the car, which was standing in front of the door,' said Breithaupt. 'I remember that I put the two suitcases of the prisoners into the luggage space of the car. Dr Spann came shortly afterwards.'

The two prisoners were handcuffed. 'During this I heard for the first time that one of the prisoners spoke German,' said Breithaupt. 'It was the bigger of the two [Bushell]. He said to Schulz that this was not compatible with the honour of an officer. To this Schulz replied while going away – he went back into the office building – that it was an order. After a short while Dr Spann and Schulz came out of the building again and got into the car. Schulz sat between the two prisoners on the back seat. Dr Spann sat in the right front seat next to me.'

Leopold Spann and Emil Schulz wore SS uniforms. Breithaupt drove to Homberg and then towards Kaiserslautern.

Nobody spoke.

In his testimony, Schulz, who was married with two young daughters, told British investigators that Dr Spann ordered Breithaupt to stop the car and to take the handcuffs off the prisoners. The Gestapo chief then got out of the car and onto the grass. 'He had a pistol in his hand,' recalled Schulz.

Breithaupt also got out of the car and stood on the autobahn, level with the front right wheel. 'He also had a pistol in his hand,' said Schulz.

'I still sat between the two officers when I took off the handcuffs of the smaller of them, Scheidhauer, who had bent forward a little and was sitting on the right beside me. Then he got out on the right and went on the grass. Then at my order, the bigger officer, Bushell, leant forward a little and I undid his handcuffs.

'I let him slip past me and got out on the right as well. He also went onto the grass. I got out of the car backwards on the left-hand side, put the handcuffs on the rear seat, took my pistol from my pocket and went round the back of the car.'

Schulz fired in the direction of Bushell.

'I do not know whether and how I hit him. I saw both officers collapse. Scheidhauer fell on his face,' said Schulz. 'I think Bushell crumpled up, fell somewhat on his right side and in lying there turned on his back. On approaching closer I noticed the dying man was in convulsions; I lay on the ground and shot him through the left temple.'

Death was immediate, said the Gestapo officer.

Lying on a grass verge just off the A6 outside the town of Kaiserslautern, his body guarded by the man who killed him, on 29 March 1944, Big X was among the first of the fifty to fall.

26

A Marked Man

The Sagan Order – Hitler's decision to execute Roger Bushell and forty-nine of his fellow escapers from Stalag Luft III – constituted the single greatest war crime committed by Nazi Germany against British servicemen between 3 September 1939 and 8 May 1945.

In fields and forests and on roadsides across Germany, Poland and the Protectorate of Bohemia and Moravia, small groups of recaptured escapers, as well as a handful of solitary individuals, were murdered by agents of the Gestapo. No mercy was shown to the fifty men on the condemned list.

Johnny Bull, the first man out of the tunnel, was captured by a German patrol while trying to climb the Reisengebirge mountain range beyond the Polish town of Boberröhrsdorf, about forty miles south-east of Sagan. Bull was travelling with Jerzy Mondschein, a Pole, and two Australians, Reginald 'Rusty' Kierath and John 'Willy' Williams.

Mondschein had flown with the Polish air force before the war but escaped to Britain after the German invasion. He had been one of Tommy Guest's tailors. Kierath organised Stalag Luft III's cricket fixtures, and was also one of the carpenters. Williams was a young squadron leader who had been responsible for collecting the bed boards needed for shoring up the tunnels, and was renowned for his sense of humour. The four men were taken to the criminal police headquarters in Reichenberg, which is now known as Liberec, in northern Bohemia.

On Wednesday, 29 March 1944, the same day as Roger Bushell and Bernard Scheidhauer were killed, the deaths of Bull,

343

Mondschein, Kierath and Williams were organised by Bernhard Baatz, the Reichenberg Gestapo chief.

If proof were ever needed of premeditated murder, Baatz provided it. He had written a letter to the local crematorium the night before the killings in which he named the four men and said that they had been shot while attempting to escape.

At thirty-five years of age, Mondschein was the oldest of the four. Kierath was twenty-nine, Bull twenty-seven and Williams just twenty-four.

Eighteen of the Great Escapers died that day.

Tom Kirby-Green, who had advocated a better deal for the native peoples of Britain's colonies during the prisoners' debate on the post-war world, was arrested on the Czech border with Gordon Kidder, a Canadian who had studied German at Johns Hopkins University in Baltimore. They were questioned by officers from the Gestapo office in Zlin and were shot a few hours later close to the crematorium at Moravská Ostrava. Kirby-Green was twenty-six years old. He had a son, Colin, whom he had never seen. Kidder was twenty-nine.

Tim Walenn, head of the forging department, was travelling with Gordon Brettell, Henri Picard and Romas Marcinkus when he was arrested near the Baltic port of Danzig. Brettell was a Cambridge graduate who had a passion for motor racing and had flown with Bushell's squadron, No. 92. Picard – another fighter pilot – was a Belgian, the third of four children, who had a flair for languages and excelled at sport. Marcinkus was a Lithuanian who had reached Britain via North Africa after the Battle of France, but had come to grief flying into a flock of seagulls after attacking the German battleship, *Scharnhorst*.

Officers from the Gestapo took the four men to a wood near the village of Gross Trampken, fifteen miles south of Danzig, and shot them in the back. Marcinkus was thirty-three and Brettell twenty-nine. Walenn was twenty-eight; Picard was twenty-seven.

Mike Casey, the Blenheim bomber pilot whose remarkable flying had won the admiration of the Luftwaffe officer who shot him down in October 1939, died on the edge of a wood near Sagan. He was one of many officers recaptured within thirty miles of the camp and interrogated by the Gestapo in the town of Görlitz, where the atmosphere was tense and threatening. According to official interviews, several prisoners were told that they would be shot. At least one was told that he would be decapitated. The Gestapo made it clear that the recaptured Allied officers could be 'made to disappear'.

Casey was shot while ostensibly being returned to Stalag Luft III. He died on Thursday, 30 March. Like Bushell, he had played a part in the mass escape from Dulag Luft in June 1941. A devout Christian who was married just a few days before he was taken prisoner, Casey was twenty-six.

John Stower, the sugar planter from Argentina who had reached the Swiss border after escaping with the delousing party the previous summer, was shot on Friday, 31 March in unknown circumstances: he was taken from a cell in Reichenberg, where Bull, Mondschein, Kierath and Williams had been held.

Stower's partner on the escape was Ivo Tonder, a Czech airman who had arrived in Liverpool by ship in August 1940 after a hazardous journey through France. Unlike his companion, Tonder survived the war.

Questioned by British investigators just over a year later, Tonder said that on the night of the escape, he and Stower had intended to board the 11 p.m. train to Lauban, close to the Czech border.

'We left the tunnel too late to catch that train and as the next was not until 0600 hours we decided to walk,' said Tonder on 25 May 1945. 'We walked together 20 kilometres to Halbau and then spent the day sleeping in the woods. The weather was bad and we were not equipped for walking. We walked on for two further nights and on 27th March we had passed Kohlfurt. We decided that owing to the weather it would be better to travel by train and we went back to Kohlfurt where we bought tickets and food.'

The two men boarded a train towards Reichenberg, but changed at Görlitz and were arrested on the journey to Northern Bohemia by two plain-clothes men belonging to the Kripo. 'Our papers seemed to them to be in order but our clothes, which were similar to those of the other escapers they had already arrested, betrayed us,' said Tonder.

'We were taken by the two plain-clothes men to the Kripo HQ in Reichenberg where we were put in a cell together. We were photographed and our personal details were taken. In this HQ we heard that Bull, Kierath, Mondschein and S/L Williams were also there. We were interrogated together and then met these four upstairs in the presence of the police and we were able to talk to them.'

The Kripo agents told Tonder that they were all to be handed over to the Gestapo. 'We went downstairs again and Bull and the other three officers signed some forms for the two Gestapo agents,' said Tonder. 'These forms merely stated that the answers that they had already given to the Kripo were correct. During this time both Stower and I had the impression that S/L Williams had learnt something about his fate. He was not normally a nervous man but he was clearly pale and scared. I have no reason to suppose that he had behaved in a provocative manner during his interrogation or that there was any cause for him to be more alarmed than the others.'

Bull, Mondschein, Kierath and Williams were taken from their cells at 4 a.m. on Wednesday, 29 March. The Kripo said they had been taken back to Sagan. 'I never saw the four again,' said Tonder.

Later that day, Stower and Tonder had their fingerprints taken and were put in separate cells. 'The same evening the two Gestapo agents looked into my cell and said words to the effect that I was a Czech and a traitor,' said Tonder. 'I therefore expected trouble and told Stower through the wall that I would probably be left behind and that on his return to the camp he was to report this as soon as possible.'

The next morning, Stower signed a form similar to those signed by the four men who had departed in the early hours of the previous day. 'He left at 0800 hours on Friday 31 March. I saw him leave but I did not see who was with him,' said Tonder. 'He was told that an escort from Sagan had arrived to fetch him. I have not seen him since that day.'

Tonder remained at Reichenberg until mid-April when he was transferred to the headquarters of the Gestapo in Prague – the Petschek Palace. He was interrogated by a Gestapo officer called Bauer, the same man who had questioned Roger Bushell two years previously. Tonder spent the rest of the war as a prisoner in Colditz Castle.

Johnny Marshall, who had helped Bull break through the tunnel exit, survived. His travelling companion, Arnost 'Wally' Valenta, a Czech intellectual who was one of Bushell's key lieutenants in the intelligence operation, did not. They were arrested at 4 a.m. on the Sunday by two members of the *Landwacht*, the German home guard, near the Polish village of Tiefenfurt, barely fifteen miles from Sagan. Interrogated by the Gestapo at Görlitz, Marshall was returned to Stalag Luft III. Valenta was shot. He was thirty-one.

Wings Day travelled as a renegade Irishman escorted by Pawel Tobolski, a Pole who was dressed in German uniform. They caught a train from Sagan to Berlin at 1.05 a.m., stayed the night in the German capital and then caught another train to the Baltic port of Stettin. Befriended by two French labourers, they found room to sleep in a workers' barracks, but were betrayed by an informer. Tobolski was sent to Görlitz and shot. He was thirty-eight.

Day was taken to SS headquarters in Berlin and interviewed by a man in a long, grey greatcoat with a red lining who appeared to be a police general.

'He was a tallish, well-built man, aged about 50–55 with grey, almost white, hair wearing an Iron Cross of the first class,' Day told investigators in London more than a year later, on 28 May 1945. 'He was clean-shaven without glasses and had a good-looking, narrow face but a cold, hard expression . . .'

Unable to identify the German officer, Day added: 'The general said in German that I and my companions had caused a lot of trouble . . . He then said that I was going to be put in a place where I would give no further trouble. I spoke quickly, pointing out that as a prisoner of war I was carrying out a duty in attempting to escape. He listened quite calmly but made no comment.'

After the interview had finished, Day was escorted by a major from the security services. 'I thought he was in the SD because he wore worsted badges and not silver ones,' Day said. '. . . he accompanied me in a car with an escort dressed in the standard Gestapo plain clothes consisting of an ordinary jacket with breeches and riding boots. During the drive I talked to the major who said that he had spent some time in England. He told me it was his duty to keep a check on all the escaping activities of prisoners of war and that he knew the records of us all. He said I had escaped four times before and this was quite correct.'

The two men discussed the other escapers, including Roger Bushell. 'I tried to find out what had happened to S/L Bushell,' said Day, 'but the major was evasive and merely said that they had found everyone.'

Day was taken to Sachsenhausen concentration camp, twenty miles north of Berlin. He was joined by Major John Dodge, the much-travelled American who was related to Churchill; Jimmy James; and one of Bushell's intelligence officers, Sydney Dowse. All four would survive the war.

At Stalag Luft III, the camp was handed over to the Gestapo: *Oberst* Friedrich von Lindeiner was relieved of his command on Monday, 26 March 1944, and court-martialled with a dozen of his staff. The court had many questions for the defendants: why were the seismographic listening devices turned off? Why was a camera loaned to the prisoners? Why did von Lindeiner's administration ignore advice on the distribution of parcels and tinned food? How could the camp staff have 'lost' the 200-metre drums of electric cables used to light the tunnel 'Harry'?

At a time when Germany was struggling to find resources, the court seemed vexed by the 'loss' of public property – the prisoners of the North Compound had stolen the following items between 15 January 1943 and 19 April 1944:

1, 699 blankets
192 bed covers
161 pillow cases
165 sheets
3, 424 towels
655 palliasses
1, 212 bolsters
34 single chairs
10 single tables
52 tables for two men
76 benches
90 double beds
246 water cans
1, 219 knives
582 forks
478 spoons
69 lamps
30 shovels

Among the leading Nazis who witnessed Hitler's demand for retribution after the mass escape, both Hermann Göring, the head of the Luftwaffe who wielded significant political power, and Wilhelm Keitel, head of the German High Command, knew there would be consequences. Many Germans despaired at the decision; the foreign minister, Joachim von Ribbentrop, demanded a cover story.

Even for the mass murderers of Nazi Germany, the execution of the RAF officers broke new ground. While Heinrich Himmler's security services tortured and murdered the people of Occupied Europe with impunity, they had, with a few exceptions, nearly always taken more care with the British.

In the first week of April, the senior officers in each of the British compounds, including Group Captain Herbert Massey, were told of the shootings. The new commandant, *Oberst* Franz Braune, read a statement, which, according to Massey, said: 'I am commanded by the German High Command to state that . . . forty-one of the escapers were shot whilst resisting re-arrest or in their endeavours to escape again after having been re-arrested.'

Asked how many of the officers had been wounded, *Oberst* Braune said none. The prisoners went into mourning, wearing black badges and holding religious services.

Whether the PoWs used their radio transmitters to alert London is not known, but the Swiss – the protecting power under the laws of the Geneva Convention – received news of the killings and worked assiduously on behalf of the British in trying to establish the facts.

In Berlin, the authorities summoned some of the men who had been involved in the killings in an attempt to shore up the stories concerning the manner in which the RAF officers died. Most of the reports submitted by the killers were remarkably similar and equally questionable.

At about the same time, General Adolf Westhoff, who was responsible for the prison camps and had opposed the killings, allowed the repatriation of Massey, the Senior British Officer in the North Compound, on medical grounds. Massey was party to all the secrets of the escape organisation. By 29 May 1944, he was giving evidence to a court of inquiry at RAF Weeton in Lancashire. So was Paddy Byrne, whose life had run along parallel lines with Bushell's since the Battle of Barking Creek in the first weeks of the war. He, too, had been repatriated on medical grounds: he had feigned madness for more than a year.

News of the killings outraged the British.

According to Geoffrey Wellum, who joined 92 Squadron just a day or so before Bushell was shot down in May 1940, the murders produced a general sense of disgust. 'Most of us in the front line realised the sort of people we were up against,' he said. 'We knew about the concentration camps, but not the intensity of what they did. We were unfamiliar with names like Dachau and Buchenwald, that sort of thing, until after the war.'

In London, a small group of men gathered at the War Office in Curzon Street House at 10.30 a.m. on Tuesday, 16 May 1944 to discuss the murders. Among those involved was Brigadier Norman Crockatt of MI9.

Crockatt told the meeting that two of the escapers, the Norwegians Jens Mueller and Per Bergsland [sometimes referred to as Rockland] had successfully reached Britain via Sweden. A third, the Dutchman, Bob van der Stock, was on his way via the Pyrenees, Spain and Gibraltar.

The meeting decided that news of the murders should be announced by a government minister in the House of Commons, and that the murdered men would all be described as 'British officers' rather than 'Air Force officers'.

An attempt was also made to drive a wedge between the German military and the security police by emphasising that those prisoners returned to the camp by the German military had received twenty-one days' solitary confinement in accordance with international law. 'MI9 suggested that it was an indication that those escapers who fell into the hands of the German Military received proper treatment, while the murders were committed by the Civilian Police or Gestapo,' recorded the minutes. 'It was thought it might be possible, by bringing out the point, to give cause to the German Military for disapproval of the Gestapo.'

Three days later, on 19 May, Anthony Eden, the foreign secretary, announced the news to the House of Commons.

The prime minister, Winston Churchill, weighed in after the issue was discussed at a Cabinet meeting on 19 June. He made three points in a memo dated 20 June as his foreign secretary prepared to make a second statement to Parliament:

1. That we should do all in our power to ascertain those who had been responsible for this deed; and to collect evidence on this point.
2. That no pains would be spared to bring to justice after the war those concerned.
3. That it would be right in the statement to emphasise the enormity of the act.

On the same day, a memorial service for the murdered officers – the death toll had risen to fifty – was held at the church of St Martin-in-the-Fields in central London.

Eden addressed Parliament for the second time on 23 June in a powerful statement that embraced Churchill's suggestions. The foreign secretary dismissed German explanations and said it was clear that none of the officers had met his death in the course of making his escape from Stalag Luft III or while resisting capture.

'His Majesty's Government must, therefore, record their solemn protest against these cold-blooded acts of butchery,' said Eden. 'They will never cease in their efforts to collect the evidence to identify all those responsible. They are firmly resolved that these foul criminals shall be tracked down to the last man wherever they may take refuge. When the war is over, they will be brought to exemplary justice.'

The British kept their word.

In August 1945, Wing Commander Wilfred Bowes was put in charge of a team from the Special Investigation Branch of the RAF. For three years, they hunted the killers and identified seventy-two of the men involved. Of these, thirty-eight were tried; twenty-one of them were executed and seventeen imprisoned.

Eleven committed suicide. Six were killed during the last year of the war, including Dr Leopold Spann, the head of the Saarbrücken Gestapo who organised the murders of Bushell and Scheidhauer. He was killed during an air raid on the Austrian city of Linz in April 1945.

A family man who had once been a miner, Emil Schulz became a police officer at the age of twenty-one and joined the Nazi party in 1938. He was caught after Frank McKenna, one of the RAF investigators, found a letter from him to his wife, Angela, at his home outside Saarbrücken. He was traced to a French prison camp and taken to London.

His lawyer told the Hamburg court that Schulz was 'breathless' after being ordered by Dr Spann to take part in the execution of the Allied officers. Spann is said to have told him: 'These are very dangerous people who already broke out by force once. The shooting has been ordered by the highest authorities, it is lawful, and must be carried out.'

Schulz's wife and two daughters appealed for clemency. They wrote to the Royal Family, but their pleas were ignored.

In a last, deeply loving, letter to his family, Schulz addressed his wife and two daughters as: 'Dear Angela, dear Ingeborg, dear Helga, you dears of mine!'

Schulz told them he was already in England and regretted that he had not been able to say goodbye to them. He was a prisoner because of an official order he had carried out in the spring of 1944.

He said he had never acted against 'the laws of humanity' on his own initiative and was waiting for justice. He hoped he would be treated fairly and judged only according to his subordinate position.

Schulz told his wife, 'dear Angela', to have courage and to live for their two girls. He said the photographs of Ingeborg and Helga were his 'faithful companion'.

As he contemplated his fate, Schulz added that he would rather be killed or executed many times over than put his family through so much pain and suffering.

These seem to be the words of an essentially decent man, a deeply caring husband and father – as the court was told at his trial – who had been in the wrong place at the wrong time.

He ended his letter: 'Ever your faithful husband, your Daddy and your Emil.'

For the prisoners of Stalag Luft III and the other camps, the world changed rapidly in the weeks after Schulz shot Bushell by the side of the A6 outside Kaiserslautern.

By the autumn of 1944, three months after the Allied invasion of northern France on 6 June, MI9 made it clear that Allied prisoners no longer had a duty to escape: the outcome of the war was not in doubt.

The thousands of prisoners remaining at Stalag Luft III left the camp in January 1945 and marched west in appalling weather on the orders of Hermann Göring, who was determined to prevent the Allied airmen from falling into Russian hands and being used to fly against Germany again. Some men died in the freezing conditions.

After nearly six years of conflict, Nazi Germany collapsed in the spring of 1945, and surrendered unconditionally a few days after Adolf Hitler committed suicide in Berlin on 30 April. Heinrich Müller, head of the Gestapo, is also believed to have taken his own life as the Soviet armies advanced into the ruins of the German capital.

27

Casualties of War

Beyond the confines of Stalag Luft III, the casualty lists included the names of many of Roger Bushell's peers, including several pilots from among 'the Millionaires' of 601 Squadron who had flown with him at the start of hostilities.

Willy Rhodes-Moorhouse, who was in the south of France with Bushell during the last days of August 1939, was killed at the height of the Battle of Britain when he was shot down by Messerschmitt Bf 109s over Tunbridge Wells. He was buried next to his father, a fighter ace from the First World War, at Parnham House in Dorset.

Michael Peacock, Bushell's friend from Wellington College who shared a flat with him in Tite Street, Chelsea, was buried in the Arras Communal Cemetery in northern France, not far from where he was shot down. His grave can be found in Plot Y, Row One.

A few survived.

Max Aitken, who was at Pembroke College, Cambridge with Bushell, took command of 601 in June 1940. He destroyed eight German aircraft that year and was awarded the Distinguished Service Order and the Distinguished Flying Cross. He finished the war as a group captain. Elected as Conservative MP for the London constituency of Holborn in 1945, he lost his seat in 1950 and eventually took over as chairman of Beaverbrook Newspapers, which included the *Daily Express*. He died in 1985, aged seventy-five.

Paddy Green, one of the two pilots Bushell took with him from 601 Squadron when he was given command of No. 92 Squadron, recovered from the wounds he suffered on the afternoon of 23

May 1940, during the unit's first day of combat. Like Aitken, he was awarded the DSO and DFC and finished the war as a group captain, with fourteen kills to his name. After the war, he returned to his home in South Africa and worked for the Anglo-American Mining Corporation. He died in 1999, aged eighty-five.

At the Bushell family home in Hermanus, Ben and Dorothe struggled to cope with the consequences of the war.

The first the family knew of Roger's death was through a news bulletin on South African radio. His last letters from Germany did not arrive until later.

In a tragic coincidence, Dorothe's cousin, Orde Wingate, commander of the Chindits, was killed in an air crash in India on 24 March 1944, the same day that Roger broke out of Stalag Luft III.

Dorothe worked with convalescing Allied servicemen, some of whom stayed at Broadmerston, and she tried to nurture the garden as she had done in Springs years earlier, but it was not a success. She painted, she wrote plays and short stories, particularly ghost stories, and read, but she never got over the death of her son. 'Essentially, she lived upstairs in her own world,' said the filmmaker Lindy Wilson, one of her grand-daughters.

A few weeks after Roger was shot, Dorothe wrote a poem, which she dedicated to her son and the 'forty-nine gallant comrades' who died with him.

> With bare, earth-stained hands and their brave hearts,
> They faced, unarmed, the bestial Nazi rage.
> Their young bodies fell, riddled with steel,
> To rest together in a common grave . . .
> And we left here who so well knew and loved them,
> Must rise above the cruel loss and pain.
> With courage we must follow in their footsteps,
> So that in freedom we may meet again.

Ben Bushell, who at times had had a strained relationship with his son, coped with his grief by putting together a chronological record of his life, which became the archive that was presented to the Imperial War Museum in 2011. He also responded to the many people who wrote to him about events in Stalag Luft III.

He lived a disciplined, organised, almost Victorian life, with a gong in the hallway announcing meals at 8 a.m., 1 p.m. and 7 p.m. He would listen to the BBC World Service on an enormous radio in his study, which always crackled with static. He cultivated a fruit and vegetable garden of about an acre, growing potatoes and carrots, beans, peas, cabbages and tomatoes, as well as boysenberries, strawberries and grapes. He delivered jars of homemade jam to his friends. He played golf and fished off the rocks.

Dorothe died in December 1964, at the age of eighty-two. Ben died three years later, shortly before his 89th birthday.

Their elder daughter, Rosemary, who was once known as Tods, had three daughters, Jane, Lindy and Caroline. She spent the last ten years of her life living at Broadmerston, but found it difficult to talk about her brother. Her sister, Lis, who was ten years younger, married a British naval officer, Commander Francis Carter. They had two children: a daughter, Ardyn, and a son, who was named Roger after his uncle.

Jaroslav Zafouk and Vlasta Christova married after the war. Zafouk smuggled his pregnant wife out of Czechoslovakia in 1948. When they arrived in Britain, the former Czech airman met Georgiana Curzon and asked Ben Bushell for help in finding a job. Although Bushell wrote at least one letter in an attempt to help him, the couple finally emigrated to Canada. Zafouk found work as a building contractor, but his marriage did not last: the Zafouks divorced in the 1970s – Vlasta felt he had never adjusted to civilian life. Jaroslav died in 1991 aged seventy-four. Vlasta lived until 2008, shortly after visiting Prague.

Petr Ginz, the fourteen-year-old boy whose diary documented the plight of the Jewish community in the Czech capital while

Bushell was in Prague, died two years later in the gas chambers at Auschwitz.

And what of the three young women who played such key roles in Bushell's war?

Blažena Zeithammelová lies in a mass grave with her brother and father in the Dablicky cemetery in northern Prague. A stone obelisk marks the place, set among trees.

Lady Marguerite Petre, the former Peggy Hamilton, flourished. Her son, John, who was born in August 1942, went to Eton, Oxford and the Sorbonne. She moved in elevated social circles and was a guest at the Queen's Coronation in 1953. She was given 'a very private, unannounced funeral' after her death in 2003. She is buried alongside her husband in the graveyard of St Mary's, Buttsbury in Essex.

The Bushell family never met Peggy Hamilton. Lis Carter felt that Peggy had behaved badly towards her brother – 'She did the dirty on him' – running off with someone else as soon as Bushell was shot down, but this was not unusual in wartime.

Whatever the truth about Bushell's relationship with Peggy, questions also remain about his relationship with Lady Georgiana Mary Curzon.

Although he did not name Bushell, Wings Day suggested in his biography that the romance between them continued after Georgie's marriage to Home Kidston in November 1935. Day's story about the love-lorn officer who asked the commandant of Dulag Luft for a car to the Spanish border can only have been about Bushell. 'He became a dedicated escaper, but his dedicated love did not survive the war,' wrote Wings Day's biographer, Sydney Smith. The claim that the affair was with "a girl whose titled parents would not let her marry him" suggests the woman was Georgie, but we shall probably never know.

What we do know for certain is that Roger and Georgie were passionate about each other and she never fully recovered from his death. Indeed, for several years, she refused to accept that he was dead at all.

In a letter dated 1 September 1944, Paddy Byrne, who had been repatriated to Britain, told Bushell's parents:

> *I knew Peggy Hamilton but Roger never mentioned Georgie to me, so I was very surprised when she told me all about it. She is a wonderful girl and would have suited Roger admirably. I never thought that Peggy Hamilton would have been a success and hoped that it would not come off. Georgie is broken-hearted, poor girl, she was absolutely living for him and had collected all sorts of things for his return.*

Robert Stanford Tuck struck a more alarming note when he wrote to Dorothe Bushell on 24 October 1945.

> *I think, firstly, a word about Georgie and the meetings and letters we have exchanged,* he wrote. *I gather from your letter to me that you have more or less accepted the fact that old Roger will not appear again. However, with Georgie it does appear rather to the contrary in that she still seems convinced that Roger is alive and possibly very ill, suffering from loss of memory, somewhere in the depths of Czechoslovakia. Her main reasons for thinking this and I know, Mrs Bushell, that you will appreciate this in the strictest confidence, seem to be that she has been in touch, over quite a long period now, with I think the term is 'a Psychic Medium' who has apparently been indicating to her, or at least giving the impression, that this is the case with Roger – namely, that he is alive somewhere and probably ill, suffering from loss of memory and is being cared for somewhere in Czechoslovakia or Central Europe.*
>
> *I tried to point out to Georgie in as gentle terms as I could, that in my opinion this was not the case and Roger was killed by the Germans.*

Lady Georgiana finally signalled her acceptance of the inevitable when she placed a personal advertisement in the memorial columns of *The Times* on 30 August 1947, nearly three and a half years after Roger Bushell's death. It read:

BUSHELL, Roger J., Sqdr. Ldr. R.A.F. 92 Squadron. On this his birthday and always in proud treasured, and ever-living memory of my beloved Roger, who was murdered by the Gestapo in March 1944, after escaping from Stalag Luft III.

And if I grieve, as lonely hearts do grieve,
I am less loyal to you, who were my sun
And moon and stars. Oh, brave and valiant one,
Have you not left me this proud legacy? –
Courage to face the future without you,
And patience to endure the loneliness.
In sure and certain faith we meet again.
Where there is no more sorrow – neither tears.

The notice ended, 'Love is immortal', and was signed 'Georgie'.

Similar notices continued to appear on the same date throughout the 1940s and 1950s.

Lady Georgiana also opened correspondence with Ben Bushell. He told her:

Your love and faith in my son make me very proud of him and I want to tell you how deeply I regret that you were unable to marry when you first wished and I knew nothing of your great affection for each other.

Ben quoted from Roger's letters and assured Georgie of his son's love for her, but he urged her to move on:

I want to have you try and beware of the danger of living too much in the past but give your present its due time and

with your amazing faith leave the future to take care of
itself . . . we are all learning to love you and look forward
some day to your coming here, please God not alone.

With her eleven-year-old son, Glen, Georgie visited the Bushells in Hermanus in 1947, returning to Southampton on the SS *Capetown Castle* in January 1948.

'She was a beautiful upper-class woman, well-groomed, clothed and coiffeured by London's best and she was protected and cared for in the manner of the British aristocracy,' said Bushell's niece, Lindy Wilson. 'As as a child of about eight, I have the absolutely clear picture of her sitting elegantly on a sofa in our house, exquisitely dressed, talking to my sister Caroline, who would have been three, about the new kittens that had just been born, which Caroline had been holding up one by one for Georgie to inspect. She was dead gorgeous in our eyes, wearing huge hats and floral summer dresses . . . but she had become quite vulnerable, had suffered hugely over her divorce and, I would think, far more over the death of Roger, whom she so firmly believed would come back.'

Lady Georgiana remarried in 1957, but there was to be no happy ending for her: she was committed to a mental institution, The Retreat in York, in the 1970s and died there aged sixty-six in January 1976. According to her death certificate, she suffered from bronchopneumonia.

She is buried in the graveyard at Holy Trinity Church in the village of Penn Street in Buckinghamshire. Her gravestone carries two lines of poetry by Tennyson:

OH FOR THE TOUCH OF A VANISHED HAND,
AND THE SOUND OF A VOICE THAT IS STILL.

28

Aftermath

Roger Bushell's gravestone stands in the old garrison cemetery in Poznan in Poland, but his ashes remain in the pine forest south of what is now Żagań. His urn, which was returned to the camp along with those of the other forty-nine men murdered by the Gestapo, was broken, probably during the Russian advance into eastern Germany. Unlike most of the other escapers, his belongings were never returned to Stalag Luft III.

All the graves of the murdered escapers can be found in the Commonwealth section of the Poznan cemetery, which is reminiscent of an English meadow, brimming with flowers and surrounded by trees, amid the steel, granite and concrete of Russian memorials.

Bushell was recommended for posthumous decorations after the war, but this amounted only to a Mention in Despatches. Even years after the Great Escape, the British government seemed remarkably reluctant to acknowledge what he had achieved, and it has become fashionable to question both Bushell's motives and the nature of his leadership. But his own letters and the many testimonies of fellow prisoners of war make clear his determination to wage war against Nazi Germany behind enemy lines – whatever the cost to himself.

After the war, Wings Day told Bushell's parents: 'I have the highest admiration for Roger and was flattered to be held as a friend by him although I am considerably older and senior.'

Wings Day's comments are what might be expected from a senior officer to the parents of a fallen soldier, but they accord with tributes paid to Bushell by his peers and contemporaries.

G. D. 'Khaki' Roberts KC, who nurtured Bushell's legal career, told Dorothe Bushell in a letter of 23 May 1944:

The Loss of such a son to you and your husband must be an overwhelming tragedy and in sending you my deepest and most sincere sympathy I fully realise how empty those expressions must seem, but with your great and heart-rending grief there must be some admixture of Pride – pride in the manner of his life, in which he so brilliantly succeeded in everything he set himself to do – and pride in the manner of his death, dying bravely and fearlessly for his Country.

'Khaki' Roberts was no idle bystander. He joined the British legal team that prosecuted the surviving Nazi leaders at Nuremberg; Wilhelm Keitel and Hermann Göring, who were both at the Berghof when Hitler demanded retribution for the Great Escape, and Ernst Kaltenbrunner, the SS chief who issued the orders for the murder of the fifty airmen, were sentenced to death.

There were critical voices, too. Hugh Falkus, a prisoner in the East Compound, condemned Bushell and the escape: 'It happened so patently near the end of the war it was a mockery, a stupid venture ... Bushell was vain, conceited, assertive and very over-confident.'

But Bushell's sacrifice is recognised in many places: on the Wellesley House memorial board at Wellington College; on the bronze panels in the chapel cloister off the first court at Pembroke College, Cambridge; at the Żagań Museum and on the site of the North Compound, Stalag Luft III; on the seafront at Hermanus on the Cape coast; and in the Swiss resort of St Moritz, where a black ski run was named after him.

Speaking in November 2012, Ken Rees, one of the last survivors of the Great Escape, said: 'Bushell was an outstanding character ... and we were very keen. We would do anything to disrupt the Germans. We were capable, well trained and well prepared. We felt almost invincible.'

The career notes of Bushell, who was still only thirty-three when he died, tell the story of a remarkable man: a Cambridge graduate, barrister, international skier, fighter pilot and intelligence asset who spoke nine languages and was embraced equally by men and women. During the war, his influence on events – both directly and indirectly – was extraordinary. The fact that his peers remember him so vividly seventy years later speaks for itself.

His squadron, No. 92, first engaged the Luftwaffe in May 1940 during the Battle of France but, imbued with Bushell's fighting spirit, became the most deadly unit in RAF Fighter Command, claiming more than 300 enemy aircraft.

For eight months he lived with members of the resistance in Prague as they struggled to survive in the face of a murderous Nazi administration, while agents dispatched by the British manoeuvred to assassinate Reinhard Heydrich, the SS commander running Bohemia and Moravia and author of the Holocaust.

As a prisoner of the Germans, Bushell helped to direct an intelligence operation that provided Britain with evidence of Hitler's secret weapons, as well as other military targets and information on Germany, in clear breach of the Geneva Convention.

The mass breakout from the North Compound succeeded in all its aims. Three airmen got back to Britain, which ranks it among the most successful British escapes of the war simply in terms of getting men home. It exacted a toll on German resources at a critical juncture of the war when the Nazis feared the consequences of elite Allied servicemen linking up with opponents of the regime. And it enraged Hitler. In terms of sheer impact, it was unsurpassed.

Group Captain Herbert Massey told Bushell's parents in a letter dated 13 February 1945:

> *His name will ever live in my memory as one of the greatest men of his generation that I have known. He was a great officer, an outstanding leader of men, quite fearless and he had a very fine brain, and for what it is worth to you I say those few brief words as the Senior British Officer of Stalag Luft III.*

As I left the remains of the North Compound on that Saturday afternoon in late September 2012, walking through the pine forest towards Żagań station, just as the escapers had done nearly seventy years before me, I recalled the prophetic words of one of Bushell's letters written from Dulag Luft in 1940 – 'that all my energies bottled up for the time being are meant to be used later on' – and the magnitude of the achievements as the men of the North Compound, Stalag Luft III, defied Hitler's tyranny.

A maverick who challenged authority all his life, Bushell broke the rules once too often. But whatever his ultimate motivation and whatever his fears for himself, Roger Bushell – Big X – gave the men under his command two great gifts: one was hope, the other was a sense of their own destiny. No man could have given more.

Afterword to the Skyhorse Edition

When the war ended in the spring of 1945, only one organisation knew the full extent of Roger Bushell's contribution toward the Allied victory, and that was the intelligence agency MI9.

In the years after I wrote this book, it has become clear that MI9 and its successors tried to ensure that Bushell received proper recognition. These efforts culminated in April 1949 when the agency, renamed AI9, lobbied for him to be awarded the George Cross, Britain's second highest award for gallantry.

In their history of MI9, published in 1979, MRD Foot and JM Langley make several references to Bushell and acknowledge the importance of the intelligence operation that he established at Dulag Luft in 1940. In the opinion of Foot and Langley, the role of the PoWs was second only to the Enigma decrypts at Bletchley Park as a source of information on what was going on in Germany – and Bushell was one of the most significant players.

Like so many aspects of Bushell's life, even honouring him posthumously was neither straightforward then nor easily followed today. I unearthed the reports and citations for Bushell's Mentions in Despatches in September 2018, five years after this book was first published, but some of the papers were ambiguous and other correspondence appeared to be incomplete. Housed at the National Archive, the documents can still be read only under supervision because the content continues to be considered sensitive.

It must be remembered that the only awards open to those killed in battle during the Second World War were the highest, the Victoria Cross and the George Cross, and the lowest, a Mention in Despatches.

On June 8, 1944, just ten weeks after the Great Escape, thirty-seven of the men murdered by the Gestapo, including Bushell, were listed in the *London Gazette* as having been Mentioned in Despatches. The naming of so many of the murdered men so soon after the escape at a time when the Nazis were still trying to cover up the crime must have sent a powerful message to the SS and Gestapo.

The documents dealing with the award can be found among the contents of a file listed as AIR/9652 at the National Archives, but it was not the end of the matter. Driven by MI9, the authorities awarded Bushell a second Mention in Despatches on June 13, 1946, this time with a detailed citation, which can be found among documents in a file called AIR2/9295. The citation highlights the leading role played by "Big X" at Stalag Luft III and elsewhere.

It reads:

Captured in June 1940, S/Ldr. BUSHELL was imprisoned in various camps in Germany. Throughout his incarceration he devoted all his energies in attempts to escape.

At DULAG LUFT he successfully eluded the attention of the guards and made his way to the Swiss frontier where he was apprehended within a few miles of the frontier. He broke away from the captors, however, but was once again re-arrested before he could cross the border.

While being transferred from LUBECK to OFLAG VIB, he and a Czech companion escaped through the floor of a cattle truck. They made their way to PRAGUE where they remained for several months until they were recaptured. After some weeks in a Gestapo prison S/Ldr. Bushell alone was returned to STALAG LUFT III.

In October 1942, he became officer i/c of all escaping activities at this camp. Although by this time the German anti-escape measures had reached a very high state of efficiency and a large number of compound police were employed, it was solely due to

S/Ldr. Bushell's organising abilities and drive that three shafts were dug, each twenty feet deep, from the bottom of which tunnels were started.

After several months' work the compound police discovered one of these tunnels but a second tunnel was completed over three hundred feet long from which 79 officers escaped on the 25th March 1944. Three successfully reached England but 50 of the others including S/Ldr. Bushell were executed by German Police Authorities.

The escapers from this tunnel were equipped to a far higher standard than ever before, with civilian clothes, with money and false identification papers. This was due to the untiring efforts and forethought of S/Ldr BUSHELL. He was gifted with a brilliant brain, great imagination, organising ability and a powerful personality which he used unsparingly in all things he undertook. Not only was he interested in escape activities but he also took part in all forms of P/W activities and utilised his outstanding gifts for the benefit of his fellow prisoners.

S/Ldr. Bushell has been highly commended for his work in connection with all escape and organising activities by the Senior British Officer and 26 of his colleagues.

One paragraph in the citation is circled in pencil and marked "Omit." It reads: "Also on numerous occasions between January and December 1941 he passed valuable information to the War Office by secret means." Another report in the same file is more general: "He also passed valuable information to the War Office by secret means on numerous occasions."

By 1949 there was a twist – and AI9 was raising the stakes dramatically. Evidence for this can be found among the contents of the file AIR2/12273, which includes papers on a number of high profile awards. Squadron Leader LA Randle, writing on behalf of AI9, stated that the department held new information on Bushell. It is dated April 25, 1949. The submission reveals: "It is considered that information held at this office justifies the reopening [of this case] ... with a view to putting forward recommendations for the award of the George Cross."

The new citation in this file includes the paragraph omitted in 1946, stating that "between January and December 1941, he passed valuable information to the War Office ..." This was a year when he was constantly on the move, starting at Dulag Luft near Frankfurt, then Stalag Luft I at Barth on the Baltic, before being transferred to a prison at Lubeck. He later escaped with Jaroslav Zafouk, reaching Prague and establishing contact with the Czech resistance, which would soon be involved in the assassination of the SS leader Reinhard Heydrich.

The response to AI9's submission in 1949, written by Miss AM Knott, an official at the Air Ministry, is dismissive. "I would like to make it clear that no useful purpose would be served by raising these cases again unless some very new material facts have come to light since the award of Mentions in Despatches to Squadron Leader Bushell on the 6th June 1944 and 13th June 1946 ... You will be aware that the only awards which may be granted posthumously (other than Mention in Despatches) are the VC and the GC and that these decorations are only awarded for very exceptional services."

No one can doubt that Bushell gave "very exceptional services" to his country. Guidance for the award of a George Cross includes "a 90 percent or more possibility of being killed in the performance of the act." Given the fact that the Gestapo had made it clear to Bushell in 1942 that he would be shot if he ever fell into their hands again – allied to the poor chances of any of the prisoners reaching a neutral country after breaking out of Stalag Luft III – it can be argued that Bushell met this criterion too.

The file contains no further correspondence on Bushell. He was not awarded the George Cross. And the secrets of Stalag Luft III would not be made public for decades to come.

More than seventy years after the Great Escape, on July 1, 2017, Bushell finally achieved the kind of international recognition that might have come with the award of a George Cross, or even the use of his real name in the Hollywood film.

At Ramstein in Western Gemany, close to the place where he and his travelling companion, the Frenchman Bernard Scheidhauer, were shot, the NATO allies unveiled a memorial to the two men. The ceremony was attended by representatives of their families and the air forces of many countries, including the United States, Britain, France, and Germany. Amid the flags and uniforms, it was an emotional moment for many of those there as the two men – one aged thirty-three, the other just twenty-three – were remembered at the place where they fell.

As for Bushell himself, he would probably have chuckled briefly at the decision by the German air force to choose as their representative that day an officer from the security branch of the Luftwaffe. He might well have said, as he did on several occasions in his letters from Nazi-Occupied Europe, "Heigh ho!"

—Simon Pearson, January 2021

My darlings – the mail continues to be appalling and this month's crop has only produced one letter from Father 30/11/43 & one from Elspa in her inimitable type-writing & dated Nov 11th. Whenever I get one of Elspa's letters a wave of sympathy for that unfortunate type-writer sweeps over me. What a pounding it must get! the Herculean force which has superimposed an e over a recalcitrant l or z that has got into the wrong place must shake its wretched bones like dice in a box. As for those slashing vertical dashes which constitute the polite fiction of erasure, they are a (~~—~~) daggers wounds that send the word to "heaven or to hell" far more effectively than did even Macbeth's Duncan. And then there are the complicated mental gymnastics (which have a charm all of their own) required

to decypher both the punctuation & the syntax. I start by taking a mental cold plunge into the middle of it, come up gasping, jump out & then wade in with deep breathing exercises from the beginning. Brushing aside obscurities in the text, I dash through, get the general sense (sic) of the thing & then start over again. Next instalment next month! Bless you all. I am very well and full of confidence as usual! Roger

This was the last letter he wrote. The tunnel was opened & the escape made on 24.3.44.

The last letter written by Roger Bushell to his parents, nearly four years after being shot down over northern France. It is dated 28 February, 1944, and was sent from Stalag Luft III just over three weeks before the mass escape from the North Compound.

Acknowledgments

A book such as this cannot be written without the generous participation of many people. I have been particularly fortunate with my companions.

With the support and encouragement of two families – the Pearsons and the Gormans – I set out on this adventure, my first book, much as Laurie Lee 'walked out one midsummer morning': rather naïve, unsure exactly where I was going and uncertain about the strangers I would meet.

My chief travelling companion on this journey was, in many ways, Roger Bushell himself. Just as in life, he continued to charm and entertain people and, in so doing, he opened doors for me. If only in spirit, he still has the knack, as Arnold Lunn once said, of making a party go.

My gratitude, however, must start at the beginning.

I would like to thank my parents: Janet, for instilling in me a love of history, and Geoff, for stimulating my interest in the Second World War – not to mention the love and support they have given me throughout my life; and my brother Guy, who shot down my Airfix kits and composed the beautiful music to which I wrote the book, and my sister Sally.

I also want to thank my wife Fiona's family – the Gormans – but particularly her brother, Edward, and his wife, Jeanna, for their generosity and interest; and Fiona's sister, the author Kate Charlton-Jones, and her husband, John, for their unstinting encouragement, constant ribbing and good humour. If nothing else, they made sure I was never able to take myself too seriously; and Jane and Peter for their support over the years.

I would not have got very far with this book without the

intervention of Roger Bushell's niece, the South African film-maker, Lindy Wilson, who responded to my first letter and encouraged the project from the outset. Treasuring the memory of Roger, she demanded rigour, but otherwise gave me free rein with the Bushell Archive, other notes and family photographs, as well as unseen footage and interviews undertaken during the making of her film, *For Which I am Prepared to Die*, a documentary about the life of her uncle. The flow of emails was almost constant.

With her husband, the brilliant and mischievous Francis, she introduced me to the town of Hermanus and engaged me in many animated discussions about Roger's life, as well as introducing me to other members of the family – David and Lynette Dicey, and Arddy Mossop – before passing me into the hands of her sister and brother-in-law, Caroline and Martin Kennard, in Johannesburg. The Kennards provided me with more notes and photographs, shepherded me around the great South African city and took me to what had been the Bushell home in the former mining town of Springs, forty miles east of Johannesburg.

On all sides of the family, I could not have asked for more generous hosts – generous with their hospitality and with themselves – during a most memorable week in South Africa, during which I got to know Roger Bushell a little better.

The book would not have appeared without the help of many people at *The Times*, where resources were made available to me and where I found a constant source of support, interest and encouragement.

The main champion was my friend Ben Macintyre, who put up with two years of muddled questioning after he had told me to get on with the book, as described in the Prologue. But there was always a smile, a joke or a knowing look, which, simply put, said: 'You silly bugger!'

The project gained momentum after the appearance of my articles in *The Times* on 26 November 2011. These described the Bushell family's decision to donate Roger's archive to the Imperial War Museum and outlined the story of his life. The articles would not have appeared without the support of Nicola Jeal, the Saturday editor, who pushed for the space and commissioned a powerful leading article from Hugo Rifkind.

I would like to thank my editors, James Harding, who was a most generous and enthusiastic supporter from the start, and John Witherow, who kindly allowed me to finish my sabbatical and complete the book when he took over as editor.

I am particularly indebted to Keith Blackmore, the deputy editor, and Anoushka Healy, the managing editor, for their friendship and unbending support from beginning to end, and to James Macmanus.

Many other friends and colleagues on *The Times* and *Sunday Times* played their part over the years. I would like to thank Roger Alton, Nicolas Andrews, Steve Bird, Roger Boyes, Grace Bradberry, David Brown, Sue Connolly, Cheryl Dickinson, Andrew Ellson, Dee Ennifer, Jack Enright, Martin Fletcher, Robert Hands, Clare Hogan, David Jack, Alan Kay, Dominic Kennedy, Patrick Kidd, Sam Lister, Valentine Low, Jack Malvern, Jo Morris, Graham Paterson, Pat Prentice, Tom Pride, Paul Sanders, Pia Sarma, Mark Shillam, David Taylor, Dave Wilson, Ian Whitbread and Kathleen Wyatt.

After the appearance of my articles in *The Times*, the Imperial War Museum weighed in. Tony Richards, head of Archive and Video, who had put me in touch with the Bushell family, nurtured the project from the start, guiding me through archives and periods of history with a keen eye and great kindness. Nothing was ever too much trouble for him. I would also like to thank his colleagues Simon Offord, Nina Smetek, Bryony Phillips, Debbie Dowden, Rob Bailey and Stephen Walton.

With a little help from his mother, Geraldine Taylor, who had read my articles, Peter Taylor, publishing manager at the IWM, decided that the story was possibly worth a book and put the proposal to me in December 2011. After a meeting with Barbara Levy, the museum's literary agent, the show was almost on the road – but Barbara probably had no inkling of the rollercoaster ride on which she was about to embark. I would like to thank her with all my heart for always believing in me, and, most of all, for the advice that helped to make me a better writer.

I would also like to thank her husband, John Selby.

Rupert Lancaster, Non-Fiction Publisher Hodder, has been a constant companion for much of the past year. His impact on the book has been decisive in terms of its structure and content. He has humoured me when I needed humouring, he has comforted me when I needed comforting, and he has found time when I needed more of it. I am extraordinarily grateful to a great editor who also happens to be a thoroughly decent human being.

Kate Miles, the assistant editor, has been a constant voice of calm and encouragement; Belinda Jones, the copy-editor, made many important changes; Meryl Evans, Hodder's legal adviser, guided me through the newly laid minefield of copyright; and Kate O'Hearn secured permission for the use of quotes from the many books, magazines and newspapers needed to tell Roger Bushell's story during a remarkable week of investigation. Rodney Paull produced a fine map of Bushell's journeys, while Ben Summers created an inspirational design for the cover.

I would also like to thank my picture editors, Scott Montgomery of *The Times*, and Juliet Brightmore from Hodder & Stoughton/ Hachette UK, for a great collection.

In South Africa, 'Mr Prince' allowed me to visit the former Bushell home in Springs, the rotting carcass of a once great house; while 'Mr Rhino' – the wonderfully enthusiastic Ronald Ryno van der Rite – showed me around the former Park Town Prep School, which has been completely restored. Dr and Mrs MacDonald allowed me to visit Broadmerston in Hermanus, which is also in pretty good shape. Ursula Mostert of the Anglo American Corporation provided me with the histories of the mines managed by Ben Bushell and the minutes of shareholders' meeting.

I am especially grateful to the Nobel Laureate, Nadine Gordimer, for sharing her memories – and her whisky – during two memorable hours at her home in Johannesburg.

The hospitality was just as generous at Wellington College, where Chris Potter, a former teacher, embraced the project and gave me access to the Bushell files. Potter is a great enthusiast who loves Wellington and wanted only to know more about Bushell. I am also grateful to the Master, Anthony Seldon, and Patrick Mileham, Ben Lewsley, Alan Loveless, Simon Pettigrew and David Wilkinson.

Daniel Scott-Davies of the Scout Association provided details of qualifications for a First Class Scout.

At Pembroke College, Cambridge, Angela Anderson and Jayne Ringrose provided material from the college and university archives.

Pat Gorman, my wife's step-mother, gave me contacts for the Lincoln's Inn Archive, as well as much encouragement and support over the writing of the book. Jo Hutchings and Guy Holborn kindly provided me with material from the archive, and Jo also read the chapters relating to Bushell's legal career. I am very grateful to her.

Many people from the Royal Air Force contributed to this book. Among them are Air Vice-Marshal Larry Lamb and his wife, Maureen, who often spend their winters in Hermanus; Sebastian Cox, head of the RAF Historical Branch at RAF Northolt; Group Captain Patrick Tootal of the Battle of Britain Memorial Trust; Wing Commander Mark Quinn; Air Commodore Graham Pitchfork; Air Commodore Charles Clarke, president of the Ex-Prisoner of War Association; Simon Morris, fighter pilot, 92 Squadron; and David Coxon, curator of the Tangmere Military Aviation Museum.

I am most grateful to Geoffrey Wellum for sharing his memories of Roger Bushell during lunch at the Mullion Cove Hotel in Cornwall, and to his daughter, Deborah Scarfe, for arranging the interview.

The staff of Ingatestone Library, Essex, and Robert W. Fletcher, a local historian, provided me with information about the life of Peggy Hamilton, also known as Lady Marguerite Petre, and the Petre family. I am grateful to Dominic Petre for engaging me at Ingatestone Hall, and to his father, John, the 18th Baron Petre, for responding to my correspondence.

Frederick Curzon, the 7th Earl Howe, Parliamentary Under Secretary at the Department of Health, put me in touch with those in his family who had known Lady Georgiana Mary Curzon. I am extraordinarily grateful to those who tried to help.

I would like to thank the author and historian Oliver Clutton-Brock and his wife, Diane – my first PoW contacts on the road to *The Great Escaper* – for their hospitality over the past two years and for sharing their research and contacts.

This book could not have been written without reference to the works of many other authors – people like Tom Moulson, Paul Brickhill, Robert Gerwarth and Aidan Crawley – and I would like to put on record my great debt to them all.

I would like to thank Charles Rollings, the PoW historian, for a highly entertaining lunch in Bognor Regis and for agreeing to read my manuscript, attempting to right my wrongs and generally giving me the benefit of his considerable knowledge. The author, Tim Carroll, generously shared his contacts.

Two of the men of the Great Escape – Ken Rees, who lives in Anglesey, and Alan Bryett, who lives in Bromley, Kent – both remembered Roger Bushell quite clearly and gave me the benefit of their memories.

I would like to thank June Bowerman, the daughter of Harry 'Wings' Day; Colin Kirby-Green, the son of Tom Kirby-Green; Teresa Wickham, the daughter of Vincent 'Paddy' Byrne; Michael Stanford-Tuck, the son of Robert Stanford Tuck; Georgina Thynne, the daughter of Brian Thynne; and my former colleague, John Blandy, the son of Graham and Mildred Blandy, who shared his memories of life on Madeira.

John North-Lewis and his wife, Alison, very generously entertained me at their home in Hexham, Northumberland, where I learned about John's grandfather – Harry North-Lewis – who was Roger Bushell's guardian. They also introduced me to Nicholas Craig, the son of George Dudley Craig, head of Intelligence in the East Compound; his wife, Dordie Craig and his

sister, Ann Pearson; and Raymond Allison, a nephew of Mike
Casey, one of the Great Escapers shot by the Gestapo.

I am greatly indebted to Luisa Dressler; Martina Voigt and
Charles Dick for their help with research in Germany; Edward
Charlton-Jones for help with research in the United States; and
to Ben Blackmore for his exhaustive work at the Royal Air Force
Museum, Hendon, and the National Archive at Kew. To them
all, I offer grateful thanks.

Marek Lazarz, director of the PoWs' Camps Museum in Żagań,
Poland, gave me a tour of his museum and made his files available
for research. The staff of the Hotel Kolegiaki in Poznan made
sure I got to the Hotel Willa Park in Żagań, where the staff helped
me to find my way to Prague!

My foray into the Czech Republic started with David Steinke,
Second Secretary at the Embassy in London, who gave me more
support than I had any right to expect. He involved Ivo Pejčoch, a
historian and author at the Military History Institute in Prague,
and introduced me to Jan Kaplan, the Czech author and film-
maker who has since become a great friend. These strangers
opened the doors to Bushell's life in Prague and gave my research
momentum I had not expected.

In Prague, the British Ambassador, Sian MacLeod, arranged
meetings with her defence attaché, Colonel Andy Shepherd, and
his assistant, Dr Radek Tomáš, which opened the door to several
Czech archives and contacts.

Many Czechs embraced this story. I would like to thank Vlasta
Měštánková, who works at the National Archive in Prague. Jan
'Honza' Červenka was the law student who earned his fees by
driving taxis and gave me a lift to the archive, but then returned to
translate the documents found by Vlasta Měštánková.

I would like to thank David and Gilly Wadmore for the use of
their flat in Prague and for their advice and encouragement; Jiřiná
Doležalová and her husband, David, and their daughter,
Leontynka, for guiding me around the Czech capital – I shall

never forget the visit to Kobylisy and the search for Blažena Zeithammelová's grave – as well as the distinguished historian, Jaroslav Čvančara, who granted me an interview; the beautifully spoken Neela Winkelmannová and her colleague, Jura Kalina, at the Institute for the Study of Totalitarian Regimes; and Emil Kulfánek, the dignified guardian of the former Gestapo cells below the Petschek Palace.

The historian, Mark Seaman, a member of the Cabinet Office, and the intelligence expert, Richard Belfield, gave me enormous help. I am grateful for their correspondence. I am also grateful to the military historian Michael Tillotson and the researcher Paul Baillie for locating the citations to Bushell's Mentions in Despatches and AI9's attempt to have him awarded the George Cross.

Crucial support came from unexpected quarters.

John Carr is an American lawyer who fought in Iraq. As a boy, rather like me, he was inspired by Brickhill's book and the Hollywood film, and embarked on a quest to find Bushell. He became friends with the Bushell family and wrote a book. He was a rival who helped me. I will never forget his great generosity.

As a family, we could not have coped without the support of Ann Ainscow, otherwise known as Raggie; our neighbours in West Norwood, south London; our friends from Rosemead and Trinity schools, Beckenham Swimming Club, Beacon Water Polo at Crystal Palace and Old Alleynians Rugby Club. They all helped while I went AWOL with the book, and never has an excuse – 'He's still writing' – worn so thin.

Without the support of my oldest friends, Andrew Semple, Nigel and Sarah Street, John Trewick, R. V. 'Bob' Williams, Phil Fairchild, Barry Parker and Jon Marsh, over many years, this book would never have been written.

My greatest thanks go to my greatest friend, my wife, Fi, who has helped me with research and editing, held the fort as I travelled, and continued to encourage our very own Escape Committee – Harold, Fred and Archie. To them all, my grateful thanks for a wonderful adventure.

Text Acknowledgments

Extract from Winston Churchill is reproduced with permission of Curtis Brown, London on behalf of the Estate of Sir Winston Churchill. Copyright © Winston S. Churchill.

Extracts from *The Flying Sword – The story of the 601 Squadron* by Tom Moulson, published by McDonald & Co, © 1964. Reissued and updated as *The Millionaire's Squadron – The Remarkable Story of 601 and the Flying Sword,* published by Pen and Sword Books, © 2014. Used by kind permission of Tom Moulson.

Extracts from the '*Minutes of the Seventh annual general meeting of Springs [gold mine] shareholders*', Johannesburg, May 26 1924 were found at the Anglo American Corporation.

Extract from the play, *The Great Escape* by Felix Felton, produced by the BBC.

Extracts from *The Great Escape* by Paul Brickill, published by Cassell Military © 2000. Used by permission of David Higham Associates.

Speech by Neville Chamberlin is used under the Open Parliament Licence.

Extract from *Escape from Germany – A history of RAF escapes during the war* by Aidan Crawley © 1958 first published by Fontana. Used by permission of the Estate of Aidan Crawley.

Extract from *Stalag Luft III: The Secret Story* by Arthur A. Durand © 1988. Reproduced by permission of Phyllis Durand.

Address to Parliament by Anthony Eden, June 23, 1944. Reproduced under the Open Parliament Licence.

Article 'Lady Petre (Peggy Hamilton) Gives Birth to a Son' from the *Essex Chronicle* © 7 August 1942. Used by permission of the *Essex Chronicle*.

Extract from *Prisoners of War: A Study in the Development of International Law* by William E. S. Flory © 1948.

Extracts from *MI9 – Escape and Evasion 1939–1945* by M. R. D. Foot and J.M. Langley. Used by permission of Biteback Publishing (1979).

Extracts from *Fly for your Life – The Story of R.R. Stanford Tuck DSO, DFC and Two Bar,* by Larry Forrester, published by Random House. Reproduced by permission of Random House.

Extracts from *Hitler's Hangman* by Robert Gerwarth, published by Yale University Press © 2011. Reproduced with permission of Yale University Press.

Extract from *The Barbed-Wire University: The Real Lives of Prisoners of War in the Second World War* by Midge Gillies, published by Aurum Press Ltd, 2011. Reproduced with Permission of Aurum Press Ltd.

Extracts from *Moonless Night* by B.A. 'Jimmy' James, published by Pen and Sword Military © 2001. Used by kind permission of Pen and Sword Books Ltd.

Extracts from *Field Marshal Wilhelm Keitel – In the Service of the Reich* translated by David Irving. Reproduced with permission of David Irving.

Source: Arnold Lunn, The British Ski Year Book (Vol X – 1944); published on behalf of The Ski Club of Great Britain (founded 1903) and the Alpine Ski Club (founded 1908).

Article: 'Kissing Cafe Court Case' from the *Daily Mail* © 10 May 1938. Used by permission of Associated Newspapers Ltd.

Article: 'Barrister to watch, Diary' from the *Empire News* © December 12th, 1937. Used by permission of NI Syndication.

Extract from *Flak and Ferrets – One Way to Colditz* by Walter Morison, published by London Sentinel © 1995. Used by kind permission of the Estate of Walter Morison.

Extract from *Chapter Seven – The God Conclusion* by Wing Commander Reginald Piff. Published by Trafford Publishing © 2008.

Extracts from *The Diary of Petr Ginz,* by Chava Pressburger and translated into English by Elena Lappin © 2004. Used by permission of Atlantic Books.

Extracts from *Lie in the Dark and Listen* by Ken Rees © Ken Rees 2004. Used by permission of Grub Street Publishing.

Extracts from *Prisoner of War: Voices from Captivity During the Second World War* by Charles Rollings, published by Ebury Press. Reprinted by permission of The Random House Group Limited.

Extracts from *Wire and Worse* by Charles Rollings © Charles Rollings 2004. Used by permission of Ian Allan Publishing.

Extracts from *After the Battle* magazine Number 106, (1999) by Dulag Luft are used by kind permission of After the Battle Magazine.

Extracts from '*Wings Day*' by (Eric) Sydney Smith © 1968, were first published by HarperCollins and then Pan Macmillan.

Extract from Stonyhurst College Magazine, 1940–1941. Reproduced by permission of David Knight, Stonyhurst College archivist (on behalf of the school governors).

Extracts from *The Second World War – An Illustrated History* by A J P Taylor, published by Penguin Books © 1976. Used by permission of David Higham Associates.

Article: 'In Memoriam – Roger Bushell' from *The Times*, August 30 1949. Used by permission of the Times and NI Syndication.

Article: 'Wedding announcement – Petre' from *The Times*, August 14 1941. Used by permission of the Times and NI Syndication.

Article on BBC interview with Paul Brickhill was taken from *The Times*, September 16, 1945. Used by permission of the Press Association.

Article: '601 Squadron Rivalry with 600 Squadron' © 15 August 1936 from the *Daily Sketch* is used by permission of Associated Newspapers Ltd.

Extracts from *The Daily Telegraph – Book of A* written and compiled by Edward Bishop © 2002. Used by permission of Grub Street Publishing.

Extracts from 'Facsimile edition of the flying log book of Wing Commander Robert Stanford Tuck' from *After the Battle* magazine are used by kind permission of After the Battle Magazine.

Roger Bushell did not use paragraph breaks in any of the letters he wrote while he was in captivity. I have introduced paragraph breaks simply for ease of reading. I have taken care not to interfere with the meaning of his letters, but anyone involved in the research of coded letters should bear this in mind. For the same reason, I have occasionally added paragraph breaks in the content of some official reports. I hope that this helps the reader.

Picture Acknowledgments

Facsimile published by *After The Battle* Magazine: 8 above. akg-images/Ullstein Bild: 11 below. Courtesy of the Imperial War Museum/ Bushell Collection: 1, 2 below left and right, 3, 6 below, 9, 11 above, 12 above left and right and below, 13 below, 14 above, text p 367. Courtesy of Simon Morris and Roger McGowan: 5 below right. The National Archives/AIR 40/1909: text p 132-133. News International Archive: 4 below right. Simon Pearson: 10 below, 14 below, 15, text p 131. Courtesy of Ivo Pejčoch/Military History Institute, Prague: 10 above. Private collection: 16. Courtesy of Charles Rollings: 13 above. By kind permission of the Trustees of the Royal Air Force Museum: 5 above, 6 above, 7 below. Courtesy of Andy Saunders: 8 below. Courtesy of Georgina Thynne: 5 below left, 7 above. Courtesy of Wellington College Archives: 2 above. Courtesy of Lindy Wilson: 4 below left and above right, 12 below right (inset).

Every reasonable effort has been made to trace the copyright holders, but if there are any errors or omissions, Hodder & Stoughton will be pleased to insert the appropriate acknowledgement in any subsequent printings or editions.

Bibliography

Addison, Paul and Crang, Jeremy A., *The Burning Blue: A New History of the Battle of Britain*, Pimlico (2000)

Arthur, Max, *Last of the Few: The Battle of Britain in the Words of the Pilots Who Won It*, Virgin Books (2011)

Ash, William, *Under the Wire*, Bantam Books (2006)

Ashcroft, Michael, *Heroes of the Skies: Amazing True Stories of Courage in the Skies*, Headline (2012)

Attwater, Aubrey, *Pembroke College, Cambridge: A Short History*, Cambridge University Press (1936)

Beevor, Antony, *The Second World War*, Weidenfeld & Nicolson (2012)

Biccard, Jeppe C., *Gold Mining on the Witwatersrand*, Volume One, Transvaal Chamber of Mines (1946)

Binet, Laurent, *HHhH*, Harvill Secker (2012)

Bishop, Edward, *The Daily Telegraph Book of Airmen's Obituaries*, Bounty Books (2007)

Bishop, Patrick, *Bomber Boys: Fighting Back 1940–1945*, Harper Press (2007)

Bishop, Patrick, *Fighter Boys: Saving Britain 1940*, HarperCollins (2003)

Brickhill, Paul, *Escape or Die: Authentic Stories of the RAF Escaping Society*, Guild Publishing and Book Club Associates (1985)

Brickhill, Paul, *The Dam Busters*, Pan Books (1954)

Brickhill, Paul, *The Great Escape*, Cassell (2000)

Brickhill, Paul, *Reach for the Sky: The Story of Douglas Bader, Hero of the Battle of Britain*, Fontana/Collins (1981)

Brown, Malcolm, *Spitfire Summer: When Britain Stood Alone*, Carlton Books (2000)

Burian, Michal; Knížek, Aleš; Rajlich, Jiří; Stehlík, Eduard, *Assassination: Operation Anthropoid, 1941–1942*, Ministry of Defence of the Czech Republic (2002)

Burleigh, Michael, *Moral Combat: A History of World War II*, Harper Press (2011)

Carroll, Tim, *The Dodger: The Extraordinary Story of Churchill's Cousin and the Great Escape*, Mainstream Publishing (2012)

Carroll, Tim, *The Great Escape from Stalag Luft III: The Full Story of how 76 Allied Officers Carried Out World War II's Most Remarkable Mass Escape*, Pocket Books (2005)

Clutton-Brock, Oliver, *Footprints in the Sands of Time: RAF Bomber Command Prisoners of War in Germany 1939–45*, Grub Street (2003)

Clutton-Brock, Oliver, *RAF Evaders: The Comprehensive Story of Escapers and their Escape Lines, Western Europe, 1940–1945*, Grub Street (2009)

Cornwell, Peter D., *The Battle of France Then and Now*, Battle of Britain International Ltd (2007)

Crawley, Aidan, *Escape from Germany*, Fontana Books (1958)

Durand, Arthur A., *Stalag Luft III*, Louisiana State University Press (1988)

Earl of Lytton, *Antony (Viscount Knebworth): A Record Of Youth*, Peter Davies (1935)

Foot, M. R. D., *SOE The Special Operations Executive 1940–1946*, Pimlico (1999)

Forrester, Larry, *Fly for Your Life: The Story of R. R. Stanford Tuck*, Frederick Muller Ltd (1973)

Foulkes, Nicholas, *The Bentley Era – The Fast and Furious Story of the Fabulous Bentley Boys*, Quadrille (2008)

Franks, Norman L. R., *Air Battle for Dunkirk, 26 May–3 June, 1940*, Grub Street (2006)

Gilbert, Adrian, *POW: Allied Prisoners in Europe 1939–45*, John Murray (2007)

Gilbert, Martin, *Finest Hour: Winston S. Churchill 1939–1941*, Heinemann (1983)

Gill, Anton, *The Great Escape: The Full Dramatic Story with Contributions from Survivors and Their Families*, Headline Book Publishing (2002)

Gillies, Midge, *The Barbed-Wire University: The Real Lives of Allied Prisoners of War in the Second World War*, Aurum Press (2011)

Gordimer, Nadine, *The Lying Days*, Victor Gollancz (1953)

Gorlitz, Walter, *In the Service of the Reich*, Stein and Day (1995)

Graham, Burton, *Escape from the Swastika*, Marshall Cavendish Publications Ltd (1975)

Green, J. M., *From Colditz in Code*, The Glenvil Group (1989)

Hague, William, *William Pitt The Younger*, Harper Press (2005)

Handley, J. R. F., *Historic Overview of the Witwatersrand Goldfields*, J. R. F. Handley (2004)

James, B. A., *'Jimmy' Moonless Night: The Second World War Escape Epic*, Pen & Sword Books (2008)

Jeffery, Keith, *MI6: The History of the Secret Intelligence Service*, Bloomsbury (2011)

Johnson, Eric, *The Nazi Terror – Gestapo, Jews and Ordinary Germans*, John Murray (2000)

Kaplan, Jan, *A Traveller's Companion to Prague*, Robinson (2005)

Kee, Robert, *A Crowd is not a Company*, Phoenix Paperback (2000)

Keitel, Wilhelm, *In the Service of the Third Reich*, Stein and Day (1979)

Kidd, Janet Aitken, *The Beaverbrook Girl*, Collins (1987)

Lambert, Angela, *Unquiet Souls: The Indian Summer of the British Aristocracy*, Macmillian (1985)

Leage, R. W., *Roman Private Law*, Second edition, Ziegler, C. H. Macmillan and Co (1946)

Letcher, Owen, *The Gold Mines of Southern Africa*, published by the author (1936)

Lunn, Arnold, *The British Ski Year Book*, Sir Isaac Pitman & Sons Ltd (1944)

Macdonald, Callum and Kaplan, Jan, *Prague in the Shadow of the Swastika: A History of the German Occupation 1939–1945*, Quartet Books Ltd (1995)

Macdonald, Callum, *The Assassination of Reinhard Heydrich*, Birlinn Ltd (2011)

Morison, Walter, *Flak and Ferrets: One Way to Colditz*, Sentinel Publishing (1995)

Moulson, Tom, *The Flying Sword: The Story of 601 Squadron*, Macdonald & Co (1964)

Neave, Airey, *MI9: The Classic Account of the WWII Allied Escape Organisation*, Pen & Sword Books (2010)

Onderwater, Hans, *Gentlemen in Blue: 600 Squadron*, Pen & Sword Books (1997)

Piff, Reginald, *Chapter Seven: The God Conclusion, The Memoirs of Wg Cdr R. Piff* Trafford Publishing (2008)

Pressburger, Chava, (ed.) *The Diary of Petr Ginz*, Atlantic Books (2007)

Price, Alfred, *Luftwaffe: Birth, Life and Death of an Air Force*, Macdonald & Co (1970)

Ramsden, John, *The Oxford Companion to Twentieth-Century British Politics*, Oxford University Press (2002)

Ray, John, *The Battle of Britain: Dowding and the First Victory, 1940*, Cassell (1994)

Rees, Ken, *Lie in the Dark and Listen: The Remarkable Exploits of WWII Bomber Pilot and Great Escaper*, Grub Street (2004)

Rees, Laurence, *The Dark Charisma of Adolf Hitler: Leading Millions into the Abyss*, Ebury Press (2012)

Roberts, G. D., *Without my Wig*, Macmillan & Co (1957)

Robinson, Michael, *Best of the Few: 92 Squadron 1939–40*, Michael Robinson (2001)

Rollings, Charles, *Prisoner of War: Voices from Behind the Wire in the Second World War*, Ebury Press (2008)

Rollings, Charles, *Wire and Walls: RAF Prisoners of War in Itzehoe, Spangenberg and Thorn 1939–42*, Ian Allan Publishing (2003)

Sander, Ivor, *The Legend Lives On: The Country Club Johannesburg 1906–2006*, GDP Africa (2006)

Saunders, Andy, *Spitfire, Mark I P9374*, Grub Street (2012)

Sims, Edward H., *The Fighter Pilots*, Cassell (1967)

Smith, Sydney, *'Wings' Day*, Pan Books Ltd (1970)

Taylor, A. J. P., *The Origins of the Second World War*, Penguin (1963)

Thrower, Derek, *The Lonely Path to Freedom*, Robert Hale (1980)

Tuck, R. R. S., Pilot's Flying Log (*After the Battle* magazine)

Vance, Jonathan F., *A Gallant Company: The Men of the Great Escape Pacifica*, Military History (2000)

Wallace, Graham, *RAF Biggin Hill*, Universal-Tandem Publishing (1969)

Walters, Guy, *The Real Great Escape*, Bantam Press (2013)

Wellington College Register, January 1859–June 2006, *The Old Wellingtonian Society* (2007)

Wellum, Geoffrey, *First Light*, Penguin Books (2003)

Whittell, Giles, *Spitfire Women of World War II*, Harper Perennial (2008)

Wilkinson, Major David Anthony Clement, *A Lucky Life! Memoirs of David Wilkinson*, Adams of Rye Ltd (2011)

Notes on Sources

Prologue
Page:

1 'remains of a wooden hut': The POW Camps Museum at Żagań has marked the site of Hut 120 as the building where Roger Bushell lived in the North Compound. The historian, Charles Rollings, says this is wrong. Bushell lived in Hut 110, which is adjacent to Hut 120.

2 'the Hollywood epic': *The Great Escape*, directed by John Sturges, was released by United Artists, in 1963

2 'Brickhill's most popular books': *The Great Escape* (Faber & Faber, 1951), *The Dambusters* (Evans Bros Ltd, 1951) and *Reach for the Sky* (Fontana Books, 1957)

3 'It was signed "Georgie"': *The Times*, In Memoriam (Bushell, Roger Joyce) 30 August 1949

3 'gave her film the title': *For Which I Am Prepared To Die: A documentary film by Lindy Wilson* (2009). The story of the man who masterminded the Great Escape. Lindy Wilson was Roger Bushell's niece. Lindywilsonproductions.co.za

3–4 'a major decision . . . where he belonged': From articles by the author, *The Times*, 26 November 2011

4 'A leader of men': Letters between Ben Bushell and the Imperial War Graves Commission in July and August 1953. The Bushell Archive, hard-covered album entitled 'Newspaper Cuttings', p.37, Imperial War Museum (IWM)

5 'invited to have lunch': Mike Casey's nephew, Raymond Allison, and George Dudley Craig's son, Nicholas Craig, in Hexham on Thursday, 25 October 2012

5 'visited my brother-in-law': Edward Gorman and his wife, Jeanna, on Thursday, 6 September 2012. Her father was Douglas Ian Farquharson (1907–1994)

5 Wellington College in Crowthorne, Berkshire

5 Czech National Archive: Archivni 4/2257, Praha 4 – Chodovec, 149 01
5 'One of the members of staff': Vlasta Měšťánková
6 'He was a law student': Jan 'Honza' Červenka
6 'the Bushell family': Francis and Lindy Wilson, Martin and Caroline Kennard

The Great Escape

7 'a black and white photograph': Recollection of Sydney Dowse, one of the Great Escapers, in conversation with John Carr, lawyer, author and friend of the Bushell family
8 'so good to look at': Dorothe Bushell's journal, the Bushell Archive, IWM
9 'the aircraft manufacturer Focke-Wulf': Smith, *'Wings' Day*, p.169
9 'wore genuine civilian clothes': The description of Bushell on the night of the Great Escape is from Harry 'Wings' Day's letter to Dorothe Bushell dated 15 July 1945. Bushell Archive, Sketch Book Three, pp.47–52, IWM
9 'a significant intelligence asset': The phrase 'asset' rather than 'intelligence agent' or 'intelligence officer', which both signify official positions, is used after discussion with Air Commodore Graham Pitchfork, a former director of military intelligence at the Ministry of Defence, who felt this best described Bushell's role at Stalag Luft III where his work included 'the collection of information and the collation of the various individual elements to produce specific intelligence and assessments'.

Report 'X', compiled after the war by members of the escape organisations at Stalag Luft III, states that, in contrast with all other RAF camps, Bushell was both X (head of the escape organisation in the North Compound) and head of intelligence. The National Archive (TNA): AIR 40/285, p.7

The Camp History of Stalag Luft III (Sagan), the North Compound, states that 'Bushell was the expert on all information concerning GERMANY'. TNA AIR 40/2645, Part III, p.23

The 'Z' Report on the development and conduct of a military intelligence system inside Germany outlines the scope of intelligence work undertaken by RAF prisoners of war. TNA: WO 208/3245

The historical record of MI9 (Military Intelligence 9), IS9, RAF Intelligence Course B, Awards Bureau and Screening adds further information, particularly on the use of codes. TNA: WO 208/3242
10 'He would be shot': Smith, *'Wings' Day*, p.119

12 'make life hell for the Hun': *For Which I Am Prepared To Die* (Lindy Wilson, 2009)

12 'Hitler was at the Berghof': Field Marshal Wilhelm Keitel, *In the Service of the Reich,* William Kimber and Co (1965) p.260

A Taste of Freedom

13 'a deeply claustrophobic boy': Filmed interview with Elizabeth Carter, Bushell's sister, on 23 September 2004 (Lindy Wilson). Elizabeth was known as Lis, but her brother used a 'z' and also sometimes referred to her as Eliza.

13 'quick to pay tribute': West Springs Limited (incorporated in the Transvaal). Minutes of the Ordinary General Meeting, 26 May 1924, held in the Board Room, 2nd Floor, 'The Corner House', Johannesburg

14 'After hours of raging storm': Dorothe Bushell's journal, p.1; the Bushell Archive, IWM

14 'Roger's mother': Notes from Lindy Wilson.

14 'Roger's father': Notes from Caroline Kennard, Bushell's niece, including *The Rambler in Worcestershire* by John Noake, and *The Pedigree of the Family of the Bushells* by Sir Rob Atkyns

15 'a delicate baby': Dorothe Bushell's journal, p.1

15 'Nadine Gordimer': Interviewed by the author at her home in Johannesburg on Tuesday, 6 November 2012

16 'By now Roger could run': Dorothe Bushell's journal, p.2

17 'The child took': Ibid, p.5

18 'During the next few years': Ibid, p.6

18 'Roger learnt to fish': Ibid

19 'Nadine Gordimer': Interview with the author

19 'opposite side of the street': Nadine Gordimer, *The Lying Days,* Victor Gollancz (1953)

20 'He asked me to stop the car': Dorothe Bushell's journal, p.7

21 'The headmaster of PTS': Ibid, p.8

22 'The Rand Revolt': www.sahistory.org.za

23 'The exit shaft in the dining room': The building that once housed Park Town School has been taken over by the South African company, Cargo Carriers Ltd, which has restored the building to its original condition. The address is 11a Grace Road, Mountainview, Observatory 2198, Johannesburg. The school closed in the late 1950s.

England Beckons

25 'Not to know even one': Dorothe Bushell's journal, p.9

25 'Don't worry about him': Karl Stocken, housemaster of Wellesley House, Wellington College, in a letter to Dorothe Bushell, 1924

26 'an open prison for boys': Patrick Mileham, Wellington College historian and archivist. Interview with the author at Wellington College on Monday, 22 October 2012

26 'We had anxious moments': Dorothe Bushell's journal, p.10

27 'I was often criticised': Ibid, p.11

27 'David Wilkinson': Interviewed by the author at his home in Rye on Monday, 29 October 2012. He was 100 years old.

28 'Wellesley House journal': many of Bushell's activities are described in detail in reports written by his contemporaries in the house journal, which forms part of the Wellington College Archive.

28 'He has an excellent physique': Wellesley House journal, 1926

28 'a most resourceful game': Ibid

28 'As a cricketer': Ibid

29 'an unreliable catch': Ibid

29 'Shaw tried to rush Bushell': *Wellington Year Book,* 1928

30 'my darling boy': Dorothe Bushell's journal, p.11

30 'Often he was thoughtless': Ibid

31 'He liked popular tunes': Ibid

31 'A wonderful morning': From an article entitled 'The Kandahar' in *The Tower,* the Wellington College magazine, 1928

33 'indomitable spirit': Wellesley House journal, 1929

Pembroke and Piste

34 'at Grenoble University': Bushell Archive, Sketch Book One, pp.2–4

34 'I think he loved being in the house again': Dorothe Bushell journal, p.12

35 'career as a mining engineer': Pembroke College Cambridge Application for Admission dated 16 November 1926. Pembroke College Archive

36 'is believed to have occupied M7': From correspondence with Angela Anderson, Pembroke College

36 'Charles Hugo Ziegler': Pembroke Archive; *Roman Private Law, Founded on the Institutes of Gaius and Justinian* by R. W. League M.A. B.C.L., and C. H. Ziegler, LL.M., Lecturer in Law at Pembroke College, Cambridge Macmillan (1946)

37 'There are some people': Article by Hugh Saunders in the *College Gazette,* 1985

37 'In the centre of the table': Ibid

38 'There was silence': Ibid

38 'Max Aitken': From a conversation with Lindy Wilson

39 'his joie de vivre – and touch of joie de vice': Dorothe Bushell journal, p.26

39 'Roger had written to me': Ibid, p.13

39 'a pretty creature': Ibid

40 'you are full of surprises': Ibid

40 'We spent five days': Ibid

41 'When I reached England': Ibid, p.14

41 'I felt rather shy': Ibid

42 'Arnold Lunn': *The British Ski Year Book* (Vol XI, No 25, 1944), p.329; Killed in Action, p.335

42 'British ski championship': *The Times*, 22 January 1931

42 'His greatest triumph': Cuttings from various newspapers, including the *Quebec Star, The Times* and *Golf and Sports Illustrated*, but many unidentified and undated, in Sketch Book One, pp.5–33, Bushell Archive (IWM)

43 'Roger was only fifteen': Arnold Lunn, *The British Ski Year Book* (Vol X, 1944) p.329

44 'This business of your divorce': Letters from Bushell to the family dogs, Kerstie and Rubbish, while a student at Pembroke. Undated. Bushell Archive

45 'While watching a game': Ibid

45 'having a big show': Ibid

45 'The Law had always intrigued me': Dorothe Bushell's journal, p.14

46 'Both Roger and Rosemary': Ibid

46 'We were all in accord': Ibid, p.15

47 'suffering from delayed shock': Ibid, p.16

48 'difficult adolescent years': Ibid, p.17

49 'a very rare personality': Ibid, p.18

High Society

50 'Tony Knebworth invited': Dorothe Bushell's journal, p.18

50 'The squadron was founded': Tom Moulson, *The Flying Sword: The Story of 601 Squadron*, Macdonald (1964) p.15

50 'A jealously guarded elite': Louise Wilkinson's thesis on the Auxiliary Air Force (University of Teesside, The School of Historical Studies Postgraduate Forum E-Journal Edition 6, 2007/08) p.1

50 'crack cavalry regiments': Ibid, p.2

50 'Asked about recruitment': Ibid, p.7

51 'third-class honours in law': Bushell's record card, Cambridge University Archive

51 'The viscount represented': Dorothe Bushell's journal, p.18

51 'Educated at Eton': *Antony (Viscount Knebworth): A Record of Youth*, by his father, the Earl of Lytton (Peter Davies, 1935)

51 'No restrictions except': Dorothe Bushell's journal, p.18; *Antony*, the Earl of Lytton

51 'an aristocratic elite': Angela Lambert, *Unquiet Souls: The Indian Summer of the British Aristocracy* (1984) p.142

52 'eschewed the discipline': Moulson, *The Flying Sword*, p.39

52 'admitted to Lincoln's Inn . . . third-class passes': From correspondence with Jo Hutchings, archivist, and Guy Holborn, librarian, at Lincoln's Inn, 2012

52 'tragedy struck': *The Advocate*, North-west Tasmania, 3 May 1933. Trove.nla.gov.au/ndp/del/article68016573

53 'Knebworth was twenty-nine': According to a book written by his father, the Earl of Lytton, Tony Knebworth visited the family home with Bushell the night before he died. 'He came unexpectedly to Knebworth in his Moth with Roger Bushell, a brother officer.' The Earl of Lytton said it was a perfect spring day. The two men played tennis, had tea and talked to Lady Lytton while she was gardening. They flew back to London that evening. Earl of Lytton *Antony* p.358

53 'According to press reports': *The Advocate*

53 'She kept in touch': Tribute to Lord Knebworth by Arthur Bryant dated June 1933. Bushell Archive, Sketch Book One, p.37; Earl of Lytton *Antony*, p.568

53 'awarded his pilot's wings': Michael Robinson, *Best of the Few*, Michael Robinson (2001)

53 'an ambitious SS officer': Robert Gerwarth, *Hitler's Hangman*, Yale (2011) p.76

53 'recovering from flu': Dorothe Bushell's journal, p.20

54 'knew there had been trouble': Ibid

54 'the temptation': Ibid

54 'it was wrong of him': Ibid

54 'At Southampton': Ibid

55 'First of all': Ibid, p.22

55 'There was a woman': Ibid, p.23

56 'more his old self': Ibid

56 'One night, we talked': Ibid

57 'a public face': Pond's History. 'The popularity of Pond's cream is boosted by a glamorous advertising campaign featuring testimonies from the gorgeous women of the 1920s. Nobility such as Lady Georgiana Curzon . . .' www.pondsinstitute.co.uk/history.php

57 'a motor-racing fanatic': Earl Howe profiled by Dick Caesar, June 1948. 500 Owner's Association, www.500race.org/MEN/Howe.htm

57 'letters written later': Airmail letter card from Ben Bushell to Lady Georgiana Curzon, written probably in 1946 but undated. Shown to the author by Caroline Kennard, Roger Bushell's niece.

57 'Pages of a photograph album': In *For Which I Am Prepared To Die* (Lindy Wilson, 2009)

58 'he joined the Clive family': Christenings, *The Times*, 11 July 1935, p.17

58 'Hitler': www.britishpathe.com/video/hindenburgs-last-resting-place

58 'wedding of Earl Howe's only son': Wedding presents, *The Times*, 23 July 1935; Marriages, Lord Curzon and Miss Weigall, *The Times*, 24 July 1935

58 'sun-tanned and smart': Mary Evans Picture Library, ref. 10587593

58 'penniless South African barrister': Filmed interview with Elizabeth Carter, Bushell's sister, 23 September 2004 (Lindy Wilson)

58 'the forthcoming marriage': Lieutenant H. Kidston, RN and Lady Georgiana Curzon, *The Times*, 28 October 1935, p.17

59 'They were married': 'A Country Wedding', *The Times*, 28 November 1935, p.18. A film of the wedding, 'Lieutenant Kidston marries Lady Georgiana Curzon', can be seen at www.itnsource.com/shotlist/BHC-RTV/1935/. . ./BGU407200943

59 'Glen Kidston': Nicholas Foulkes, *The Bentley Era: The Fast and Furious Bentley Boys*, Quadrille Publishing (2008); Wikipedia, the free encyclopaedia, http.//en.wikipedia.org/wiki/Glen_Kidston

59 'writing some years later': Records of the Supreme Court of Judicature and related courts, Court for Divorce and Matrimonial Causes, later Supreme Court of Judicature; Divorce and Matrimonial Causes Files, Kidston G. M. & R. A., letter from Home Kidston to Georgiana Kidston from HMS *Highlander*, 30 November 1941. TNA J77/3967

59 'In his ceremonial uniform': wedding photograph in the *Daily Sketch*, 28 November 1935

Chelsea Boys

61 'The red-brick flat': *For Which I Am Prepared To Die* (Lindy Wilson, 2009)

61 'Peacock had arrived': Correspondence with Jo Hutchings, Lincoln's Inn

61 'With two bedrooms': *For Which I Am Prepared To Die* (Lindy Wilson, 2009)

61 'Looking pretty chipper': Ibid

62 'the only romantic drama': conversations with the Bushell family in Hermanus, South Africa, on Sunday, 25 November 2012
    Divorce Court File: 834. Appellant: Wallis Simpson. Respondent: Ernest Aldrich Simpson. Type: Wife's petition for divorce. TNA: J77/3574/834

62 'started work as a junior barrister': Correspondence with Jo Hutchings, Lincoln's Inn

62 'Sir Henry Curtis Bennett': Curtis Bennett, Sir Henry Honywood (1879–1936), *Oxford National Dictionary,* Oxford University Press 2004–13.

62 'G. D. "Khaki" Roberts': *Without My Wig,* G. D. Roberts Q. C., Macmillan & Co Ltd (1957). 'One day in the summer of 1900, having fallen onto some gravel, I rose covered with brick-dust, which matched a swarthy complexion. "You look a Khaki-Roberts," exclaimed my fellow mudlark. The dust came off; but the nickname has stuck'. p.29

63 'interesting days': *Empire News,* 12 December 1937, Bushell Archive, Sketch Book One, pp.38–9

63 'The Kissing Café': The *Daily Mail,* 10 May 1938; Bushell Archive, Sketch Book One, pp.38–9

63 The *Daily Mail*: Ibid

64 'Congratulations': Letter from Dr J. Anthony Gorsky, 29 June 1938, in Bushell Archive, Sketch Book One

64 'welcomed into the East End': Filmed interview with Elizabeth Carter, Bushell's sister (Lindy Wilson, 2004)

64 'offered their services': Moulson, *The Flying Sword,* p.42

65 'Bushell was briefed to': Moulson, *The Flying Sword,* p. 42

65 'Mike Peacock reversed': Ibid

65 'saw law as conflict': Ibid

65 'joined at 601 Squadron': Moulson, *The Flying Sword,* pp.40–41; Janet Aitken Kidd, *The Beaverbrook Girl* (1987) p.157

66 'The Honorary Commodore': unidentified and undated newspaper

cutting – 'Clubmen formed own air squadron, The Soty of 601 (A. A. F) – in the Bushell Archive. *Sketch Book One*, pp.40–41

66 'making a party go': Lunn, *British Ski Year Book*, p.329

66 'Photographs and film': *For Which I'm Prepared To Die* (Lindy Wilson, 2009)

66 'explosively happily': Moulson, *The Flying Sword*, p.41

66 'An officer of the 600th Squadron': *Daily Sketch*, 15 August 1936

67 'the Spanish Civil War': A. J. P. Taylor, *The Origins of the Second World War*, Penguin Books (1964); en.wikipedia.org/wiki/Bombing-of-Guernica

67 'Herman Göring': Ibid; www.spicgel.de › English Site › Europe › World War II

67 'The Condor Legion': en.wikipedia.org/wiki/Condor_Legion

67 'Guernica': en.wikipedia.org/wiki/Guernica_(painting)

67 'Stanley Baldwin': John Ramsden, *The Oxford Companion To Twentieth-Century British Politics*, Oxford University Press (2002), p.36

68 'The *Anschluss*': Robert Gerwarth, *Hitler's Hangman: The Life Of Heydrich*, Yale (2011) p.118

68 'exceptional from the start': Letter from Brian Thynne, former commander of 601 Squadron, to Dorothe Bushell, dated 18 May 1944; Bushell Archive, Sketch Book Three, p.44

68 'Then came Czechoslovakia': Gerwarth, *Hitler's Hangman*, p.131

68 'Thousands of miles away': Telegram from Bushell, received in Springs on 26 September 1938. Bushell Archive, Sketch Book Two. 'War Years and Letters from PoW Camps', p.1

69 'Two days later': A. J. P. Taylor, *The Origins Of The Second World War*, Penguin Books (1961) pp.228–31; Gerwarth, pp.132–3

69 'The Hawker Demon': Moulson, p.58

69 'In the House': Neville Chamberlain, House of Commons, 3 October 1938 (Hansard)

69 'The Slovaks': Taylor, *The Origins of the Second World War*, p.249; Gerwarth, *Hitler's Hangman*, p.132

70 'Within two hours': Gerwarth, pp.133–4

70 'The invasion': Ibid

70 'Watching from the American Embassy': Gerwarth, p.134, quoting from Chad Bryant, *Prague in Black: Nazi Rule and Czech Nationalism*, Cambridge, MA (2007) p.167

71 'boarded a ship': Dorothe Bushell's journal, p.26

71 'my most vivid memory': Filmed interview with Elizabeth Carter (Lindy Wilson, 2004)

71 'My children are detached': Dorothe Bushell's journal, p.26

72 'Roger has matured early': Ibid

On the Brink

74 'Hitler's next target': Gerwarth, p.141

74 'Poland's fate': A. J. P. Taylor, *The Origins of the Second World War* p.319.

Taylor, *The Second World War: An Illustrated History*, Penguin Books (1975) p.34

74 'Bushell was appalled': Letter from Bushell to his parents, 25 August 1939, shown to the author by Caroline Kennard, Bushell's niece, in November 2012

75 'We had a great party': Ibid

75 'Willie Rhodes-Moorhouse': Moulson, p.50

   Battle of Britain London Monument – F/Lt. W. H. Rhodes-Moorhouse www.bbm.org.uk/Rhodes-Moorhouse.htm

75 'helped in all matters': Bushell letter, 25 August 1939

75 'She was the sister': Moulson, p.61

76 'we set out': Letter from Bushell, 25 August 1939

76 'Bushell wired ahead': Ibid

77 'By the time': Ibid

77 'Bushell's parents . . . photographs of Roger': Conversations with Francis and Lindy Wilson during a visit by the author to Broadmerston on 27 November 2012

78 'Outside, Dorothe cultivated': Ibid; Beatrix Potter, *The Tale of Peter Rabbit*, F. Warne & Co (1902)

78 'Just back by flying-boat': Telegram from Bushell, received in Hermanus on 26 August 1939. Bushell Archive, Sketch Book Two, p.2

78 'Germany invaded Poland': Taylor, *The Second World War: An Illustrated History,* p.35

78 'Heydrich's SS action squads': Gerwarth, *Hitler's Hangman,* p.141

79 'posted to Biggin Hill': Moulson, *The Flying Sword*, pp.59–60

79 'Winston Churchill visited': Graham Wallace, *RAF Biggin Hill*, Universal-Tandem Publishing (1969), p.89

79 'Address to the Nation': The transcript of Neville Chamberlain's 'Declaration of War', 3 September 1939, BBC Archive

79 'The world has gone mad': Letter from Bushell to his mother, 5

September 1939 (Caroline Kennard)

79 'ready for action': Wallace, *RAF Biggin Hill,* p.90

79 'splendid lunches': Moulson, *The Flying Sword,* p.61

80 'director of Shell': Moulson, p.60

80 'The squadron is grand': Letter from Bushell to his father, 5 September 1939 (Caroline Kennard)

80 'My darling': Letter from Bushell to his mother, 5 September 1939

81 'night duty squadron': Ibid

81 'started to write': Letter from Bushell to his parents, 11 September 1939 (Caroline Kennard)

82 'The Russian business': Ibid

82 'first combat of the war': Patrick Bishop, *Fighter Boys,* HarperCollins (2003), pp.106–9

83 'Battle of Barking Creek': Ibid

83 'new identification system': Interview with Sebastian Cox, head of the Air Historical Branch of the Royal Air Force, and a director of the RAF Centre for Air Power Studies, at RAF Northolt on 12 December 2012

83 'There is very little news': Letter from Bushell to his mother, 3 October 1939 (Caroline Kennard)

84 'All the boys are well': Ibid

84 'verge of being promoted': Letter from Bushell to his parents, 11 October 1939 (Caroline Kennard)

84 'F/Lt Bushell was posted': Operations Record Book, No. 92 Squadron. The National Archive (TNA): AIR 27/743

85 'Best of all possible wars': Ibid

Flying High

86 'daring raid': Moulson, *The Flying Sword,* pp.64–6

86 'There was a cool silence': Ibid

87 'Five German seaplanes: *Morning Bulletin,* Rockhampton, Australia, 2 December 1939. trove.nla.gov.au/ndp/del/article/56055018

87 'many obstacles in the way': Operations Record Book, No. 92 Squadron. TNA: AIR 27/743

87 'No. 92 Fighter Squadron': Ibid

87 'squadron had last seen action': B1569 Historical Notes on No.92 Squadron [cg], Royal Air Force Museum, Hendon, H/332/4103/00002 (System ID 79709)

87 'thoroughly modern aerodrome': Correspondence with David Coxon, curator, Tangmere Military Aviation Museum, Tangmere,

Nr. Chichester, PO20 2ES

88 'Five days later': Ibid

88 'his beautiful wife': Rachel Verney (née Wrey), Lady Willoughby de Broke
www.npg.org.uk › Collections

89 'In his combined capacity': Operations Record Book, No. 92 Squadron. TNA: AIR 27/743

89 'Charles Patrick Green': Battle of Britain London Monument – F/Lt. C P GREEN www.bbm.org.uk/Greencp.htm

89 'Indeed the commanding officer': TNA: AIR 27/73

91 'Nov 8: S/Ldr Bushell': Ibid

93 'Christmas Day': Ibid

94 'F/Lt Byrne took': Ibid

94 'first experience of the Spitfire': Simon Morris, jet-age fighter pilot, 92 Squadron, *A Cobra In The Sky* (unpublished), with a foreword by Robert Stanford Tuck, drawing on material from Larry Forrester, *Fly For Your Life: The Story of R. R. Stanford Tuck, D.S.O., D.F.C. and Two Bars*, Frederick Muller (1956), with the permission of Tuck. www.sirius1935.wix.com/92squadron

97 'a familiar figure': In her biography, Max Aitken's sister, Janet, says that Peggy Hamilton, one of the 'Dorchester cabaret girls', had an affair with her husband, Drogo Montagu, which sealed the end of her marriage. Janet Aitken Kidd *The Beaverbook Girl* p.147–48, 156–57, 162.

97 'Bushell and Hamilton': Wing Commander Reginald Piff, *Chapter Seven, The God Conclusion*, Trafford Publishing (2008), p.74

97 'likely to have met members of MI9': The historical record of MI9, IS9, RAF Intelligence Course B, Awards Bureau and Screening adds further information, particularly on the use of codes. TNA: WO 208/3242

98 'MI9 was borne out of': M. R. D. Foot and J. M. Langley, *MI9: Escape and Evasion 1939–1945*, The Bodley Head (1979), p.21

98 'On 23 December 1939': The historical record of MI9, TNA: WO 208/3242. p.15

99 'Crockatt's natural grace': Foot and Langley, MI9, p.25

99 'assessing MI9's role': Foot and Langley, MI9, p.26; TNA: WO 208/3242, p.2

99 'Crockatt's principal aims': Foot and Langley, MI9, p.48

100 'a fighting man remained a fighting man': Ibid, p.14

101 'registration took place': Charles Rollings, *Wire and Worse: RAF*

Prisoners of War in Laufen, Biberach, Lübeck and Warburg 1940–42, Ian Allan Publishing (2004) pp.24–30; Camp History of Dulag Luft (oberursel) December 1939–June 1941. TNA: AIR 40/1909 (Chapter V, Code-Letter Mail, p.26)

First Combat

102 'Bushell gave them dual instruction': Operations Record Book, No. 92 Squadron. TNA: AIR 27/743

102 'Clear to the Nazi leadership': A. J. P. Taylor, *The Second World War: An Illustrated History,* pp.45–8

102 'Hitler knew of the plans': Christos military and intelligence corner: B-Dienst vs Bletchley Park . . .

chris-intel-corner.blogspot.com/. . ./b-dienst-vs-bletchley-park-invasion-o . . .

102 'a "real war" in the West': Taylor, *The Second World War,* p.48

103 'blood, toil, tears and sweat': Churchill, House of Commons, 13 May 1940 (Hansard)

103 'Six Spitfires': No. 92 Squadron. TNA: AIR 27/743

103 'At about noon': Ibid

103 'Robert Stanford Tuck': Posted to No. 92 Squadron, 1 May 1940, Pilot's Flying Log, R.R.S.T. (Facsimile Edition, *After the Battle* magazine)

104 'we'll be getting a crack': Larry Forrester, *Fly For Your Life,* pp.81–4

105 'Am very fit': Telegram from Bushell to his parents, 15 May 1940 (Caroline Kennard)

105 'At 1400 hours': No. 92 Squadron. TNA: AIR 27/743

105 'Escorting Prime Minister': Pilot's Flying Log, R.R.S.T., 16 May 1940

105 'Broken through at Sedan': Taylor, *The Second World War,* p.53

105–6 'The French Prime Minister . . . bases in Kent': Martin Gilbert, Winston S. Churchill, Vol. VI 1939–41 Heinemann (1983), pp.349–54

106 'Escorting Prime Minister back': Pilot's Flying Log, R.R.S.T., 17 May 1940

106 'Two days later': No. 92 Squadron. TNA: AIR 27/743

106 'One of the casualties . . . first day in command': death of Squadron Leader M. F. Peacock, 20 May 1940; Peter D. Cornwell, *The Battle of France Then And Now, Six Nations Locked in Aerial Combat September 1939 To June 1940 (After The Battle,* 2007)

106 'Poor Mike': Letter from Bushell to G. D. Roberts, 8 June 1940, Bushell Archive, Sketch Book Two, PoW letters, pp.11–47

106 'tribute to Peacock': Roberts, *The Times*, undated, Bushell Archive, Sketch Book Two

106 'Geoffrey Wellum': Interview with the author at the Mullion Cove Hotel, Mullion, Cornwall, 21 July 2012

108 'kind of madness': Ibid

108 'described in several books': Larry Forrester, *Fly For Your Life*, pp.84–9; Edward H. Sims, *The Fighter Pilots*, Corgi Books (1967) pp.68–75; Norman Franks, *Air Battle For Dunkirk, 26 May–3 June, 1940*, Grub Street (2006), pp.23–4

109 'his first report': Pilot's Flying Log, R.R.S.T., 23 May 1940

109 'The whole squadron left at dawn': TNA: AIR 27/743

110 'a more measured document': M10429 Combat reports for 92 Squadron, 1940–41 [cg]; H/332/0501/00002 (System ID 209483)

111–12 'Pilot Officer Wellum . . . very much alive': Interview with the author

112 'immediate: deeply regret': Telegram from the Under Secretary of State, Air Ministry, London, to Ben Bushell in Hermanus, 24 May 1940. Bushell Archive, Sketch Book Two, p.6

112 'highest opinion of him': Letter from Group Captain S. J. Vincent, station commander, RAF Northolt, to Ben Bushell, 25 May 1940. Bushell Archive, Sketch Book Two, p.7

113 'I do hope': Letter from Brian Thynne, former commander 601 Squadron, to Ben Bushell, 28 May 1940. Bushell Archive, Sketch Book Two, p.7

113 'Information now received': Telegram from Air Ministry, London, to Ben Bushell, Hermanus, 13 June 1940. Bushell Archive, Sketch Book Two, p.8

114 'advised the Bushells': Letter from Director of Personal Services, Air Ministry, London, to Ben Bushell, 20 June 1940. Bushell Archive, Sketch Book Two, p.8

114 'our hearty congratulations': Letter from Group Captain Vincent to Ben Bushell, 15 June 1940. Bushell Archive, Sketch Book Two, p.9

114 'worked like super-men': Letter from George Irvin to Ben Bushell, 16 July 1940. Bushell Archive, Sketch Book Two, p.10

115 'a letter from Germany': Letter from Roger Bushell to his parents, 31 July 1940. Bushell Archive, Sketch Book Two. PoW Letters, pp.11–47

Prisoner of War

116 'count myself lucky': Letter from Bushell, 31 July 1940. Bushell Archive.

116 'Karl Langenberg': Peter D. Cornwell, *The Battle of France Then And Now*, p.351; Luftwaffe Officer Career Summaries, Section L–R, (Henry L. deZeng and Douglas G. Stankey, updated April 2013); Karl Langenberg, Pilot Profile: Karl Langenberg www.militaryshop.co.uk/aces.php?PilotID=3926

116: 'badly shot up': Letter from Bushell, 31 July 1940. Bushell Archive

117 'Bushell was trapped': Taylor, *The Second World War*, p.55

117 'I had great admiration': Letter from John Gillies to Ben Bushell, 14 October 1945. Bushell Archive, Sketch Book Three, p.41

117 'A long journey': Letter from Bushell to John Brinton, 8 June 1940. Bushell Archive, PoW letters, pp.11–47

117 'march through France': Letter from John Gillies, 14 October 1945

118 'I wrote to you twice': Letter from Bushell, 31 July 1940

118 'Built on the site': TNA: AIR 40/1909, Chapter 1, p.1; Charles Rollings, Dulag Luft, *After The Battle* magazine (No. 106)

119 'Major Theo Rumpel': Ibid, p.7; Smith, *'Wings' Day*, pp.37–44; Tim Carroll, *The Dodger*, Mainstream Publishing (2012), pp.134–8

119 'Top Secret': Camp History of Dulag Luft (oberursel) December 1939–June 1941. TNA: AIR 40/1909

120 'Solitary confinement': Aidan Crawley, *Escape from Germany: A History of RAF Escapes During the War*, Fontana (1958), pp.33–4

121 'the Senior British Officer': Smith, *'Wings' Day*, p.26–27

122 'when Roger first arrived': Letter from Harry 'Wings' Day to Dorothe Bushell, 15 July 1945. Bushell Archive, Sketch Book Three, pp.47–52

123 'As soon as the battle started': Letter from Bushell to Brinton, 8 June 1940, Bushell Archive

123 'I did most of the journey': Ibid

123 'I was told by some soldiers': Ibid

124 'von Massow's staff': Smith, *'Wings' Day*, p.48

124 'We are very well treated': Letter from Bushell to G. D. Roberts, 8 June 1940. Bushell Archive

125 'and other friends': Letter from Tony Page in Zurich to Ben and Dorothe Bushell in Hermanus, 6 September 1940. The letter is signed 'George H. Page', but George Page and Tony Page appear to be the same person. They have the same address and the handwriting is identical.

125 'run by the German Air Force': Letter from Bushell to his parents, 31 July 1940. Bushell Archive

126 'Peggy Hamilton': Letter from Bushell to his family, 30 September 1940

127 'sudden change of mood': Ibid

127 'wrote to Uncle Harry': Letter from Bushell to Harry North-Lewis, undated but probably written in September 1940. Bushell Archive

128 'the organising genius': Letter from Peter Cazenove to Ben Bushell, 6 June 1945

128 'Jimmy Buckley': Smith, *'Wings' Day,* p.56

129 'Roger handed over': Letter from Day to Dorothe Bushell, 15 July 1940

129 'all military information': Camp History of Dulag Luft (oberursel) December 1939–June 1941. TNA: AIR 40/1909, Chapter II, p.10, Chapter V, p.26

129 'mainsprings of escape': Aidan Crawley, *Escape from Germany,* p.35

129 'developing MI9's coding system': TNA: AIR 40/1909, Chapter V, p.26

129 'for four days – from July 20 to July 23': Information supplied by the historian Charles Rollings

130 'code called Amy': TNA: AIR 40/1909, Chapter V, p.26

134 'certain pre-arranged signals': Foot and Langley, MI9, p.50

134 'Censorship was asked': The historical record of MI9 (Military Intelligence 9), IS9, RAF Intelligence Course B, Awards Bureau and Screening adds further information, particularly on the use of codes. TNA: WO 208/3242, p.82

135 'Crockatt added': Ibid

135 'this was valuable intelligence': Smith, *'Wings' Day,* p.48

136 'most fighter pilots': Charles Rollings, *Wire and Worse,* p.28

136 'muddled start': Although Hunkin played the crucial role in introducing an operational code to Dulag Luft, several other people, including John Gillies, John Casson, and Neil Prendergast all probably contributed as the system developed over a number of weeks, with Bushell and Day pulling the coding operation together during the summer of 1940.

137 'the snowball': MI9, WO 208/3242, p.83

137 'We had failed': Ibid

137 'relatively content': Letter from Bushell to his family, 28 October 1940. Bushell Archive

138 'The BEF stock of whisky': Ibid

Man of Letters

139 'lost 1,733 aircraft': Taylor, *The Second World War*, p.71

140 'My dear old John': Letter from Bushell to John Brinton, 29 November 1940. Bushell Archive

143 'several Irish prisoners': Rollings, Dulag Luft, *After The Battle* magazine (No. 106), p.15

143 'immaculate script': Smith, *'Wings' Day*, p.57

144 'My Darlings': Letter from Bushell to his family, 30 November 1940. Bushell Archive

In Pursuit of Peggy

148 'The first snow': Letter from Bushell to Erik Hvalsoe, 10 December 1940. Bushell Archive

148 'Day suffered blood poisoning': Smith, *'Wings' Day*, p.64

149 'surrounded by barbed wire': TNA: AIR 40/1909, Chapter 1, p.7

149 'described the digging': Letter from Day to Dorothe Bushell, 15 July 1945. Bushell Archive

150 'the first tunnel': TNA: AIR 40/1909, Chapter II, p.13

150 'Buckley suspended work': Rollings, Dulag Luft article, p.15

150 'Primitively forged *Ausweiss*': TNA: AIR 40/1909, Chapter II, p.11

151 'Michael Casey': Jonathan F. Vance, *A Gallant Company*, Pacifica Military History (2000), pp8–9

151 'vivid account of the action': Stonyhurst school magazine, December 1939

152 'John Dodge': Tim Carroll, *The Dodger*, pp.17–114

153 'far too friendly': Smith, *'Wings Day'*, pp.65–6

154 'male nudity': Ibid, pp.54–5

154 'women problems': Letter from Bushell to his family, 31 January 1941. Bushell Archive

155 'I still have not heard from Peggy': Letter from Bushell to his family, 27 February 1941. Bushell Archive

155 'I'm gloomy about Peggy': Letter from Bushell to his family, 26 March 1941. Bushell Archive

155 'Nothing to worry about': Letter from Bushell to his family, 31 January 1940. Bushell Archive

156 'hope like hell': Ibid

156 'Identification Friend or Foe (IFF)': Charles Rollings, Dulag Luft, *After The Battle* magazine (No. 106)

156 'Erich Killinger': PWIS(H)/LDC/749 and PWHIS9H0/LDC/750: reports on the interrogation of PW LD 639 Obstlt Erich Killinger. TNA: WO 208/3657, WO 208/4642, AIR 40/2317

157 'keen student of psychology': Ibid

158 'Buckley and his team': Rollings, *After The Battle*, p.16

158 'tunnel was completed': Smith, *'Wings' Day*, p.71

159–60 'tackled familiar themes': Letter from Bushell to his family, 29 April 1941. Bushell Archive

161 'a hilarious evening': Smith, *'Wings' Day*, p.69

161 'fingers crossed': Letter from Bushell to his family, 29 April 1941. Bushell Archive

The Goat Shed

162 'go it alone': Crawley, *Escape from Germany*, p.37

162 'The reason': Letter from Day to Dorothe Bushell, 15 July 1945. Bushell Archive

162 'stash of German currency': Smith, *'Wings' Day*, p.70

163 'all three authors': Brickhill, *The Great Escape*, p.7; Smith, *'Wings' Day*, p.72; Crawley, *Escape From Germany*, p.37

165 'biographical documentary film': *For Which I'm Prepared To Die* (Lindy Wilson, 2009)

165 'a long time ago': Letter from Day to Dorothe Bushell 15 July 1945

166 'sporting attitude': Letter from Bushell to his family, 10 July 1941. Bushell Archive

166 'My darlings': Ibid

166 'escape attempts': Testimonies of British prisoners, TNA: AIR 40/1909, Chapter II, pp.16–22

169 'first mass escape': Crawley, *Escape From Germany*, p.39; Smith, *'Wings' Day*, pp.78–9

170 'a fine military record': Carroll, *The Dodger*, p.134–7

170 'a case of champagne': Smith, *'Wings' Day*, p.79

170 'defeatists like Rumpel': Ibid

171 'Rumpel's departure': Rollings, *After The Battle*, p.17

171 'Rommel's Afrika Korps': Taylor, *The Second World War*, pp.88–9

171 'In Poland . . . a free hand': Gerwarth, *Hitler's Hangman*, pp.184–90

172 'fight to the death': Ibid, p.185

Journey to Prague

173 'guard towers looked uglier': Charles Rollings, *Prisoner Of War: Voices from Behind the Wire in the Second World War,* Ebury Press (2008), p.82

173 'Among the prisoners': B. A. 'Jimmy' James, *Moonless Night: The Second World War Escape Epic,* Pen & Sword Books (2002), pp.42–3

174 'ill-disciplined': Smith, *'Wings' Day,* pp.82–3

174 'an optimistic note': Letter from Bushell to his family, 10 July 1941. Bushell Archive

174 'News from Peggy Hamilton': Ibid

174 'appeared to be irritated': Letter from Bushell to his family, 31 July 1941. Bushell Archive

175 'You'll be speechless': Ibid

175 'a striking portrait': Ibid

175 'Day took over': James, *Moonless Night,* p.43

176–7 'reputation as a goon-baiter': Filmed interviews with 'Jimmy' James and M. R. D. Foot in *For Which I Am Prepared To Die* (Lindy Wilson, 2009)

177 'Very naïve of you': Letter from Bushell to his family, 13 August 1941. Bushell Archive

177 'Heard from P': Ibid

178 'Miss M. Hamilton': Forthcoming marriages, *The Times,* p.7, 14 August 1941

178 'Joseph William Lionel Petre': Person Page 3629 www.thepeerage.com/p3629.htm

178 'a "bon vivant" relationship': Wing Commander Reginald Piff, *Chapter Seven: The God Conclusion,* p.74

179 'reached his 31st birthday': Letter from Bushell to his family, 31 August 1941. Bushell Archive

179 'Another tunnel': Ibid

180 'In September': Letter from Day to Dorothe Bushell, 15 July 1945. Bushell Archive

180 'a real bastard': Rollings, *Wire and Worse,* p.152

180 'extreme personal hostility': Rollings, *Prisoner of War,* p.144

181 'I have moved again': Letter from Bushell to his family, 29 September 1941. Bushell Archive

181 'Madeira': Conversations and correspondence with John Blandy, Mildred Blandy's son

182 'being an old PoW': Letter from Day to Dorothe Bushell, 15 July 1945. Bushell Archive

182 'to dig a tunnel': Rollings, *Wire and Worse*, p.154

182 'The intelligence organisation': The historical record of MI9 (Military Intelligence 9), IS9, RAF Intelligence Course B, Awards Bureau and Screening. TNA: WO 208/3242, p.83

182 'code correspondents': Ibid, p.85

183 'We were very careful': Ibid, p.85

184 'surprise visit by diplomats': Rollings, *Wire and Worse*, pp.155–7

184 'a last squeeze': Ibid

184 'a terrific shouting match': Ibid

185–9 'Bushell was ready . . . arrived in Prague': Letter from Jarsolav Zafouk to Ben Bushell, 12 November 1946. Bushell Archive, hard-covered album entitled 'Newspaper Cuttings' (IWM Collections)

Reinhard Heydrich

191 'born into a musical family': Gerwarth, *Hitler's Hangman*, p.14

191 'six years at sea': Ibid, p.33

191 'Lina von Osten': Ibid, p.39

191 'fan of detective novels': Ibid, p.51

192 'aggressive sexual encounters': Callum MacDonald, *The Assassination of Reinhard Heydrich*, Birlinn (2007), pp.52–3

192 'Ernst Rohm': Gerwarth, *Hitler's Hangman*, p.78

192 '*Kristallnacht*': Ibid, p.125

193 'the Hangman': Ibid, p.282–3

193 'the *Einsatzgruppen*': Ibid, p.184–93

193 'plans for the Holocaust': Ibid, p.209–17

194 'acting Reich Protector': Ibid, p.218–26

195 'ruthless mission for the SS': Ibid, p.226; The Killing of Reinhard Heydrich! http://www . . . www.holocaustresearchproject.org/nazioccupation/heydrichkilling.html

195 'Heydrich took action': Gerwarth, *Hitler's Hangman*, p.227

196 'generated panic in London': Ibid, pp.2–3

196 'plans for Anthropoid': Ibid, p.2

196 'so many spies': Filmed interview with Vlasta Zafouk, Jaroslav Zafouk's former wife, in Prague on 13 June 2007 (Lindy Wilson)

197 'My brother provided food': Letter from Zafouk to Ben Bushell, 15 July 1946. Bushell Archive

198 'According to documents': I was given three batches of documents relating to this story by staff at the Czech National Archive; the first

two concerned personal details of Otto Zeithammel, his daughter, Blažena Zeithammelová, and his son, Otokar Zeithammel, and those of Vojtěch Přidal and his wife, Ludmila. Among other things, they included passport applications, mortgage applications and police character references.

The files were: PR1941-50 ka13048signZ773-11; PR1941-50 ka9082signP3569-7; PR1941-50 ka13049sign773-10; PR1941-50 ka13049signZ776-10; and PR1941-50 ka5934signK5600-3

The third batch of files contained papers relating to the interrogation and trial of Miloslav Kraus after the war, including those from the Regional Criminal Court in Prague (LS 520/1945) and the Extraordinary People's Court in Prague (Tk XV 15695/1947). Others were: PR-EO; Státní Soud signOrl-III41-50 Kraus Miloslav; and Vězenská Služba and ČR. Kraus Miloslav.

I was also given one loose, two-page German military report, with three sheets of Czech translation, which related to the Zeithammels and the Pidals: Dokumentč. VI/27 – Praha, 1942, červen, 30.: hlášení o provedení popravy v Praze – Kobylisích 30. Června 1942.

Family at War

199 'romantic affair': Filmed interview with Vlasta Zafouk (Lindy Wilson)

199 'Blonde, voluptuous': Ibid

199 'The Zeithammels were important': Interview in Prague, 1 October 2012, by the author with the Czech historian, Jaroslav Čvančara, an authority on the assassination of Heydrich.

199 'hundreds of bombs': Michal Burian, Aleš Knížek, Jiří Rajlich, Eduard Stehlík, *Assassination, Operation Anthropoid 1941–1942*, Ministry of Defence of the Czech Republic (2002), p.52

200 'Blueprint for the Tiger Tank': Barbara Mašín, *Gauntlet*, Naval Institute Press (2006)

200 'Berlin-Anhalt railway': Burian, Knížek, Rajlich and Stehlík, *Assassination, Operation Anthropoid*, p.52

200 'the Three Kings . . . code name, A-54': Ibid

200 'Otto, the father': Czech National Archive, see notes on 'documents' for p.198

200 'His son, Otokar': Ibid

200 'Blaza was born': Ibid

201 'applied for a job': Ibid

202 'also a member of Sokol . . . three addresses': www.valecnehroby. army.cz/zeithammel (then see XLS]List1 – Praha 5 www.praha5.cz/ cs/priloha/3387)

202 'the German traitor, A-54': Burian, Knížek, Rajlich and Stehlík, *Assassination*, p.52; MacDonald, *The Assassination of Reinhard Heydrich*, pp.173–7

202 'an SS state': Gerwarth, *Hitler's Hangman*, pp.230–55

203 'The Mautners': *The Diary of Petr Ginz*, ed. Chava Pressburger, Atlantic Books (2007), p.46

203–6 'As tragedy unfolded . . . I never saw them kiss': Filmed interview with Vlasta Zafouk (Lindy Wilson)

205 'The trouble with Bushell': Tom Moulson, *The Flying Sword*, p.41

206 'resistance cells': Czech National Archive, see notes on 'documents' for p.198

207 'Sigmund Neudorfer': Ibid

207 'Přidal and his wife, Ludmila': Ibid

207 'After three months': Letter from Zafouk to Ben Bushell, 12 November 1936. Bushell Archive

208 'Roger remained in Prague': Letter from Day to Dorothe Bushell, 15 July 1945

208 'the evening of 28 December 1941': Burian, Knížek, Rajlich and Stehlík, *Assassination*, p.44

209 'Ron Hockey': *The Daily Telegraph Book of Airmen's Obituaries*, Bounty Books (2002), p.296–9

210 'the Luftwaffe monitoring service': Burian, Knížek, Rajlich and Stehlík, *Assassination*, p.49

210 'God and my pistols': Ibid, p.52

210 'From the preparations': Ibid, p.58

211 'Fears also grew': *The Diary of Petr Ginz*, p.98

211 'We exercised in shirts': Ibid, p.99

212 'aware of the plot to kill Heydrich': According to the authors of *Assassination, Operation Anthropoid*, the book published by the Ministry of Defence of the Czech Republic, Gabčik and Kubiš established contact with the 'Sokol resistance organisation' in Prague. Blažena Zeithammelová was a member of Sokol.

212 'One Czech source': A Czech website, Blog.Respekt.CZ, issued a guide to memorials associated with those who died in the wake of the Heydrich assassination. Referring to a plaque on the wall of the Zeithammel flat, an awkward translation reads: 'On this

day, a very busy street Strakonická close to the railway bridge lived in number 1564/23 Mr. Otokar Zeithammel. For example, helped keep the family Khodlových and burn one of the parachutes. The whole family ended up on Zeithammelových Kobylisy [the execution ground].' The family mentioned in this caption, the Khodls, played a significant role in the plot to kill Heydrich, and were killed in Mauthausen concentration camp in October 1942. I can find no other sources to back up this claim. www.pavel.blog. respekt.ihned.cz/c1-45958120-pamet-pametnich-desek

212 'asked Bushell for a promise': Filmed interview with Vlasta Zafouk (Lindy Wilson)

Love and Betrayal

213 'become an informer': Czech National Archive, see notes on 'documents' for p.198

213 'Blaza told Kraus': Ibid

213 'a black and white photograph': The description of Kraus is taken from a photograph that appeared with an article by Ivo Pejčoch of the Military History Institute in Prague. The article, which appeared in 2009, is entitled: 'Military personnel executed in the period of the political trials in Czechoslovakia in the years 1948–1955'. The Czech signature reads: Ivo Pejčoch, Vojenské osoby popravené v období politických procesů v Československu v letech 1948–1955, VHÚ Praha, Praha 2009

213 'joining the underground movement': Czech National Archive, see notes on 'documents' for p.198

214 'It was against the law': Interview with M. R. D. Foot in *For Which I Am Prepared To Die* (Lindy Wilson, 2009)

215–16 'Roger Bushell . . . gangster movie': Letter from Zafouk to Ben Bushell, 12 November 1946

216 'taken to police headquarters': Letter from Day to Dorothe Bushell, 15 July 1946

216–17 'Petschek Palace . . . surface of the body': Guided tour and lecture by Emil Kulfánek on 4 October 2012

217 'Two years later': Statement of 8323 Flight Lieutenant I. P. Tonder, 25 May 1945. TNA: AIR 40/2645

218 'Bushell's interrogation': *For Which I Am Prepared To Die* (Lindy Wilson, 2009)

218 'the last I've seen of Roger': Letter from Zafouk to Ben Bushell, 12 November 1946. Bushell Archive

218–19 Blaža's father . . . other details': Czech National Archive, see notes on 'documents' for p.198

219 'It was inexcusable': Filmed interview with Vlasta Zafouk (Lindy Wilson)

219 'According to witnesses': Czech National Archive, see notes on 'documents' for p.198

220 'After the interrogation': Letter from Zafouk to Ben Bushell, 12 November 1946. Bushell Archive

220 'to witness events': Letter from Vincent 'Paddy Byrne' to Dorothe Bushell, 1 September 1944. Sketch Book Three, pp.31–2

221 'Josef Gabčík and Jan Kubiš . . . determined to press on': Gerwarth, *Hitler's Hangman*, pp.8–9; Burian, Knížek, Rajlich and Stehlík, *Assassination*, p.64

221–2 'The black Mercedes . . . a passing truck': Gerwarth, pp.10–11

222 'a lacerated wound': Burian, Knížek, Rajlich and Stehlík, *Assassination*, p.64

222 'Himmler': Ibid, p.65

222 'recorded events': *The Diary of Petr Ginz*, p.108

223 'The next day': Ibid

223 'Another diarist': Gerwarth, p.11

223–4 'At that moment . . . had all fallen': Taylor, *The Second World War*, Chapter 6 (Germany and Japan at their zenith)

224 'destabilised the Nazi regime': MacDonald, *The Assassination of Reinhard Heydrich*, p.221

224 'disastrous': Gerwarth, p.13

224 'the impact': British intelligence assessment of the attack on Heydrich. TNA: WO 208/4472

224 'Heydrich's condition deteriorated': Gerwarth, p.13

225 'taken to Berlin': It is not known for certain where Bushell was held – Harry Day referred to an 'Officers' Military jail' – but it is possible he was held at Tegel Prison in the western suburbs of the German capital. See Day's letter to Dorothe Bushell, 15 July 1945

225 'Events developed in Prague . . . was disbanded': Czech National Archive, see notes on 'documents' for p.198

225 'terrible things': Filmed interview with Vlasta Zafouk (Lindy Wilson)

226 'The Nazi regime': Burian, Knížek, Rajlich and Stehlík, *Assassination*, p.68

226 'Heydrich's coffin': MacDonald, *The Assassination of Reinhard Heydrich*, pp.3–4

226 'Lidice': Burian, Knížek, Rajlich and Stehlík, *Assassination*, pp.70–5

226–7 'Gabčík and Kubiš . . . were cremated': Ibid, pp.76–80

227 'they caught the assassins': *The Diary of Petr Ginz*, p.114

227–8 'Several miles from . . . would not be in vain': Czech National Archive: German military document on the execution: Dokumentč. VI/27 – Praha, 1942, Červen, 30.: hlášení o provedení popravy v Praze – Kobylisích 30. Června 1942.

228 'Josef Mašín': Interview by the author with the Czech historian, Jaroslav Čvančara

Holding Out

229 'A series of letters . . . he wants for nothing': Exchanges between Ben Bushell and 'Countess Reichenbach', March–August 1942. Bushell Archive, Sketch Book Two

233–4 'a precarious position . . . when they visited us': Letter from Day to Dorothe Bushell, 15 July 1946. Bushell Archive

235 'a very difficult time': *For Which I Am Prepared To Die* (Lindy Wilson, 2009)

235 'suave belligerence': Paul Brickhill, *The Great Escape,* p.5

236–7 'Here I am again': Letter from Bushell to his family, 19 June 1942. Bushell Archive, Sketch Book Two, PoW letters, pp.11–47

237 'I do hope': Letter from Bushell to his family, 29 July 1942. Bushell Archive

238 'gave the secret away': Filmed interview with Vlasta Zafouk (Lindy Wilson)

238 'A son and heir': *Essex Chronicle*, p.1, 7 August 1942

239 'the Zafouks searched for Georgie': Filmed interview with Vlasta Zafouk (Lindy Wilson)

240–41: 'collapsed in scandal . . . I am sorry about it all': Records of the Supreme Court of Judicature and related courts, Court for Divorce and Matrimonial Causes, later Supreme Court of Judicature; Divorce and Matrimonial Causes Files, Kidston G. M. & R. A., letter from Home Kidston to Georgiana Kidston from HMS *Highlander*, 30 October 1941. TNA J77/3967

241 'sank the German submarine': HMS *Highlander*, destroyer www.naval-history.net/xGM-Chrono-10DD-33Brazil-Highlander.htm

242 'not happy in her marriage either': Records of the Supreme Court of Judicature and related courts . . . letter from Home Kidston to Georgiana Kidston from HMS *Highlander*, 30 November, 1941. TNA J77/3967

242 'a harsh settlement': Divorce and Matrimonial Causes Files. TNA
   J77/3967
243 'it all goes to P': Letter from Bushell to his family, 20 August 1942.
   Bushell Archive
243 'had for a sucker': Letter from Bushell to his family, 3 September
   1942. Bushell Archive
244 'The information you received . . . Your loving son, Roger': Letter
   from Bushell to his family, 10 September 1942. Bushell Archive
244 'The last act': Letter from Day to Dorothe Bushell, 15 July 1945.
   Bushell Archive
246–7 'some silly row . . . optimism once more': Letter from Bushell to
   his family, 30 September 1942. Bushell Archive
247 'The Germans kept me in Berlin . . . which is not unfunny': Letter
   from Bushell to his family, 30 December 1942. Bushell Archive

Big X
250 'We all decided': Letter from Day to Dorothe Bushell, 15 July 1945
250 'he would be shot': when Bushell was sent back to Stalag Luft III
   in the autumn of 1942, he found himself in the "cooler" with a
   prisoner called Derek Thrower. In his memoirs, Thrower wrote that
   Bushell had told him that the Gestapo had demanded his execution.
   He thought he would be shot. *The Lonely Path to Freedom* (Robert
   Hale, 1980), p.87–89
250 'The SS were concerned': The historical record of MI9 (Military
   Intelligence 9), IS9, RAF Intelligence Course B, Awards Bureau and
   Screening adds further information, particularly on the use of
   codes. TNA: WO 208/3242, p.16
251 'The city of Cologne': Taylor, *The Second World War*, p.130
251 'Allied air crew . . . German civilians': RAF Bomber Command
   lost 55,573 men during the campaign against Germany between 3
   September 1939 and 8 May 1945. About 600,000 Germans are estimated to have lost their lives as a result of Allied bombing. Air
   Historical Branch of the Royal Air Force
251 'Stalag Luft III': The Camp History of Stalag Luft III (Sagan).
   TNA AIR 40/2645, Part I, Chapter I
252 'As part of a diverse strategy': Ibid; Midge Gillies, *The Barbed-
   Wire University*, Aurum Press (2012)
253 'Flight Lieutenant Alan Bryett': Interview with the author, 24
   August 2012

253 'Sport': Gillies, *The Barbed-Wire University*, p.56

253 'theatre': Ibid, p.291

254 'a university education': Ibid, p.292

254 'Games and gambling': See exhibitions at the POW Camps Museum at Żagań. museum@um.zagan.pl

255 'a very different Bushell': Forrester, *Fly For Your Life*, p.324

255 'he was moodier': Brickhill, *The Great Escape*, p.20

255 'the weather has been simply astonishing': Letter from Bushell to his family, 31 October 1942

256 'You need have no fear': Ibid

256–7 'News from the front lines': Taylor, *The Second World War*, Chapter 7, The turning point

257 'described the escape': *The Times*, 17 September 1945

257–60 'a play': *The Great Escape*, adapted by Felix Felton from Paul Brickhill's book, broadcast by the BBC, 4 March 1951

260 'Floody . . . Peter Fanshawe . . . Tim Walenn': Vance, *A Gallant Company*

260–1: 'he did lie low': Letter from Day to Dorothe Bushell, 15 July 1946, Bushell Archive

261 'took over the escape committee': Report 'X', compiled after the war by members of the escape organisations at Stalag Luft III. The National Archive (TNA): AIR 40/285, Appendix A

261 'hell for the Hun': *For Which I Am Prepared To Die* (Lindy Wilson, 2009)

261 'a clear brain': Ibid

261 'brought order and discipline': Ibid

262 'As the narrator': *The Great Escape*, broadcast by the BBC, 4 March 1951

262 'Group Captain Herbert Massey': Anton Gill, *The Great Escape Review* (2002) pp.96–7

263 'Breathtaking in its scope': Crawley, *Escape from Germany*, pp.136–7

264 'He took over': Letter from Byrne to Dorothe Bushell, 1 September 1944. Bushell Archive

264 'did not exactly radiate joy': Letter from Bushell to his parents, 30 December 1942. Bushell Archive

264 'bubbling over': Letter from Bushell to John Brinton, 30 December 1942. Bushell Archive

Going Underground

265 'deputy leader of the Labour Party': William Ash, *Under the Wire*, Bantam Press (2005), p.323

265 'a mind like a filing cabinet': Brickhill, *The Great Escape*, p.26

266 'a new emphasis on the security of the project': The Camp History of Stalag Luft III (Sagan). TNA AIR 40/2645, Part I, Chapter II, p.18. The 'Z' Report. TNA: WO 208/3245. Appendix ZI

266 'aggressive pursuit of all kinds of intelligence': The Camp History of Stalag Luft III (Sagan), Part I, Chapter VIII, p.78; 'Bushell was the expert on all information concerning GERMANY.' Part III, p23. TNA AIR 40/2645. The 'Z' Report on the development and conduct of a military intelligence system. TNA: WO 208/3245

266 'the escape committee': The Camp History, Part III, Chapter II, p.7. TNA AIR 40/2645

266 'each of the nineteen members': Ibid

267 'monstrous tyranny': Churchill, House of Commons, 14 May 1940

267 'I have taken to the boards': Letter from Bushell to his family, 28 February 1943. Bushell Archive

268 'made the most of his opportunity': The Camp History, Part III, Chapter II, p.27. TNA AIR 40/2645.

269 'Many prisoners': Ibid, p.41

269 'Notices were posted': Crawley, *Escape from Germany*, p.138

270–2 'the sites for the three traps': The Camp History, Part III, Chapter II, pp.28–30. TNA AIR 40/2645

274–5 'solved by Peter Fanshawe': *The Great Escape*, broadcast by BBC radio, 4 March 1951

275 'Sand excavated': The Camp History, Part III, Chapter II, p.32–4. TNA AIR 40/2645

275 'obsessed by security': Ibid, p.12

275 'The trap of each tunnel': Ibid, pp.38–9

276 'fullest possible details': Ibid, p.12

277 'the magnitude of these undertakings': The Camp History of Stalag Luft III, Part III, Chapter II, p.98. TNA AIR 40/2645

277 'A new camp': Letter from Bushell to his parents, 29 April 1943. Bushell Archive

278 'the only bachelor': Ibid

Love of a Lady

279 'relationship with Georgie': Letter from Bushell to his parents, 30 October 1943. Bushell Archive

279 'passionate love scene': Elizabeth Carter, filmed interview with Lindy Wilson, 2004

279 'Earl Howe': Divorce and Matrimonial Causes Files. TNA J77/3967

280 'In legal documents': Ibid

280 'Day told his biographer': Smith, *'Wings' Day*, p.54

281 'Vlasta Christova's assertion': Filmed interview with Vlasta Zafouk by Lindy Wilson, 2007

281 'The mail is rotten': Letter from Bushell to his parents, 26 May 1943. Bushell Archive

282 'Newcomers very optimistic': Ibid

282 'an SA party': Ibid

282 'It is quite untrue': Letter from Bushell to his parents, 28 June 1943. Bushell Archive

283 'shocking letter-writer': Ibid

283 'James Little has been killed': Letter from Bushell to his parents, undated but probably July 1943. Bushell Archive

284 'nothing to get fussed about': Letter from Bushell to his father, 29 August 1943. Bushell Archive

284 'I wrote with some care': Ibid

284 'a caring, loving brother': Letter from Bushell to his sister Lis, 29 August 1943. Bushell Archive

285 'dear old Father': Letter from Bushell to his father, 29 August 1943. Bushell Archive

285 'time on your side': letter from Bushell to his father, 28 September 1943. Bushell Archive

Secret Agent

287 'a hard man': Filmed interview with Alex Cassie for *The Making of the Great Escape* (Steve Rubin, 1993)

287 'cool, logical and ruthless': Filmed interview with Walter Morison, *For Which I Am Prepared to Die* (Lindy Wilson, 2009)

288 'operational outpost of British Intelligence': The 'Z' Report on the development and conduct of a military intelligence system inside Germany. TNA: WO 208/3245

288 'parcels containing': The Camp History of Stalag Luft III, Part I, Chapter III, p.56. TNA AIR 40/2645

289 'Crockatt always insisted': The historical record of MI9 (Military Intelligence 9), IS9, RAF Intelligence Course B, Awards Bureau and Screening, pp.88–9. TNA: WO 208/3242

289 'We had been notified': the historical record of MI9, p. 77. TNA: WO 208/3242

289 'The most ambitious demand': Smith, *'Wings' Day*, pp.153–4

290 'intelligence mission to the Baltic': Ibid

290 'The great majority of Germans': Report 'X', pp.35–6. TNA: AIR 40/285

291 'Dowse's contact': Eberhard Hesse is named as Dowse's contact in many books, but Hesse's genuine source for the information on Peenemunde is not. In *Wings' Day*, Sydney Smith wrote: 'An Austrian baroness, Hesse's girlfriend, had been somewhere near a place called Peenemunde on the Baltic . . . it appeared to be stiff with scientists engaged on war work involving rocket-propelled missiles.' B. A. 'Jimmy' James also refers to an 'Austrian baroness' in his memoir. The truth is established by Guy Walters in his book, *The Real Great Escape*, Bantam Press (2013) in a chapter on collaboration called 'An Anglo-German Affair'. Hesse's source was, more credibly, a German scientist – his brother. WO 311/171 and WO 311/759

291 'back to England': B. A. 'Jimmy' James, *Moonless Night*, p.90

291 'site was bombed': Peenemünde – Royal Air Force www.raf.mod. uk/bombercommand/peenemunde.html

291 'experiments with new weapons': The Camp History of Stalag Luft III, Part I, Chapter VIII, pp.78–9. TNA AIR 40/2645

292 'breach of international law': William E. S. Flory, *Prisoners of War: A Study in the Development of International Law*, Washington DC, American Council on Public Affairs (1942)

292 'It became apparent': The 'Z' report on the development and conduct of a military intelligence system inside Germany outlines the scope of intelligence work undertaken by RAF prisoners of war, Appendix Z.A. TNA: WO 208/3245

292–3 'It cannot be stressed . . . reached the camp: Ibid

293 'Infiltration': Ibid

294 'The chief coding officer': Ibid, Appendix Z. C.

294 'known as "Plug"': The Camp History of Stalag Luft III, Part I, Chapter IX, p.83

295 'The campaign worked': Ibid, p.84. But there was also a downside. The prisoners lost access to newspapers and magazines, which were a useful source of information.

295 'resentment of British prisoners': The historical record of MI9 (Military Intelligence 9), IS9, RAF Intelligence Course B,

Awards Bureau and Screening. SS Report on Questions of Internal Security (12 August 1943), p.16, Appendix B. TNA: WO 208/3242

296 'warned senior Allied officers': Smith, *Wings' Day*, pp.156–7; also see statement by Günther von Massow WO 311/997

297 'On one occasion': The Camp History of Stalag Luft III, Part II, Chapter II, p.16

297 'the "contact" system': Report 'X', compiled after the war by members of the escape organisations at Stalag Luft III, Intelligence section, p.15. TNA: AIR 40/285

298 'Harry was a genuine Democrat': Crawley, *Escape from Germany*, pp.48–9

299 'Another German': Report 'X', Intelligence section, p.16. TNA: AIR 40/285

299 'scale of the great endeavour': *The Great Escape*, broadcast on BBC radio, 4 March 1951

300 'Eberhard Hesse': TNA: WO 311/759. Bushell appears to have become contemptuous of the Germans. In a letter written to his parents, probably in July 1943, Bushell writes: 'Do you remember what Sir Richard Wemyss told the Lyttons at the luncheon party at the Crillow? It is in "Antony". If not, look it up. It is so true of today.' On p.50 of the Earl of Lytton's book, *Antony*, Admiral Sir Rosslyn Wemyss, who had just returned from the signing of the Armistice at the end of the First World War, told the Lyttons that the Germans whined. 'One of them read a prepared document describing the terrible state of their country, and almost begging for mercy.'

Treading the Boards

301 'George and Margaret': Letter from Bushell to his parents, 28 September 1943

301 'Bushell took several parts': Brickhill, p.124

302 'Even better': Crawley, *Escape from Germany*, p.124

303 'Roger did not take part': Letter from 'Wings' Day to Dorothe Bushell, 15 July 1945

303 'escape attempt went ahead': The Camp History of Stalag Luft III, Part III, Chapter II, p.43

304 'All the escapers': Ibid, pp.43–4

304 'De Wever': Morison *Flak and Ferrets: One Way to Colditz* London Sentinel Publishing (1995) p.116

305 'John Stower': *Flak and Ferrets*, p.117; *A Gallant Company*, pp.88–9

305 'to Colditz': *Flak and Ferrets*, pp129–50

306 'The Germans were pretty smart': Interview with Sydney Dowse, *For Which I Am Prepared To Die* (Lindy Wilson, 2009)

306 'Herman Glemnitz . . . escape, escape!' Smith, *'Wings' Day*, pp.121–2

307 'fateful consequences': Crawley, *Escape from Germany*, pp.148–50

308–9 'caught the mood . . . Harry as well': *The Great Escape*, broadcast by BBC radio, 4 March 1951

309 'Tom progressed until': The Camp History of Stalag Luft III, Part III, Chapter II, p.30. TNA AIR 40/2645

310 'The Germans were especially incensed': Smith, *'Wings' Day*, p.155

310 'Tom gained celebrity status': Crawley, *Escape from Germany*, p.149

311 'to blow it up': Ibid

311 'called a halt': The Camp History of Stalag Luft III, Part III, Chapter II, p.31. TNA AIR 40/2645

312 'South Compound was neat': Arthur A. Durand *Stalag Luft III: The Secret Story*, Louisiana State University Press (1988), p.296

312–13 'Alan Bryett': Interview with the author, August 2012

313 'Duff Cooper's *Life of Talleyrand*': Letter from Bushell to his parents, 30 October 1943. Bushell Archive

313 'childishly easy': Ibid

314 'The mail gets worse and worse': Ibid, 30 November 1943

314 'My sergeant rigger': Ibid

315 'I wouldn't worry about the photograph': Ibid, 30 December 1943

315 'whose face is the window of their spirit': Dorothe Bushell's journal, p.17. Bushell Archive

Eve of Battle

316 'primary motives': Smith, *'Wings' Day*, p.164

316 'torturing people': Brickhill, *The Great Escape*, p.20

317 'a last Xmas': Letter from Bushell to his parents, 30 December 1943. Bushell Archive

317 'Big X ordered "Harry"': Camp History of Stalag Luft III, Part III, Chapter II, p.31. TNA: AIR 40/2645

317 'When digging had ceased': Crawley, *Escape from Germany*, p.154

317 'It was in good condition': Camp History of Stalag Luft III, Part III, Chapter II, p.31. TNA: AIR 40/2645

317 'It was necessary': Camp History of Stalag Luft III, Part III, Chapter II, p.35. TNA: AIR 40/2645

318 'If there were no Germans': Camp History of Stalag Luft III, Part III, Chapter II, p.36. TNA: AIR 40/2645

319 'Morale was closely': Camp History of Stalag Luft III, Part I, Chapter I, p.12. TNA: AIR 40/2645

319 'At the beginning of 1944': Taylor, *The Second World War*, Chapter 9, Year of Liberation, p.188

319 'Now, what am I': Letter from Bushell to his parents, 31 January 1944. Bushell Archive

320 'the best place to be': Rees, *Lie in the Dark and Listen*, p.170

321 'a wave of sympathy': Letter from Bushell to his parents, 28 February 1944. Bushell Archive

322 'Tuck chuckled': Forrester, *Fly For Your Life*, p.336

323 'Instead of damping': Crawley, *Escape from Germany*, p.158

323 '"The Bullet Order", Plan Kugel': Treatment and Disposal of Recaptured Officers and NCOs, other than British or American. TNA: 311/36

324 'escape penalties': TNA: 309/527. WO 235/424 and WO 311/995

324 'warning to Bushell': IWM Sound Archive, Sydney Dowse 27731

324 'construction work was completed': Camp History of Stalag Luft III, Part III, Chapter II, p.31. TNA: AIR 40/2645

324 'The diggers knew': Crawley, *Escape from Germany*, p.160

325 'The break would have to be soon': Smith, *'Wings' Day*, p.167

325 'The first thirty places': Camp History of Stalag Luft III, Part III, Chapter II, p.45. TNA: AIR 40/2645

326 'esprit de corps': Prisoner of War interrogation section (Home) London District Cage: interrogation reports, L.D.C. 765-790. WO 208/3659

326 'one vital factor': Letter from Keith Mountfort to Ben Bushell, 18 August 1945. Bushell Archive, Sketch Book Three, pp.33–4

327 'I was completely overwhelmed': Bryett, interview with author, August 2012

327 'the cross-country boys': *The Great Escape*, broadcast on BBC radio, 4 March 1951

329 'Somebody came to me': Albert Clark, US Air Force Museum, Colorado, R00ls 235–7

329 'Roger was dressed': Letter from Day to Dorothe Bushell, 15 July 1945

Goodbye, Harry

331 'All their passes': Letter from Peter Cazenove to Ben Bushell, 6 June 1945. Bushell Archive, Sketch Book Three, p.39

331 'The exit shaft': Camp History of Stalag Luft III, Part III, Chapter II, p.46. TNA: AIR 40/2645

332 'The first 20 out': Statement of 36103 H. C. Marshall

332 'More things began': Rees, *Lie in the Dark and Listen,* p.178

333 'Per Ardua Ad Astra': IWM Sound Archive, B. A. 'Jimmy' James 4987

333 'I shall never forget': Rollings, *Prisoners of War,* p.269

334 'a slight squeeze': Anton Gill, *The Great Escape,* p.183

334 'Eventually it was decided': Camp History of Stalag Luft III, Part III, Chapter II, p.47. TNA: AIR 40/2645

335 'I remember hearing the shot': Albert Clark, US Air Force Museum, Colorado, R00ls 235-7

336 'We also met S/L Bushell': Statement of Freddie Dvorak, Czech inspectorate general. WO 311/993

336 'commandant threatened': Camp History of Stalag Luft III, Part III, Chapter II, p.48. TNA: AIR 40/2645

336 'red with controlled anger': Rees, *Lie in the Dark and Listen,* p.180

336 'Hitler was informed': Wilhelm Keitel, *In the Service of the Reich,* Stein and Day (1966) pp.259–60

337 'Hell for the Hun': *For Which I Am Prepared to Die* (Lindy Wilson, 2009)

337 'In his memoirs': Keitel, *In the Service of the Reich,* p.260

338 'Gentlemen, this must stop': Interrogation of General Adolf Westhoff by Colonel Curtis L. Williams, US Army, 2 November 1945

338 'the Sagan Order': Air Ministry, Directorate of Intelligence and Related Bodies: Intelligence reports and papers. TNA: AIR 40/2268

339 'Their arrest': Air Ministry, Directorate of Intelligence and Related Bodies: Intelligence reports and papers. TNA: AIR 40/2284 and AIR 40/2489

340 'Schulz told British investigators': Air Ministry, Directorate of Intelligence and Related Bodies: Intelligence reports and papers. Sagan, Stalag Luft III Camp: Murder of Fifty Officers. Reports Nos. 301–368. TNA: AIR 40/2493

340 'It all went very quickly': Voluntary statement by Walter Breithaupt. WO 309/530

341 'He had a pistol': Voluntary statement by Emil Schulz. WO 40/2490

A Marked Man

343 'Small groups of recaptured escapers': Camp History of Stalag Luft III, Part III, Chapter II, testimonies, pp.51–77

345 'We left the tunnel too late': Statement of 8323 Flight Lieutenant I. P. Tonder. TNA: AIR 40/2645

347 'He was a tallish, well-built man': Statement of Wing Commander H. M. A. Day. TNA: AIR 40/2645

348 'The court had many questions': Camp History of Stalag Luft III, Part III, Chapter II, pp.78–98

349 'the prisoners had stolen': Crawley, *Escape from Germany*, p.248

350 'I am commanded by the German High Command': Ibid, p.175

351 'Most of us in the front line': Wellum, interview with the author, 21 July 2012

351 'Crockatt told the meeting': War Office, Curzon Street House, 16 May 1944

351 'Anthony Eden': 19 June 1944, House of Commons (Hansard)

351 'Churchill memo': referring to Minutes of the War Cabinet, 20 June 1944, signed by K. E. Bridges.

352 'cold-blooded acts of butchery': Eden, 23 June 1944, House of Commons (Hansard)

352 'they hunted the killers': Brickhill, *The Great Escape*, p.248

353 'His lawyer told the Hamburg court': Stalag Luft III case, September 1947. WO 235/424

353 'In a last letter to his family': *Daily Mail*, 21 October 2009

Casualties of War

356 'Essentially, she lived upstairs': Wilson, correspondence with the author, March 2013

356 'With bare, earth-stained hands': Bushell Archive

358 'A very private, unannounced funeral': Piff, *Chapter Seven: The God Conclusion. The Memoirs of Wg Cdr R.* p.170

358 'She did the dirty on him': Elizabeth Carter, filmed interview with Lindy Wilson, 2004

358 'He became a dedicated escaper': Smith *'Wings' Day*, p.54

359 'I knew Peggy': Letter from Paddy Byrne to Bushell's parents, 1 September 1944. Bushell Archive, Sketch Book Three, pp.31–2

359 'a word about Georgie': Letter from Robert Stanford Tuck to Dorothe Bushell, 24 October 1945. Bushell Archive, Sketch Book Three, p.36

360 'And if I grieve': *The Times*, 30 August 1947

360 'Your love and faith': Letter from Ben Bushell to Lady Georgiana Curzon, shown to the author by Bushell's niece, Caroline Kennard, November 2012

361 'a beautiful upper-class woman': Wilson, correspondence with the author, March 2013

361 'her death certificate': Ref 4781037/2 of 2 – 11232510, 12 January 1976

Epilogue

363 'highest admiration': Letter from Day to Dorothe Bushell 15 July 1945. Bushell Archive, hard-covered album entitled 'Newspaper Cuttings'

364 'The loss of such a son': Letter from G. D. Roberts. Bushell Archive, hard-covered album entitled 'Newspaper Cuttings'

364 'a stupid venture': Hugh Falkus, Rollings, *Prisoner of War*, p.270

364 'an outstanding character': Rees, in conversation with the author, November 2012

365 'His name': Letter from Massey to Bushell's parents, 13 February 1945

366 'all my energies': Letter from Bushell to his parents, 30 November 1940

Index